Heirs to Forgotten Kingdoms

"As the al-Qaeda splinter group, ISIS, storms across Syria and Iraq and attempts to destroy the Yazidi religious sect, now comes Gerard Russell, an erudite, polylingual former British diplomat, who documents the fates of the ancient religions of the Middle East, many of which are on the brink of extinction. Russell writes beautifully and reports deeply, and his account of these 'disappearing religions' will be an enduring anthropology of largely-hidden worlds that may disappear within our own lifetimes."

> —PETER BERGEN, author of *Manhunt: The Ten-Year Search for Bin Laden from 9/11 to Abbottabad*

"Oxford and Harvard, fluency in Arabic and Farsi, postings with the British Foreign Service in the Middle East and Afghanistan—as a scholar-diplomat Gerard Russell seems almost too good to be true. He brings these gifts to his beautifully written account of some of the most fascinating and little known communities facing the challenges of globalization. Read it to understand the complexity of—and hope in—our world."

> —AMBASSADOR AKBAR AHMED, Ibn Khaldun Chair of Islamic Studies at American University in Washington, DC, and the former Pakistani High Commissioner to the United Kingdom

"An eloquent and sensitive portrayal of the Middle East's lesser known religions, whose existence is severely threatened by the strident nationalisms and proxy wars that are currently tearing apart a region once renowned for its tolerance. Gerard Russell gives a voice to those who cannot speak for themselves, those whose traditions—handed down through many centuries—are being disregarded and indeed obliterated in a blaze of violence and hatred. He lifts the 'veil of ignorance' and reveals just what is at stake—both in the Middle East and around the world. Through extensive and meticulous research, and encompassing years of travel to distant places to meet in person those whose lives have been turned upside down, Mr. Russell's passionate message touches the heart and reminds us of the value and beauty of tolerance."

> —ALI ASANI, Professor of Indo-Muslim and Islamic Religion and
> Cultures, Director, Prince Alwaleed bin Talal Islamic Studies Program,
> Harvard University

"At a time when minorities—and even majorities—are being persecuted across the Middle East, ancient faiths continue, just barely, to survive. Gerard Russell not only recalls a more tolerant past through his sketches of now exotic tribes and rituals, but also paints a deep and complex relief to help us understand this troubled region's evolution. Russell is a true classical diplomat: explorer, linguist, scholar—and master storyteller."

> —PARAG KHANNA, author of *The Second World: Empires and*
> *Influence in the New Global Order*

"Gerard Russell's beautifully written book provides wonderful insights into the Middle East and the beauty of the different cultures that have flourished there for centuries. It is a welcome respite from the usual portrayal of violence in the region, and at the same time a wakeup call of what will be lost if a perverse form of violent extremism is allowed to prevail. At a time when religion is so often seen as a cause of war, this book shows how lives can be enriched by maintaining rituals and beliefs through generations."

> —EMMA SKY, Senior Fellow at the Jackson Institute for Global
> Affairs, Yale University

HEIRS *to* FORGOTTEN KINGDOMS

Heirs *to* Forgotten Kingdoms

JOURNEYS INTO *the* DISAPPEARING
RELIGIONS *of the* MIDDLE EAST

GERARD RUSSELL

BASIC BOOKS

A Member of the Perseus Books Group

New York

Copyright © 2014 by Gerard Russell

Published by Basic Books,

A Member of the Perseus Books Group

All rights reserved. Printed in the United States of America. No part of this book may be reproduced in any manner whatsoever without written permission except in the case of brief quotations embodied in critical articles and reviews. For information, address Basic Books, 250 West 57th Street, New York, NY 10107.

Books published by Basic Books are available at special discounts for bulk purchases in the United States by corporations, institutions, and other organizations. For more information, please contact the Special Markets Department at the Perseus Books Group, 2300 Chestnut Street, Suite 200, Philadelphia, PA 19103, or call (800) 810-4145, ext. 5000, or e-mail special. markets@perseusbooks.com.

Designed by Pauline Brown
Typeset in Times New Roman

A CIP catalog record for this book is available from the Library of Congress.

LCCN: 2014948120

ISBN: 978-0-465-03056-9 (hardcover)

ISBN 978-0-465-05685-9 (e-book)

10 9 8 7 6 5 4 3 2 1

To my parents
And to Linda Norgrove, Vadim Nazarov,
and others who shared my journeys
but are no longer here to read this book

Contents

Foreword by Rory Stewart ix
Timeline xv
Map of the Forgotten Kingdoms xvi
Introduction xix

CHAPTER 1: Mandaeans   1

CHAPTER 2: Yazidis   39

CHAPTER 3: Zoroastrians   75

CHAPTER 4: Druze   113

CHAPTER 5: Samaritans   147

CHAPTER 6: Copts   181

CHAPTER 7: Kalasha   219

Epilogue: Detroit   257

Sources and Further Readings 281
Index 301

Foreword

RORY STEWART

By the early eighth century, Muslim rulers controlled most of the land between Afghanistan and the edge of North Africa. But Islamic states—which
developed in Europe a reputation as fierce and exclusive—proved ultimately
more tolerant of other religions than Western Christianity. In Europe, "pagans" were eliminated so completely and so rapidly that the details of the
pre-Christian religion of somewhere like Britain can barely be recovered.
In the Muslim world, however, complete "pagan" religions were allowed to
survive intact into the twenty-first century, and it is still possible to interview
their believers.

There are the Yazidis of northern Iraq, whose temples include a statue
of a peacock, somehow associated with the devil. There are the Kalasha
of the Afghan-Pakistan border, whose faith incorporates wooden statues of
ancestor-heroes. From Lebanon to Iran religions survive—some with a special relationship to fire, others that center on immersion in water, others with
focus on the sun and the moon. Some of these faiths long predate the birth
of Christ.

The subject is wonderful. These groups are not just symbols of religious
sensibilities and possibilities now faded. They suggest a great deal about the
origins and evolution of the major world religions. And they are challenging
components of a modern world: intricate compressed identities, rooted in

history and landscape, but also systems of belief that have changed dramatically over time, incorporated rival religions, and been exported to new lands.

But the subject is almost impossible. These religions are formidably difficult to access, understand, or describe. They survived partly because they are located in some of the most remote, mountainous, and dangerous regions of the Middle East. The believers sometimes speak obscure, archaic languages. The archives and scholarly accounts of the faiths are intimidating. In some cases the religions are esoteric: it is forbidden to record, discuss, or reveal their beliefs. In other cases, the religions are persecuted, and believers have had to learn to conceal the details of their faith, to avoid being murdered. They rarely can or will speak to outsiders. It is, therefore, very difficult to imagine someone qualified to address the subject.

Gerard Russell is one of the few people able to write a book of this kind. Born in 1973 in America to British parents, Gerard Russell studied classical languages and philosophy at Balliol College, Oxford. He then joined the British Foreign Service, which sent him to Cairo to learn Arabic. His Arabic became sufficiently fluent for him to become the UK public spokesman on Arabic news channels. He was posted to Iraq after the US invasion, became consul general in Jeddah, and then was political counselor in the embassy in Kabul. In those posts, when many diplomats remained isolated from the local populations, he developed strong friendships with Arabs and Afghans outside the compound, aided by his linguistic skills, and became an ever greater expert on the countries and people with whom he lived. In 2009, he joined a group of Afghan specialists at the Carr Center for Human Rights Policy, at Harvard's Kennedy School.

He is so modest that it can be tough to remember just how difficult it must have been to produce this book. He presents himself again and again as simply a bemused tourist, clattering around on rural buses. But he is an erudite scholar with patience and a very nimble mind. He has an extraordinary capacity for synthesizing and presenting complex information. He has a great knack for winning the trust of interviewees. When he interviews people in Iran or Lebanon, he is doing so in fluent Arabic or Farsi. When he traces the influences on the Yazidis or the Mandaeans, he does so with a deep knowledge of Islamic history and Christian doctrine. When he writes about the bombs and attacks in Iraq and Afghanistan, he writes as someone who has worked and lived through the politics and violence of those insurgencies. The network of friends on which he relies to move through dangerous areas or gain access to religious leaders has been developed over years. This—his first book—is the fruit of two decades of experience and reflection.

Each of these religions has been shaped by a dozen other religions, living, evolving, and vanished. Theology is a subtle and tough discipline, where apparently "trivial" disagreements prove to have vast and often fatal consequences, frequently provoking sectarian killings. Many of the most basic facts about these faiths are still subjects of fierce debate, some driven by new data, some simply by new politics and fashions in anthropology or world religion. Thousands of books and articles demand to be read. Unpublished manuscripts in archaic languages need to be consulted. Some of the best accounts are a century old but need to be filleted for the prejudices of their authors. Much of this information is—inconveniently—relevant and good.

And "modernity," conflict, and "the West" overshadow everything. Many of the religious homelands of these faiths are today in active conflict zones—Iraq, Afghanistan, the edge of Syria—that have been swept up in the fortunes of regimes supported or toppled by the United States, Iran, Saudi Arabia, Russia, and Qatar. "Pagan" families have experienced occupation, proxy wars, honor killings, kidnappings, and giant truck bombs. The "pagans" are now clean-shaven men in suits or young professional women. In the last three decades, unparalleled numbers have left their rural homes, lost their links to their original landscape and extended family, and begun to marry out and forget their old religion. And perhaps the majority of believers have now fled as refugees to the West. So an honest portrait of a contemporary faith requires a description not only of a three-thousand-year-old temple and its ancient priest but also of a converted cinema in London or a community center in Detroit, all surrounded by the juddering fantasies and pressures of contemporary Western culture.

Russell navigates all of this, creating an almost effortless narrative, so that twenty years of dedication, study, imagination, and care are left very much in the background. It is tempting at times to hope for a more romantic account, more focus on his own emotional responses, a clearer glimpse of his own faith or views on God. There could have been space for Wordsworth's fascination with paganism as another energy or possibility:

> —*Great God! I'd rather be*
> *A Pagan suckled in a creed outworn;*
> *So might I, standing on this pleasant lea,*
> *Have glimpses that would make me less forlorn;*
> *Have sight of Proteus rising from the sea;*
> *Or hear old Triton blow his wreathed horn.*

But Russell resists this, just as he resists the temptation of boasting about his discoveries or of turning the story of the decline, persecution, and scattering of these religions into a prolonged lament.

Instead, he achieves something perhaps ultimately more valuable and more lasting—a careful chronicle. He truthfully and exactly records encounters with these religions in the twenty-first century. He introduces us in detail to his informants, gives us their context, and hints at their prejudices. He is never afraid to admit ignorance, uncertainty, or contradiction. He hints at a deep problem that the theologies of some of these religions no longer exist, if indeed they ever did. Some worshipers appear to continue their rituals without clear doctrines of sin or redemption; without clarity about the meaning of the words, or the objects and symbols in their temples; without any remaining memory of the stories of their gods. He links all his discoveries to contemporary landscapes.

This combination of linguistic skill, deep cultural understanding, courage, classical scholarship, and profound love of foreign cultures was once more common. Russell is in the direct tradition of British scholars/imperial officers such as Mountstuart Elphinstone, Macaulay, or even T. E. Lawrence. But it is now very rare. It is not an accident that Russell has now moved on from the British diplomatic service and Harvard University. Academics seem to be absorbed in ever more intricate internal arguments, which leave little space or possibility for a project of this ambition and scope. Foreign services and policy makers now want "management competency"—slick and articulate plans, not nuance, deep knowledge, and complexity.

Russell instead, brings older, less institutionalized virtues to bear. This book is a patient and nuanced challenge to grand theories and abstract ambitions. He is rigorous in his focus on the details of culture and history. He uncovers and helps to preserve the diversity and bewildering identities and commitments under the surface of a "global world." He demonstrates how the autonomy, dignity, and ability of alien cultures can challenge Western vanities and preconceptions. And above all, he manages to link his love and his learning to living landscapes and living people. There is much to learn from this book.

Timeline

c. 2560 BC	Great Pyramid built in Egypt
c. 1900	Indo-Europeans arrive in India, perhaps including ancestors of Kalasha
1842	Babylon emerges as an independent city-state
c. 1000	Date of composition of the Zoroastrian scriptures, the Avesta
740/722	Assyrians attack Israel, take the Ten Tribes into captivity
597	Nebuchadnezzar sacks Jerusalem, deports leading Jews to Babylon
331	Alexander the Great conquers Persia; shortly after, he passes the Hindu Kush
AD 70	Sack of Jerusalem by the Romans and destruction of the Second Temple
274	Death of Mani, founder of Manichaeism; Mandaeans already exist in Iraqi Marshes
313	Constantine issues Edict of Milan, granting recognition to Christianity
529	The Byzantine emperor Justinian closes Plato's Academy
634–654	Arab Muslims conquer all lands from Morocco to Iran
635	The first Christian missionary arrives in China from the Middle East
1017	The Druze faith is first taught openly in Cairo
1095	Pope Urban II preaches the First Crusade
1160	Death of Sheikh Adi, a key figure in the Yazidi religion of northern Iraq
1258	Sack of Baghdad by Genghis Khan
1263	Birth of Ibn Taymiyyah, conservative critic of Druze and other heterodox Muslims
1501	Beginning of the reign of Shah Ismail I of Iran, who converted the country to Shi'a Islam

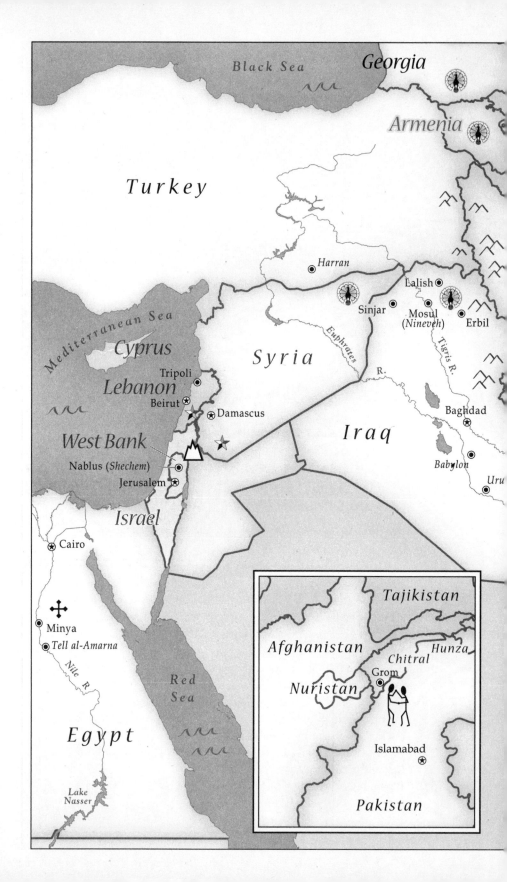

Introduction

Imagine that the worship of the goddess Aphrodite was still continuing on a remote Greek island, that worshipers of Wotan and Thor had only just given up building longboats on the coasts of Scandinavia, or that followers of the god Mithras were still exchanging ceremonial handshakes in subterranean Roman chapels. In the Middle East, in contrast to Europe, equally ancient religions survived—often in marshes, wildernesses, mountains, and other remote or impenetrable places, and sometimes under the veil of a strict code of secrecy.

These religions might have dominated the modern world if history had taken different turns. A follower of the austere vegetarian preacher called Mani almost became emperor of Rome. Had he done so, the Roman Empire might have spread Mani's teachings, not Christianity, across Europe; instead of going to Bethlehem, European pilgrims might head instead to the Iraqi Marshes, where Mani first preached. Instead, the Manichees became extinct, but their closest cousins, the Mandaeans, are still living in Iraq. Had it not been for the invasions of the Mongols and Tamerlane, Baghdad might still be a world center of Christianity, for there was a time when the Iraq-based Church of the East had bishops and monasteries as far east as Beijing.

In the course of fourteen years as an Arabic- and Farsi-speaking diplomat, working and traveling in Iraq, Iran, and Lebanon, I encountered religious beliefs that I had never known of before: a taboo against wearing the color blue, obligatory mustaches, and a reverence for peacocks. I met people who believed in supernatural beings that take human form, in the power of the planets and stars to steer human affairs, and in reincarnation. These religions were vestiges of the pre-Christian culture of Mesopotamia but drew as well from Indian traditions that had been transmitted to the Middle East through the Persian Empire, and from Greek philosophy. They preserved, too, the customs of ancient civilizations of which they were the last, frail descendants. These are some—and only some—of the groups described in this book.

As I met these different religious groups, I was inspired and amazed at their constancy in faith. They have held on to practices and traditions without change for more than a thousand years—sometimes preserving them for many millennia, under constant pressure to convert. Most of these groups, though, are now more vulnerable than ever, and this book aims to give them a voice. They are worth hearing for other reasons as well: they connect the present to the past, bringing us within touching distance of long-dead cultures. They link the Middle East with European culture by showing how the two emerged from shared roots. They follow their religions differently than Europeans and Americans do—the Copts, for example, take on a burden of prayer and fasting that exceeds even that of monks in the West; the Druze have a religion that makes no demands of them at all, save that they marry within it. Thus the groups featured in this book seem to me to address three things that troubled me during my time in the Middle East: humanity's collective ignorance of its own past, the growing alienation between Christianity and Islam, and the way the debate about religion has become increasingly the preserve of narrow-minded atheists and literalists..

WE HAVE INTELLECTUAL COUSINS in unexpected places. Greek philosophy is not a European phenomenon, for example, but a Mediterranean one and it influenced the Middle East as much as it did Europe. To give another example, when Alexander the Great marched through what we now call Afghanistan and Pakistan, he felt that he could see echoes of his own culture—and he was right, because Europe and North India share a common

Indo-European heritage. Such links exist with people who live even farther east. The Christians of Iraq a thousand years ago shared their church with Mongolians; they had a Chinese patriarch and a bishop of Tibet, and influenced the modern-day Mongolian and Tibetan alphabets. Everywhere in the Old World, at least, apparent differences can conceal unexpected connections and commonalities. As I wrote this book I was always delighted to find these: they disprove the theories and beliefs of those who want to corral people into separate cultures and civilizations and set them at war with each other.

At the same time I enjoyed finding differences, too: ideas that differed from my own and challenged me to reflect on what I myself believed and why. The Lebanese–French writer Amin Maalouf, in a book called *On Identity,* called for a fight "for the universality of values" but also against "foolish conformism . . . against everything that makes for a monotonous and puerile world." I agree with him—though I could never in my own mind decide whether cultural diversity should be treasured whatever the price. Should we be sad if a community grows rich and abandons its customs, or if a religious belief is defeated in argument? I don't pretend to know the answer: I just believe that we happen to be fortunate that they have survived, and that today religions that have been sincerely observed for many generations are able to examine each other's ideas and learn from them.

How did they survive so long under Muslim rule? Very often Islam is presented as an intolerant religion, and some of its own followers regrettably want it to be so. The existence of the minority religions described in this book shows that image of intolerance to be untrue, for they survived under Islam, while no equivalent faith survived in Christian Europe. The reasons for this, though, are complex. For the remainder of this introduction, let me try to summarize them.

One reason goes back well before Islam or Christianity. There were religions in the Middle East that were more sophisticated than the pre-Christian religions of Europe and which had common roots with Christianity and Islam. So whereas Christians had no hesitation about putting an end to the Norse or Celtic religions and relatively quick success in doing so, some Middle Eastern pagans—deeply learned in Greek philosophy and Babylonian astronomy, and possessing a complex theology—clung on much longer.

Also, though the Prophet Mohammed certainly wanted to put an end to the traditional religious practices of the Arabs, which involved worshiping multiple deities, the Koran was by contrast relatively benign toward religions that were monotheistic and had religious texts, such as Jews, Christians, and Zoroastrians. These groups were called "people of the book." Several of the groups discussed here survived because they managed, somehow or other, to secure this label for themselves.

The early Muslims were not systematic about suppressing even openly pagan practices in the first three or four centuries of Islam, when Muslims remained the minority in many parts of the Middle East. When Muslim preachers did seek converts more aggressively, some of them were prepared to tolerate a wide range of beliefs and practices that elided the difference between Islam and the old religions it was supplanting. A group of newly converted Muslims, for example, might say that their rites of reverence to the stars were legitimately Islamic because the stars were angels—and so they could preserve some parts of the older, pagan heritage that they were giving up by adopting Islam.

None of this means that minority faiths were treated well. This was a time when to disagree with the ruler about theology was also potentially to challenge his right to rule. It was understood, in both the Byzantine and Arab empires, that those who rejected the ruler's religion would be disadvantaged. The "people of the book" were legally inferior to Muslims and paid an extra tax. When they rebelled against the imposition of taxes, as the Copts did in the ninth century AD, the state might begin to regard their religion as a subversive force and take measures to undermine it.

In the tenth and eleventh centuries, as Islam became the majority faith, communities that were not "people of the book" came under greater pressure. The tenth century saw the mass persecution and virtual extinction of the Manichees. In the eleventh century, the temple of the sun god Shamash at Harran, which had existed since Babylonian times, was demolished and the scholar al-Ghazali pressed for Muslims to abandon their fascination with pre-Islamic philosophers. Even then, though, scholars such as Biruni and Ibn Nadim were writing about non-Muslim religions with an objectivity that still impresses modern readers.

Conflict between Muslims and the followers of other faiths—Crusaders in the west, Mongol invaders in the east—further undermined tolerance, as Arabs looked for the enemy within. By the thirteenth century the fundamentalist cleric Ibn Taymiyyah was issuing every execration and encouragement to violence that he could against sects such as the Druze and Alawites. By this time, though, some of the Middle East's minority religions had taken refuge in places where the authorities could not reach them, such as mountains and marshes. Central government did not become as strong in the Middle East as it did in Europe, and military force was usually deployed against rebels or outside conquests, not in suppressing religious divisions at home. It was not until the nineteenth century, for the most part, that these remote religious communities faced widespread interference from the state, and by the middle of that century the governments of the Middle East had begun to change their approach toward minorities and (sometimes under Western pressure, sometimes just inspired by progressive ideals) to offer them something like equality. The Ottoman Empire gradually granted its non-Muslim subjects near-equality in the nineteenth century. The fifty years from 1860 to 1910 revolutionized the status of the Copts in Egypt. The Iranian revolution of 1906 gave Zoroastrians a seat in the country's parliament. All this proves that Muslims in the Middle East were perfectly capable of valuing diversity. In fact, it was sometimes the Europeans who did not. When asked by Lebanese Christians what his country might do to help them, the German kaiser replied: "You are three hundred thousand Christians among three hundred million Muslims. Why not turn Muslim?"

So why today are the Middle East's minorities on the retreat? Why are attacks on Christian churches in Egypt or Baghdad, or on Yazidis in northern Iraq, more common now than they have been for 150 years? (Not forgetting minorities within Islam—even the largest Islamic group, the Sunnis, can find themselves a minority under pressure in Iran and Iraq, while massacres of Shi'a Muslims are common in Pakistan.) There are several factors at play here.

For one, the diversity of the Middle East is partly because its governments were too weak to impose their religion. Today governments have more power, and when they choose to evict a religious minority or impose orthodoxy they can do it more effectively than ever before. The Ottoman Empire was able to organize, between 1915 and 1917, the killing of more than a million of its Armenian subjects when it perceived that the Armenians were siding with Russia—"giving the death warrant," as the American ambassador to the empire later wrote, "to an entire race." Civil wars, too, can reach deep into the territory of a religious group that might only want to be neutral—as the Yazidis of northern Iraq found in 2007, when they became the victims of one of the world's deadliest terrorist attacks. There are no safe places anymore.

Religious groups in the Middle East have a high degree of internal cohesion. Marriage to an outsider is generally frowned on; people within the group may prefer to employ other members from the same group; converting to another religion is not an intellectual choice but a much more profound change, because it usually means leaving behind one's community and joining a new one. Some religious groups (such as the Yazidis and Assyrians, for example) enjoyed a high degree of autonomy for many centuries, outside the reach of governments; a few still speak their own language. This internal cohesion means there is a tendency to hold such groups collectively liable for the actions of anyone who has their religion. Hence the past attacks on the Armenians and Jews, and the present ones on Shi'a and Christians. In itself, this is not new. In the complex and ever-shifting political landscape of the modern Middle East, though, it is easy to end up being loyal to the wrong people. The Samaritans, living on a mountain in the West Bank, try hard to avoid alienating either the Israelis or the Palestinians; the Yazidis of northern Iraq are being pressed to choose between Arabs and Kurds; the Egyptian Coptic Church has had to decide whether to back military or Islamic rule. Each choice makes enemies for the whole community, not just its leaders.

Although governments have become strong enough to crush troublesome minorities, some of them are hesitant to expend political capital and risk wider confrontation by protecting smaller communities from attack. In southern Egypt, if a Coptic family comes up against a Muslim tribe, it will lose the fight—whether that be over money, land, or "honor" (love affairs, as described in Chapter 6, are a particularly frequent cause of conflict). Some Coptic communities are big and tough enough to turn the tables. Those that are not rely on the police and courts to protect them—but even those institutions, which often lack moral authority, may be afraid of the belligerent tribe and prefer not to punish them. This is not only a religious issue. Racial minorities often have the same problem. Religious minorities in the twentieth-century Middle East, however, became detribalized, urbanized, and middle-class, meaning that they are now well placed to benefit from stability and economic growth, but also that they are usually not well enough organized to defend themselves, and so they become especially vulnerable in times of conflict.

Finally, the past few decades have brought a change in the behavior of some Muslims in the Middle East toward other religions, and toward rival interpretations of Islam itself. In Egypt, the past fifty years have seen much more violence against Copts than the previous fifty years had. In Pakistan, a country founded by a Shi'a Muslim, violence against the Shi'a has become common. Iraq, a country ruled in the 1950s by a man of mixed Shi'a-Sunni parentage, is now a maelstrom of communal violence. Weakness and vulnerability make for closed-mindedness and, in turn, closed-mindedness holds back societies. Anger and hatred toward outsiders strengthen the communal identity of a group, perhaps satisfy some atavistic human urge for companionship in the face of an external threat, and may be cultivated by the group's leaders as a way to strengthen the group's sense of identity and mutual loyalty. There is no quicker way to build a sense of group identity than to point to a common enemy who is wicked and powerful yet can be defeated—to be David defeating Goliath. In the Middle East, such anger and hatred—which sometimes boil over into violence and at other times simmer unnoticed, perpetuating themselves through virulent propaganda—are also the product of specific circumstances. Islamism's secular competitors from the twentieth century, Communism and nationalism, have declined. In their time, all these ideologies appeared to offer opportunities for peoples in the Middle East to regain the dignity and power to which they felt entitled, and of which they felt European colonialism, American dominance, Israeli military strength, and Arab governments' weakness and corruption were depriving them. Communism's appeal and its external funding ceased when the Soviet Union collapsed; nationalism's popularity has declined since the end of the anticolonial struggle of the early twentieth century. Both movements offered minorities a cause in which they could stand side by side with Muslims. With the decay of postcolonial nationalist movements, religious divisions became easier to exploit. The idea that Iraq, or Egypt, was a country for all of its citizens has given way, for some Muslims, to the older idea that the natural community is one based on religion. As Suha Rassam wrote in *Christianity in Iraq,* "All minorities . . . have become vulnerable in the absence of a unifying Iraqi identity."

Outside attempts by a secularized Christian West to interfere in the Middle East have strengthened this religious tension—particularly when that interference has all too obviously not served the interests of the people of the Middle East. "We do not even propose to go through the form of consulting the wishes of the present inhabitants of the country," wrote Arthur Balfour in 1919 about the British scheme to establish a Jewish national homeland in what was then Palestine. That attitude has not greatly changed, as the ill-considered Coalition plans for postwar Iraq (including a failure to safeguard the country's precious archaeological heritage) demonstrated in 2003.

Nor do state institutions often enjoy the moral authority that might help them face down extremists without resorting to the use of force. State-backed religious institutions and clerics are discredited in the eyes of some Muslims by the presumption that they have been given preferment and money in return for toeing the government line. Radicals can exploit this by presenting themselves as bolder, less corrupt alternatives. Confronted with religious radicals who are more popular than they are, governments often prefer to buy off the radicals rather than confront them.

The currency with which religious extremists have usually been bought off is the opportunity to radicalize future generations through the education system. Islamists did this successfully in the 1970s, when they were seen (including by Israel and the West) as a valuable antidote to Communism and radical nationalism; they have since benefited from the fact that oil and gas wealth has enriched the Middle East's most conservative societies. In Egypt, they have used their influence over the past forty years to make the country's laws more explicitly Islamic. This has created an environment where minorities feel unwanted; as one Egyptian Christian told me, "If the constitution makes Islamic law *the* source of legislation, then I feel marginalized." Some Islamist groups use violence, too—usually for political motives, rather than just for the sake of encouraging conversions. Christians were targeted by Egyptian Islamists in the 1980s not just as a way to force conversions and remove an obstacle to religious homogeneity but also as a means to put pressure on the government. After the fall of the Muslim Brotherhood government in Egypt in 2013, and in revenge for it, radicalized gangs of young men burned dozens of churches.

At the same time, it is important not to exaggerate. There are plenty of cases of Muslims protecting Christians in Egypt, and in Lebanon—where a terrible civil war ended only about twenty years ago—polling suggests that religious tolerance is higher than it is in many European countries. The progress the twentieth century brought toward religious equality in the Middle East has not been wholly undone: not even Ayatollah Khomeini went so far as to restore the old penal laws that oppressed non-Muslims in nineteenth-century Iran. But minorities feel increasingly unloved. And it is easier for minorities to emigrate from the Middle East than ever before, since they have used the last century or so to educate and enrich themselves, and generally find it easy to emigrate to Australia, Canada, the United States, or Europe. So the prospect that some of these religions will diminish or even disappear from their homelands is a serious one. Nobody would lose from this more than the Muslims of the Middle East, who I hope therefore will welcome this book, which attempts to memorialize the diverse faiths their ancestors brought to the world.

One thing remains to be said, about belief. The communities in this book have refused every inducement to abandon their religious beliefs and customs, and have often endured insult or violence in order to stand by them. In some cases those religious customs are in themselves very demanding, as they are for the Copts who fast most of the year round, or indeed for Muslims during Ramadan. If people in the Middle East fight about their beliefs more than Europeans and Americans do, it is partly because those beliefs are so precious to them. While the fighting is something that should be stopped, the religious spirit that motivates it may have something more attractive to offer. So the chapters that follow may perhaps prompt a reflection: as well as all the lessons that the West wants to teach to the people of the Middle East, have we something to learn from them?

———————

I HAVE CHOSEN IN THE BOOK to use modern names of countries in the Middle East, even when referring to the distant past. So when I say that something happened in "Lebanon" a thousand years ago—a time when there was no such country—I just mean that it happened in a place within what is now Lebanon. This is simply for convenience's sake. I have also used AD and BC instead of CE and BCE because, in a region where every community has its own calendar, there is not yet such a thing as a "Common Era." To give an example, this year is AD 2014. In the Samaritan calendar the year is 3652, measured from the day when the people of Israel entered the Promised Land; in the Muslim calendar it is 1435, measured from Mohammed's migration to Medinah; in the Zoroastrian calendar it is 1383, measured since the last Zoroastrian king was crowned. Given this plethora of different dating systems, it seems more honest to say that 2014 is a year reckoned on the European Christian system.

On the same note, I want to make it clear that this book is a series of informal and personal investigations. They are necessarily subjective and selective, colored by my own interests and by the encounters and scenes that I have chosen to depict. My own perspective is that of a British-American Roman Catholic speaker of Arabic and Farsi. Like the members of the other religions portrayed here, I also come from a culture in the process of transformation, whose older customs and traditions are being abandoned. There are other ways of looking at these communities, other stories that might cast a different light on them, and other interpretations of their histories. Anyone who wants to take a more thorough look at any of these communities should read certain books listed in the Sources and Further Readings section. Attempting to write this book based on only four years of research and ten years of traveling in the Middle East, I was awed by the dedication of someone such as E. S. Drower, who spent her whole life studying the Mandaeans.

I could never compete with her knowledge or that of the many experts who have been kind enough to help me with this book. I have named and thanked them in the Sources and Further Readings.

In respect to Drower, and still more with Biruni and his medieval contemporaries, I am reminded of the praise given to Sir William Jones, the proponent of the idea that European and Indian languages had one common source. "Blessed are the peacemakers," commented political economist James Anderson, "who by painful researches, tend to remove those destructive veils which have so long concealed mankind from each other." I cannot claim any credit for doing anything so significant—but at least this book can remind people of the work of those who have.

———————

TO RETURN TO THE SPECULATION with which I began the introduction: how might the world have been different if (let's say) the emperor Constantine had not become a Christian in 312, the event that led to the empire adopting Christianity as an official religion? There would still be many Christians, of course, though their numbers might have been diminished by persecution. Judaism would be a major world religion, based in Iraq, squaring off from time to time against the Samaritans (who would number millions, dominating what is now Israel, and maybe southern Syria, too). Greek philosophers would not just be read; they would be worshiped by some. As for the rest of us, we might be following a mystery religion, one that vouchsafes its truths only to selected elders. What such a religion offers is not so much a personal relationship with God as the opportunity to benefit from the powers enjoyed by those few austere and pious elders who do have such a relationship. Several of these religions were among Christianity's early competitors, including the Manichees. The following chapter gives an idea of what having such a religion might be like.

1

Mandaeans

I N THE FADED CAFETERIA of Baghdad's al-Rashid Hotel, the Mandaean high priest, his brother, and his cousin all looked at me, asking for my help. They did not know how honored I felt to meet them. Here, in front of me, were the representatives of one of the world's most mysterious religions. Because they worshiped one God, practiced baptism, took Sunday as their holy day, and revered a prophet called John, the Mandaeans had been mistaken by sixteenth-century European missionaries for yet another of the region's many and varied Christian sects. In fact, their religion is wholly separate from Christianity. They believe in a heaven, but it is called the Light-World; in an evil spirit, but one that, unlike Satan, is female, and called Ruha; and in baptism as a necessary condition for entering the Light-World, though for them it must be in running water, while babies who die unbaptized are comforted for eternity by trees bearing fruits shaped like their mothers' breasts. Their John is the Baptist, not the Evangelist, and although the Baptist is presented in Christian texts as a follower of Jesus, the Mandaeans see him as a greater prophet. After hearing the Christian gospel in which John the Baptist says he would be unfit to undo the strap of Jesus's sandals, one nineteenth-century Mandaean convert to Christianity became indignant. "Aren't Isa and Iahia"—the Arabic names for Jesus and John—"cousins, and

A Mandaean baptism in the River Tigris. © Oleg Nikishin/Getty Images

therefore equal?" he demanded of the priest after the service. "Aren't they in the Light-World together?"

Mandaeans claim descent from Seth, son of Adam, and to have received secret teachings passed on from Adam in the garden of Eden. When a Mandaean priest whispers into the ear of one of the faith's followers, on the day of that individual's first baptism, the person's sacred name, the name that he or she must never disclose except to the closest family members, he says it in the language of ancient Babylon. When he takes down from his shelf one of the sacred books, containing legends and dialogues that were so secret that for many centuries they were not written down at all, he reads words that have been repeated by Mandaeans for more than fifteen centuries. When he ingests a sacred meal, performing the rituals in the precise order required for the salvation of souls, he is doing as his ancestors did for generations. These rituals connect the present day with the distant pre-Christian past, the funerary banquet of the Mithraists and the Egyptians, and the teachings of the Manichees, the now extinct religion that in its day had followers as far away as China and competed with Christianity for the loyalty of St. Augustine.

I encountered this extraordinary religion in the least promising of circumstances. In 2006 I was stewing in the dusty heat of Baghdad, suffering not from fear but from frustration. Barbed wire circumscribed my world—the Green Zone, a five-square-mile twenty-first-century dystopia filled with concrete berms and barbed wire, highway bridges that ended in midair where a bomb had cleaved them, and tunnels walled off to block intruders. In this place, which once had been a suburb specially built for the former dictator Saddam Hussein and his closest henchmen, swimming pools had now been dutifully filled in, gaudy palaces had been partitioned, and a private zoo had been evacuated to make room for an ever-expanding legion of Western bureaucrats who, exhausted by long days at their computer screens, occasionally fortified themselves with lobster flown in from America or with liquor served in bars closed to Iraqis, where the overwhelmingly male clientele swayed and shifted their feet collectively whenever a woman entered.

I had at least the distraction of working in an office wholly staffed by Iraqis. During Ramadan, when they neither ate nor drank during the day, I sometimes slipped surreptitiously into the kitchen, anxious not to offend but in need of sugary soft drinks to stave off torpor. Otherwise, I tried to do as they did—up to the point where they had to leave the safety of the Green Zone. In the evenings during Ramadan we ate *iftar* together, the pleasure of the dates and simple soup magnified if I had managed to survive the day without eating. I tried to mimic the deep-voweled, complex Baghdadi accent, learned to navigate the shabby corridors of various government departments, and steeled myself to the ghastly news that came in every day from the world outside that office, where Sunni and Shi'a Muslim gangs were fighting for control. Each day new tragedies were reported: the decapitated head of a girl, implanted with explosives so that it became a booby trap for her family when they tried to recover it; men kidnapped and released for ransom, but with their eyes gouged out and their hands and feet cut off.

All this was happening in the place where civilization began more than seven thousand years ago. In the landscape of recorded history, Iraq is Everest: just as Everest makes other mountains seem small, Iraq makes even ancient history seem recent by comparison. Noah's ark? Ancient Iraqi legends speak of a great deluge, and of a man called Utnapishtim who survived it in a great boat. The legend, which influenced the biblical account of Noah, was based on fact. Iraq's low-lying cities were exposed to devastating inundations.

The archaeologist Leonard Woolley discovered evidence of one such flood as his team dug down through the ruins of Ur in the 1920s and found eight feet of clean soil between two layers of pottery and flint implements. As he drily recorded, "My wife came along and looked . . . and she turned away remarking casually, 'Well, of course, it's the Flood.'" It might be truer to say that it was *a* flood, but the basis for the biblical story is certainly Iraq, whose civilization therefore is older than the Flood.

The pyramids? Spry youngsters compared with south-central Iraq's cities, which appeared as early as 5300 BC—three thousand years before Pharaoh Cheops built the Great Pyramid. Iraq's cities were almost as ancient for him as Tutankhamun is for us. It is the Iraqi habit of building in mud brick, in a climate much less dry than Egypt's, that has caused its great monuments to collapse while Egypt's have been preserved.

Homer's *Odyssey*? The golden age of Iraq was almost over by Homer's time. Iraqi epic stories survive from as early as around 2000 BC. One is about a hero called Gilgamesh, his relationship with a man called Enkidu, and their joint slaying of the monster Humbaba. It deals with eternal themes: friendship, sex, death. It even has comedy. A bawdy curse aimed at a prostitute goes, "May wild dogs camp in your bedroom . . . may drunkards vomit all over you . . . may angry wives sue you!" Odysseus himself might have heard this epic poem and recognized in it some similarities to his own travels—but even in his time, it was already old.

The most famous and maybe greatest of all the cities of ancient Iraq was Babylon but this once-great city is now a huge expanse of almost featureless mud by the side of the Euphrates River, fifty miles south of Baghdad. All that remain are low walls and the foundations of gateways. These were once part of temples so tall that people thought they reached up to heaven itself. Among these unprepossessing ruins language was supposedly invented. "Therefore is the name of it called Babel," says the Bible, "because the Lord did there confound the language of all the earth."

In their ceremonial religious processions, Babylonians carried effigies of the lion, the animal form of the sun god, Shamash, and of the dragon, the form of the moon god, Sin. Ishtar, goddess of love (whose name survives today as Esther), was symbolized by the dove. A temple almost as large as

St. Paul's Cathedral was dedicated to the city's chief god, Marduk; its doors were decorated with motifs of dragons, mythical creatures that were half goat and half fish, and dogs. The city was reputedly home to the Hanging Gardens, one of the seven wonders of the ancient world. It was here that Daniel and his companions escaped from the fiery furnace, Belshazzar was weighed in the balance and found wanting, and Alexander the Great died in the palace of Nebuchadnezzar, thwarted in his ambition to conquer the world.

It is now four thousand years since Babylon was founded, and for more than half that time it has lain abandoned, exposed to rain, flood, and the pillaging of later generations. After Alexander's death in 323 BC his huge empire was split between his squabbling lieutenants. Their civil war devastated Babylon's economy, and the city entered a period of decline. Apart from sporadic sacrifices, we hear no more of its great temples. The Hanging Gardens of Babylon disappeared, and today no trace of them can be found. One grandiose project exists among the ruins—but it is new, not old. It is one of the ancient city's palaces, reconstructed. Its bricks bear an inscription: "In the era of President Saddam Hussein, all Babylon was reconstructed in three stages. From Nebuchadnezzar to Saddam Hussein, Babylon is rising again."

All around, Ozymandias-like, is an expanse of decaying mud brick. Saddam's reconstruction of Babylon was pastiche, derided and deplored by serious archaeologists. Most of what had remained of the actual Babylon was taken long ago as building material for the city of Baghdad, or plundered or bought for a song by foreign archaeologists and shipped to museums in London, Berlin, and Paris. Saddam's new palace was not built to please archaeologists, though. By building it, Saddam was laying claim to Iraq's ancient past, which could help to legitimize Iraq's existence as a country and his own rule over it. Instead of being a set of Turkish provinces wrested from their Ottoman rulers in the aftermath of World War I, unified by neither religion, language, nor ethnicity, he could present his oppressive police state as the successor to the Babylonian and Assyrian empires. Conveniently, in that glorious past, it had been ruled not by Muslim clerics, whom Saddam hated and feared, but by capricious and brutal monarchs—just like Saddam.

By 2006, Saddam was under American guard and Iraq was in chaos. The time when it was a capital of world civilization could not have seemed more distant. Once Christian patriarchs in Iraq had signed their letters "From my cell on the river of the garden of Eden" because they believed that it was the site of the original paradise where Adam and Eve had lived. Now that same river carried the bodies of the dead down toward the sea, past Abu Nawas Street, where Baghdadis in happier days used to sit, eat fish, and smoke *narghileh* pipes. Most Iraqis tried simply to stay safe: they headed home as quickly as possible after work and then stayed indoors. If they wanted to try to live as they had before the war and sit at one of the city's cafés, they had to harden themselves. One woman told me how she and a friend had been drinking tea from the elegant tea glasses that Iraqis call *istikhana*s—wide at the rim, thin at the waist; similar examples survive from the fifteenth century—when they heard a man blow himself up further down the street. They looked around briefly, and when they realized there was no immediate danger, they turned back to their *istikhana*s and resumed sipping their tea. A mere suicide bomb was an everyday thing.

In the months that I had spent in Baghdad as a diplomat, speeding along the city's highways in an armored car or looking out from a helicopter scudding over Iraq's farmland with a machine gun hanging out the side, I had seen no trace of the country's history. Its ancient palaces and mosques and churches had been destroyed in multiple wars, invasions, and ill-considered rebuilding schemes; mud-brick houses had been dissolved by centuries of rain. Wars, neglect, decay, and an oil-fueled twentieth-century construction boom had all helped modernize Baghdad, which was now ringed by vast suburbs of small two-story houses with tiny yards.

A guidebook bravely written around the time of the 2003 war for the few tourists who might want to visit (under the section "Entertainment," it said, "The news is bad") recommended just a few mosques and one palace that remained from the city described in *The Arabian Nights*, where the caliph Haroun al-Rashid had wandered at night in the company of his faithful servant Jaafar. *The Arabian Nights* was fiction, but the real city had been remarkable enough: built by the Arab caliph al-Mansur in AD 734, designed by Persians, and at one time staffed by Hindu astronomers who had been brought from India by a Jewish envoy. This monument to the fertile links between cultures and religions was now buried in concrete somewhere underneath the main railway station. Iraq had not been kind to its own history.

———————

THE MANDAEANS, THOUGH, were living history. Their religious texts dated back at least to the third century AD, and they preserved customs and traditions that were far older—dating back perhaps to Babylon itself. For the surprising fact is that neither Christianity nor Islam fully suppressed Iraq's older religions. Certain areas of Iraq remained predominantly pagan after the Muslim conquest. A book called *Nabatean Agriculture,* written by an Iraqi called Ibn Wahshiyyah in around AD 904, described a contemporary culture so little changed from ancient times that Victorian scholars for a while thought that the book dated back to ancient Babylon and was thus the oldest ever written. It describes encounters with worshipers in temples to the sun and moon; fruits, vegetables, and trees that, invested with the power of the gods, are able to speak; insects brought into being by the evil deeds of men; soothsayers; golems formed by Greek science from Chinese clay; ascetic bands dedicated to the old gods, but resembling Christian monks or Sufi mystics, with henna-dyed hair and long beards; and philosophical speculation about the origin of the world. Against such a backdrop, Babylonian culture could easily have survived—and indeed, the Muslim writer al-Mas'udi wrote in the tenth century AD that the "remnants of the Babylonians" were still living in the Iraqi Marshes, which once covered over 7,000 square miles of southern Iraq.

Why had the Muslims, who had been ruling Iraq for more than two centuries, not suppressed these un-Islamic cultures? One reason was that the first generation of Arab conquerors, who in the decades following AD 632 beat back the forces of Byzantium and smashed the Persian Empire, did not work particularly hard to impose Islam on their new subjects, since they saw it as essentially an Arab religion. The caliph Omar wept, it was said, when he learned that his non-Arab subjects were adopting Islam. From a practical point of view, non-Muslims also paid more tax, so the state lost income when its subjects adopted Islam.

Even when they wanted to, the Arabs could not impose their will over

A village in the Iraqi Marshes, whose maze of rivulets isolate its inhabitants from the outside world. At least three religions originated there. © Nik Wheeler/Corbis

every square mile that they conquered. They began by being a small proportion of the population, at most 20 percent in Iraq. Geography stood in their way, too. In the 1990s, for example, Saddam had to dam the rivers feeding the Marshes before he could suppress rebel groups that had taken refuge there. For rulers in the past such a crackdown was not worth the trouble.

Furthermore, there was a tradition of tolerance in Islam. Although the Koran denounced idol worshipers, it praised "people of the book," who were monotheists and possessed written scriptures. The latter explicitly included the Christians and the Jews. Other religions singled out for positive mention in the Koran were Zoroastrians and "Sabians." A few centuries after Islam's beginning, the precise identification of this last group was unclear, providing a loophole by which several other Middle Eastern religions escaped persecution—including the Mandaeans, who were identified as Sabians by the great eleventh-century Muslim anthropologist Biruni in one of his 142 books. Incidentally, Biruni, described by George Sarton as "one of the greatest scientists in world history" for his open-mindedness, is a good example of the tolerance some Muslim intellectuals displayed toward the religions they discovered in their midst. Another was al-Mas'udi, who was the one who spotted the Babylonians living in the Iraqi Marshes—and who studied peoples as distant and diverse as the Russians and the French. Despite the reservations of religious conservatives, these intellectuals were prepared to learn even from those who did not share their faith, acting on an Arab saying: "Knowledge is the stray camel of the believer: it benefits him regardless from where he takes it." Although this spirit of tolerance waned in subsequent centuries, and the Mandaeans were frequently harassed and sometimes persecuted, it was only rarely that the Muslim authorities put great effort into converting their subjects forcibly; and the Mandaeans had the Marshes to protect them, right up into the twentieth century.

The Babylonians had been living in the Iraqi Marshes; so had the Mandaeans. Might they be connected? I had loved reading about Babylon when I was a child, and it was exciting to think the Mandaeans were the last frail remnant of Babylonian civilization. When I was telephoned by the high priest of the Mandaeans and asked for a meeting, therefore, it was like being summoned to meet one of the Knights of the Round Table, or discovering that in a small village in a remote part of the English countryside a community still worshiped Odin and had invited me to tea. So I said yes: I would see the high priest. This was the spring of 2006.

There was only one place in the Green Zone to which the average Baghdadi might easily gain access. In its heyday the al-Rashid Hotel, an eighteen-story concrete building from the 1970s, had a hundred eavesdroppers sitting in its basement, connected to a network of cameras and microphones that recorded everything done and said in its every room. After the 2003 war the cameras and microphones apparently were stripped out, and the mosaic of George H. W. Bush that had been the hotel's official doormat was covered over. The hotel remained a strange place. The waiters at the café, in fake bow ties and waistcoats, stood slightly too close to the tables for slightly longer than was necessary, listening intently. This was where I met the high priest, who was known as Sheikh Sattar (*sheikh* is an honorary Arabic title, used widely in Middle East religions and tribes to indicate respect). He was sitting at a table with two men who turned out to be his brother and secretary.

"Ours is the oldest religion in the world," said Sheikh Sattar. "It dates back to Adam." He traced its history back to Babylon, though he said it might have some connection to the Jews of Jerusalem. The Mandaeans believed in Adam, he said, who was the first man, and they accepted some other prophets who featured in the Hebrew Bible, such as Seth and Noah. Above all, they revered John the Baptist. But they rejected Abraham and had their own holy books that were quite separate from the Bible or the Koran. The sheikh handed me one of these books, which had been published in Arabic with a white cover.

The book was called the Ginza Rabba; the title means "Great Treasure." I leafed through the pages, right to left, and realized that it could also be turned upside down and read back to front, revealing another text back-to-back with the first. Both versions were laid out like the Koran, divided neatly into verses and chapters. At the start of each chapter, where the Koran has the phrase "In the name of God, the merciful, the beneficent!" the Ginza Rabba declared, "In the name of the Great Life!" On each page was what seemed to be a cross, crowned with a myrtle branch, over which a white scarf had been draped. This was not a cross, Sheikh Sattar assured me, but the *darfesh*. It is a symbol of the immersion in the Tigris, the Mandaean "baptism" and one of the religion's most sacred rites. Its four arms represent the four directions of the world. It is a glimpse on earth of the Mandaean heaven, in which the spirits of the good have eternal bliss. It was placed on earth on the day when Hibil Ziwa, the angel of light, baptized John—who then in turn became John the Baptist and performed miracles recorded in one of the Mandaean holy books, the Drasa da Yehia (Book of John). John the Baptist, the book says, was a far greater miracle worker than Jesus.

Baptism was a particular focus of the Mandaeans. "We practice baptism not just once in a lifetime, like Christians," said the sheikh, "but before all big occasions. Before a wedding, for instance, both the bride and groom are baptized." The baptism is more than just a cleansing process. It is seen as giving energy and spiritual contentment, and as purifying sin and healing the body. Mandaeans preferred to wear white, Sheikh Sattar added, and to live near rivers, because baptisms had to be performed in clean running water. They were also pacifists. "We don't believe in fighting even if we are attacked," he insisted. Our conversation was in Arabic, but I learned that the Mandaeans had their own language, which today is used only for names and rituals. The name *Mandaean* came from this language's word for wisdom, *manda*. They believed in one God, *manda da hiya*, the Great Life. They called heaven the Light-World, *malka da nhura*.

The group had not come just to tell me about their religion. They had a request for me. "My family are gold merchants," the secretary told me, and so they were attacked not just for their religion but also for their money. All the male members of his family, he added, had been killed. "Please," the high priest said, "there are only a few hundred of us left in Iraq. And we all want to leave. We want your country to give us all asylum." Britain did not grant them asylum as a community, which is what they were hoping for, but I knew that it would not be hard for them to apply as individuals, in Britain or elsewhere, and that one by one they would leave Iraq. I had encountered the link to the ancient culture of Iraq that I had been looking for, and it was vanishing almost before my eyes.

AS I WOULD SEE, the Mandaeans do preserve Babylonian customs, but their religion is not the same as that of the ancient Babylonians: they do not worship the Babylonian sun god Bel or the fertility goddess Atargatis, for instance. Their earliest surviving religious texts date back to the late second or early third century AD, according to historian Jorunn Buckley. That dates them to a time of unprecedented intellectual ferment in the Middle East, when new cults and philosophies swept through the Middle East, bringing new deities, ideas, and legends to replace the traditional ones. Why did this intellectual revolution happen at that particular time? It was mainly because of politics and empire. East and West had been brought together more closely than ever before, thanks to the expansion of huge empires such as those of Persia, Alexander, and Rome. Persia had India on its eastern border and Greece on its west; Rome touched Persia on the east and Britain on the west. So cultures that previously had been isolated from each other could meet. Even in an earlier era, stories of Indian asceticism had reached the early Greek philosophers and inspired the practices of the Cynics, who believed that the only path to true happiness lay in abandoning all possessions and living in complete poverty. In later centuries (especially after sea travel was easier) this kind of contact became even more common. Urbanization, too, threw different religions into a melting pot. It was no longer enough for a people to hold on to the gods they had had for a thousand years: new gods were wanted, and new philosophies to justify their worship.

What resulted was an era of fervent religious belief and radical intellectual debate that makes the modern world, whose five largest religions are now all more than a thousand years old, look static by comparison. Hinduism and Buddhism entered the Persian Empire. Middle Eastern faiths reached Rome, such as the clannish cult of the god Mithras and the worship of the Egyptian goddess Isis (the latter notorious because its initiation rites allegedly involved ritual sex). A man called Elagabalus from the Syrian city of Homs became emperor in the third century, supplanted the old cult of Jupiter with worship of a Levantine sun god, and installed a black meteorite from his hometown as focus of the Rome's largest temple. In the other direction, the cult of the Greek philosophers spread across the Middle East. Another religion that moved from west to east was Judaism. Perhaps some Jews had remained by the waters of Babylon after their exile there in the sixth century BC; certainly there was an established Jewish community in Iraq in the early first century AD, when the king of the northern province of Adiabene, his wife, and his mother were all separately converted to Judaism. In AD 70 the Jews of Iraq were joined by others fleeing eastward from the Roman armies that had sacked Jerusalem and demolished its Temple. Babylonia (the region where Babylon had once stood, and which kept its name: the city itself was ruined by this time) became the heartland of the Jewish religion. Estimates of the Jewish population of Iraq go as high as two million by the year AD 500—perhaps something like 40 percent of its population.

The oldest surviving Mandaean scriptures were written in a language very close to that used by the Jewish scholars who compiled the Babylonian Talmud, one of the most important collections of Jewish law, which was assembled between the third and fifth centuries AD. The Mandaean books show an interest in Judaism and a close knowledge of its practices, but a lot of hostility too. The Mandaeans have adopted John the Baptist but dislike Abraham. They utterly reject circumcision—a practice that marked out the

Jews from the Babylonians even during the Jewish exile in Babylon. The Mandaeans take Sunday, not Saturday, as the Sabbath. The legend of Miriai is about a Jewish woman who leaves her community in order to marry a Mandaean man. Jews and Mandaeans knew each other but were rivals.

Mandaeanism was not alone in being heavily influenced by Judaism: several versions of Christianity were, too. Some tried to keep Jewish law while following Jesus, while others were more hostile. For example, a breakaway Christian group called the Marcionites, founded in what is now northern Turkey in about AD 144, accepted that the events described in the Hebrew Bible (adopted by Christians as the Old Testament) were true, but were appalled by some of them. Why would God, for instance, forbid Adam to eat from the tree of knowledge in the Garden of Eden? Why would he ask Abraham to kill his own son? So they believed that the God described there was in fact an inferior deity, unworthy of worship. The material world this inferior deity had created was something to escape from. That included the human body and its urges: elite Marcionites were unmarried and had no children. The Marcionites' scriptures included only the Gospel of Luke and the Epistles of Paul, and even those were changed somewhat. The name of Abraham, for example, was removed almost everywhere it appeared, because Abraham not only was willing to kill his son but also slept with his maid and allowed Pharaoh to sleep with his own wife.

It was in such an environment—where Jews were numerous, Christian groups proliferated, and the old religions were giving way to new ideologies— that a man called Patik prepared to offer a sacrifice to one of the old gods at a temple in a city south of where Baghdad stands today. It would have been a bloody affair, the slaughter of a goat or a sheep perhaps, after which he might receive a portion of the flesh to eat. But he suddenly heard a supernatural voice telling him never to eat meat again. Nor to have sex. Nor to drink alcohol. The year was around AD 215.

Asceticism was a common theme of the new religions of the Middle East. This may have been in part a reflection of Indian influence or a reaction to the self-indulgence of the older religions (Syria, where pagan temples once housed sacred prostitutes, was also the country where a Christian saint lived on top of a pillar for thirty years without once coming down). There was a philosophy behind the self-denial as well. Society was technologically advanced: in the second century AD Ptolemy drew a map of the world that would be used for more than a thousand years, and Galen wrote a medical textbook that would be used until the nineteenth century. Yet cesspits had to be cleaned out by hand, diseases such as typhoid were common, and wounds might easily develop gangrene. The body's weakness and foulness were in strange contrast to the intellect's amazing achievements. Since at this time it was not generally understood that the intellect had any connection with the brain (Galen realized that it did, but Aristotle had thought the brain existed just to release heat from the body), it was easy to suppose that the mind, or soul, could survive without the messiness of the body.

Religions that instructed their followers to punish or subordinate the body so that the mind could be made free are often called "Gnostic," and there were several such at this time. Patik discovered that a number of austere communities had recently been established in the Iraqi Marshes. The Mandaeans were one of these, but their rules perhaps were not strict enough for Patik. (Although the Mandaeans may have been vegetarian at some point in their history, they never favored celibacy.) A nearby community fitted better with the instructions that the voice had given him. Not only did they never eat meat, have sex, or drink alcohol, but they also avoided art and music. Otherwise they tried to strictly follow both Jewish law and the Christian gospels. Each family seems to have had a plot of land where they grew vegetables and fruit to eat. Later writers called them the Mughtasila, which in Arabic means "the washers," because of their practice of baptism in the rivers of the marshes. It was the Mughtasila that Patik and his already pregnant wife joined, and shortly afterward their only child was born. They named him Mani.

As Mani grew up, he went through a period of rebellion. It did not involve sex or alcohol. Instead, he chafed at the restrictions on art. He was a talented artist and longed to express his ideas visually as well as with musical hymns. The Mandaeans, living nearby in the marshes, were an inspiration: although they rejected Jesus, whom Mani admired, he appreciated their music and borrowed one of their hymns. In other ways, however, he found his own community's rules too lax. Giving up meat was not enough, he said. To

A modern representation of Mani, a third-century founder of a religion that competed with early Christianity and whose division of the universe between good and evil gave rise to the term "Manichean." He was preceded and influenced by the Mandaeans.

kill and eat vegetables was cruel to plants, and he could even hear the fig tree weep for the fruit that was cut from its branches. The springs of fresh water complained, he said, when the Mughtasila bathed in them, because they were polluting the water. (His own followers in later years apparently would wash themselves using their own urine instead.) Eventually Mani claimed to have received a new revelation—an account of a cosmic battle between light and darkness.

According to St. Augustine, who followed Mani's teachings for a time before becoming a Christian, Mani taught that the universe contained "two antagonistic masses, both of which were infinite"—one good, the other evil. "Evil was some . . . kind of substance, a shapeless, hideous mass . . . a kind of evil mind filtering through the substance they called earth." Evil was the source of all darkness in the universe, including eclipses of the sun and moon and the alternation of day and night. To Mani, day following night, and night following day, were signs of a constant battle between light and darkness. To this day, we speak of a "Manichean worldview" to mean one that divides the world into the forces of good and the forces of evil. (*Mani chai* was what Mani's followers cried in Aramaic: it means "Mani is alive." So his followers came to be called Manichees or Manicheans.)

For religiously enlightened Manichees, the highest calling was to free the spirit from the bonds of matter. For the truly committed—the "elders," as they were called (the same word, *sheikh* in Arabic, is applied to Mandaean priests)—this meant never having children, eating only fruit, and atoning for plucking that fruit. Wasting water was a sin. Killing animals was unthinkable. Strict Manichees would not kill a fly. "Let [the country] . . . with smoking blood change into one where the people eat vegetables," as a Manichee prayer declared. The religion also offered a chance of salvation, however, to people who wanted to follow Mani without observing all his rules: after all, someone had to commit the sin of plucking the fruit for the elders to eat. The elders absolved their followers of this sin by digesting their food according to a strict ritual, which was meant to liberate the fragments of light trapped inside the food. This structure of elders and followers meant that the religion had people of exemplary austerity who were capable of interceding with God on behalf of the whole community, leaving their followers free to live as they chose, provided that they maintained and respected the elders. As we will see, this structure is still used by some Middle Eastern faiths today.

In around the year 240 Mani left the marshes and the community where he had been brought up and traveled east to the capital of the Parthian Empire. He was a distinctive figure in his multicolored coat, striped trousers, and high boots. Helped by his family's aristocratic connections and the general laissez-faire attitude of the Parthians toward religion, he almost succeeded in converting the emperor to his cause—and was executed for his efforts. But his religion continued to spread. As his followers went east from Iran, they relied on Buddhist iconography to explain their message. Mani was presented as "the Buddha of Light." A Manichee kingdom was established among the central Asian Uyghurs. In later centuries, Manichees became numerous in China, where they were best known for their refusal to eat meat. "Vegetarian demon worshipers" was the way the authorities described them in an edict in 1141. Official persecution winnowed their numbers, but they may have survived in southern China until the turn of the twentieth century. Indeed, it appears that Mani is still worshiped in one place in China today, though accidentally: at a temple in eastern China, a statue of a Buddha with a beard and straight hair dates back to the time when the temple was built by Manichees—and was probably originally a statue of Mani.

In the West, Manicheism taught reverence for Jesus and was a serious competitor to early Christianity. A Manichee called Sebastianus almost became the emperor of Rome in the middle of the fourth century: if he had, world history would have been very different. Instead, Manicheism largely disappeared in the lands of the empire, as Christianity became the state religion of Rome and Roman authorities began to stamp out rival faiths. It survived longer among the Muslims, and Manichees even worked in the center of government—until the eighth-century caliph al-Mahdi decided that its adherents had become too powerful, and crucified large numbers of them. The Muslim scholar Ibn al-Nadim, who left the account of Mani's life on which the above is based, knew a few Manichees in Baghdad in the tenth century, but they do not seem to have survived much longer than that under Islamic rule.

Manicheism nevertheless left a lasting mark on European civilization. There is some evidence that Christians felt the need to imitate the unsurpassed austerity of Mani's holy men and women. Inspired by their belief that matter was permeated with evil and was a prison for the soul, the Manichee elect tried to thwart all bodily impulses—and Christian hermits followed suit, denying themselves sleep, eating only grass and fruit, and sometimes castrating themselves. Christian monasticism was particularly strong in Egypt, where Manichee monasteries had already been established. St. Augustine, a strong believer in original sin and an advocate of chastity, had been a Manichee and felt the need to combat its appeal. In short, modern Christian asceticism and monasticism may still owe a debt to Mani.

The Mandaeans are neither Manichees nor Mughtasila. Unlike both of those groups, they reject Jesus and believe that marrying and having children are moral obligations. But in other ways they have many things in common with the Manichees. They reject Abraham and believe that the body is a prison for the soul. They believe in an angel of light, Hibil Ziwa, who is always contending with darkness. Mandaeans believe themselves to be sparks of the cosmic light that have detached themselves from it and become trapped in a material home. When liberated by death from their bodily prisons, these sparks of light can ascend back to the great light from which they once came. So at a funeral, a Mandaean priest may address the soul of a dead man as follows: "You have left corruption behind and the stinking body in which you found yourself, the abode of the wicked, the place which is all sin, the World of Darkness, of hatred, envy, and strife, the abode in which the planets live, bringing sorrows and infirmities." And the Mandaeans believe that the manner in which a priest eats a sacred meal at the funeral of a deceased member of the faith can make a difference to that person's fate in the afterlife. All of these are ideas and practices that would have been familiar to the followers of that other Iraqi religion, Manicheism. The Mandaeans therefore are a link not only to the ancient history of the Middle East but to the history of Christianity as well.

———

THE MANDAEANS PROBABLY NUMBER fewer than a hundred thousand in the whole world, and until 2003 most of them lived in Iraq. Not all of them are religious, as I discovered when I had my second encounter with a Mandaean—this time in a café in Manhattan, in 2009. Nadia Gattan was visiting the United States from Britain, which had given her asylum. Though she had left Iraq, she remained, as she put it, "hard-core Iraqi. We're matter-of-fact people, not interested in glamour. I'm emotional, passionate, not like Europeans." Brought up in a left-wing family in the Baghdad suburbs, Nadia saw herself as Iraqi first and Mandaean second. Her friends came from many different religions, and her parents were not especially observant. "I was taught nothing about religion," she went on, "only moral rules: not to lie, not to steal, always to remember that I was a woman."

The Mandaean holy books were not available for Nadia to read, as they were kept by priests in a chapel called the *mandi*. Her family did not pray, and in their home in Baghdad, which she described to me, it would have taken a sharp eye to spot anything that marked them as different from other middle-class, secular Iraqi families. It was an absence, not a presence, that would meet the eye at first. The walls were not decorated with the sacred writing of the Koran, nor any photograph of the great Ka'aba of Mecca with thousands of white-clad pilgrims circling it, nor (as the Shi'a Muslims tend to have) a portrait of Imam Hussein. On a closer look, a privileged visitor might have seen more evidence of Mandaeanism. A discreet picture of the *darfesh* hung on the wall of the living room. The family's white baptismal robes and girdles, used for sacred immersions in the water of the Tigris River, were stored in a cupboard kept free from all impurity, ready for the rare occasions when they would be needed.

Nadia was brought up in Baghdad, but her family had only moved there in the 1970s. Before then they had lived in a small town in the south of Iraq called Suq ash-Shuyukh (literally, "the elders' market"). Nadia's father had been a teacher there, with a small gold shop as a side business. And it was when the family went back there for Mandaean festivals that Nadia really experienced her religion properly, spending time with her devout grandparents. In an old photo that Nadia showed me, I saw her grandfather: surrounded by children dressed in Western-style clothes, he was an old man with a long beard and a red-and-white *keffiyeh*. He ate meat only if it had been taken from an unblemished male animal that had been slaughtered while facing north and then bled dry, and only his wife was allowed to prepare it. She was next to him in the photograph: an equally devout woman, dressed all in black and wearing a veil over her hair. He was a blacksmith and she practiced traditional medicine, treating the eye diseases that local farmers would get during the rice harvest. When she visited these grandparents, Nadia was told that if she was menstruating, she had to sit at a separate table. This was the strict enforcement of a rule shared by both ancient Babylonians and Jews (in Babylon a man who touched a menstruating woman was impure for six days). With Nadia it came to an end. She refused, and eventually her grandparents stopped complaining that she was violating the rules.

This couple had arrived in Suq ash-Shuyukh in 1949. Before that they had lived out in the Iraqi Marshes, the vast maze of small islands, reedbeds, and shallow rivulets that bordered the town on its eastern side. The majority of the population consisted of fiercely independent Muslim tribes. The British traveler Wilfrid Thesiger lived there in the 1950s and described it as a "world complete in itself," with minimal interference from the outside. He was fascinated by the tribes, among whom he found a curious mix of tolerance (accepting tomboy women who slept with other women, for example) and rigidity (the laws governing cleanliness were so strict that a man might see his son bleed to death and not touch him for fear of making himself ritually unclean).

Thesiger only briefly mentions the Mandaeans who lived alongside the Muslims in the marshes. He comments on their long beards, red-and-white checked head cloths, silver work, and habit of keeping ducks, which to local Muslims were unclean animals. Who knows: Thesiger might have met Nadia's mother's father, who worked for the leaders of the tribes fixing weapons for their hunting trips. "He could disassemble a gun and put it back together," Nadia told me. Her father's father made small, simple boats that the local people used for transport, as it was easier to move around the marshes

Wilfrid Thesiger took this picture in 1950 of Arabs from the Iraqi Marshes using the *belem*, a type of boat dating back to Sumerian times, to move through the marshes, which were so isolated that he called them "a world in itself." Photo courtesy Pitt Rivers Museum

on water than on land. These boats were called *belem,* a word with Sumerian roots.

One of the Mandaean festivals is called the White Days and commemorates the five days during which Mandaeans believe the world was created. During Nadia's childhood this festival was in April (the Mandaean religious calendar contains no leap years, so its festivals move very slightly from one solar year to the next), and Nadia's parents took her and her brother back to their hometown to celebrate with their extended family. Nadia described to me the town's small houses, some the same shade of brown as the fields and the rivers, others made of reeds. The town's Mandaeans all lived together in one district. The children

A Mandaean man pictured by Wilfrid Thesiger in the Iraqi Marshes, applying pitch to a boat—just as Nadia's grandfather once did. Photo courtesy Pitt Rivers Museum

played in the road and went from one house to another to ask for food or sweets. If they were lucky, they might be given the Mandaean specialty, wild mallard duck stuffed with cinnamon and cardamom, chopped onions, nuts, and sultanas, and boiled with dried limes and turmeric. To keep the children in line, the adults warned them that if they misbehaved, the wild horsemen of the desert would seize them and carry them off.

The White Days are a joyful festival, but the Mandaean New Year is a feast day with a more frightening side to it. Evil is said to walk the earth for thirty-six hours in the form of a female spirit called Ruha. In line with tradition, Nadia's parents tried to make her stay indoors at this time, but without success. "I didn't take it seriously," she told me. "But I was told Ruha might take the form of a wasp, a bee, a tree, or a bird and would try to harm me. Or I might be hit by a car. It was an unlucky time to be outside." Even in her secular household, this particular taboo still had some force.

In addition to a happy festival and a frightening one, the Mandaeans have a sad one, too. On the same day that Shi'a Muslims mark Ashura—the day of mourning for the death of the Prophet's grandson Hussein and their own failure to come to his aid—the Mandaeans mourn as well, preparing a special meal of pearl barley soup, called *abul harith*. Sometimes they even join the Shi'a processions. They have various explanations for what exactly it is that they are remembering that day—"It's in memory of a very stressful time," was all that Nadia knew—but some Mandaeans believe that it commemorates the drowning of Pharaoh's soldiers in the Red Sea. While Jews regard this incident as cause for celebration, the Mandaeans—for some reason that they themselves do not know—have come to empathize with the Egyptians. (Such days of mourning were once common across the Middle East. The Babylonians used to berate themselves once a year over their abandonment of the body of a pagan prophet, an act that they believed had caused the Great Flood.)

Nadia and her family also turned up with the rest of the community to give moral support to Mandaean men who were trying to enter the priesthood. The initiation ceremony is an arduous process. An aspirant must spend seven days in a reed hut without food or sleep. This is when he needs the support of the community: some of them stand outside the hut beating drums and chanting to make sure he stays awake, and women ululate. A *ganzibra,* the equivalent of a Mandaean bishop, stays with the aspirant and carves twenty-one words of power with his olivewood staff on the earthen floor of the hut: they are too secret to be said out loud, and when they have been learned the *ganzibra* sweeps over the dust to ensure that nobody else can read them. To complete the initiation the aspirant must eat a ritual meal, following an intricate and precise set of instructions. From then on, he must grow his beard long and keep strict rules of purity.

But there is a higher level of holiness and knowledge, available only to those who, like Sheikh Sattar, had been appointed to the rank of *ganzibra*. This is an appointment that in the Mandaean tradition no living man can confer. A messenger must be sent into the afterlife to seek permission for it. The would-be *ganzibra* finds a person on the verge of death and stows a bottle of holy oil in the pocket of the garment adorned with gold and silver that dying Mandaeans are obliged to wear. "I have brought it to you," the priest must say, "and you bear it to Abatur." The ritual is complete after the messenger dies and his soul reaches Abatur, the judge of the dead, from whom he receives confirmation of the aspiring *ganzibra*'s request.

Only men can enter the Mandaean priesthood, and only men can marry non-Mandaeans and still pass on the religion to their children. A woman who marries out is debarred from baptism and cannot have her children baptized. Nadia thought that this inequality between the sexes was not the original spirit of Mandaeanism. For corroboration she looked back to the Mandaean scriptures: instead of Eve being made from Adam's rib, as is told in the Book of Genesis, the Mandaean version says that both were made together. "I am sure there was a time," she told me, "when Mandaean women could be priests, not just men." She was right: in the Drasa da Yehia, a Jewish woman converts to Mandaeanism and becomes a priest. (Similarly, in ancient Babylon women could serve as priests. For that matter, women occasionally achieved secular positions of power in the ancient Middle East. The ancient Persian navy had a female admiral—Artemisia, back in the fifth century BC— and in the third century AD Palmyra had a powerful queen, Zenobia.)

———————

THE MOST IMPORTANT Mandaean ceremony of all is baptism. One view of the Mandaeans has it that they adopted this practice from Jewish followers of John the Baptist fleeing eastward from Roman persecution; another has it that immersion in the waters of the river Tigris might have been an ancient practice in Iraq itself, as it was in Egypt. Certainly the traditions attached to the ceremony are distinctively Mandaean. As priests had done for the children of Iraq in pre-Christian times, a priest read the stars when Nadia was born and used them to devise a horoscope for her. And when she reached the age of seventeen, another priest in Baghdad used that horoscope to choose a secret name for her, called a *milwasha*. As she crouched in the waters of the Tigris, a girdle around her waist, a ring of myrtle leaves on her finger, and a white garment enveloping her head and body, he immersed her in the water three times, signed her forehead with water three times, made her swallow the river water three times, crowned her with myrtle,

Nadia (far right) prepares for her baptism in Baghdad in 1991.
She is veiled because of the holiness of the occasion, and carries
a myrtle sprig. Behind the group, a picture shows a baptism being
performed. Photo courtesy Nadia Gattan

prayed over her, and named her. "It will be my name in religion," she told
me, "for as long as I live and beyond."

Four aspects of that ceremony would have been familiar to any Babylonian of the first millennium BC. The first was the language in which it was
performed. I got to see this language when I went to examine Mandaean holy
books kept at the Bibliothèque Nationale in Paris. Because of the books'
fragility, it took some persuasion before the staff would allow me to look
through one of them. As I turned its pages I reflected that the Mandaean
scribe who had copied it out with great care in the seventeenth century,
spacing his lines out and crafting each calligraphic stroke, would have been
horrified to see me reading it. Only Mandaean initiates into the priesthood
were meant to be shown these texts.

The scribe would have been still more appalled by the volume's leather cover, embossed with a fleur-de-lis, which the French royal librarian had put on the book when it entered the collection of King Louis XVI. Mandaean priests never used animal products such as leather to bind their books—a relic, some scholars say, of a time when their religion used to forbid meat altogether. They used calico as a binding material, or they engraved the pages on wood or even etched them onto lead with acid. The sharp-angled words that sloped from right to left across the page, black ink on the thick fibrous paper, were in a strange script: to my untutored eye it was similar to Arabic but with some extra letters and fewer of the dots that mark the Arabic alphabet. This was a specifically Mandaean dialect of Aramaic, the language of Iraq before Arabic.

Early Muslim writers, knowing that Aramaic had preceded their own language, Arabic, assumed that Aramaic was as old as the world itself and that Adam had spoken it after the Fall. In fact, when Babylon first emerged four thousand years ago, its official language was Sumerian, which was gradually displaced by a language called Akkadian—we can tell that for some time Akkadian was regarded as something like slang, because a four-thousand-year-old comic poem complains about what happened when the poet, as a boy, was caught speaking Akkadian at school (as well as breaking every other rule): "The door monitor said, 'Why did you go out without my say-so?' He beat me. The jug monitor, 'Why did you take water without my say-so?' He beat me. The Sumerian monitor, 'You spoke in Akkadian!' He beat me." Only in the last centuries of Babylon's existence did Aramaic become the city's everyday language. A form of Aramaic is also spoken by Mandaeans in Iran, and a closely related language, with a distinct but similar script, is still in use among Christians in northern Iraq.

NADIA'S RELIGIOUS NAME was given to her after her priest's careful study of the stars—the second Mandaean inheritance from the Babylonians, who were dedicated astronomers. It was the Babylonians who first divided the sky into the twelve signs of the zodiac, choosing twelve to match the number of cycles of the moon in every year. Such diligent watchers of the skies saw early on—certainly by 1500 BC—that some stars behaved differently than others. They were brighter and moved through the sky in a different way. The observers called these *lu-bat*, meaning "wandering sheep." The term was translated into Greek as *aster planetes,* meaning "wandering star," which in turn gave us our word *planet.*

Babylonian astronomers identified five planets—Mercury, Venus, Mars, Jupiter, and Saturn (not Uranus and Neptune, which were invisible to the naked eye). They put the sun and moon in this group as well—making seven—and named each one after a god, such as Marduk, Ishtar, and Nebu. They then invented the week as a period of seven days, one for every planet god. (Rather neatly, seven days made up a quarter of a moon cycle, too.) We have inherited from the Babylonians the habit of naming the planets and the days of the week after gods: Mercury, Venus, Pluto; Saturday for Saturn, Thursday for Thor, Sunday and Monday for the sun and moon. For the Babylonians, one day in seven was an evil day, when activity should be avoided—which may have been the origin of the Sabbath day adopted by Judaism.

Because the planets were gods, their behavior was a sign of the gods' intentions. The stars, too, were divine beings. Skilled astrologers called *umannu,* rather like Mandaean priests, advised the king on the omens they saw in the night sky and how to avert any ill they boded. They prayed to the stars ("O great ones, gods of the night . . . O Pleiades, Orion, and the Dragon") before examining them. Eventually the Babylonians made predictions for people's lives based on the disposition of the gods at their birth. For instance, a clay tablet survives that tells us of the birth of a boy called Aristokrates in 235 BC: "That day: Moon in Leo, Sun in 12° 30' of Gemini, Jupiter in 18° Sagittarius. The place of Jupiter means that his life will be regular, he will become rich, he will grow old, his days will be numerous." The tradition has survived for millennia: in the back pages of European and American newspapers today are predictions that the old Babylonian astrologers might have recognized.

More to the point, Mandaean priests and *ganzibra*s have a similar custom of making astrological measurements in order to determine the propitious hours for various activities. When a Mandaean couple are married, they may not have intercourse until the right time, determined in advance by the *ganzibra* through observation of the stars. Afterward they are considered unclean—and, just as the fifth-century Greek historian Herodotus says Babylonian couples used to do, "at daybreak they both wash. Before they have washed they will not touch any household utensils." (For Mandaeans, the washing is the ritual of baptism. For Babylonians, too, it probably meant washing in the river.)

The numbers seven and twelve still have a special significance in Western culture: seventh heaven, lucky number seven, twelve apostles, twelve knights of the Round Table, twelve Greek gods on Mount Olympus. For the Mandaeans, though, "the Seven" and "the Twelve" had their original Babylonian meaning, referring specifically to the stars and planets as supernatural, quasi-divine beings. In the Mandaean Book of John appears this phrase: "The Seven sent him their greeting and the Twelve made obeisance before him." They still believe, as the scholar of Mandaeanism E. S. Drower wrote, that "the planets are creatures of God and each has a spirit in it." In the 1930s Drower knew a Mandaean named Hermez bar Anhar, who told her, "I worship all the *melki*"—meaning the heavenly beings—"but my especial worship is of the sun." Hermez seems to have regarded the sun as a kind of angel; "worship" implies that it is a kind of god, but the Mandaeans do not see themselves as polytheists and vigorously reject any suggestion that they are "star worshipers." Unlike the Babylonians, the Mandaeans do not have temples to the sun and moon. Still, they have clearly preserved many Babylonian customs and beliefs with respect to the stars and planets.

AT NADIA'S BAPTISM, as she stood in the waters of the Tigris, the name the priest said to her was meant to remain a secret, and this is the third aspect of the ceremony that links her community with ancient Babylon. Secrecy has been a guiding principle of the Mandaeans and of the cultures from which they came. When Ibn Wahshiyyah was compiling the *Nabatean Agriculture* in the ninth century AD, putting on record the agricultural knowledge of the pre-Islamic inhabitants, he encountered many obstacles in his research, for the Nabateans had a strict code of secrecy. "Do you want to argue against the way of our elders and forebears," he was asked, "and their admonitions to us to keep hidden our religion and habits?" So he reached a compromise: he would tell readers some of the Nabatean "science" but nothing about their religion. To make doubly sure that he did not spill secrets, the writer tells us that he mixed lies in with facts to confuse the lay reader. He gives an example of the code he developed: "The eggplant will disappear for three thousand years" apparently means that there were three months of the year when the eggplant should not be eaten.

E. S. Drower was a good friend of the Mandaean community (a "dear sister in faith," as one Mandaean priest called her). Yet even she only managed to see their holy texts after nine years of asking. When the head priests of the community found that she had succeeded in deciphering some of their scriptures, they reacted, in her account, with "resentment and anger. These scrolls, they said, contain 'secrets,' knowledge imparted to priests only at ordination and never to laymen or outsiders." As she read the manuscripts, she found that their introductory pages were inscribed with curses on anyone who revealed them to the uninitiated.

The books that Drower read can today be seen in an underground vault belonging to the Bodleian Library in Oxford. In those books, and in Drower's published transcriptions of oral legends told to her by Mandaeans in the 1930s, I discovered more about their radical mythology and the amazing characters that populate it. There is Krun, the flesh mountain, who sounds a bit like Jabba the Hutt; as Drower wrote, "The whole visible world rests on this king of darkness, and his shape is that of a huge louse." There is Abraham, who appears as a failed Mandaean guided by an evil spirit to leave and found his own community. There is the dragon Ur, whose belly is made of fire and who sits above an ocean of flammable oil. There is Ptahil, "who takes souls to be weighed and sends his spirits to fetch souls from their bodies." My favorite was the demon Dinanukht, who is half man and half book and "sits by the waters between the worlds, reading himself."

The reason for the secrecy, Nadia said, was bound up with belief in magic. "Some people think that if they reveal their name, it can be used for black magic. But I trust you. And," she chuckled, "you don't have access to the black magic books." Magic is the fourth and final link between the modern Mandaeans and the ancient Babylonians. The *Nabatean Agriculture* included a great number of magical spells in its list of agricultural techniques. (Some examples: averting hail by placing a tortoise on its back in the middle of a field, or having three menstruating women bare their vulvas at any approaching hailstorms to make them go the other way, using the apotropaic power of menstrual blood.)

In the seventh century, the Christian writer Yohannan bar Penkaye (who lived near where the Turkish-Iraqi border is today) said that sorcery was more common in his town than it had been in ancient Babylon. In the 1930s, E. S. Drower was fascinated by the survival of magic in Iraqi society. Magicians—of all different religions—told people's future and also produced love charms. She wrote of a modern spell that could easily have come from *Nabatean Agriculture*: "To cure a Baghdad boil . . . take a sparrow, kill it, and apply his body so that the fresh warm blood touches the sore. Then hang the sparrow up. As the body dries so will the boil dry up and disappear."

Jews and Mandaeans, Drower writes, were particularly famous for spells. Mostly they gave out amulets and good-luck charms, but occasionally they used darker arts. Drower's collection at the Bodleian includes a book of "black magic"; Drower justified using the term because, she said, even in the Mandaean language this book was described as "evil," as it contained spells for breaking up marriages, inflicting illness, and bestowing curses. I leafed through its pages and saw diagrams of the human body, numerological charts, strange symbols, and unreadable letters repeated over and over again, all blotched with ink (suggesting, perhaps, a lack of skill on the part of the scribe; or perhaps the pages had been wetted as part of a ceremony, for in some magical rites in the Middle East, water that has touched the ink of a sacred book is drunk as a ritual). It describes amulets made from bat's wings inscribed with hoopoe blood and the blood of a rabid wolf; for a person who has been possessed by a demon on a Sunday (the Mandaean holy day), an ointment should be made from horse saliva, monkey and pigeon blood, the juice of mint and purslane, and olive and sesame oil, and then stuck into the victim's nose.

Some of these spells had clearly been handed down over the generations since Babylonian times. Drower discovered for sale a Mandaean magic scroll that could be buried beside a grave in time of plague to avert the disease's spread; it began with "In the name of Libat, mistress of gods and men," an invocation to the Babylonian love goddess Libat (also known as Ishtar). Drower was told by Mandaeans in her day that Libat was consulted for oracles and invoked for love spells. She also found a recent Mandaean amulet designed for separating lovers, which declared: "Sundered is Bel from Babylon, sundered is Nebu from Borsippa." Nebu was the god after whom the king Nebuchadnezzar was named, and Borsippa has been a ruin for more than two thousand years.

The commonest amulet among Mandaeans today is the *skanduleh,* which Nadia has hanging on her kitchen wall. It is placed under the pillow or mattress of small children, she told me, and is also placed in a basket of clothes belonging to a bride on her wedding day. (Remedies for the evil eye, in European tradition, are used in the same contexts; a traditional English poem tells a bride to wear "something borrowed" and "something blue" on her wedding day.) The *skanduleh* consists of a round disk with four animals pictured on it: a lion, a snake, a scorpion, and a wasp. These represent the forces of darkness and are used to frighten away evil spirits. In Uruk, in southern Iraq, German archaeologists discovered a scorpion amulet dating to the thirteenth century BC. The Ishtar gate of Babylon was decorated with mosaics of a snakelike creature with feline forelegs, possibly because it could evoke the sinister powers of both the lion and the snake.

Nadia's aunt had made a living in Baghdad from spell casting, as Nadia told me. The walls of this aunt's house were thin, and when the young Nadia was playing there with her cousins, they could all hear the consultations in the next room between the aunt and her various clients. People would come to her desperate for something that might improve their lives; often they wanted their daughters to marry rich men, and they hoped an amulet might help. Once the aunt enlisted Nadia's help. She asked the girl to scribble on paper whatever came into her head, and then she took away the bits of paper and gave them to customers as magical amulets. Nadia's aunt believed in the effect of these things, because so often the customers really did find life improved for them afterward.

Nadia's aunt was a gentle, lovable character, which helps explain why people opened up to her. As a result, she had insight into every layer of Iraqi society—enough, even, to attract the attention of the secret police.

"They tested me," Nadia's aunt said. "They sent undercover girls who sat down and checked exactly what I was doing. They told me I was in the clear because I did everything aboveboard." Maybe they were trying to determine whether anything subversive was going on, for a soothsayer could be in a position to recruit conspirators. Or perhaps they were looking for evidence of the use of black magic (meaning curses; amulets and fortune-telling were considered harmless white magic), which might well have been punished.

Nadia's aunt was still casting spells in the 1990s, when Nadia was studying languages at Baghdad University and working part-time at a printing shop so that she could pay her university fees. Those were tough times: after Iraq invaded Kuwait in 1990, United Nations sanctions destroyed its economy. Per capita income declined by 85 percent. Chocolate had become so rare that a friend of Nadia's celebrated her university graduation by giving a small piece of chocolate to each of her friends; Nadia took her piece home and split it with her sister. The teachers at the university had to work as taxi drivers half the day, and one of them even drove his own pupils to class—he needed the fare to supplement his meager salary. Children were sent out to find work instead of going to school. This, in a country that once had $35 billion in foreign exchange reserves, whose middle class in 1990 made up over half the population, and which had reduced illiteracy among those under age forty-five to less than 10 percent.

One day Nadia's aunt came out of one of her spell-casting consultations with a troubled expression. Nadia and her cousins asked her what was wrong. "Oh, it was that client who just left," she said. "She wanted an amulet for her daughter. She's only fifteen, but the mother wants an amulet to help her daughter find a rich man to marry. The grandfather is ill, and the uncles are out of work. And as the woman took the amulet, she told me she had been dressing her daughter up with makeup and sending her out to knock on God's door. So I was wondering what that might mean." "Knocking on God's door" was a phrase that a laborer might use to refer to standing in line with other workers waiting to be hired. "And I realized she must be sending her daughter out as a prostitute."

It was not only the poor and desperate who wanted spells. So, as Nadia related, did Saddam Hussein. Saddam's Ba'ath party had begun its rule with a brutal crackdown on political opponents, who included Iraq's most distinguished Mandaean, Abdul-Jabbar Abdullah. Born in a village in southern Iraq in 1911, Abdullah had been able to travel to America and study at MIT; he also worked under Albert Einstein, who was impressed enough with his pupil's talent that he presented him with his own Parker pen. Abdullah was a meteorologist (a branch of science particularly suited to the Mandaeans, who have inherited the Babylonians' fascination with the stars). When the left-wing nationalist Abdul-Karim Qassem deposed the Iraqi monarchy and took power in 1958, Abdullah became the first president of Baghdad University. He was, however, a Communist—a common thing then among minorities in Iraq, who saw Communism's secular ideology as a protection against religious bigotry. So when the anti-Communist Ba'ath party seized power in 1963 they sent men to arrest Abdullah; they burst into his office at the university, announced his dismissal, and arrested him. But only when they seized Einstein's pen and snapped it in front of Abdullah did he burst into tears. Later freed, Abdullah fled to the United States, where he died.

Saddam was not an enemy to all Mandaeans, though: he employed one as a poet, and—seeing plots everywhere and fearing supernatural as well as human enemies—he also turned to the Mandaean high priest of the day for spells of protection. Perhaps because of this man's spells—and the rumors of the Mandaeans' powerful curses—Saddam looked after the Mandaeans. For a time he even extolled them as symbols of Iraqi identity. Like the palaces he built on the ruins of Babylon, the Mandaeans helped reinforce the idea that Iraq was a nation-state with a proud history rather than a province carved out of the Ottoman Empire. They did not represent a serious political threat, and they were not rich enough to be worth targeting for their money. Like Jews and Christians, they were identified as "people of the book": the Mandaeans are identified as the "Sabians" mentioned in the Koran as deserving special leniency (as opposed to polytheist pagans, who were to be fought and killed). The Mandaeans even took care to publish one of their holy books in 2001 in a classical Arabic translation, a form designed to make it acceptable to Muslim readers. The Mandaeans knew they needed friends in high places. Their history was full of grim encounters with unjust rulers.

A Hebrew schoolbook and dusty typewriters are almost all that remained in 2003 of Baghdad's Jews, who once made up as much as a third of the city's population. Photo by the author

And although in the twentieth century ideologies such as Communism and Arab nationalism held out the promise of equality, the fate of Iraq's Jewish population showed that governments, more powerful now than ever, could penalize minorities as never before.

———————

IN THE 1940s there were still over a hundred thousand Jews in Iraq. In 2003, when I visited Baghdad for the first time, I saw what little remained of them. In a quiet road in an old quarter of Baghdad a dusty house sat empty; when I knocked at the door, a curtain opposite twitched. This was Baghdad's Jewish community center. It had been abandoned in rather a hurry, from the look of it. In an upstairs room I found Hebrew-language schoolbooks heaped on the floor. A ledger sat next to them, wedged between old typewriters. The latest entry was dated December 21, 1969. What happened to Iraq's ancient

Jewish community, so that by 2003 nothing remained but a pile of dusty schoolbooks? I asked this question of Moshe and Yvonne Khadhouri in a comfortable flat in London. Back in 1940, when Iraq was still a monarchy, Moshe and Yvonne were both living in Baghdad. As they remembered it, it was a Jewish-friendly city. "On Saturday, the banks in Baghdad were closed for the Sabbath," Yvonne said, "because all the banks but one were Jewish-owned. The textile trade was all Jewish. We were a third of the inhabitants of Baghdad." Both of them lived through the ghastly events of June 1941 when the monarchy was briefly overthrown and, for three days, a mob whipped up by Nazi-sponsored anti-Semitic propaganda attacked the city's Jews. It was called the *farhud*.

"The Muslims are not bad people," said Moshe. "The Nazis came to Baghdad. And Israel made a lot of trouble between Jews and Muslims. If not for politics—"

"It was religion that was the problem," interrupted Yvonne. "And there were only a few that were nice people."

They both agreed, though, that more than seven hundred Jews were killed during the *farhud*. And although things then returned to normal, with British troops entering the city to forcibly restore the monarchy, the situation deteriorated after the foundation of Israel in 1948 and the final collapse of the monarchy in 1958. In the years that followed, many Jews were denounced, and some were hanged—nine of them in January 1969, a few months before the community center was abandoned. Many were sacked from government jobs and saw their property expropriated. Moshe stayed till the 1960s and Yvonne till the early 1970s. He missed Iraq more than she did. "My daughter wants to look for roots," he said. "There are no roots anymore. The cemeteries were razed. All my heritage is there, but our communities are lost. I want to feel patriotic. Not in Israel. Not in England. I am Iraqi. I feel I've been robbed."

Until 2003, the Mandaeans escaped the fate of the Jews. In the following ten years, however, their fortunes would change, and Nadia would hear from a Jewish Iraqi exile a glum verdict comparing the two communities' fates with the sequence of their different sabbath days: "We were on Saturday, and you are on a Sunday. Now your Sunday has come."

BAGHDAD IN EARLY 2003 was a place simmering with suspicion and fear. From time to time demonstrators (paid, everyone knew, by the government) would parade through the streets, shouting their support for Saddam. Once a crowd of excited men thought they had seen an American soldier hiding in the thick reeds that lined the Tigris, which runs through the city, and beat the reeds with heavy sticks as they tried to hunt the intruder down. Nadia was not interested in campaigning for or against Saddam. She only wanted to keep her brother safe. He had just received call-up papers from the Iraqi army; he was to join the force that would resist the American-led invasion. If he obeyed the draft, she feared, he might be killed. If he did not, he risked a brutal punishment: the amputation of an ear. And so, in their family's small house in southern Baghdad, the two of them argued over whether he should enlist. She thought not. She was the older sibling and had no interest in conforming to traditional ideas of feminine meekness. If she was going to persuade him, she knew, she had to be more intimidating than Saddam. "If you ignore those papers, I'll pay every bribe you need," she said. "And if you obey the call-up, then I'll break your arm." He relented.

Nadia told me that she had almost never encountered discrimination from Muslim Iraqis. At school she had met one pupil who declined to eat her food and called her *nejas,* an Islamic word meaning "unclean." But otherwise she felt that, if anything, being a Mandaean meant that she was treated with extra respect. (This was in a middle-class part of Baghdad; in rural areas, things might have been different. In Suq al-Shuyukh even now, there are eating places and coffeehouses that refuse to serve Mandaeans because they are believed to pollute the utensils they eat with.)

Educational standards dropped during the era of sanctions, as Nadia had described to me, and Iraqi society became coarser—but it was only after the US-led invasion in 2003 that she began to sense danger. She was drawn into arguments at work. "Saddam was like a crown on our head and the invaders are *kuffar,*" said one colleague—*kuffar* being the plural of *kafir*, a word that legitimizes violence against nonbelievers.

"I think he was like a pair of slippers. You put him on your head if you want to!" Nadia replied.

As time went on, she found it harder to sustain her bravado. The conflict gave plenty of opportunities for religious bigotry to fester. "We started to hear of people being kidnapped, hijacked, killed just like that," Nadia told me. Her own workplace, the Red Cross, was bombed in October 2003. The violence struck even closer to home four months later. On January 18, 2004, she was on her way to assist at an international charity in Baghdad when she heard an explosion. Not only heard, but felt—the car she was in shook with the force of the blast. "The sky was cloudy," she remembers, "and I got a strange feeling afterward, as if someone I knew had been caught in the explosion. So I called Hadeel." Nadia and Hadeel, a Christian woman, knew each other from working together in a print shop in Baghdad in the 1990s. In 2003 Hadeel had taken a job with the American embassy and had also managed to find her ideal husband—an Iraqi dentist working in Denmark. Nadia and her other friends had bought her an engagement ring, which Hadeel wore on the same finger as the ring given her by her fiancé.

"I called Hadeel's house; her little brother said she had gone to work. I called her mobile phone, and the mobile phone of a friend who used to go to work with her. No answer. I called her colleague, and he said she had never arrived. When I went home I called her family. They said she had just disappeared. Hadeel's mother called me later—she knew I worked for the Red Cross—and she said, 'I want you to get good news about my daughter.'" News came, but it was not good. The car Hadeel had been in turned out to have had a bomb planted under the driver's seat. It was detonated, and killed the driver; two other women in the car had been injured. But there was no news of Hadeel. Nadia took a day off work and toured the hospitals looking for her. She found nothing. It was only later that she heard. The body had been hard to identify, the hospital said. It was badly burned. The only things that remained uncharred were two rings on one of its fingers.

Hadeel's family went ahead with the wedding party anyway and sang the traditional celebratory chants and ululations. But they did it after having buried the bride. "And they said, 'This is not the wedding we wanted.' I couldn't bear seeing them again. It was such a pointless waste of life. I think people should be aware of these stories before they go to war." The death preyed on Nadia's mind and made her want to leave. "I thought, I don't want to be killed like my friend. I don't want to break my parents' heart."

Nadia had never defined herself by her religion. "I see myself first as a human being, second as an Iraqi, and only third as a Mandaean," she told me. But humanism and patriotism did not help her in postwar Iraq, where more atavistic loyalties came to the fore. Religion was not the only thing that put her in danger: so did her ability to speak English, and the facts that she did not wear a veil or belong to a tribe. "I realized the power of the tribes," she said. "And we, as Mandaeans, don't have a tribe." In the past Mandaeans had used the time-honored tactic of attaching themselves to a tribe not as members but as dependents, an "annex." The tribe would agree to protect them, but since they remained outside the tribe proper, they did not have to accept its religion. In the frightful horrors of Iraq after 2003, Nadia's family had a tribe to protect them, but, as she said, "they don't provide as much protection to their annexes as to their own people." Mandaeans were exposed to kidnapping, forced conversion, and murder. Between 2003 and 2011, the Mandaean Human Rights Group documented 175 murders and 271 kidnappings. In 2004, the group reported, thirty-five Mandaean families living in Fallujah were forced to convert to Islam.

Nadia got on a plane leaving Baghdad on March 18, 2004. Her identity papers—she had no passport and had never been on a plane before—were stamped for the first time. Her parents were worried for her: if she lived abroad on her own, no man would marry her afterward, they fretted. She found London so expensive that she had to pawn her jewelry to pay the rent, and she was startled by the "much milder culture." She missed Iraq and nostalgically sought out the fragrance of orange blossoms. Going with her friends to Iraqi concerts, she was quizzed by Iraqi Jews who had left Baghdad forty years earlier and wanted to hear the latest news about their favorite places there.

Despite the nostalgia, she abandoned thoughts of returning home. "I love it there," she said, "but I can't live it." She was not the last Mandaean to leave. Two years after her departure the high priest Sheikh Sattar fled to Australia. By the time of this writing, more than 90 percent of the Mandaean population of Iraq has emigrated or been killed. It is only in southern Iran that one can find their communities intact. Nadia believed that the Mandaeans' departure was a loss for Iraq. "We were the fulcrum in a pair of scales—holding Iraqi society together. And when the Mandaeans and other minorities left, the scales were broken." And after what we had both seen from looking back in the Mandaeans' history, Nadia and I could agree: with their departure, Babylon has truly fallen.

2

Yazidis

ON A STREET IN A CITY IN CANADA, looking up at an apartment block any day at dawn, one may see a window lit: Mirza Ismail is praying, as he also does at noon and sunset. No outsider may witness his prayers, and since no other member of his own community lives nearby, he performs them alone. Each time he prepares himself carefully. He washes his hands and face and winds a special girdle called a *pishtik* around the white shirt he always wears. Then he prostrates himself toward the sun and begins praying in Kurmanji, the language of his people, to an unknowable God. "There is no god but God," the prayer declares, "and the sun is the light of God." He prays that God may give the world peace.

Mirza is a soft-spoken Iraqi man with a neatly trimmed salt-and-pepper mustache, and because he prays at regular intervals during the day, colleagues and acquaintances often wrongly assume he is Muslim. He is instead a Yazidi, a follower of an esoteric religion that has superficial similarities to Islam but is very different from it. Although his people are often thought of as Kurds and speak the same language (Kurmanji) as their Kurdish neighbors, he insists that they are a separate people. Sometimes called Ezidis, they number hundreds of thousands in northern Iraq and in parts of Syria, Georgia, Armenia, and northwestern Iran. Yazidis believe in reincarnation,

Mirza Ismail and his friend Abu Shihab in Sinjar, northern Iraq. Photo courtesy
Mirza Ismail

sacrifice bulls, and revere an angel who takes the form of a peacock. Their
traditions forbid them to eat lettuce or wear blue; men must grow a mustache,
though few have beards. They are also victims of an ancient calumny—
the accusation that they worship the devil. And even before 2014, they were
the victims of the second-deadliest terrorist attack in history.

Mirza was born in a village on well-watered, oak-forested hills in the Sinjar region of northwestern Iraq (a place far to the north of the Iraqi Marshes,
in which the Mandaeans live; the two communities know about each other
but have very little contact). Long ago this region was part of the Assyrian
Empire, which culturally had much in common with the Babylonians—but
it changed hands many times since, being conquered by Babylon, Persia, the
Romans, the Arabs, and finally the Turks. When Mirza was a young boy, his
family was relocated by Saddam Hussein's government to a housing development called Qahtaniyah. Saddam was trying to bring the restive northern
provinces under tighter government control in order to crush a growing rebellion there by Kurdish separatists who wanted to found their own breakaway
state. Although not all Yazidis saw themselves as Kurds, Saddam was taking

no chances. In Qahtaniyah the Yazidis would be easy to control, especially as without their land they were dependent on government food handouts.

Mirza therefore grew up in one of Qahtaniyah's simple mud-brick single-story homes. Water dripped through the ceiling during the infrequent rainstorms of the winter season. The streets were dirt, and there was no sewage system, but the schools were good, the settlement's one clinic did at least offer treatment for free, and the nearest city, a long but practicable journey away, had a hospital. At the front of the house each family had a garden, where they grew food—radishes, tomatoes, eggplants, and sunflowers for their seeds. The gardens were a reminder of a time when these families had lived in their hill villages, cultivating rich crops of figs and olives. Mirza went back to the hills from time to time, to pray at conical-roofed Yazidi shrines and sometimes to admire the sacred hidden caves where Yazidi families had sought refuge from persecution in past centuries.

Yazidis keep a list of the seventy-two persecutions to which they have been subjected over the centuries. In particular, in the nineteenth century the Ottoman authorities several times hunted them down as heretics—heretics who were particularly vexing because they evaded military conscription and paid no tax. The Ottomans did not find their task easy, though. Even by the easiest road, Sinjar was a day's walk from the nearest city before motorized vehicles were invented. The Yazidis were usually a match for the Ottomans—using their knowledge of the local hills and caves, they could fend off invaders and loot passing caravans. Even when forced to convert to Islam, they could go back to their own religious practices as soon as the outsiders had gone. As subsistence farmers, they could survive without much goodwill from the outside world.

Yazidis and Christians lived alongside each other for centuries and made common cause in past centuries against Muslim overlords. People would convert from one religion to the other; one Yazidi even came to believe that in a former incarnation he had been a Christian priest. (Recently a Christian man in Germany called up a Yazidi woman, claiming to have been her father in a former life. The Yazidis were skeptical.) Yazidis have no special objection to praying at Christian shrines, and they sometimes wear crucifixes—though as amulets to protect against evil, not as signs of belief.

When Mirza was four or five years old he was taken many miles east to a place called Lalish. Located in a wooded valley just under three hundred miles north of Baghdad, it consists of a collection of old stone buildings. The Yazidis insist that this place is the very center of the earth, where creation began. Under one of the buildings of Lalish, in a place closed to non-Yazidis, a white-robed sheikh (the Yazidis use the same word as Mandaeans and Muslims for a member of their priestly caste) dipped Mirza into a sacred spring called Zemzem—a ceremony performed, like Christian baptism, once in a lifetime.

Mirza himself had been born into the caste of sheikhs. "When I was very young," he told me, "I was told how to be a sheikh. It's a prestigious position; people who are fighting each other must make peace when a sheikh comes among them." Sheikhs were one of the classes of religious figure that the Yazidis respected, along with self-denying *faqir*s, the *kawwal*s who recite the religion's sacred songs, the *kochek*s who guard the shrine at Lalish, and the *pir*s, who are a priestly caste junior to the sheikhs. Sheikhs traditionally had been looked to for miracles as well as spiritual guidance. One family of sheikhs cured eye diseases using saliva or dust from the tomb of their ancestors; another charmed snakes. All eschewed manual labor and lived off charity. The Yazidi community had traditionally been averse to reading and writing (something that we know was true of the ancient Persians as well), and a century ago Mirza's family had been distinguished among other sheikhs by their literacy.

Mirza's family was dedicated specifically to Melek Sheikh Hassan, who Yazidis believe was a superhuman being and vice-regent of the angels whose will governed the planets and the stars. Under the name Sheikh Hassan, the Yazidis believe, he had once assumed human form, and his tomb was at Lalish. Mirza always swallowed the first syllable of the name Hassan, I noticed, so the name sounded like "Sheikh-san" or "Sheikh-sin." *Sheikh* means "elder" or perhaps "lord," and in Babylonian and Assyrian times the people in and near Sinjar worshipped a Lord Sin, the moon god. Similarly, the Yazidis revere Sheikh Shams, whose name resembles that of Shamash, the Assyrian sun god. His name is not the only point of resemblance, for Sheikh Shams's tomb is the venue for a ceremony that thousands of years ago honored Shamash: the great bull sacrifice.

The sacrifice is intended to bring rain in winter, and fertility in the spring that follows. A small bull not less than a year old is brought inside the sanctuary of Lalish, and then chased, by men whose tribe have had this honor as long as anyone can remember, to the shrine of Sheikh Shams. The men carry thin sticks to drive the bull; other men carry machine guns, to fire in the air in celebration. When the bull reaches the shrine of Sheikh Shams, it is captured and a sheikh is at hand to whisper in its ear and then cut its throat. The event almost could be described by the words of the four-thousand-year-old epic of Gilgamesh: "And when they had killed the bull, they tore out its heart, and placed it before Shamash the sun / They stepped back and fell down before Shamash in homage." This is not the only sun-related festival of the Yazidis. They observe a fast of three days in December, followed by a feast day called Eid al-Sawm (the feast of the fast). Long ago when the sun failed to appear, three days of prayer and fasting by Yazidis led God to restore the sun; this event commemorates that occasion.

The Yazidi faith, like the Mandaean one, is a mystery religion. Far from being anxious to communicate its inner messages and convince others of them, the Yazidi clergy want to keep them secret. Since Mirza belonged to the caste of sheikhs, he was entitled to learn them—but he would have to earn the right to this knowledge. If he made the commitment to dress entirely and always in white, and to fast twice a year for forty days each time, giving up all food during daylight hours and staying indoors, then he would gain the ability to foresee the future, and those who had taken this step before him would teach him the unwritten scriptures of the Yazidis. Mirza told me that these scriptures had once been written down but that Western scholars had stolen the manuscripts; all that remained was a leather scroll with gold writing on it, which he believed would show him the history of his people. (In fact, the manuscripts that Western scholars once thought were the Yazidi scriptures have since been shown to be fakes, and it turns out that the real scriptures are orally transmitted. The religion's secrets have been kept well, even from its own followers.)

What Mirza knew already was that the first prophet had been Abraham and the last Mohammed, but that the four elements were more important than any prophet. Of these elements the greatest was fire, and the sun was the main intermediary between humans and the unknowable God. "Yazidis and Assyrians both worshiped the sun," he pointed out. He knew, too, that Yazidis expected to be reincarnated—as men, or possibly as animals. (I found it odd that Mirza was unsure on this point, but many Yazidis appeared to be incurious about the afterlife, or else perhaps secretive about their beliefs.) They regarded the Greek philosophers as prophets. And a crucial figure in their religion was the figure of the Peacock Angel, as I would discover when I went to Lalish myself.

I HAD WANTED TO GO TO LALISH ever since hearing about it when I lived in Baghdad. It was 2011 by the time I made the journey there, beginning it in an unglamorous suburb of Istanbul where I caught a bus for the first leg of the thirty-hour, thousand-mile journey to Iraq. Over the following day, I watched the landscape around me change as we traveled from the north-western corner of Turkey to the far southeast, where the road crosses into Iraq. Istanbul, where I started, is Turkey's biggest and richest city; the land in Turkey's coastal areas is fertile, and the climate a temperate Mediterranean one. The country's southeast, by contrast, is hot, poor, and sparsely popu-lated. It is here that the city of Sanliurfa sits in what is effectively a huge oasis surrounded by semidesert. Once known as Edessa, Sanliurfa was visited in the fourth century AD by Christian pilgrims keen to see a letter that Jesus had supposedly written during his lifetime to the king of Edessa, Abgar. Among the pilgrims was a diarist named Egeria, from whose writings we can see that there were also pagans still living in Edessa who regarded the fish in the local rivers as sacred and refused to kill them. As a Christian, Egeria made a point of eating these fish ("very tasty," she commented).

Today Sanliurfa is a Muslim city, and its heart is an ornate mosque sur-rounded by a park where families and couples stroll in the relative cool of the evening. After reaching the city and installing myself in a local guesthouse, I joined them, thinking about the city's past. There has been a settlement on the site for thousands of years—for instance, between 2000 and 600 BC in the time of the Assyrian Empire, whose legendary king Nimrod features in the Bible and whose capital, Nineveh, stood where Mosul is today. The modern city was founded by one of Alexander's lieutenants and subsequently changed hands many times as Romans, Persians, and Byzantines—and, in a later era, Arabs, Crusaders, and Turks—fought over it. Above the mosque, on a ridge, a tall pillar still stands with an inscription in the extinct language Syriac, a reminder of this history.

There turned out to be another relic of the past in the park: Egeria's tasty fish. A small stream ran through the park, and I noticed it was full of carp—thousands of carp, as thickly gathered together as if they had been caught in a net. They thrashed about, writhing past each other, three or four deep. A man came to stand next to me, his head draped in a black-and-white *keffiyeh*. Every so often one of the people walking in the park would come scurrying up to him, half kneel, press the man's hand to lips and then forehead, and mutter briefly in Kurmanji. Each time this happened, the man would scowl with feigned annoyance and maybe move his hand out of the way in a condescending gesture. But he never turned the supplicants away.

Eventually the man addressed me. "Maybe you are wondering how there are so many fish here?" he asked. "Nobody here will kill or eat them. When the evil king Nimrod wanted to punish the prophet Ibrahim, he ordered him to be burned alive on a pyre of flaming coals. But God turned the fire into water and the coals into fish. This is why we regard these fish as holy." Ibrahim was Abraham, who is claimed by Muslims as well as Jews as a prophet. But the tradition of Sanliurfa's sacred fish was older than Islam, dating back at least to Egeria's time and perhaps much further. The people standing around that pool once spoke Aramaic, then Greek, then Arabic, and now Kurmanji, and Christianity has come and gone, but the fish remain.

"My name is Mahmoud," the man said. He was a Muslim, and a Kurd like many of the people of Sanliurfa. He explained that he was a man of some standing locally. And as we talked he told me about a ruined city to the south of Sanliurfa, called Harran. That evening I read about Harran and discovered that, though now abandoned, it had once played a major part in history. It was allegedly where Abraham lived before adopting Yahweh as his God. (This has now been called into question: the biblical account certainly places him in a town called Harran, but it may have been a town of the same name much further south.) It was definitely the place where the Romans experienced one of their most famous defeats. In 53 BC the Roman plutocrat Crassus launched what he hoped would be a lucrative military campaign against the Parthian Empire (the successor to Cyrus's Persian Empire), coveting its gold and its monopoly on the traffic of Chinese goods to the west. Tricked by a local Arab who was a double agent for the Parthians, Crassus and his legions were annihilated by a numerically inferior Parthian army. It was the first encounter in history's longest war. Hostilities between Rome and Persia continued, with intervals of truce, for nearly seven hundred years.

We have forgotten this longest war, for both protagonists are extinct, but it shaped their world and ours. In its last phase, when the Roman emperors had moved to Byzantium, the Persians found allies among the Byzantine Empire's Jewish communities; the Byzantines, meanwhile, employed Arabs, some of them Christians, to fight against Persia. News of the war even reached remote Mecca, where the Prophet Mohammed was converting Arabs to the new religion of Islam. At one point, after a Persian victory at Antioch in AD 613, it seemed as though the Byzantine Empire was on the verge of utter defeat. The Persian emperor wrote to his Byzantine rival, "Even if you take refuge in the depths of the sea, I will stretch out my hand and take you," while the Byzantines issued coins inscribed "God help the Romans." The Prophet Mohammed and his followers were troubled, because Christian Rome was meant to have God on its side. A Koranic verse offered comfort. "The Byzantines have been defeated in a nearby land," it acknowledged, "but after their defeat they will overcome . . . And that day the believers will rejoice." The Byzantines did recover, dealing the Persian empire a mortal blow—and cutting payments to their Arab mercenaries, dismissing them as "dogs." The Muslim Arabs changed their mind about Byzantium and marched north to seize its southern territories and ultimately conquer the Persian Empire, too. The seven-hundred-year war had exhausted both empires; without it, Islam might not be the world religion that it is today, and the Christian West, with its capital at Istanbul, might have a Zoroastrian-dominated culture as its Eastern rival.

In the course of that war, a curious cultural encounter took place. In the first century AD southern Turkey fell into Roman hands for the first time.

Legionaries posted to this area encountered a religion that was wholly alien to them. It seems they found it attractive: when they went back to Rome, they took a version of it with them. It was the worship of the god Mithras. And it had some similarities to the religion of the Yazidis, the nearest of whom now live 120 miles east of Harran. Underground chapels dedicated to Mithras—built around a spring or stream, like the underground chamber at Lalish where Mirza was baptized—were constructed in great numbers across the Roman Empire. Initiation into the cult was intentionally difficult, and only initiates were allowed to learn the cult's unwritten teachings (which were kept so secret, in fact, that we know very little about them today). This was not the only point of similarity between the Yazidis and the Mithras worshipers. Both religions involved praying three times a day, revering the sun, wearing girdles, and sacrificing bulls. Finally, the Mithras worshipers called themselves "those united by the handshake." To the modern ear that sounds unremarkable: what was so special about a gesture that was so ordinary? But it was not then the standard gesture of greeting that it has since become in the West. It appears that it became so thanks to the Mithraists—for whom it was a ritual of bonding, as it is for the Yazidis. Mithras's cult eventually disappeared when Christianity became popular in the Roman Empire, but the gesture has survived. Completely shorn of all its mystical associations, it is now the universal gesture of friendship.

No scholar knows the full history of the Yazidis. The remoteness and secrecy that kept them safe from outside interference also kept them out of most history books. Unlike the Mandaeans, who lived in relative isolation in the Iraqi Marshes, the Yazidis have been exposed to and influenced by many different religions and cultures over the past two thousand years. It would be a mistake to think that they are "the same as" this or that ancient religion just because they have cultural characteristics in common. There are differences between Yazidis and Mithraists: the Yazidis have three main castes and the Mithraists had seven, for example; Sanliurfa in Roman times did not speak Kurmanji; and ethnically, the modern Yazidis may not be linear descendants of the people of Sanliurfa. But our experience of religion is so conditioned by Christianity, Judaism, and Islam (the Abrahamic faiths) that we forget that in the Middle East there has been, and remains, a wholly separate family

The god Mithras, depicted in the act of killing a bull; a snake, dog, and scorpion are also shown, which all feature in different ways in some contemporary Middle Eastern religions. From a subterranean chapel at Santa Maria Capua Vetere, Italy, dating to the second or third century AD. Digital image courtesy of the Getty Museum's Open Content program

of religions to which, loosely speaking, the Yazidis belong. Although the Roman soldiers who popularized the handshake had not met the Yazidis themselves, clearly they had encountered a religion from the same family.

ALL THE WAY TO HARRAN, along a road with desert on either side, Mahmoud puffed incessantly at one cigarette after another. When we reached the ruined city, it proved to be a peculiar place. The modern-day settlement, built by Arab migrants who came from Iraq a few centuries ago, is made up of a group of beehive-shaped huts, their conical roofs smudged with smoke, grouped around a ruined stone fortress. Pale stones scattered across the hillside nearby were the remnants of a medieval mosque. Thousands of years ago, however, when Harran was one of the region's largest and best-known settlements, the same pale stones were part of a temple dedicated to the moon god Sin. The Babylonian king Nabonidus, who rebuilt the temple in the sixth century BC, was especially proud of the stones' color and declared that he had made Harran "as brilliant as moonlight." His 2,500-year-old inscription was uncovered in the 1950s, when an archaeologist turned over one of the steps of the ruined mosque and found that the mosque's builders had recycled Nabonidus's stones instead of quarrying new ones.

Long after the Roman Empire had become Christian, and even after their city had become part of the Muslim Arab empire, the Harranians stubbornly continued to worship the seven planets (true to Babylonian tradition, they regarded the sun and moon as planets, and were aware of Mercury, Venus, Mars, Jupiter, and Saturn) and to allocate each one of them a holy day. Their ancient customs were coupled with sophisticated philosophy and scientific knowledge. The temples to the planets, for example, were arranged in order of the planets' distance from the earth. And the worship of those planets was justified by an elaborate theology. The Harranians agreed with the Greek philosophers who had concluded that there was a supreme God who was the ultimate explanation for why the universe exists but who was far beyond the grasp of the human intellect. Since God was literally indescribable, mere human beings could hope only to see and revere the projections of God in the material universe.

As the eleventh-century Muslim theologian Shahristani put it, trying to explain the Harranians' beliefs, God "multiplies himself in persons before the eyes of men. These bodies or persons are the seven planets which govern the world." Thus Babylonian and Assyrian religious practices could survive with a new ideology to underpin them: the planets could legitimately be worshiped as projections of God. So could some people, as the writer goes on to explain: there could be "a descent of God's essence" into a human being, "or a descent of a portion of his essence, which takes place according to the degree of the preparedness of the person." When this essence descends in its fullest form, it might make a person into a sort of projection of God on earth. Shahristani recorded that the Harranians believed in reincarnation, which meant that these projections of God might die and then be reborn, returning to earth in successive eras.

The Muslim armies that seized the city from the Byzantines in AD 638 were unsure what to do with the Harranians. According to the Koran, "people of the book"—including Christians, Jews, and the so-called "Sabians"—deserved special tolerance. Polytheists, on the other hand, were generally thought to deserve death if they did not convert. It was not clear to which of these categories the Harranians belonged. So when the Arabs were confronted with a temple to the moon god, some among them—especially those who had been Jewish or Christian before adopting Islam—wanted to destroy it immediately. Another group of Arabs, though, had relatives who practiced something similar to the Harranian religion. This group defended the right of the Harranians to worship as they had before. Their view prevailed, and the temple survived for two hundred more years.

At the end of that time the caliph himself happened to pass through Harran. The people were terrified. The caliph might condemn them as pagans, and strip them of legal rights or even condemn them to death. Then they spotted the reference to "Sabians" in the Koran and latched on to it: they declared that they were the Sabians, and in doing so won another three hundred years of peace. (Only the perceptive Biruni pointed out that there were Mandaeans in the southern Iraqi Marshes who were the real Sabians.) The Harranians were also protected by their knowledge of Greek science, which made them useful to their Muslim rulers. A Harranian called Thabit ibn Qurra was employed by the illustrious "House of Wisdom" in Baghdad, an institution founded by the Muslim caliphs as a repository of the world's scientific knowledge. He calculated the length of the year to within two seconds and proved that Pythagoras's theorem of triangles had a wider application than had previously been demonstrated. He made an eloquent defense of his culture: "Who was it that settled the inhabited world and propagated cities, if not the outstanding men and kings of paganism? Without the gifts of paganism, the earth would have been empty and impoverished, enveloped in a great shroud of destitution."

So it was not until the eleventh century that Harran's luck ran out and a mob tore down the shrine, scattering its stones, "brilliant as moonlight," on the hillside. A hundred years later the Mongols destroyed the city and its people, wiping out two thousand years of history. But the Harranians' ideas can still be found in a belt of land south of the ruined city, stretching from the mountainous Iranian province of Azerbaijan westward to the Mediterranean Sea. On the Syrian coast, for example, a community of Alawites have practiced for many centuries a very unusual form of Islam permeated with customs and ideas that the Harranians would have recognized. Though technically they are Shi'a, Alawites have as little in common with orthodox Shi'a as Unitarians do with evangelical Protestants. The Alawites followed eleven of the twelve imams who led the Shi'a in the first two centuries of Islam. Then their ideas developed in a very radical direction.

In 2012 I set out to interview an Alawite sheikh in northern Lebanon, in the hope that he might talk to me about his religion. My expectations were low. Not even his own flock were entitled to know the secrets that he held, and I was an outsider who represented two undesirable nationalities (British and American) at once. At the time of my visit the Alawites were especially controversial because the Syrian government and its Alawite president, Bashar al-Assad, were involved in brutal repression and mass killings. So I was unsure how easy it would be to reach them, let alone get them to talk. But, armed with a cheap mobile phone, some phone numbers, a grizzled taxi driver from Beirut's southern suburbs, and a car that had seen better days, I was going to try.

The Sunni Muslim city of Tripoli is located right up in the north of Lebanon, and it is in one of its suburbs (originally a hill village, which the city has now swallowed up) that the Alawites live. It was obvious when I had entered this suburb: there were huge portraits of Bashar al-Assad hanging from every lamp-post. I had arranged the meeting through a local strongman who was accused of organizing the militia that led the local Alawites in battles against their Sunni Muslim neighbors. Men standing in the street quizzed the taxi driver who brought me and were satisfied only when they found that he was Shi'a. That made him an ally, in their eyes—a rare thing.

After a full-body search to make sure I had no concealed weapons, I was ushered into the study of an Alawite sheikh whose head was encased in a red-and-white turban. "None of our beliefs are hidden," he assured me. "There are a few things that are private, that is all—ancestral customs and suchlike." These included a ban on eating camel or rabbit meat, and on eating meat from any animal of a different sex from oneself: women ate the meat of

female animals and men the meat of male animals. Did they attach a sacred
significance to groves of trees, as the British ambassador had suggested to
me? No. Did they regard Ali as divine? No, just as a lawgiver and successor
to the Prophet. As for Syria, he claimed, what was going on there was the
work of terrorists acting in the service of Israel. As I left, the sheikh was
willing to share with me one last observation about his religion. "There are
no Alawites in hell," he said with a smirk. "Only the terrorists are in hell,
suffering torment."

The sheikh was being less than frank according to an Alawite who
asked to remain strictly anonymous. The Alawites' most secret ritual involves the drinking of consecrated wine and shows very clear Christian
influences—they call it the Mass, and their books make references to
Jesus—but also draws on traditions that come from Iran: the core of the
ritual is inherited from Zoroastrianism, in which wine is regarded as a means
to achieve communion with God. People can be reincarnated as plants or
animals; perhaps this is why certain types of tree have a sacred significance,
though the sheikh denied this. The Alawite holy books (which, though no
non-initiate may see them, have been published by Western scholars) teach
ideas that were justified by early Muslim philosophers but which also continued the traditions of Harran. The books list many figures from history
as having been the human equivalents of God's celestial servants: not just
ones familiar from Islam and Christianity, such as Mohammed and Jesus,
but also others drawn from classical traditions, such as Plato and Alexander
the Great. The greatest of them, in their tradition, is Ali, the son-in-law of
Mohammed. He was a glimpse or image of God, and the closest thing to
God on earth that the limited human mind could conceivably grasp. It would
be right to exalt Ali by saying that he was God, but wrong to limit God by
saying God was Ali. (The Alawites actually say "the image is God but God
is not the image," a phrase that resembles that used by Nestorian Christians
in a text dated to AD 550: "The Messiah is God but God is not the Messiah.")

The Alawites, too, share the Yazidi and Harranian reverence for the
planets. One of their tribes is named after the sun, and another after the
moon. Adoration for the sun and moon was considered a virtue, at least by
some Alawites. "They do not *love* the moon," complained members of one

Alawite tribe of another tribe when talking to a nineteenth-century British missionary called Samuel Lyde, who later wrote a book of his experiences among the group. They also told him that Ali, who had been the closest thing to God on earth, had hidden himself in the eye of the sun; that was their argument for facing toward the sun at prayer time. (A similar belief was once held about the god Mithras; it is possible that at some point the name Ali was substituted for Mithras, either as a pretense or as a deliberate syncretism, and that over time the original association was forgotten.)

When Neil Armstrong set foot on the moon it provoked a theological crisis among Alawite scholars. Like the Harranians, they believed that the moon was a physical manifestation of a spirit that stood in the heavenly hierarchy as an intermediary between God and man—but how could that be true if it was a lump of rock, and not even the only moon in the universe but one of many? So an Alawite sheikh named Ahmad Mohammad Haidar wrote a book called *After the Moon,* which attempted to explain the problem. This, at least, is what I was told by my anonymous source. And although I found that the book had indeed been published, and I found a review of it that confirmed that it discussed the nature of the stars and planets, all copies of it had mysteriously disappeared, so I was never able to discover the sheikh's proposed solution to the problem. This thoroughgoing secrecy fit with what Jacob de Vitriaco, a Crusader bishop of Acre in the thirteenth century, wrote about the Alawites' secret doctrines, which he called their law: "If any son were to reveal the law to his mother, he would be killed without mercy." The Alawites remain rigidly secretive today. They are even more so, in fact, because of their political power and their associations with the controversial Assad regime. I did not press my inquiries too far into the Alawites' beliefs.

The Yazidis, who have no power, are less embarrassed. Sheikh Shams, Mirza told me, "is responsible for" the sun. But he is also an angel who came to earth and took human form in order to spread divine wisdom. There are other similarities between Harranians, Alawites, and Yazidis. All three believe in reincarnation and have a reverence for fire. (A nineteenth-century British missionary, Percy Badger, commented that Yazidis "never spit into a fire, and will frequently pass their hands through the flames, and make as though they would kiss and wash their faces with them.") Yazidis and Alawites pray three times a day toward the sun; the Harranians prayed three times a day facing south, Biruni tells us, but the sun does stand to the south at midday. Some Yazidis share the taboo against killing fish, which they see as sacred because they live in water. (A friend of Mirza Ismail's, Abu Shihab, told me that a Yazidi saint pitched his tent at Damascus "1,350 years ago" and that fish came out of the river to be his tent pegs; ever since then, Yazidis have not killed fish. Damascus, he added, used to be Yazidi. And indeed, a thousand years ago Biruni recorded that the Harranians had a shrine at Damascus.)

————————

THE ROAD EAST FROM SANLIURFA heads toward the land where the Yazidis still live. The poverty of the places that we were passing became more and more evident, even just from the roadside restaurants at which we stopped. At the last of these there was only a bare kitchen with a few disappointed men queuing by empty soup tureens, waving away flies. It felt unimaginably far from the tourist resorts of Turkey's Mediterranean coast, but at least one thing was more familiar to me here: the language I heard being spoken had an echo of other places I knew. *"Panj dakka,"* said the driver when we stopped. I recognized that phrase: "five minutes." It was the same that I had heard in Iran, and in Afghanistan. *"Choni?"* asked one man of another, meaning "how are you"; *"Bashi,* I am well," was the reply.

This was Kurmanji, the Kurdish language, which has for a hundred years survived consistent efforts by the Turkish government to suppress it. When the charismatic Mustafa Kemal, called "Ataturk," was trying after World War I to shape the decaying remnants of the Ottoman Empire into the modern state of Turkey, he felt that his new country's diversity was a source of weakness and division. He attempted to suppress the many local and regional identities, and in some cases succeeded—but not with the Kurds. He and his successors banned Kurmanji in schools, but it survived (and the ban has now been lifted). Kurds were taught that they were Turks, but they held on to their Kurdish identity, and a strong separatist movement demanded a separate Kurdish state on the basis that they were a people whose language and ethnicity distinguished them from the Turks to their west and the Arabs to their south.

In Iraq that particular dream has come close to fruition. When we reached the frontier I could hardly be sure that it was Iraq I was looking at across the reedbeds, the thin river, and the wire border fence. A huge flag hung on the other side of the border, its tip almost hanging over the Turkish side of the border, but it was not the Iraqi flag. Red, white, and green with a yellow sun in its center, this was the flag of Kurdistan. For decades this flag was a banned symbol of the Kurds' desire for independence. Only after 1991, and only in Iraq, did the Kurds feel strong enough to fly their flag. This period saw the Western powers set up a no-fly zone in northern Iraq, which enabled the Kurds to defy Saddam with impunity. Since the fall of Saddam in 2003, in the three provinces of the country that they now call Iraqi Kurdistan, the Kurds have raised their flag by constitutional right.

For as long as I was on Turkish soil, however, "Kurdistan" was a forbidden word, suggestive of separatism and the breakdown of Turkey into its separate ethnic parts. Spotting the word on my computer screen, a fellow passenger wagged his finger at me until I deleted it. Yet "Welcome to Kurdistan!" were just about the next words I heard, as soon as I was across the border. What was heresy in one place was orthodoxy in the next. Once in Iraq, I found that people said "Kurdistan" as often as they could. Iraqi Kurds used it emphatically, assertively, as though it had a magic force, as though its use were the source of their freedom and growing prosperity.

Iraqi Kurds are enjoying unity without uniformity. They are divided among dozens of tribes, three languages, and two political factions that once fought a civil war against each other and even now work together uncertainly, but they have cooperated effectively enough to win a high degree of autonomy, reduce terrorist attacks in their territory to a minimum, and gain a 17 percent share in Iraq's oil revenue, worth billions of dollars every year. The Kurds have never before experienced such wealth. Theirs has been a long history: there are references to "Kurti" in those hills three thousand years ago, and some scholars trace their origins back even further. But they were never rich and left little trace of their culture—perhaps because the mountains and hillsides that they farmed were ungenerous, even if they provided excellent shelter from enemies. In Marco Polo's time they were highwaymen, if that intrepid or possibly fraudulent traveler is to be believed. "The Kurds are lusty fighters and lawless men," he grumbled, "very fond of robbing merchants."

Now, by contrast, it is in the areas where Kurdish is spoken that a foreigner is safest. On a map I saw during my visit showing a red dot for every violent attack in the past year, Kurdistan was an empty space. Red dots were spattered around its edges, especially in a strip of land on its western border called the Plain of Nineveh. Nearer to the site of biblical Nineveh itself, which is now within the limits of Iraq's second-biggest city, Mosul, the red dots thickened. Mosul itself—"the most dangerous city in the world," as a newspaper once called it—was just one large blood-red stain.

When I had been to Mosul before, as an election observer, it had been in a car so fully armored that the only view of the outside was on video screens. Even then, we apparently came close to being hit by a roadside bomb. "I wasn't expecting to see you," the base commander told our little group when we reached his outpost on the edge of the city. "I had a report one of our vehicles was hit, and I thought it was yours." The next day in the city we were met with cold, quiet stares from its people. No, I had no wish to go back to Mosul. And yet the bus from Istanbul seemed to be headed there: certainly it was now careening along the road under Saddam-era signs saying "Mosul," past harvested fields and shorn hilltops.

I could see now—rather too late—how much geography was going to matter to my safety. I had gotten onto this bus on an impulse and had done little planning other than buying a map of northern Iraq. It was supposed to be the best available, but it gave me just enough information to worry me. My destination was Erbil, the Kurdish capital. And on the map the thick red line of the main road to Erbil went through Mosul. My heart sped up, and I gripped the window frame. I tried to ask my fellow passengers whether that was the way we were going, but they were Kurdish and Turkish merchants and could not understand me in Arabic or Farsi.

I started to look anxiously out of the window, willing the bus to turn off onto a side road, to find a shortcut across the fields. I took off my glasses and was wondering how I could change my shirt, duck out of sight, or hide my British passport, when—at what felt like the last moment—the bus finally swung left, off the main highway and onto a narrow, newly built road not on my map. It seemed that Kurds were just as keen to avoid Mosul as I was, and had built a web of new roads to circumvent it. Indeed, as I realized later, years of fighting have reshaped not just the roads but the landscape of the region.

As the bus sped along this new shortcut, sharing the road with daredevil drivers and at least one wrecked car, I was given another lesson in the geography of danger. It turned out there was one man on board who spoke enough Arabic to understand me. He was called Hajji Abbas and lived in the city of Kirkuk, just outside the borders of Kurdistan. I learned from him that a referendum was going to decide whether his city, along with a whole swath of land bordering Kurdistan—"the disputed territories," which also include Mirza's birthplace, Sinjar—would be run by the Kurdish regional government in Erbil or by the Iraqi central government in Baghdad. In the meantime, Kirkuk had become a quiet and half-deserted city plagued by religious and racial violence. "Do not forget the Turkmen of Iraq," were Abbas's parting words to me; I supposed he must be one himself, a descendant of conquering armies from the steppes of central Asia who had preserved their Turkic language over the centuries and were now a distinctive Iraqi community. I would hear many more appeals in the next few days from other vulnerable groups: the Shabak, who are Muslims who practice a ceremony of drinking wine and confessing their sins; the Assyrians, who are the last remnant of the Church of the East, a Christian sect that once reached as far as China; and the Kakais, a group like the Yazidis but who reject the Yazidi caste system and, instead of following Sheikh Adi, follow instead Sultan Sahak. The "disputed territories" were home to most of Iraq's beleaguered minorities, all of them nervous about what might happen next.

———————

THE BUS DROPPED ME AT ERBIL, Kurdistan's capital, at a shopping mall full of electronic goods. I drank a bad cappuccino, glad of the chance to stay out of the burning sun while I pondered my next move. Erbil had expanded rapidly in just a few years, with housing developments and new roads everywhere I looked. A friend was staying in the city, and when I reached him on the phone he helped me find a driver named Taha, a gruff former Kurdish militia fighter who kept his car in immaculate condition; the crinkly plastic wrapping was still on its seats. In halting Arabic he told me that he had never been to Baghdad. He stayed within Kurdistan. He was happy, though, to take me to Lalish and to some of the other places where Yazidis lived—though not to Sinjar, which was outside Kurdistan and which he said was less safe.

Lalish is where one of the two founders of the Yazidi faith is buried. His name was Sheikh Adi bin Musafir, and he was a Sufi preacher; his holiness and asceticism are much celebrated by Yazidis. Traditionally he is seen as the reformer of the Yazidi faith, which was founded by a mysterious figure called Sultan Ezid. Mirza told me that "Ezid" was just another name for God. A more controversial reading has it that Ezid is the caliph Yazid, one of the early Sunni rulers of Islam and a figure despised by Shi'a Muslims. The Yazidis are at pains in Shi'a-dominated Iraq to deny this account.

There is less controversy over Adi bin Musafir, a historical figure who appears in non-Yazidi sources. He was born in around the year 1075, a descendant of the onetime rulers of Islam, the Umayyad caliphs. His birthplace was near Baalbek in the Beqaa Valley of Lebanon—where at that time the Harranians may still have had an outpost. So he may already have had some acquaintance with customs like those of the Yazidis when, from that remote village, he set out on a journey hundreds of miles long to study mysticism in Baghdad. Then, instead of staying in the imperial capital and enjoying a comfortable life as a scholar, he went as a missionary to the Kurdish areas, which at the time were untamed, dangerous, and resistant to Islam. He founded an order of Sufis (self-denying mystical preachers who resembled, and maybe inspired, the wandering friars of medieval Europe, and who wore wool—*suf* in Arabic) called the Adawiyyah. Sufi preachers who converted people on the frontiers of Islam often gave themselves flexibility to accept aspects of their converts' old beliefs, sometimes grafting Islamic names onto them and reshaping them so that they could sit alongside Muslim practices. The intention was that eventually the converts would see themselves as Muslims. Sometimes, though, the new teachings did not take root; some aspects of Islam were adopted, but they were superficial ones, and deep down the supposed converts never saw themselves as Muslims but remembered their older identity. Perhaps some such process happened to Adi's converts, who eventually abandoned any pretence of being Muslim at all.

Adi himself had, in the view of his Muslim contemporaries, somewhat outlandish views. A poem that was attributed to him by the Yazidis in the nineteenth century certainly sounds unorthodox. "My wisdom knoweth the truth of things," it begins innocuously; "I have not known evil to be with me." But the poem goes on to make grander claims: "All creation is under my control . . . and every created thing is subservient to me. I am he that guideth mankind to worship my majesty . . . and I am he that pervadeth the highest heavens." Some Yazidis also seem to have regarded him as having a godlike status. "Who is the author of good?" said the attendant at the Lalish shrine to a British missionary, Percy Badger, in the nineteenth century. "God or Sheikh Adi."

Sheikh Adi is not the figure that most Yazidis will mention, though, when asked what their religion is all about. Nor is it his picture that hangs on their walls. He was merely the earthly manifestation of Melek Taoos, who is the true ruler of this world, God's lieutenant in the knowable universe, and the closest figure to God that our limited human minds can grasp. Since the Yazidis' view of God is a very abstract one—nothing can be said of God with any certainty, they say, except that he exists—it is Melek Taoos who is the focus of their cult. In former centuries seven bronze images of Melek Taoos (called *sanjaks*) were ceremoniously carried around Yazidi villages for people to revere. The missionary Badger described the *sanjak* as follows: "The figure is that of a bird, more resembling a cock than any other fowl . . . fixed on the top of a candlestick, around which are two lamps, placed one above the other, and each containing seven burners, the upper being somewhat larger than the lower." Five of the *sanjaks* have been lost; two survive. Yazidis also believe that Melek Taoos comes down to earth every year on a day called Charsema Sor, "Red Wednesday," to initiate the new year. This festival is marked by the painting of eggs, just like the Christian Easter. The Yazidis regard the egg as symbolizing the creation of the world, which in their creation myth was once liquid and (like a cooked egg) became solid, and which was colorless until Melek Taoos laid his peacock feathers on it, bestowing their blue and green shades to its seas and forests.

More controversially, Melek Taoos is also identified by the Yazidis with

Azazael or Iblis, which in the Muslim tradition (and the Jewish and Christian ones, for that matter) are names for the greatest of the angels, who rebelled against God and was cast down into hell—in short, the devil. The peacock has similar associations. The Druze in Lebanon believe that it was the peacock, not the serpent, that was the tempter in the Garden of Eden. Some Zoroastrians in Iran believed that the peacock was the one good thing that the devil made, as a way of showing that he had the power to do good if he so chose.

An Armenian Yazidi girl kisses a representation of the Peacock Angel, Melek Taoos. Melek Taoos is also called Iblis, or Azazael, but is thought by the Yazidis to be good rather than evil. AFP/Getty Images

The Yazidis, however, will never call the Peacock Angel by the name Satan (Sheitan in Arabic), for it is a word that is prohibited to them with the sternest and most unbending taboo. In the nineteenth century the Yazidis wrote a letter to the Ottoman authorities describing a terrible practice that they had to carry out on hearing the name of Satan: to kill the person who said the name, and then kill themselves for hearing it. After the Iraq War the sole Yazidi member of the Iraqi parliament did not go quite so far when he heard the prime minister curse Satan at the beginning of his speeches. But he did make a stir when he rose to object to the practice, or rather specifically to the fact that other parliamentarians gave him accusing looks every time the curse was said. The accusing looks came because those other parliamentarians considered him a devil worshiper.

So did the taxi driver Taha, as he revealed to me as he drove me north toward a town called Dohuk, where I was due to meet a Yazidi scholar and Kurdish official named Khairi Buzani. "You'll see that I won't eat any of their food," Taha warned me as he drove. "People say that Muslims used to eat the Yazidis' food. Not anymore. That Melek Taoos that they worship—that's the devil." Younger Yazidis would later tell me that it has become common for Muslim Kurds to refuse to eat with them. Early European visitors were also chary of the Yazidis because of Melek Taoos. Austen Henry Layard, an archaeologist who traveled through northern Iraq in 1840, found the Yazidis to be better-behaved than their neighbors; he particularly noted their "quiet and inoffensive demeanour, and the cleanliness and order of their villages." Still, he hesitated to take up their invitation to take part in a naming ceremony for one of their children. "Notwithstanding my respect and esteem for the Yazidis . . . I was naturally anxious to ascertain the amount of responsibility which I might incur, in standing godfather to a devil-worshiping baby."

WHAT THE YAZIDIS REALLY BELIEVE about Melek Taoos is far more intriguing and thought-provoking than devil worship. Back in the ninth century AD, Muslims, Christians, Zoroastrians, and others were all jostling against each other in the Muslim-ruled Abbasid Empire. Islam's theology was not as fixed then as it since became, and Sufis were particularly given to developing inventive and daring new interpretations of religion. One of these Sufis was Hussein ibn Mansour al-Hallaj. Hallaj's grandfather had been a Zoroastrian, a believer in dualism, the notion that the universe is the locus of a battle between good and evil. His grandson had the opposite idea. One day he knocked on a friend's door. When the friend asked who was there, Hallaj replied, "*Ana al-Haqq*—I am God." "There is nothing in this cloak but God," he said at another time.

Hallaj's words won him admirers. The poet Rumi said that it showed a spirit of greater humility than calling oneself a "servant of God" because Hallaj's phrase represented a total denial of self, a willingness to be absorbed completely by God. "When you destroy your own heart," as Hallaj wrote, God "enters it and discloses His holy revelation." Some Christians had had a similar idea: a former pagan priest called Montanus, who went on to found his own breakaway Christian movement, had claimed to be possessed by God and declared, "I am Father, Son, and Holy Spirit." Yusuf Busnaya, a ninth-century Christian priest, described his own mystical experiences by saying that a person's "spirit itself becomes Christ . . . it becomes God and God is no longer God." Hallaj, though, was making a wider philosophical point. He meant that everything was God. "It is You that I see in everything," as he wrote in a poem. This was the ultimate monotheism: for everything, literally, to be made of God to a greater or lesser degree.

As a complete monotheist, Hallaj wrestled with the idea of Satan. In a world that was made of God, the devil was a piece that could not fit. In the orthodox Islamic tradition, which was shared by Jews and Christians, the devil was pure evil—a rebel against God who could never repent and could never be reconciled. Didn't that mean that the creator God was either unjust or not as all-powerful as religion taught? Zoroastrians, too, had spotted this particular question. If God was all-powerful, they challenged their Christian neighbors, then why does he allow the devil to do evil in the world? Why can't he redeem Satan as he redeemed mankind? One of those Christians, Isaac of Nineveh, came up with a reply. At the end of the world every creature would indeed be redeemed and even devils would enter heaven. Hell would disappear. "Demons would not remain demons, nor sinners sinners."

Hallaj developed his own reply to the Zoroastrians. The Koran, like the Christian and Jewish scriptures, said that Satan had been the prince of angels; he had refused to bow down before Adam and rebelled against God, and for this he was cast down into hell. But Hallaj gave this story a startling twist. It was out of jealous and uncompromising love of God, he said, that Satan refused to bow to Adam. Satan was the archetype of all those Sufis and others who focused only on contemplating God and had no time for other people. But, said Hallaj, Satan was more misguided than evil. Today Hallaj's view would be regarded by most Muslims as very unorthodox. In the religion's early centuries, though, there were other Muslim mystics who similarly wrestled with the question of how Satan fitted into the world. One of these, Rabi'a of Basra, shocked her hearers by refusing to say that she hated Satan and by threatening to burn heaven and quench hell because fear of punishment or hope for reward came between people and the true love of God.

The Yazidis' view of Melek Taoos fits into this tradition. By referring to him as Azazael or Iblis, they are identifying him as the rebel angel, but not as the prince of darkness. They justify this by saying not just that de-mons will be changed into angels at the end of time but that it has already happened. Khairi Buzani explained this to me when I reached his office in Dohuk, surrounded by houses painted in pastel colors with metal poles sticking out of their roofs, ready for when the next story would be built for the next generation. "After his rebellion, Azazael"—he carefully avoided the forbidden name, I noticed—"was punished but repented," Khairi said. In seven thousand years of exile, Azazael had extinguished the fires of hell with his tears, and so he was restored to favor as the chief of all the angels. This gives the Yazidis a different view of the universe, one in which hell does not exist. Buzani told me more: "We have an idea about the One God which the heavenly religions do not have: evil and good both come from God. There are not two struggling powers that fight each other for dominance in the universe." Far from worshiping the devil, the Yazidis believe that there is no such thing.

They may possibly have been directly influenced by Hallaj's followers. The radical preacher came to a cruel end: after backing a slave rebellion in southern Iraq, he was captured by the forces of the Abbasid caliph and cut into pieces. His devotees fled into the north and took refuge in the moun-tains there, not far from where Sheikh Adi would later preach and where the Yazidis now live. Their ideas could have filtered through to the ancestors of the Yazidis, either in the time of Sheikh Adi or even earlier, and been fitted into their religious life alongside the remnants of much older traditions and beliefs.

The tradition of propitiating malevolent deities was a very old one in Iraq. The *Nabatean Agriculture* (mentioned in the last chapter) records a prayer, in use in ninth-century Iraq, that seems to show traces of Islamic influence but quickly reveals itself to be from quite a different tradition: "There is no god but Allah alone and there is no companion to him . . . all might, majesty and greatness belong to him . . . blessed art thou, lord of the Heaven and everything else . . . by my life, we ask you to have mercy on us. Amen. . . . While you are praying this prayer give a burnt offering to his idol consisting of old hides, grease, strips of leather and dead bats. Burn for him fourteen dead bats and an equal amount of rats. Then take their ashes and prostrate yourself on them in front of his idol." The prayer was addressed to the god Saturn, the "lord of evil and sin and filth and dirt and poverty," and intended to persuade him to leave the supplicants alone.

Saturn's role in ancient Assyria was played by the god Nergal, who was identified as god of the fierce noontime sun, the plague, and the dead; lion-headed colossi guarded his temples. It may be significant that he took the form of a cockerel, which the *sanjak* somewhat resembles. In later centuries Mithraists set up lion-headed statues labeled "Deo Arimanio"—a reference to Angra Mainyu, the Zoroastrian spirit of evil, whom it seems the Mithras worshipers wanted to propitiate. Propitiation of evil, according to the first-century AD Greek historian Plutarch, took place in his time in Iran, and involved offerings of the intoxicating plant extract haoma mingled with the blood of a sacrificed wolf and poured out in a dark cave. Yohannan bar Penkaye, the seventh-century Christian writer who came from the Syrian-Turkish border close to where some Yazidis still live today, said that people in his region worshiped the sun, the stars, and also Baalshamin and Baalzebub—the former being an ancient sky god, the latter being Lucifer.

Whatever his origins, Melek Taoos was a constant companion as Taha drove me to Lalish: the peacock emblem, painted on doors and gateways, was visible everywhere as I entered the Yazidi town of Ain Sifni, not far from Lalish. The head of a bird was even carved into the top story of a block of apartments. There was a branch of an institution called the Lalish Cultural Center in this town. It was a simple place, with a good library and a small museum. In the library I met Ayad, one of a new generation of Yazidis, reading a magazine. He could read and write in four different languages and had a degree in political science. Like many of the Yazidi intellectuals I spoke with, he was fascinated by the history of his own religion. I was getting used to every Yazidi giving me a slightly different account, which was not surprising, given that they have no catechism or publicly available religious texts. Instead, every person tells the Yazidi story in a slightly different way, though there are themes that are common to every version.

Ayad's theory of his people went as follows: "We are one of the peoples of the sun. Once the people of Syria, Russia, Armenia, Iran, and Turkey all considered the sun as a god. That was the first stage of our religion, which

The temple at Lalish. Photo by the author

was nature worship; then it became monotheist; and last came the teaching of Sheikh Adi." The Yazidis did not worship the sun anymore, Ayad said. But they did continue to bow to it when they prayed. When the first Yazidi member of parliament took his seat in the new Iraqi assembly, he took his oath of office not on the Koran or the Bible but on the flag of Kurdistan—and specifically on the image of the sun at its center. Ayad did not see that as a coincidence. "We are the original Kurds," he said. Some Yazidis fear that assimilation among Kurds will threaten the Yazidi identity, but Ayad felt that the safest and truest course was to place his people right at the heart of the Kurdish identity.

———————

THE DRIVE FROM AIN SIFNI to Lalish was described in a 1940s travel book as a painful experience, one that could give a car a broken axle. Things have improved: now there is a smooth paved road that winds down through a wooded valley to the temple. The day I traveled this road, cars were parked along it, and I could hear Kurdish pop music and teenage laughter. As Taha and I approached to the shrine, we passed a stone effigy of the sun. The shrine turned out to be an assortment of stone buildings resembling an old monastery (a Christian priest in the Middle Ages claimed that Lalish had once indeed been a Christian church) and nestled in a wooded valley. The day of my visit was a Friday, the Islamic weekend. Many families were at Lalish to picnic under the mulberry and fig trees that shaded its flagstone courtyards. The Yazidis' holy day is Wednesday, when they do not work in the fields, travel, bathe, or wash their clothes. Few keep this old tradition, though, which may date back to the old taboos of pre-Christian Mesopotamia. Friday, being the Muslim day for communal prayer, has now become more popular as a weekly holiday than Wednesday.

Leaving Taha in the car—he said he would meet up with us later—Ayad and I joined one of these families and sat beneath the trees, with sliced watermelon on a plate between us. The family we sat with spoke no English or Arabic. The father, his head swathed in a red-and-white *keffiyeh,* smiled in friendship, but my attempts to turn a broken phrase or two of Kurmanji fell flat. His sons sat with him, while his wife and daughters had their own picnic a few paces away, protected from the sun by the stone walls of a small building topped by a twisted conical spire, a familiar characteristic of Yazidi shrines. (The spire's twisting lines, radiating down from the tip of the cone to its base, may be designed to resemble the rays of the sun.) Ayad volunteered to show me the temple itself, the building at the center of the complex. We walked along a roofless passage overlooked by a balcony, on which a woman dressed in white regarded us silently. As well as studying the Mandaeans, E. S. Drower used her time in Iraq to visit the Yazidis at Lalish. She mentions "the white-clad, nun-like attendants of the shrine" who never married, spending their lives spinning wool and tending the shrines and the gardens around them. This, I thought, must be one of those attendants. In Babylonian times there were consecrated women who likewise spent their time within temple precincts, spinning wool.

We reached the sunlit courtyard of the temple after walking through an arch surmounted by a carving of an ibex head. Beside the temple's door, a large black snake was embossed on the stone wall, head pointing upward, acting as an amulet to prevent evil from entering. The door had a huge lintel. Ayad motioned that I should remove my shoes and step over the lintel without touching it, as the Yazidis do, for the lintel is kissed by the faithful who regard it as holy. We thus entered a dark, stone-flagged room that smelled of dust and antiquity, light filtering through small windows, the only decoration some rolls of brightly colored silk—yellow, red, light blue—that hung from its central pillars. Passers-by could tie or untie knots in them for good luck. A few family groups were walking about the room, cheerful-looking but quiet.

We descended a set of stairs, and I encountered Melek Taoos again: a curtain in front of a niche concealed one of the surviving *sanjak*s, the brass representations of the Peacock Angel. When we reached the lower floor, we found ourselves in a room reeking of the stale oil that was oozing from bottles stacked against the wall. Teenagers were throwing a bundle of silk over their shoulder and seeing if they could gain a bit of luck by hitting a particular stone in the wall, which I thought might be a statue so worn away by time that its features were unrecognizable. (Later I was told by Yazidis that this stone was miraculously suspended in midair. "But," they said, astonished at the stupidity they were about to describe, "some years ago, people who lacked faith insisted on putting up a wall behind it.") When I backed out of the room I saw a stone sarcophagus covered in a green cloth. Yazidis were walking around it, left hands trailing on the tomb. A black woolen cloak, typical of Sufis, was spread reverently nearby. Only a very pious

Yazidi would be allowed to don it. Sheikh Adi, I was told, wore such a cloak. Was he a Muslim? I asked. A group of Yazidis were listening, and they all chorused: "No!"

Ayad told me I was lucky: a body called the Spiritual Council, which included some of the most influential laymen and top clergy, was meeting at the temple that day. To ask them for an audience I had to walk from the temple to an alcove of a neighboring building. As was required, I removed my shoes before entering. There were no women inside. A group of young men sat on stone benches running along the side of the alcove walls. Beyond it a courtyard opened up, leading to a room where the Spiritual Council was holding its meeting. I could overhear snatches of conversation from the men on the benches, who were earnestly discussing (in English) the history of Kurdish nationalism. When I talked to them I found that many of them had foreign passports, mostly from Germany or Sweden. They were sheikhs, the topmost of the three Yazidi castes. According to tradition, sheikhs should marry within their own caste. Wasn't this hard, I asked one of them, for Yazidis living in Europe and America? "I preserve the customs," he replied, "and I managed to find a wife who was a sheikh. But when my daughter is twenty I won't be able to control what she does!"

I could see the members of the council gathering in the courtyard; evidently the meeting had ended. Some were wearing suits, but five men, with long gray beards and traditional dress, held themselves with particular dignity. They could easily have passed for Arab tribal chiefs, with their white headdresses fixed on their heads by black circlets; some of them wore the gossamer-thin cloak called a *bisht* in Arabic and signifying high rank. One of these was the Mir, the temporal leader of the Yazidis. Another man was dressed a little differently, in the red-and-white turban of a cleric and cream-colored robes. This was the Baba Sheikh, who technically was the chief spiritual leader of the Yazidis (though, at least while I was there, he left the talking to the Mir). The men in the courtyard were, collectively, the leaders of the Yazidi faith. I asked if they would grant me a brief audience, and they asked for my questions in writing and then sent me away to wait for their decision; I sat for a time in a stone-floored upper room until I was summoned back. They had decided that it would be safe to talk to me.

The Mir's answers were bland. He told me the Yazidis wanted to live in peace with all religions and to keep their own distinct traditions; relations with Muslim and Christian clergy were good, and they would visit each other for festivities; the Yazidis rejected missionary work and would never seek to convert others. "In our prayers," he said, "we ask for good for others first, and then for ourselves. People will be judged for their actions, not for their beliefs. The spirit that God breathed into Adam passes down to all humans. In the wrong kind of people it is repressed, and in the best it shines out." After he finished, the five gray-bearded elders stood up, shook their robes, and went out for a cigarette break. Roast chicken and rice were brought in. Ayad and Taha the driver joined us. There were no chairs. The Mir gestured for me to stand beside him. He ate without talking, crossing his hands on his belly whenever he set his fork and knife down. Taha, I saw, stood there and ate nothing, as he had told me he would.

I left Lalish with many questions still unanswered. The Yazidis were endlessly intriguing. Why was it forbidden to wear blue, for example, or eat lettuce? When I asked Yazidis about this, they had vague answers, mostly suggesting that these were meaningless rules that perhaps had been imposed by past Yazidi leaders because the hated Turks wore blue, or just because they disliked lettuce. Mirza dated the rule against lettuce quite specifically to 1661. I was more inclined to see ancient roots in these traditions, seeing parallels to them among other religions in the area. For the Mandaeans, blue is the color associated with the evil Ruha. Among the Druze, blue is the color of robes worn by the most respected sheikhs. The taboo against lettuce has a counterpart among the Druze, whose elders sometimes eschew a similar vegetable called *molokhiya.* The Harranians avoided eating beans. But I could not see how these traditions had originated. No matter how hard I tried, the Yazidi faith still guarded at least some of its secrets.

IN THE MODERN WORLD, the Yazidis can no longer count on being left to their own devices. With the rise of far-reaching government bureaucracies and modern technologies, there are now fewer places where a people can hide. Sometimes a new idea of citizenship has developed in tandem with the bureaucracy and technology, and has resulted in minorities being treated generously when they are not perceived to pose a threat. But when they are seen as a threat, or when old prejudices have come to the fore, the results have been bloody and sinister.

In Mirza's hometown, Qahtaniyah, on a summer's evening in 2007, a crowd of men in off-white cotton *jelaba*s and black-and-white head scarves gathered when they saw a truck drive into town. They hoped it had come to distribute food. Instead, it delivered a blast so powerful that it knocked down houses, scattered people across streets, and left corpses stripped of their clothes. The bare facts were terrible enough: four trucks, with explosives hidden probably inside their doors, had blown up, leaving approximately eight hundred dead and around fifteen hundred homes damaged or destroyed. Furthermore, ambulances and earthmoving machines had never arrived because the roads were considered too dangerous; clothes hung from sticks as memorials to children whose bodies were never found. It killed more people than any other terrorist attack save that against the Twin Towers on 9/11. The immediate reason for the bombing was the killing of a Yazidi woman called Du'a Khalil Aswad, who was murdered by her relatives for wanting to marry a Muslim man. A rumor spread that she had converted before she was killed, and so she was adopted as a Muslim martyr by various groups that then began to carry out reprisals against Yazidis.

These clashes happened in a context, though, in which resentments between all the ethnic groups in the area had been deliberately stoked by Saddam's government, which tried to maintain control of the population by inciting Arab against Yazidi, and Yazidi against Kurd. In the years since 2003, furthermore, intolerant and violent varieties of Islam had spread, according to Dakheel, an elderly and distinguished Yazidi. "Religious hatred" lay behind the Qahtaniyah attack, he said to me sadly as we sat in the new lobby of Erbil's Sheraton hotel. "It was pure religious hatred." After the Ba'ath came to power in the late 1950s, he said, religious divisions had deepened, but this was a small change in comparison to the decline in tolerance since 2003. Salafi Muslims, fundamentalists who want to mimic as closely as possible the behavior of the first Muslims and are particularly hostile to heterodox groups such as the Yazidis, had grown in influence. Dakheel was gloomy about the future. The Yazidis would one day cease to exist, he thought, as they were less well-organized than the Mandaeans and the Druze. They were also fractured geographically. Most Yazidis in Iraq lived in Sinjar, to the west of Erbil, outside direct Kurdish control. This was traditionally the area where they were strongest, and where for several centuries they had held off the Ottomans. Around 15 percent of the Yazidis lived around Lalish, north of Erbil. The remainder lived farther north, around Dohuk.

On the other hand, Dakheel added more optimistically, Yazidis were also becoming better educated. Before World War I, a British writer observed that only one Yazidi family could read and write. In the 1940s, Dakheel's uncle had been the first-ever Yazidi to become a schoolteacher. In 1973 the community's first doctor graduated. "Now there are plenty of Yazidi doctors in medical school. There are more than 3,000 Yazidis at university. We have no other way to survive except through learning," Dakheel told me. The cost of living in the Kurdish areas had soared since the region had stabilized, attracting migrants from the rest of the country. Amid the general rise in religious fervor across the country, though, the Yazidis had if anything become less fervent. "Ten or fifteen years ago in Sinjar, cutting off one's mustache was punishable with death," Dakheel added, reminding me that wearing a mustache was a religious obligation for a Yazidi man. "That's not true anymore. And people no longer wear special clothes when they make the pilgrimage to Lalish."

Later, back in Erbil, I visited the rocky plateau on which the city was originally built, and which has now been turned into a heritage site. From the edge of it I looked down toward a newly refurbished square in which young Kurds sat and chatted around fountains. Then I looked beyond, to the dusty western horizon. Out there lay Sinjar. To its west were Syrian villages where Kurds, Arabs, and Yazidis lived. Beyond that were Harran and the lands to its south, and then the wooded hills of the Syrian coast. All of this territory has historically been a haven for minority groups of all kinds—adherents of ancient religions that somehow made their peace with Islam; heterodox Muslims; and believers in faiths that mixed old folk traditions with Islamic practice to produce fascinating and curious hybrids.

That territory now sits on the edges of the self-declared Islamic caliphate, declared in 2014 by a terrorist group famous for its brutality and
religious intolerance. It only adds to the awful dilemmas that the Yazidis
face, now that their territory is no longer remote from its neighbors. They
additionally face the challenge of maintaining a secret religion, whose truths
are known only to a priestly caste, at a time when members of the faith live
side by side with people of other religions in cities rather than in remote
villages—meaning that they are exposed to questions about their religion
that they are often not well equipped to answer. For those who have moved
abroad, it is likewise not easy to keep children from marrying outside their
faith or caste.

Mirza is now confronting those challenges, because he left Iraq long
ago—in 1991. The Gulf War had begun, bringing with it the threat of conscription into a doomed army. He joined a group that included a friend
of his called Abu Shihab, who was trying to escape with his whole family.
They crossed the border that Iraq shares with Syria at a place a short distance west of Sinjar. It was a summer's evening, and the terrible heat of
the daytime was subsiding. Because of the war, the army had been diverted
elsewhere; forces on the border between Iraq and Syria were stretched thin.
Once inside Syria, the group was going to head for a Yazidi village whose
people were friendly—but miles lay in between, and in crossing them they
would have to keep an eye out for land mines and for guards who had orders
to shoot on sight.

Mirza started walking. He ducked and crept along where he had to.
Halfway through the journey he heard gunfire. He thought Abu Shihab, who
was trying a parallel crossing a mile away with his wife and all his children,
had run into trouble—and so he had. Abu Shihab's family had been spotted
by the border guards. These had shouted warnings and then started shooting.
The bullets came close, and one of Abu Shihab's sons was hit in the neck.
But then they were across the border, and nobody came after them. They did
not celebrate for long, for they soon realized that the family's two youngest
children were not with them. These two, too small to walk, had been riding
on a donkey, and somehow, in the rush across the border, nobody had noticed that the donkey had not kept up. The two children were captured and

returned by the government to their grandfather—on the condition that if they escaped, the grandfather's life would be forfeit. Abu Shihab did not see them again for seventeen years.

Abu Shihab, the rest of his family, and Mirza all migrated to North America—Abu Shihab to the United States, Mirza to Canada. They remained close. Perhaps it was their shared experience at the border that led Abu Shihab to approach Mirza and ask him to be his "brother in the afterlife," or spiritual mentor. In former generations this relationship was an almost feudal one, involving a layman's absolute obedience to the sheikh. The relationship is sealed by taking soil from Lalish, rolling it into a ball, which represents the world, and mixing it with water from Lalish's sacred Kaniya Spi, or "White Spring." The two spiritual brothers then clasp each other's hands with the moistened earth in between. This fraternal gesture is not only one that binds Yazidis together. It also is a reminder of a past time when cultures learned and adopted customs from each other. It is the Yazidis' original contribution to Western life—for this is the custom that, thanks to the cult of Mithras, has become our handshake.

IN 2014 I RETURNED to northern Iraq after the Yazidis had been driven out of Sinjar by the so-called Islamic State terrorist group. I talked to refugees who had fled their homes, walking 25 miles nonstop to escape the murder, rape, and kidnap that had been inflicted on those who had not been lucky enough to get away. All the Yazidis who packed around me in their tiny shelter, desperate to tell their stories, had one request: they wanted to leave Iraq. "It's broken," one of them said. "Our honor is gone, our livestock are gone, our women are gone. We have no future in Iraq." Their white-robed sheikh, who proudly told me of his descent from the one-time Yazidi ruler of Sinjar, said the same. Surrounded by followers who believe in his power to foretell the future, he predicted the end of his religion in Iraq. In the background, I saw the pointed white spires of a Yazidi temple, reminding me of how long this religion has been practiced, in one form or another, in this ancient and bloodied land. Perhaps no longer.

3

Zoroastrians

L AAL SHAHRVINI WAS BORN IN THE 1920s in the city of Yazd, an
oasis in the heart of Iran surrounded by low and barren hills. Today,
the whole of Yazd's old city has been declared a UNESCO World Heritage
Site. Mud-brick walls frame alleyways and streets down which no car can go.
Tall wind towers—shaped like huge chimneys, these are early and picturesque
forms of air-conditioning that capture summer breezes and filter them down
to the sweltering houses below—loom overhead. Mysterious stairways lead
down to cisterns where people once took shelter from the heat, which in summer can reach 114 degrees Fahrenheit. In the main square sits a wicker wheel
bigger than a man, a replica of Hussein's tomb that Muslims carry around
the city on their shoulders once a year as an act of penitence.

Laal never went to watch these Islamic passion plays, or to pray at
the mosque with its turquoise faience domes and tall minaret. She was not
a Muslim: hers was a smaller and older community. Her people had their
own festivals and commemorations, such as the winter solstice, when they
would stay up through the year's longest night, bringing watermelons and
pomegranates out of storage to eat as they told stories until dawn. The spring
solstice, when the day finally became longer than the night, was the most
important festival of their year. Purity was central to their lives: to achieve

The old city of Yazd, built from mud brick and dating back many centuries, still partly survives. To the left is the *nakhl,* representing the death of Hussein, grandson of the Prophet Mohammed; it is used in yearly parades. Photo by the author

it, Laal went through a ritual requiring nine nights of wakefulness, during which a priest sprinkled bull's urine over her body and gave her a few drops of it to swallow. She declared that of her own free will, she was joining "the brotherhood and sisterhood of those who do good."

Instead of despising dogs, as the Muslims of Yazd did, she was tasked by her family with putting out food for them every night, before she and her family could have their own meal. Instead of praying at a mosque, her family offered litanies and burned sandalwood in front of a sacred fire in a nearby temple. Each night her father, a priest, climbed onto the roof of their mud-brick house; she would see him standing there with a sextant and astrolabe, taking measurements of the stars. In the family's prayers they used Avestan, a language that was last used in everyday speech in the Iron Age. At home they spoke their own language, which others pejoratively called "Gabri": it was spoken and understood only by those who shared their religion.

Laal's traditions were practiced by most Iranians before the coming of Islam. When the horsemen of Pars province in the sixth century BC rode north, east, and west to conquer their neighbors and build the largest empire that the world had yet seen, which they named Pars or Persia, Laal's was the religion they followed. It had reached them from central Asia, where it was founded perhaps around 1000 BC by a prophet named Zarathustra. His followers are called Zoroastrians in the West. Arabs call them Majoos, after their priests, the Magi (also called *mobeds*). In India they are known as Parsees, the name given to them after they arrived as refugees from Persia shortly after the Islamic conquest. Early Christians often depicted the Three Wise Men who were said to have visited Jesus as Persian Zoroastrians: although this is never specified in the account in the Gospel of Matthew itself, it was a lucky choice. When the Persian armies conquered Bethlehem in AD 614, it is said that they spared the Church of the Nativity from the destruction they visited on the rest of the town, because they saw a depiction of three Magi at the church's entrance.

Once the dominant religion of Iran, by Laal's time Zoroastrianism had dwindled: her community, one of the last to survive centuries of mistreatment, numbered only eighty-five families living in the same quarter of the city, a group small enough that Laal knew them all. In all, there are fewer than a hundred thousand Zoroastrians in the world today. But their contribution to world religion, including our own, makes them more important than this figure suggests. According to Nietzsche, Zarathustra invented morality. More certain is that Zarathustra taught that the world was formed by the ceaseless struggle between good and evil. "Between these two," he declared in his Gathas, poems that form the oldest and most important part of the Zoroastrian scripture, the Avesta, "let the wise choose aright." The worshipers of false gods had chosen evil, and his followers were to abandon those gods, worship instead the wise lord Ahura Mazda, and do good in his service.

In subsequent centuries this theology developed into an explanation of the world's imperfections. Why do night, winter, sickness, and vermin exist? Zoroastrians explained them as the work of Angra Mainyu, the Adversary, who sent down evil animals to harm the good ones made by Ahura Mazda. Ahura Mazda created light; Angra Mainyu polluted it by inventing darkness. Ahura Mazda brought life; Angra Mainyu partially spoiled it by introducing sickness. Ahura Mazda represented fertility; Angra Mainyu brought the desert. Ahura Mazda's kingdom was one of eternal joy; Angra Mainyu's was one of torment. Although Zoroastrians looked forward to the ultimate victory of good over evil, they had to help make it happen.

The good animals included the horse, the ox, and the dog. Angra Mainyu's servants in the animal kingdom, called *khrafstra*s, included flies, ants, snakes, toads, and cats. A Zoroastrian Persian emperor called Shapur condemned Christians because they "attribute the origin of snakes and creeping things to a good God." For him, such things could only be the creation of a separate, malign creator. The great Persian national epic the *Shahnamah* begins with a great army of fairies and animals that had chosen the side of good over evil, setting out for battle with Angra Mainyu. (If this sounds like C. S. Lewis's *The Chronicles of Narnia*, that is because he was a great admirer of the *Shahnamah*—and he called Zoroastrianism his favorite "pagan" religion.)

The battle between good and evil was one in which human beings could take part if they chose. The concept of free choice is especially important in Zoroastrianism, which holds that even Angra Mainyu is bad by choice. (This is why the story is told that Angra Mainyu created the peacock just to show that if he wished to, he could make beautiful things instead of ugly ones.) Virtuous acts such as telling the truth were means to defeat Angra Mainyu—the forces of darkness in the Avesta are called "the lie"—and the Greek historian Herodotus, who studied the Persians in the fifth century BC, tells us that they were brought up to "ride horses, shoot straight, and tell the truth." But there were also physical battles to undertake against Angra Mainyu's servants. Herodotus tells us that "the Magians kill with their own hands all creatures except dogs and men, and they even make this a great end to aim at, killing both ants and serpents and all other creeping and flying things." Even in the 1960s, Iranian Zoroastrians observed a day every year during which they killed *khrafstra*s, especially ants.

Loving dogs, meanwhile, was obligatory. In the Avesta, the Chinvat bridge, across which a soul must pass safely if it is to enter paradise, is said to be guarded by two dogs. When a dog stared intently into the middle distance, it was thought to be seeing evil spirits invisible to humans, and so was often chosen to sit by the bedside of a dying person. In turn, when such a dog died it was accorded special funeral rites, as described by the scholar Mary

Boyce in her observation of traditional Zoroastrian life in the 1960s. An announcement would be made as the dog died: "The soul is taking the road." The dog would be dressed like a Zoroastrian—in a girdle called the *kushti* and muslin vest called the *sedreh,* which were always worn by the faithful (the first around the waist and the other over the shoulders)—and its body would be treated like that of a Zoroastrian man or woman who had died: it would be exposed in a deserted spot for the birds to eat. For three days after its death its favorite food would be put out for the dog's spirit to enjoy.

To maltreat a dog is prohibited by the Avesta. "When passing to the other world," the soul of a person who has hit a dog "shall fly howling louder and more sorely grieved than the sheep does in the lofty forest when the wolf ranges." A man who kills a dog is required by the Avesta to perform a list of penances eighteen lines long. One of the penances is to kill ten thousand cats. Because Muslims preferred cats over dogs, which they think of as unclean, disputes over the treatment of dogs often led to fights between Zoroastrians and Muslims.

Dog-cat rivalry in the West has never gone so far. In a different way, though, the Zoroastrian division of the earth's animals has found its way into European culture. The word "magic" comes from the name for the Zoroastrian priests, the Magi; the distinction between black and white magic (one evil, the other good) parallels the difference between Angra Mainyu and Ahura Mazda; and the animals that accompany a practitioner of black magic, such as snakes, toads, and of course cats, are all creatures of Angra Mainyu.

Zoroastrians bequeathed to us a more influential legacy, too. They believed that those who fought on the side of good could hope after death to enter the House of Song, which they also called the Abode of Light. Egyptian wall paintings had portrayed a glorious afterlife, but only for the pharaoh and perhaps his servants. The Greeks fighting in the siege of Troy hoped for nothing after their death except fame: their shade might remain in Hades, but that was at best a shadowy existence. Zarathustra taught that any person who followed a certain code of conduct on earth could live forever, that the soul mattered, and that a good deity exerted power over the world. Those who served Angra Mainyu, on the other hand, would be punished with misery and darkness. These notions of good and evil, and heaven and hell, were to prove very influential.

In the early Jewish scriptures (the Pentateuch, the first five books of the Torah), for example, there is no reference to Satan. Evil is represented instead by a serpent in the garden. After death, all souls, without differentiation, went to a place called Sheol; there was no heaven and hell. When the Jews were liberated from Babylon by the Persian king Cyrus in 539 BC, this changed. In the Book of Job, perhaps written at around that time, Satan is a powerful being, able to intervene in the world, inflicting plagues on an innocent man—the exact kind of action that Angra Mainyu undertakes in Zoroastrian belief. In the second-century BC Book of Daniel, heaven and hell appear: "Many of those who sleep in the dusty ground will awake— some to everlasting life, and others to shame and everlasting abhorrence."

Centuries later, Jesus's description of Satan resembles Angra Mainyu, in that a good God sows wheat, but God's enemy scatters weeds in the wheat field; only at the end of time can the weeds be separated from the wheat and burned. Similarly, it was after the Greeks encountered the Persians that the Greek philosopher Plato suggested souls went to reward or punishment after their death, depending on what they had done in their lives. Religion had been fundamentally changed. The nineteenth-century German philosopher Nietzsche, looking back at these events, judged that "Zarathustra created this most portentous of all errors—morality." (Consequently, he wrote a book in which Zarathustra returns and abolishes moral law. Richard Strauss was so impressed by the book that he named a fanfare after it: in this roundabout way the name Zarathustra lives on in concert halls around the world.)

Laal and her fellow Zoroastrians knew that their community was small and vulnerable. From time to time they experienced disrespect and hostility from their neighbors: Laal's brother was attacked once by boys throwing stones and shouting the word *gabr,* a derogatory term for Zoroastrians. But they had the consolation of knowing that their own ideas had shaped the way those neighbors thought.

They had also the sight of some very concrete achievements left by Zoroastrians long ago. Persepolis is a city of white marble with a royal palace at its heart, two hundred miles southwest of Yazd, built in the sixth century BC when the Persian Empire stretched from the west coast of Turkey to the deserts of Kazakhstan. The emperor Xerxes supposedly gave the order for the invasion of Greece while in the palace, and when Alexander the Great conquered the Persian empire in 330 BC he wrecked it in a drunken fit of revelry and revenge. Now, all around the marble staircase are scattered remains of pillars, half-destroyed walls, and the occasional fine sculpture that survived the fire because it was in storage at the time. As an inscription written by a medieval visitor on one of its pillars asked, "How many cities which have been built betwixt the horizons / Lay ruined in the evening, while their dwellers were in the abode of death?" To this day, Alexander has never been forgiven. The name Sekandar is common among Muslims in Kashmir, and in the Arab world Alexander is remembered as Dhu'l Qurnein, a heroic figure mentioned in the Koran. Not so in Iran, where Zoroastrians still call him "Alexander the Accursed."

Even in its present ruined state Persepolis has a power to impress, as a monument to the onetime power of the Persian Empire. It was "the richest city under the sun," according to the Sicilian historian Diodorus. All over its remains are the signs and emblems of Zoroastrianism, especially the bird-man motif, the *fravahar*. "Everything we have constructed that looks beautiful," declared an inscription left at the top of the staircase by Xerxes, "we have constructed through the grace of Ahura Mazda." When I visited this palace in 2006 these Zoroastrian symbols did not stop my guide, a young Iranian woman in a *hejab,* from taking obvious pride in the empire that had built it. She took special pleasure in explaining the meaning of the grand staircase, a masterpiece of carving with twenty-three panels, each representing one of the empire's subject nations. "Twenty-three peoples," she said. "Look, here are the Arabs . . . the Armenians . . . the Scythians . . ." Each delegation had a distinctive characteristic: Arabs bringing a camel, Armenians bringing wine, Scythians bringing horses. All were offering tribute to Persepolis as a sign that they accepted Persian hegemony. In the course of the few decades that preceded the making of these panels, Persian armies had conquered the great kingdoms of the known world—Babylon, Lydia, Egypt.

The second and last of the Pahlavi shahs who ran Iran in the twentieth

The *fravahar,* the winged figure that is a symbol of Zoroastrianism, atop the pillars of Persepolis—which was built by the emperor Darius in the sixth century BC. Photo by the author

century, Mohammed Reza Shah, oversaw in 1971 an opulent celebration at Persepolis of 2,500 years of Iranian civilization. Kings, presidents, and an emperor were entertained with 2,500 bottles of wine, 92 imperial peacocks, and processions of soldiers dressed in historical garb, and the guests slept in 52 silk-lined, air-conditioned tents with marble en suite bathrooms, specially built for the occasion. The festival was intended to encourage Iranian national pride as an alternative to the religious sentiment on which the shah's Islamic opponents, such as the Ayatollah Khomeini, based their appeal. It also was a reminder to Iranians that in their greatest era they had been ruled by monarchs. The sheer extravagance of the festival contributed to public disaffection and the shah's downfall in the Islamic Revolution of 1979. Yet even under the ayatollahs, Iran has not forgotten its former empire. When Warner Bros. produced the film *300,* which glorified the Greek resistance to the imperial Persian armies at Thermopylae in 480 BC, Iranians were outraged. "Three hundred against seventy million!" declared an Iranian newspaper headline at the time—meaning the seventy million citizens of Iran, almost all of them Muslim, united in nationalist outrage at the insult to their Zoroastrian predecessors.

IN THE AFTERMATH OF THE 2003 IRAQ WAR I was sent to Basra, in southern Iraq. Driving along the coastal road south of Basra city, along the Shatt al-Arab—the vast estuary where Iraq's rivers meet before they flow into the Gulf—I found that the road was decorated with a hundred statues of men pointing accusing fingers across the water toward Iran. A territorial dispute over the estuary waters had led to a state of near-warfare between Iraq and Iran in the 1970s, and when Iran's secular ruler, the shah, was overthrown and Ayatollah Khomeini ascended to power, the dispute erupted into a war that cost a million lives. The statues were erected by Saddam after the war to encourage people to see Iran, not their own government, as the enemy. Each statue was modeled on an Iraqi soldier who had died in the war.

I knew that it would not be easy to visit the other side of that estuary. Just as the Persians, when they were Zoroastrians, would ritually execrate Angra Mainyu, the supernatural creator of all that was evil, so now the Islamic government of Iran organized demonstrations at which protesters recited, "Death to America! Death to Britain!" For Iranian revolutionaries, who overthrew the Western-backed monarchy in 1979, America was the "Great Satan" and Britain was the "Little Satan." Yet Britain's standing in the demonology was older than America's, or Israel's for that matter. A well-loved Iranian book, *My Uncle Napoleon,* features an eccentric old soldier who sees British plots everywhere. That book is set in the 1940s, and the old soldier's paranoia dates back to events at the start of the twentieth century, when Russia and Britain set up spheres of influence in Iran and dominated its economy. When the Islamic Revolution came in 1979, the Ayatollah Khomeini blamed the British for being a power behind his enemy the shah—even though the monarchy had already blamed the British for being the power behind the Ayatollah. ("If you lift up a mullah's beard," the shah of Iran had said, "you will find MADE IN BRITAIN stamped on his chin.")

In 2006, when I was working in Baghdad, I thought I might have my chance. I encountered the Iranian ambassador at a reception given by the president of Iraq, and introduced myself in rather bad Persian before lapsing briefly into Arabic. He thought I was Iraqi, and engaged in friendly conversation. But then he asked where I worked—and when I told him it was the British embassy, a grimace crossed his face, as though I had a contagious disease. He backed away. Someone might have seen him talking to me; the report might go back to Tehran and destroy his career. I guessed that it would be a bad time to ask him for a visa. I applied instead at the Iranian embassy in London (there was one at that time), where I was given a rather stiff interview and, to my surprise, a visa. The temporary thawing in the British-Iranian relationship must have helped: the reformists were still theoretically in power in Iran, under President Khatami. Still, when I visited I expected to be followed everywhere by intrusive Iranian intelligence agents and the infamously thuggish *basij* militia.

The border between Iraq and Iran runs along the Shatt al-Arab estuary northward, through the Iraqi Marshes, and then along the western ridge of the Zagros Mountains. Because it is aligned with these natural barriers to movement, it has always marked a division between cultures: to its east, for three millennia at least, have lived mostly Indo-European peoples; to its west the people have been and are predominantly Semitic. Today Iran still speaks Farsi, while the language of most Iraqis is Arabic. *Ajami,* meaning "Persian," is still a derogatory term in parts of Iraq; nor is it hard to find Iranians who look down on their Arab neighbors. It does not help that both sides fought a terrible war in the 1980s in which a million people died.

In Zoroastrian tradition, human history is cyclical—the events of one era are repeated in some form in the next. And certainly the Iran-Iraq border has been a focus of conflict since long before the 1980s. The Persians crossed it westward in the sixth century BC, led by a king called Cyrus, to smash the kingdoms of Babylon and Anatolia and build the largest empire the world had yet known. The massive army, led by Cyrus's grandson Xerxes, that fought the Greeks at Thermopylae marched across it. Only twice did armies come east across it to occupy Iran. The first was led by Alexander the Great in 331 BC; the second was sent by the Muslim caliph Omar in AD 642 and would ultimately subdue Persia completely and pave the way for its conversion to Islam. (Both men, as it happens, are reviled by Iranians today; a Muslim Iranian is more likely to be called Kouroush [Cyrus] than Omar.) Neither the Romans during their seven hundred years of war with the Persians nor the Turks who fought them for more than three hundred years succeeded in capturing any part of modern-day Iran. The Turks sacked an Iranian city once and then withdrew, while the furthest east the Romans ever reached was a port near Basra, where the emperor Trajan stood wistfully watching ships full of Indian spices as they docked and wishing that he might sail east on one of them, to reach India by sea, for he knew the way by land through Persia was impassable. The border has always been more than a line on a map.

I did not want simply to fly over this historic border, so I made my way to eastern Turkey and prepared to cross into Iran on foot. Just before the border crossing I exchanged my dollars for Iranian riyals. Within Iran itself international sanctions meant that I would have no access to my bank account and that my credit cards would be useless, so I had to take with me all the money I might need. The largest Iranian note they could give me was worth a dollar, and so I ended up with a plastic bag full of them. Carrying this bag of cash in one hand and with a rucksack on my back, I walked up to the Iranian frontier. A huge banner hung there, showing the Ayatollah Khomeini and his successor Khamenei scowling at those walking underneath, as if to say to those entering from liberal Turkey, "Here you leave secularism behind."

"Welcome!" said a voice as I stepped onto Iranian soil. An old man sitting in a chair seemed to be the only border force deployed here. He looked delighted to see a foreigner among the small crowd of locals. Did he know, I wondered, that I came from the "Little Satan"? I fingered my British passport nervously as I moved on toward the customs queue. I was sure that the staff here, after seeing my passport, would summon the secret police, who would then have me tailed conspicuously wherever I went. But the customs police waved me through, and on the other side there was no sinister escort. In fact, I found myself in an emptying parking lot with no means of onward transport. It seemed I was beneath the Islamic Republic's notice.

I walked from the terminal along the road. A driver passed by and called out to me, "Ten imams!" I was puzzled. *Imam* was a name for the Ayatollah Khomeini. But then the man stopped his car and took a 10,000-riyal note out of his wallet. It had a picture of Khomeini on it. "Ten of these," he said, "to take you to the town." I asked him instead to drop me at an old house nearby, now a museum, which once had belonged to a Kurdish aristocrat and whose reception rooms were decorated in best Iranian early-twentieth century style, with bright blue shutters and walls covered with shimmering mirrored glass. It had been built in 1912. Iran at that time was undergoing rapid social change, illustrated by two paintings on the ceiling of the dining room. In one, a turbaned patriarch eats with his hands from a bowl while all around him men with mustaches, beards, and black *tarbush* hats do likewise, or drink tea. In the other, a clean-shaven man in a dinner jacket raises a glass of wine, while his wife, who sits next to him, does the same. Their guests are men and women in smart European fashions. One of the women is shown looking over her shoulder at the *tarbush* wearers in the other painting.

The pictures were meant to celebrate the change from the old to the new. With hindsight it could be read differently: the Westernized elite were wise to be looking over their shoulders at the traditionalists, because the turbaned patriarchs would eventually take their revenge. In January 1979 Iran's secular ruler, Mohammed Reza Shah, gave in to the demands of revolutionaries and went into voluntary exile. The following month, his longtime critic Ruhollah Khomeini returned from exile to Tehran, and moved swiftly to take power. As an ayatollah—a senior Shi'a cleric—he claimed divine authority for the new government he established. "The commandments of the ruling jurist," he declared, meaning his own, "are like the commandments of God." The shah and his father had done much to help the Zoroastrians; under the ayatollah's rule, the authorities became more hostile to non-Muslims, and laws were changed in ways that disadvantaged them.

When I reached the nearest town I went to eat at its kebab shop, and two Muslim Iranians at the next table decided to adopt me. They were brothers. "Come to our village," they said, and I said yes, hoping to see Iranian family life. As we drove through the cherry orchards near Lake Orumiyeh, with Iranian music of exquisite sadness playing on their stereo, I learned that the brothers were Azeris, a Turkish people who have been assimilated into Iran over the past seven hundred years. There were Kurds and Assyrian Christians and Armenians also living in this part of the country, and though each group had its own language, the majority spoke Azeri. At the village, my new hosts asked me to slide down in my seat to avoid being seen, because they were forbidden to entertain foreigners. "It is because I belong to the *basij*," one of them told me. So, I realized, I was in the hands of the *basij*—if not in the way I had feared. The brothers gave me dinner and a bed for the night. I met their wives and small children, who ate with us.

The next morning, when I sat on the red woolen rugs that had been laid out on the floor of the living room and consulted my map, I saw that I was close to a Zoroastrian landmark. So after the brothers surreptitiously dropped me off at a bus stop ("Keep down!" they said as the car passed people they knew on the street), I caught a bus for a short ride out of town, past snow-capped peaks, to a steep, cone-shaped hill with dust-colored sides. On the winding track that led to its summit were various Iranian couples, some young boys, and an old man. I followed them, and at the top all of us stared down into the crater of an extinct volcano. This, they told me, was Zendan-e-Soleyman, Solomon's prison.

THE JEWISH KING SOLOMON features prominently in the Koran, where he is said to have had power over the unseen spirits that Muslims call *djinn.* In one of the fables that make up the *Arabian Nights,* a fisherman opens a bottle that has the seal of Solomon on its stopper, and a *djinni* is released and tells how Solomon, "to punish me . . . called for this bottle and imprisoned me in it, and closed it with a leaden stopper, and he stamped the lead with the Most Great Name." Apparently local tradition held that Solomon had done something similar at Zendan-e-Soleyman, imprisoning rebellious spirits within its deep, steep-sided crater.

The spirits of the place might well have resisted Solomon. Before the coming of Islam this volcano was one of the greatest and most important shrines of Zoroastrianism. It may have been a site for sacrifices: Herodotus tells us that when the Persians wanted to sacrifice to Ahura Mazda, they went up on a high mountain. They also then sacrificed, he added, "to the sun and the moon and the earth, to fire and to water and the winds." I imagined them climbing the same path that I had come, exhausted from carrying a

This ruined temple at the foot of Zendan-e-Soleyman once housed the Gushnasp fire, sacred to warriors, which was visited by Persian emperors prior to their battles with the Romans. Photo by the author

sacrificial lamb or goat all the way up the mountainside. Three of the four elements remained: wind still swept over the plain, bringing a chill even in springtime; the earth was there, brown and ungenerous; and a nearby lake was still a beautiful deep blue. But the fire had gone.

Herodotus adds that the Persians rejected the common practice of depicting gods in human form and worshiping them in temples: "They have no images of the gods, no temples nor altars, and consider the use of them a sign of folly." Later, though, the Zoroastrians did build temples, perhaps under the influence of Babylonians and other peoples they conquered, but they housed no statues of gods, only an ever-living flame. As I looked down from the crater's brim I could see the ruins of one of the greatest of these temples. It had been built nearly two millennia ago to house what must have seemed a truly supernatural fire—a flame that was kept perpetually alight by the natural gas seeping from the volcano's base. The Zoroastrians called this fire Gushnasp and regarded it as one of the three most sacred fires of Persia.

Gushnasp was known as the warriors' fire, and Zoroastrian tradition held that it was as old as the world. Persian kings would visit it to make an offering before going out on campaigns against the Romans and later the

Byzantines. By the seventh century AD constant warfare had exhausted the Persian Empire. A successful campaign that took the Persians as far west as Egypt proved to be their empire's last gasp. In AD 627 the last royal visitor came to the Gushnasp fire. His name was Khosro, and he made his visit at a time of despair. He and his forces were in retreat from the advancing Byzantines, who were employing local Arab tribes as mercenaries. The Byzantines were Christians who were known to treat the holy fire with disrespect, and rather than let it fall into their hands Khosro removed it from the shrine and took it with him. Fifteen years later his empire fell—not to the Byzantines but to the Arabs, unified now by Islam.

The Arabs did not want to confront the Persian armies, which they feared would win any military encounter. But when the Arabs were finally drawn into a battle with the Persian army they successfully pressed their opponents back to a place called Nihavand, where the Persians decided to make a stand. As the great Persian epic the *Shahnamah* describes the scene, an Arab envoy in rags comes to deliver an ultimatum to the Persian knights, all of them dressed in splendid gold armor, a sign of their glory and decadence. Rustam, son of the Persian king, reads the stars and sees into the future: "The stars decree for us defeat and flight. / Four hundred years will pass in which our name / Will be forgotten and devoid of fame." After their defeat the emperor and the remnants of his court did indeed flee eastward into central Asia, taking their religion with them. It survived there as the dominant faith for another generation or so. From Nihavand onward, Islam became the state religion in Iran. The fire of Gushnasp was never rekindled.

Opinions differ over how fast the Iranians abandoned Zoroastrianism, but some members of the royal family appear to have become Muslims early on. Converts would have found that some aspects of the new religion meshed well with Zoroastrian custom. Both religions required their followers to pray several times a day (Zoroastrians three times, Muslims five), revered cleanliness, and were based on a set of divine scriptures. Islam offered an escape from the Zoroastrian caste system, in which priests and warriors were at the top; the lower castes were taught less about the religion and were quicker to abandon it, as is apparent from the high proportion of priestly families among those who have remained Zoroastrian. Converts could have it both

ways, adopting Muslim practices but also keeping up some of the most popular traditions of Zoroastrianism, such as the celebration of the New Year
(Nowruz), which is still a major two-week festival in Iran. During my visit,
I spotted many Iranian families sitting outdoors with picnics in celebration
of Sizdah Bedar, the last day of Nowruz.

Whether the Iranians adopted Islam quickly or slowly, they clearly did
not easily accept being ruled by Arabs. In countries further to the west, the
Arab invasion transformed the entire culture of the conquered peoples, many
of whom eventually began to call themselves "Arabs" and forgot their former
identities and languages. It likely helped that the conquered peoples were
also Semites, with languages that resembled Arabic, not to mention that they
were already subjects of the Byzantine Empire and, with the Arab conquest,
were only swapping one set of rulers for another.

Persia was different. An imperial people now were reduced to subser-
vience. The Arab poet al-Ja'di gives us a poignant image of their changed
fortunes: "O men, see how Persia has been ruined and its inhabitants humil-
iated: they have become slaves who pasture your sheep, as if their kingdom
was a dream." The worst insult that the Zoroastrian priests could throw at
someone who left their religion for Islam was that he or she had "ceased
to be Iranian." The Arabs in turn regarded Zoroastrianism with suspicion,
often denouncing it as fire worship and hesitating to extend to its followers
the same level of tolerance they offered to Christians and Jews.

As an early Arab governor in Iran warned his fellow Muslims soon
after the conquest: "This is the religion of the Persians—to kill Arabs." In
Bukhara the Arabs attempted to spread Islam by offering money to those
who came to prayers, and by forcibly settling Arabs among the inhabitants;
the city repeatedly rebelled nonetheless, and those who adopted Islam apos-
tatized. The man who was caliph of Islam at the time of Iran's conquest,
Omar ibn al-Khattab, was assassinated by an Iranian slave. Even in subsequent centuries a spirit of rebellion seems to have persisted, especially in the
havens that rebel movements could find in the Iranian mountains. Two centuries after the Arab conquest a group called the Khorramiyah and its leader,
Babak, operated north of Maku, preaching redistribution of property and
free love and waging war on the government. Then in the twelfth century a

dynasty that claimed to be descendants of the Prophet Mohammed operated from a fortress called Alamut on a formidable pinnacle of rock standing high above a remote valley. From their mountain stronghold they sent out their followers, known as the Assassins, to kill senior figures in the government that ruled Iran at the time. One of the dynasty declared the abolition of all religious laws: "What was forbidden is now licit," he said, "and what is licit is now forbidden."

Iran was in those days mostly Sunni rather than Shi'a. It became majority Shi'a only in the sixteenth century. Yet it seems more than a coincidence that this fallen empire has ended up with a version of Islam that has embedded within it a sense that all is not right with the world—that the true order of things has been inverted. Shi'a Islam began with twelve imams, who were meant to be the successors to the Prophet Mohammed (from whose family they were all descended; one of the points on which the Shi'a insist is that the rulers of Islam must be from the Prophet's family). Only the first of these Shi'a imams was accepted by the majority of Muslims, and many of them died amid accusations of foul play. For the Shi'a this embedded in their faith a contempt for worldly governments and a pious hope that the last of the twelve imams would one day return as the Mehdi—the equivalent of the Jewish and Christian Messiah—to usher in the end of the world. The medieval rulers of Iran even had a horse always ready in their stable for the Mehdi to ride, should he return.

Thinking about this belief of the Shi'a, I was tempted to compare it to music in a minor key, like the haunting Iranian song I had heard earlier that day on the car stereo. The notes of the elegiac melody of the twelfth imam might have been familiar to any Zoroastrian, pining for the restoration of the old order. And the Mehdi, according to legend, will be descended from the ancient emperors of Persia. For Shahrbanu, daughter of the last emperor of independent Persia before it became Muslim, was said to have married Hussein, grandson of the Prophet Mohammed: had this been true, all the subsequent imams would have been descended not only from the Prophet but also from the Persian royal family. Perhaps this story helped shore up support for Islam among Iranians who pined for the old order.

The Avesta, too, prophesied a Messiah—the Saoshyant, the redeemer who will lead the armies of good in their final battle, after which will come the end of the world and the resurrection of the dead. This Zoroastrian concept, which fits neatly into their belief that the world is a battlefield for the forces of good and evil, appears to have predated both the Jewish belief in the Messiah and the Muslim belief in the Mehdi; some scholars think that it inspired them both, though in truth the idea of a historical figure rising from the dead to rescue his people is one that might appeal to any society whose past was greater than its present. In later legend, a great lake in southeastern Iran was said to contain the seed of Zarathustra, capable of giving the world seven more prophets like himself to bring the world to a new level of wisdom each time. This concept was adopted by some Muslim groups, which sometimes suggested that Mohammed was the seventh prophet. Breakaway groups from Islam claimed that Mohammed had only been the fifth or sixth, and that their own founder was the seventh.

In the ninth and tenth centuries the Arab Abbasid Empire's grip on Iran weakened and local dynasties gained control over parts of the country. It was one such dynasty, called the Samanids, who sponsored the writing of the Iranian national epic, the *Shahnamah*. The writer, Ferdowsi, was officially a Muslim, but the poem is saturated with Zoroastrian ideas. The history it tells of the Iranian people, for example, begins with a battle against Angra Mainyu. The poet may also, by using the Persian language, have helped to preserve it. Iran never adopted Arabic for everyday speech and continues proudly to enjoy its own quite separate literature, especially a rich corpus of poetry.

FROM ZENDAN-E-SOLEYMAN I headed for a city that represents more than any other the Shi'a Islamic side of Iran. Qom is home to the country's premier shrine and seminary, where Muslim clerics are trained. The shrine in the city was built around the tomb of the sister of the eighth imam, Fatimah al-Maasoumah. It is not as important a site as the cities of Najaf and Karbala in Iraq, where the Prophet's son-in-law Ali and grandson Hussein are buried. Qom, however, has often been much easier for Iranian pilgrims to reach, and so has become immensely popular. The green lights of the shrine illuminated the parking lot where we stopped, and I could see where devout pilgrims had pitched tents among parked cars, to get as near as possible to the shrine. At a hotel overlooking the square, where I hoped to find a room, the receptionist—after showing me my room—told me not to stay there. "It's much too expensive here," he said confidentially; "you should stay instead with my friend Mr. Jehangir. He loves to meet visitors!" He placed a call and confirmed that the mysterious Mr. Jehangir could give me a bed for the night, and then told me how to find him. I wandered off down a series of little roads and alleyways till I found Mr. Jehangir's cellar apartment.

Mr. Jehangir turned out to be a newly fledged Shi'a cleric, though he was not wearing his clerical clothes. After ushering me into his home he introduced me to three of his friends who were all sitting on his floor (his wife, wearing a white face veil, sat demurely in the background, but his toddler daughter was less restrained). They were all at various stages of clerical study in one of Qom's seminaries: he was the most senior of them and proudly showed me a picture of himself in the white turban of a sheikh, the title for a man who has attained a certain level of religious learning but who does not have the extra distinction of being a black-turbaned *sayyid,* a descendant of the Prophet. I was quizzed for hours by the clerics about Britain—though more about society, and how to get a visa, than politics. We didn't finish until around 1:00 A.M., and even then they clattered away on their laptops for another hour as I lay on a nearby mattress trying to sleep. At five in the morning they rose to pray. I had to rise with them and—bleary-eyed but delighted to have this opportunity—made myself ready to be shown around Iran's top seminary by its own students.

First they gave me a tour of the shrine, whose golden domes and shiny new blue ceramic tiles were visible signs of how much support and funding it received. Non-Muslims were not allowed to enter, but my companions ushered me in. They went to pray; I stood waiting for them as the crowd of worshipers flowed past me. When they returned, they said they had another place to show me. We filed out of the mosque and walked along a tree-lined street to a large seminary. This seminary was special: it was where the Ayatollah Khomeini once studied. The two-story arcade that surrounded its wide, leafy courtyard was topped by a picture of the ayatollah. My new friends guided me to the room that once had been Khomeini's small bedroom-cum-study, and they stood as Westerners might when their national anthem is played, reverently gazing at the simple furniture and the ayatollah's picture on the wall. I fidgeted uncertainly. By resisting the temptations of wealth and power as an absolute ruler, Khomeini had shown great strength of character. Yet he was no friend to the Zoroastrians of Iran, who had prospered under the secular monarchy he overthrew.

We sat in the seminary courtyard for a while; a black-clad *sayyid* and a black cat walked slowly by, as if in stately procession. One of Mr. Jehangir's friends told me he hoped to study at the seminary. First he had to pass his entry exams; Plato's philosophy was one of the core subjects on which he would be tested. In the seminary he would study Aristotle, attending tutorials in which he learned through debating with fellow students (a technique that itself resembles that of the Greek philosophers). It was years since I had studied Aristotle and Plato myself, and I had not expected to find them a useful introduction to the Ayatollah Khomeini's classmates, since that was what my friends had turned out to be. There was a certain historical irony to it: the classical philosophers, who had inspired the European Enlightenment, were fashionable with the reactionary clergy of Iran? Plato the Athenian, and Aristotle the mentor of Alexander, were popular in Persia—which famously had been the enemy of Athens and Alexander?

But this was ignorance on my part, because as I learned, the much-hated Alexander the Great did in fact leave a legacy in Persia of affection for Greek culture. Iran's Parthian rulers in the first century BC were addicted to Greek theater. (When the unlucky Roman general Crassus was killed at Harran, his head was brought to the emperor and used as a stage prop in Euripides's *Bacchae*.) Greek science was so much revered in Persia that even after the West had adopted newer ideas, the Persians continued to follow the Greeks. Into the nineteenth century, anyone going to a doctor in Persia would have had his or her humors analyzed, based on the prescriptions of the second-century Greek doctor Galen. (*Unani-tibb*—Arabic for "Greek medicine"—has now been abandoned in Iran, though it is still practiced in India.) The astronomy that Iranian clerics were still being taught at the start of the twentieth century was that of Ptolemy, a second-century Greek scientist. A man called Ahmad Kasravi once studied to be a cleric and then went on to become one of the major anticlerical writers of modern Iran—and his disillusionment with Shi'a Islam began not with the Koran but rather with a flaw he spotted in Ptolemy.

Because of this enthusiasm for Greek learning, it was natural that when in the sixth century AD the last pagan members of Plato's Academy—whose practice it was to teach students first Plato's philosophy and then Aristotle's—were expelled by the Byzantine emperor Justinian, the Persians offered them refuge. They were housed at a town called Gundeshapur, where they joined scholars from one of the Byzantine Empire's religious minorities, who had likewise been expelled; in later years the Persians brought Chinese and Indian scholars to join them. Gundeshapur became a great university whose curriculum included Greek, Sanskrit, and Chinese texts; it had a hospital that was the greatest medical center in the region, and doctors even took examinations there (a startling innovation at that time). Byzantium's intolerance became Persia's gain.

Khomeini would have studied Plato in the seminary. In fact, his idea that Iran should be run by the "most learned cleric" not only marked a sea change from the traditional Shi'a view that government was intrinsically wicked but is not found in the Koran. Instead it is perhaps the closest approximation on earth to Plato's vision, set out in his *Republic,* of a state that is run by the "wisest philosopher." Khomeini always denied that there was a connection, although he approved of Plato and once said that he considered him "sound."

———————

MY JOURNEY FROM QOM took me through the fabulous city of Esfahan, whose central square was designed to double as a polo field, whose blue faience mosques are among the most beautiful buildings in the world, and in whose bazaar artists carefully paint tiny china boxes with love scenes and images of poets. And south from Esfahan I went to Shiraz, a city where in the 1840s a conservative Muslim *sayyid* called Ali Shirazi declared himself to

be the Mehdi and won a hundred thousand followers before he was brutally
put to death by the authorities, who regarded him as a blasphemer. His followers, who included Zoroastrians, declared that he was also the Saoshyant.
They called themselves the Babis, because Shirazi was the "Bab," the mystical
gateway to God. In the late 1880s, the British scholar Edward Browne visited
Iran. Later one of the greatest Western experts on the country (and still the
only British man to have a street named after him in modern Tehran), he
went deep into Iranian society and became adept at deciphering the secret
codes Iranians used—such as the code that Iranian men employed when
puffing smoke from their water-pipes, each series of puffs representing a
letter. Despite his skill and his keenness to meet the Babis and quiz them
about their beliefs, he was unable to penetrate the secrecy with which they
surrounded themselves. Every time he approached someone who seemed
plausible, the man would claim to be an orthodox Muslim.

Clearly enough, the Babis were watching him during this time, because
they eventually decided that they could trust him. "The 'Friends' are everywhere," a Babi man told him after revealing his own affiliation, "and though
hitherto you have sought for them without success, and only at last chanced
on them by what would seem a mere accident, now that you have the clue
you will meet them wherever you go." He learned about their customs, some
of which showed clear Zoroastrian influences: Babi men took only one wife
each, Babi women did not veil, and Babis adopted a new fast in place of
Ramadan, held in the run-up to Nowruz. The secrecy was justified: Iran's
nineteenth-century government slaughtered thousands of Babis and enslaved
their wives. The Babis' religion eventually morphed into Baha'ism. In recent
years the Baha'i leaders have been imprisoned and their followers systemat-
ically harassed, excluded from government jobs, and sometimes arrested on
the grounds that they are apostates from Islam. Since the Islamic Revolution,
two hundred Baha'is have been killed.

Shiraz is a city much celebrated in Iranian poetry, and most of all in the
poems of the fourteenth-century Hafez, Iranians' favorite poet—though one
whose work does not survive well in translation. "Oh, come to Shiraz when
the north wind blows! / There abideth the angel of Gabriel's peace / With
him who is lord of its treasures; the fame / Of the sugar of Egypt shall fade

and cease, / For the breath of our beauties has put it to shame." Hafez's *Diwan* is one of the two books that every traditional Iranian family owns—the other being the Koran. His tomb in Shiraz is a place of pilgrimage. I saw a young man kneel at it and stay there for a long time in silent prayer, while several women stood nearby, heads bowed. Perhaps it was not just Hafez they honored and longed for but the vivacious and liberated culture that he proclaimed: "Hail Sufis! Lovers of wine, all hail! For wine is proclaimed to a world athirst."

Hafez's poetry is rife with references to wine. Embarrassed by this, because wine is forbidden in Islam and Hafez was the favorite poet of Iranian Muslims, the pious interpret these references as being metaphors for spiritual delight. On that basis even the Ayatollah Khomeini wrote a poem declaring, "Let the doors of the tavern be opened, and let us go there day and night." Hafez's taverns, however, were kept by the Zoroastrian priests, the Magi. As one of his poems says, "I placed my difficulty before the old Magi last evening, / Who with the help of his glance could solve the problem. / I found him happy and smiling with a glass of wine in his hand." It shows that Hafez's mentions of wine are references to the Zoroastrian belief that drinking wine is a way to communicate with God. At a Zoroastrian prayer ceremony, wine is among seven fruits of creation that are placed in front of a priest (who is sometimes also called a Magus). In Zoroastrian tradition Zarathustra gave the saint-king Vishtaspa wine to drink, which put him into a trance. In that trance he ascended to heaven and glimpsed the glory of God. Herodotus said that the Persians made a decision only if they had considered it twice—once when sober and once when drunk. So if they made a decision while sober, they would then get drunk and see if it still seemed a good idea. If it did, they would go ahead. When I first read this, I assumed it was a joke—but in fact it makes sense. If wine gives a special kind of mystical insight, then it would seem to be a good idea to get drunk before making decisions. And a few bad experiences would have taught the value of thinking the decisions over when sober, too.

The verses quoted above are just one example of how Hafez's writing was deeply suffused with Zoroastrian thought. No wonder, then, that a Zoroastrian named Khosro wanted to honor Hafez. When he saw an earlier

A dervish circumambulates the tomb of the poet Hafez, in Shiraz, Iran. Photo by the author

memorial to him in a shabby state, he tried to build a new one around his grave. That was back in 1899, and the effort came to an end when a local Muslim cleric led a mob to destroy the monument because it had been built by a Zoroastrian. The tomb has since been rebuilt magnificently by the poet's Muslim admirers. Where, I wondered as I stood by the stone pillars of this new tomb, were Hafez's Magi now? As I did so, a dervish in ragged clothes walked past me and proceeded to circumambulate seven times around the monument. It is an old Zoroastrian custom. But as well as brown robes and a tall round hat, this holy man was wearing a green scapular, the color of Islam. He was a Muslim, not a Zoroastrian; Iran has been deeply influenced by Sufism, and some Sufis pay respect to dead saints by walking around their tombs. Of course, there might have been some Zoroastrians among the young men and women who were praying at the tomb or sitting in the café attached to the tomb. But I did not think so. Hafez's Magi had shut their taverns long ago.

There was one place where I was confident of finding the Zoroastrians: Yazd, where Laal had been born. The road there went for a hundred miles through the desert, past jagged ridges of rock and fields of sand and dust, before it reached Yazd's oasis. A huge tiled façade of pointed arches called a *tekyeh*, several stories high, greeted me on arrival; it was decorated in light blue and cream-colored Iranian faience, and next to it was a wicker wheel called a *nakhl*. These were used to stage the yearly Shi'a passion plays that commemorate the death of Ali's son Hussein, who in Shi'a eyes was the third imam and who fell in battle with his Sunni Muslim opponents.

Browne came to Yazd and described his delight when he "had at length succeeded in isolating myself not only from my own countrymen, but from my co-religionists," and was mistaken for a Zoroastrian himself. He reported that the community was "less liable to molestation now than in former times," though they "often meet with ill-treatment and insult at the hands of the more fanatical [Muslims], by whom they are regarded as pagans." When a bad governor held office, or when there was nobody in charge at all, he added, they were treated worse.

Browne was encountering the Zoroastrians at a time when their fortunes were on the mend. Despite the pervasive influence of their ideas, they had been treated with great harshness through the Middle Ages and beyond. A visitor to Iran in 1854, Maneckji Limji Hataria, wrote, "I found the Zoroastrians to be exhausted and trampled, so much that even no one in this world can be more miserable than them." The community then was subject to a special *jizya* tax, imposed on all non-Muslims. Zoroastrians were also denied the right to testify against a Muslim in front of a judge, which put them at a great disadvantage in disputes over land or trade. In addition, they were reeling from what has been called "the last mass forcible conversion of Zoroastrians to Islam"—an episode that saw a mob attack a village in the 1850s and threaten its residents with death if they did not convert. Hataria was from a family of Parsees, descendants of Zoroastrian refugees who had left Iran a thousand years before for Gujarat in northern India. The Parsee community had originally looked to Iran for religious guidance, but it had become larger and wealthier over the centuries, and Hataria was there not to receive aid but to give it. He and his fellow Parsees sent money to the poorest Zoroastrians in Iran, founded modern schools, and helped persuade the Iranian government to abolish the *jizya* in 1882.

More improvements in the situation of Yazd's Zoroastrians soon followed, and after 1906, when a constitutional revolution forced the monarchy to accept a set of liberalizing measures, including the creation of a parliament, one Zoroastrian was elected to the new body. The monarchy reasserted itself soon afterward but was eventually replaced by the dictatorship of Reza Khan, who took the title of shah and the surname Pahlavi. Despite these political changes, the community continued to flourish for the next seventy years. Zoroastrians entered government, and one of their own, Farhang Mehr, even rose to become deputy prime minister. They were particularly successful in business. As a result, fewer and fewer went into the priesthood, a profession that paid little and involved spending much time learning texts in ancient Avestan (an archaic language that itself could take years to learn). Laal's father—the priest who used to stand on the roof of his house studying the stars—told her brothers to become doctors, not priests, if they wanted to escape a life of poverty. Other Zoroastrians clearly felt the same way. In the 1930s there were two hundred priests in Yazd; by 1964, there were fewer than ten.

Laal's father was not only a priest—who eked out a small income as an itinerant preacher and small trader—but also a poet and thinker who took enthusiastically to the new ideas that were then spreading in Iran. When Reza Shah forbade the wearing of the head scarf in Iran in the 1930s, Laal's mother wanted to stop her from attending school—for, though not a Muslim, she had her own strict idea of how a girl should dress in public. It was Laal's father who insisted that she should be schooled again. When Laal chose to be a midwife, a profession that involved regular contact with human blood—taboo in a religion that placed great value on ritual cleanliness—he supported her, as he did when she chose for her husband Shahriar after being introduced to him by her brother.

It was a traditional courtship: at her first meeting with her future husband, she was accompanied by her mother and sister and did not look him in the face. She had to ask her sister what he looked like. Eventually she sneaked a look at him when they were sitting together on their third date, at a cinema, when she hoped that he was concentrating on the film and would not notice her sideways glance. She liked what she saw, and agreed to marry him. The family by that time had moved to Tehran, but after their marriage Laal and Shahriar did return occasionally to Yazd, to visit a small house they owned in the mountains; they rented out its lands to local farmers in return for a yearly supply of almonds and fruit. Their move to Tehran was a trend followed by many Zoroastrians as the Pahlavi shahs liberalized Iranian society. Laal's brother no longer had to hear shouts of *gabr*—he went on to be a doctor in Iran's air force. Shahriar was an army officer, later decorated for valor. For the first time since Nihavand, Zoroastrians could fight for Iran.

I saw no priest on the roof of any Yazdi house in 2006. At first I struggled to find any trace of Zoroastrians at all. Obituaries pasted to lampposts on every street had the Arabic Muslim heading *bismillah* (in the name of God) above photos of the recently dead. On one street corner, though, I found a notice with a different heading. *Ba nam-e-Ahura Mazda,* it declared in Persian: "in the name of Ahura Mazda." Beneath it was the symbol of the bird-man, a man with a Persian cap and wings to his left and right and beneath him. I had seen the same symbol at Persepolis. Here at last were the Zoroastrians. A grocery shop along that road was festooned with pictures.

Just as Middle Eastern Christians plaster images of St. George or the Virgin Mary to their walls and Muslims display photos of the shrine at Mecca or (in Iran) of Hussein, these pictures were of Zarathustra and the *fravahar.* They were stuck on the glass of the counter, the cash register, and the walls of the shop. At the end of the road there was even a shop selling Zoroastrian souvenirs. I contemplated whether to buy a clock with the Zoroastrian motto "Good thought, good word, good deed" written on it in Persian.

Opposite the shop, set back from the road behind a small garden, stood a fire temple. I was allowed inside, into a small clean room: behind a glass window, I could see a small flame burning. A picture of Zarathustra was on the wall of the room, and alongside it ran various excerpts from Zoroastrian scriptures—reminding the visitor that the Zoroastrians, too, have a holy book, which, along with belief in a single God, is traditionally a prerequisite for toleration under Islam. The "people of the book" are spoken of highly in the Koran, and in Iran the Zoroastrians are counted among their number. The regime derides them, however, because of their reverence for the sacred fires in their fire temples, alleging that they "worship fire." This is something that the Zoroastrians deny, saying that they do not consider the fire God, but instead worship God by means of the fire. I asked the temple's caretaker how many Zoroastrian families remained in Yazd. Very few, he said. Life was hard: the economy was bad and the government unfriendly. The numbers of Zoroastrians in the whole country, I later learned, had dropped since the revolution from thirty-three thousand to ten thousand (these are approximations, as no definitive statistics exist).

Perhaps it was appropriate that after visiting the fire temple, my next appointment was with the dead. On the opposite side of the city were two dusty hilltops surmounted by ruined towers. Called "towers of silence" by tourists, these were known to Zoroastrians as *dakhma*s. The road leading up to these hills, along which young men were racing all-terrain vehicles, used to be the route for Zoroastrian funeral processions. The body of the deceased would lie in the family home for three days, while a dog was kept nearby to deter evil spirits. Then the body would be carried on an iron bed, by men specially trained for the task, up this road and into the *dakhma.* Here the bier carriers would address the dead man: "Fear not and tremble not! This

An *ateshkadeh,* or fire temple, at Yazd. Photo by the author

is the place of your ancestors, and of our fathers and mothers, and the pure and good, for a thousand years."

"What follows," Herodotus wrote in his account of this ceremony, "is reported about their dead as a secret mystery and not with clearness, namely that the body of a Persian man is not buried until it has been torn by a bird or dog." In fact, the body was exposed until it was wholly eaten by birds or dogs. The birds, usually crows or vultures, could pick a body clean within minutes. The custom was abandoned in Iran some decades ago, apparently by choice, though it continues to be practiced among Parsees in India. The practice may predate the Zoroastrians by centuries. At Catalhuyuk in Turkey, where a human settlement from the eighth millennium BC has been excavated, there is some archaeological evidence that dead bodies may have exposed to the elements before burial.

I climbed the *dakhma* nearest to the road, and from its wall looked down to see a Zoroastrian funeral in progress down below. Since the *dakhma* had now been abandoned, the funeral was heading instead for a nearby cemetery.

A *dakhma* in Yazd, where Zoroastrians once exposed their dead for the birds to eat. Photo by the author

There bodies were placed in stone and concrete to prevent them from polluting the earth. After the funeral, the participants would go home and wash themselves with bull's urine. (The ammonia this urine contains makes it a good disinfectant, and apparently after years of storage it loses its smell—which is just as well, as sometimes Zoroastrians are expected to drink it, for example during coming-of-age ceremonies, although the squeamish now substitute pomegranate juice for the urine. Plutarch, in the first century AD, refers to this ceremony, so it is certainly very old.)

I tried to imagine what it would be like to see the collision of cosmic forces in one's daily life. All people, I suppose, have a conceptual understanding of pure and impure. Few people are comfortable buying a house where someone has died a violent death, and not many of us would like to be on an airplane journey seated next to a corpse. Immorality has been discovered by scientists to elicit the same physical reactions as physical disgust; indeed, sin and immorality are often described in terms of uncleanness ("immaculate" literally means "unstained"). Zoroastrians believe that the impurity in the world has been put there by an active and malign supernatural power, so cleanliness has a moral force, and the uncleanness of a burial ground must be taken very seriously. The death of a good person represents a great victory for Angra Mainyu and his servants, and makes the place of the burial especially unclean. A dead body attracts the corpse demon, the *nasu*. Wandering about in a *dakhma* would not be the Zoroastrians' idea of a holiday: to them it is one of the most supernaturally polluted places on earth.

I rode in a taxi from the *dakhma* back to the center of Yazd. "Zoroastrians are good people," said the driver, Hassan. Hassan was a devout Muslim, wearing a purple shirt to mark the fact, he told me, that the day was the anniversary of an Islamic martyr. "Islam came to Iran through war," he said, "from the Arabs. Before that we were all Zoroastrians." Every year people like Hassan are reminded of their heritage when they celebrate Nowruz, the spring festival, when the day becomes longer than the night (in Zoroastrian thinking, this marks a victory by good over evil). The spring festival lasts two weeks in modern Iran, and Muslims celebrate it more exuberantly than the Zoroastrians' own quiet and more religiously oriented ceremonies. Common to both groups is the custom of placing on a table seven fruits of creation, corresponding to seven virtues and the seven planets. For Zoroastrians the fruits can include wine, milk, water, sprouting cereals, the oleaster berry, and sweets; a mirror and coins can also be included, the former representing the future and the latter prosperity. Muslim Iranians tend to use wheat, apples, lotus fruits, garlic, a spice called *somak,* a pudding called *samanu,* and vinegar. A lesser festival called Charshanbeh-e-Suri, which occurs just before Nowruz, involves leaping over fire. It, too, is practiced by Muslims. The Iranian religious establishment has tried to discourage Nowruz, and in 2010 Ayatollah Khamenei tried to completely ban Charshanbeh-e-Suri on the basis that the celebrations "have no basis in Islam," but Hassan and many other Iranians across the country, though many of them are deeply religious, ignored him. I could see why. The event is fun, deeply entrenched in society, and distinctively Iranian: it is not celebrated by any culture that has not been influenced by Iran.

LAAL'S HUSBAND, the army officer Shahriar, was sent after World War II to fight a Soviet-backed insurgency in northwestern Iran (the province where I first entered the country, near Zendan-e-Soleyman). During the fighting he was wounded and left for dead on the battlefield; when he was finally found to be alive and taken to a hospital, he had lost his sight. The shah decorated him and sent him to Britain for treatment. A war veterans' charity adopted him, taught him Braille, and helped him find a job as a telephone operator. There were few Zoroastrians in Britain at this time: their daughter Shahin was brought up singing Christian hymns at school ("My father wanted us to fit in," she told me) and could explain to her puzzled classmates what her religion was only by talking about the Three Wise Men of the Bible.

Though few and not well known, the Zoroastrians were already a prosperous and influential community. The Parsee Zoroastrians had been preferred by the British over all other groups in their Indian empire: "the most intelligent, as well as the most loyal of the races scattered over our Indian possessions," as one nineteenth-century cricket commentator wrote, inspired by the visit to England of a Zoroastrian cricket club in 1887. The Zoroastrian cricketers (whose club had been formed in 1850 in Bombay) were not uncritical in their response. They complained about how dirty England was and how shocking it was to see such a gap between rich and poor: "men and women living in a chronic state of emaciation, till they can hardly be recognised as human."

Britain was a good place to do business, though, and a number of India's top trading families were Parsee; some of these began to put down roots in Britain. In fact, the first Indian to enter the British parliament was a Parsee called Dadabhai Naoroji. In the 1880s he had helped to found the Indian National Congress, which would eventually be post-independence India's ruling party. Mahatma Gandhi had called him an "inspiration"; Naoroji had had the future founder of Pakistan, Mohamed Ali Jinnah, as his assistant. Then, since India had no parliament of its own, Naoroji stood for the British one. He was selected as the Liberal candidate for a northern suburb of London called Finsbury Park in the 1892 general election. The odds did not favor him: the Conservative prime minister Lord Salisbury famously said he doubted that a "black man" could be elected to the British Parliament. One newspaper attacked Naoroji's religion, denouncing him as a fire worshiper.

So when Naoroji won by a slender majority, a delegation of his supporters made the journey all the way from India to see him sworn in. This was only a few years after Parliament had agreed to admit non-Christians at all. On the day that he was due to take his oath of office, therefore, Naoroji took his place as a lone Indian in a long line of top-hatted Victorian gentry, queuing up in the Chamber of the House of Commons. He was carrying a small copy of the Zoroastrian Avesta in his pocket, intending to take the oath on it instead of the Bible. A few days later he found himself speaking in a debate shortly after Gladstone and Balfour, warning Britain that injustice toward the people of India would end its rule there. He sat in Parliament for three years but never felt quite at home there, speaking of the "peculiar position" in which he found himself. There were in all three Zoroastrian MPs elected before India achieved its independence (none since—though one member of the British House of Lords is a Parsee). But the community never grew to any huge size. In 1980 it numbered two thousand people.

In their last twenty-five years Laal and Shahriar made no more visits back to Yazd or Tehran, out of fear of the new Islamic regime. Instead they became mentors for a new wave of Iranian Zoroastrians arriving in Britain. Between 1980 and 2001 the Zoroastrians of Britain doubled in number, from two thousand to nearly four thousand—including both Parsees and Iranians. In 2004, the Zoroastrians themselves estimated their numbers in the United States at ten thousand and in Canada at five thousand. Numbers in Iran itself have declined, though official statistics do not show this, because however badly the Zoroastrians are treated, the Baha'i fare worse, and so many Baha'is have begun to register themselves officially as Zoroastrians.

Professor John Hinnells of Liverpool Hope University interviewed and polled hundreds of Zoroastrians across the world in the late 1990s for a massive study of this diaspora. He found that many felt caught between cultures. One Zoroastrian woman in Britain told him: "My mind says I should behave like a Zoroastrian, but my body says Western." Another, in America, complained that "nowhere in the world are the social pressures to conform as great as in the United States." Yet in fact nearly three-quarters of Zoroastrians in the United States and United Kingdom said they prayed daily, and almost half those in Britain said that living there had not had an effect on their beliefs. Hinnells also recorded fierce opposition from senior clergy to the idea that those who have married outside of the religion should be allowed to take part in any of its rituals or receive a Zoroastrian burial. A marriage between a Zoroastrian woman and a non-Zoroastrian man, said the high priest in Bombay, "hurts and distresses Ahura Mazda," because women who marry outside cannot observe the rules of purity laid down by the religion. Those born to such marriages are also not counted, by traditionalists, as Zoroastrians.

Laal and Shahriar's daughter Shahin follows a more liberal interpretation of Zoroastrianism. She is a spokesperson for the World Zoroastrian Organisation, which celebrates Zoroastrian heritage and tries to keep the culture and religion alive. She also organizes events for Iranian Zoroastrians in Britain such as the yearly water festival Tirghan, when Zoroastrian children are encouraged to throw buckets of water over each other—just as their ancestors in Yazd once playfully threw water from the rooftops over passers-by. Because the water (one of the four sacred elements) is a blessing, those who are hit by it cannot complain. Such events are a way of keeping up traditions in a society where the Zoroastrians face the new challenge of secularism. "We find life in the West comfortable because people here have embraced humanistic values," Shahin told me when we met at an artists' club in a fashionable suburb of London. "We get assimilated into that because they're in tune with what we've been taught." But this is a tricky balancing act, as Shahin acknowledged: "Our children might hold on to the cultural baggage of our faith. But they might not." She was looking for a way to adapt her faith to modern times—welcoming scientific progress as, in Zoroastrian terms, the slow triumph of good thought over evil. She has even worked out a progressive approach to death that marries her interpretation of Zoroastrian principles with contemporary mores. "Exposure to vultures is about being useful in death to living creatures. Personally, I've gone for recycling," she told me cheerfully; "I have offered my body to a research institute."

We exchanged stories about Yazd, which she has not visited since the

Islamic Revolution. She was involved in a charity there, but it was largely engaged in providing care for the elderly; hardly anyone else was left. "Very few homes in Yazd have Zoroastrians in them now," she said. "Yazd is pretty much abandoned. We try to keep *gahambars* [prayer services] in them for what is left of the community. And when the mud roofs fall in they pay for repairs." Younger Muslim Iranians, such as my Yazdi taxi driver Hassan, are less prejudiced than earlier generations were—but the Islamic government has introduced newly discriminatory laws. Zoroastrians who convert to Islam in Iran today, for example, can take their parents' inheritance at the expense of their unconverted brothers and sisters.

———

THE STORY OF ZOROASTRIANISM TODAY, though, is not just about decline and growing secularism. This ancient faith has in recent years accepted its first converts in fourteen centuries. Carlos is a convert whom I met at a concert of Indian and Iranian music put on by talented young Zoroastrians in London. I had encountered Zoroastrians who had converted to Christianity and who attributed their decision to what they saw as the ritualism of their native religion. What had made Carlos, originally an unreligious Spanish Catholic, go in the other direction? Glancing briefly at his wife, Carlos explained: "We wanted to fight evil. In our religion we help God and he helps us. We're not his servants. This world isn't a test, where we get told at the end if we have passed or not." He had read about Zoroastrianism as a small boy and been attracted to it, but he had not realized any Zoroastrians still existed. After watching a BBC documentary about the fire temple at Yazd, he searched on the Internet for a community that might initiate him as a Zoroastrian, and discovered one in Scandinavia. There he put on the *kushti*, alongside a group of panicky converts from Afghanistan who wanted to return to their ancestral religion but were understandably nervous about the consequences for them when they returned home.

I noticed, though, that Carlos and his wife stood alone for much of the evening, while others at the gathering had known each other since childhood. I saw the same when I met two Zoroastrians who had adopted the religion from a nominally Muslim background (both said that their families were not religious): they were not excluded, but neither did people go out of their way to make them feel welcome. Some Parsees in particular admit that they are a clannish group, defining their identity not always by belief but also by race, and only some more liberal Zoroastrians countenance the admission of converts.

Though the Zoroastrians are few, they have internal divisions. Liberals and conservatives disagree about how to tackle intermarriage (tradition-alists want to exclude altogether the children of mixed marriages, whereas liberals want to include them) and whether to admit non-Zoroastrians to the most sacred parts of the fire-temples, where the ever-living flames are kept. There are also disagreements about how to interpret the Avesta. For the most part, Zoroastrians today are much less likely to emphasize the independent power of evil than, for example, their Sasanian forebears would have done. There are also cultural distinctions between Iranians and Parsees: Iranians speak Farsi and prefer Iranian dishes, while Parsees speak Gujarati and pre-fer Indian food.

Nonetheless, at the London fire temple that is the religion's chief social and religious focal point in Britain, an effort has been made to accommodate all varieties of Zoroastrians. In the entrance hall of the temple, which once was a movie theater, an Iranian tapestry depicts imperial Persian soldiers from the era of Darius; in what used to be the principal screening room and is now the main prayer hall, a picture of Dadabhai Naoroji celebrates the most famous Parsee to have lived in Britain. A picture of Zarathustra, on the prayer hall's left wall, faces a picture of the Queen on the opposite wall. The stage, where the screen once was, is still faced by a few rows of com-fortable seats left over from the building's days as a theater. A piano on the stage shows that the temple is used for secular entertainment as well as prayer services. Above the stage in gold letters affixed to the wall, the Zoroastrian motto is displayed: "Good thought, good word, good deed."

I visited this temple when I attended the memorial service for Laal and Shahriar, who died within months of each other in 2004. (They are buried at the Zoroastrian cemetery at Brookwood, where a prayer service is regularly held in a small chapel. The chapel is surrounded by neatly tended graves, their stones often marked with the *fravahar*, while grander stone tombs in Persian style house the dead of the wealthiest families.) At the ceremony a priest, his mouth veiled by a cloth mask that came down well below his chin—its purpose being to prevent contamination of the holy fire by breath or spittle—chanted rhythmically for ninety minutes in old Farsi, with his wife seated beside him, a scarf partly covering her hair. On the table in front of them were wine, milk, water, fruit, and white and purple blossoms, the last used as symbols of the spirits of the dead. Also on the table were pictures of Laal and Shahriar themselves; other photos showing their life in Iran and Britain were beamed onto a screen by a projector. Sandalwood twigs were burning in a small brazier, which was carried at intervals around the congregation, who waved their arms to waft the scent toward them. Afterward a selection of food was served, including both Indian and Iranian dishes.

As I talked to the Zoroastrians afterward over wine in plastic cups, I realized: at last, in this northern suburb of London, in a disused movie theater, I was in the tavern of Hafez's Magi.

4

Druze

L EBANON'S CAPITAL CITY, Beirut, is a twenty-mile-long, million-resident stretch of modern buildings on the eastern coast of the Mediterranean sea—dotted here and there with an old, honey-colored, red-roofed house that has survived from when the city was smaller and more picturesque. Walking in 2011 along its Corniche past discreet lovers and seaside clubs, I heard everywhere the pounding of waves against rocks. Another metaphorical sea was obvious as well. Up by the colder waters of the English Channel a century ago, Matthew Arnold heard the sea of faith's "melancholy, long, withdrawing roar." At Beirut, that sea was still at the full, and stormy.

Though Lebanon's fourteen-year civil war officially ended in 1989, the various religious groups whom that war pitted against each other still eye each other warily. The war wounded one in four Lebanese and killed one in twenty. All groups committed atrocities; all suffered them. But Lebanon's diversity is not only a source of conflict. This country, whose five million people are divided between eighteen recognized sects and religions, offers the closest thing to religious equality that exists in the Middle East—a constitution declaring that "the State respects all creeds" and a people more tolerant of religious diversity than most others in the world, according to Gallup polling.

"Pity the nation that is full of religions and empty of faith. Pity the nation that is divided into fragments, each fragment deeming itself a nation," wrote the Lebanese poet Kahlil Gibran in the *Garden of the Prophet,* referring acerbically to this multiplicity of sects. The reason for all this variety, though, is a virtuous one: these groups were safer in Lebanon than in most other places, because it consisted largely of mountainous areas that government forces could enter only with difficulty. Meanwhile, its location on the Mediterranean Sea made Lebanon part of both West and East. It was the Mediterranean, not the landmass of Europe, that was the heart of ancient Western civilization: around it the ancient Greeks lived, as Socrates once put it, "like frogs around a pond." Traders shipped spices, wheat, dyes, and slaves across the sea. Philosophers and saints traded ideas and knowledge across it. The eighth-century Greek poet Homer, the fifth-century Greek historian Herodotus, and the Greek mathematician Euclid were none of them from mainland Greece: they were from an Aegean island, southern Italy, and Egypt, respectively. The Greek philosopher Pythagoras was born on the Aegean island of Samos to a Lebanese father and ended his days teaching in southern Italy. I was in Lebanon to meet members of one of its eighteen religious groups, called the Druze. I wanted to see if they might be the modern-day successors to Pythagoras's followers, an ancient and secretive group of Greek philosophers called the Pythagorean Brotherhood.

PYTHAGORAS FEATURED IN THE PHILOSOPHY syllabus that I had studied at university, as he may have been a teacher of Socrates, but I could not remember anything he had written. In a Beirut bookstore I bought a book about the philosopher that had been translated into Arabic from a French original. As I read the book, I realized why I had seen so little of his work: he never wrote any of it down. Although Lebanon was part of the Greek world, it was also seen by the Greeks as exotic and mysterious (rather as it was by nineteenth-century Orientalists) because of the ancient civilizations that had existed there. Pythagoras played on this exoticism and the perception that the Orient contained esoteric wisdom passed on from the ancient Chaldeans and Israelites: legends spread that he had been taught by Jewish rabbis, Egyptian priests, and Chaldean astrologists. He was not willing to reveal what he had learned, however, except to the chosen few who were allowed to join his school. These pupils apparently had to keep absolute silence for five years, and only at the end of that time were they even allowed to catch a glimpse of their teacher. Those who gave away the secrets of Pythagoras's teaching could expect merciless vengeance from the other members, who considered any breach of secrecy to be an unforgivable betrayal. This extended even to some of their more inexplicable teachings. Everybody knew, for instance, that the Pythagoreans were not allowed to eat beans, or even tread on them. Nobody understood why, because the Brotherhood would rather die than explain. Their spirit of secrecy, denounced by others at the time as charlatanry, was summed up by a motto at the beginning of the book, put there by its French writer: "Come near, you few philosophers, the Pythagorean way of life embraces you! But you, ordinary mass of everyday people, are far from it."

Enough people did betray those secrets, though, for at least some Pythagorean beliefs to emerge. The Pythagoreans believed in reincarnation, and this drove them to purify the soul, which was immortal, and neglect the body, which they viewed as only its temporary casing. They wore white, undyed garments as a symbol of their commitment to living austere, self-denying lives. (When Julius Caesar encountered the Celtic Druids in Gaul, he thought they, too, must be Pythagoreans, because they also believed in reincarnation, dressed in white, guarded their teachings, and studied the stars. It is possible that he was right, since the Gauls had been exposed to Greek ideas for centuries.) Some Pythagoreans held their possessions in common, and they tended to avoid eating meat, animal products, or even cooked food. They were so unified that they were capable in their early years of taking over entire cities, and even in later centuries they were known for their solidarity. They identified themselves to each other through secret phrases and symbols deriving from their fascination with numbers and geometry. A Druze magazine that I had found completed the story. In an article titled "The Wise Pythagoras," it noted that "persecution suppressed the sect and scattered its members, but Pythagoreans preserved their teachings over the generations."

It might seem more natural to look for the successors to these Greek philosophers in Greece, not Lebanon. But that would be to neglect an event some historians regard as the end of antiquity and the beginning of the Middle Ages. In the year AD 529 the Academy of Plato closed its doors for the last time. Nine centuries had passed since Plato founded it in Athens. The idea of the Academy—a place where people might study at no cost, and which kept alive a certain interpretation of Greek philosophy—had survived the philosopher's death, the burning of the city by the Romans, and the dispersal of its teachers. Its professors tried to combine the teachings of the ancient philosophers they most revered: Pythagoras, Plato, and Aristotle. They taught that there was an ultimate cause for the existence of the Universe, which they called "the One." But this One really was like the number 1—utterly timeless, and free from human imperfections such as mind or will.

Such ideas were anathema to Christianity, which believed in a God who created the world through an act of will. The Byzantine ruler Justinian, a devoutly Christian emperor, decided that the existence of the Academy was an insult to his religion and to his imperial power. In Athens, he ordered, "no one should teach philosophy nor interpret the laws." The Academy's seven last professors, the "successors of Plato," sought refuge in Persia. Athens's schools fell into decay.

It was a dramatic conclusion to the reign of Greek philosophy in the Mediterranean world, where philosophers had sometimes been treated as prophets or even gods. Plato had attracted a religious cult that claimed to have access to unwritten doctrines of the philosopher; it had its own initiation ceremony. The mysterious mathematician Pythagoras, Socrates's teacher, had ended up regarded as a miracle worker, able to see the future and be in two places at once. These cults had a strong ethical dimension: Pythagoras's followers in particular (the Pythagoreans) were encouraged to examine their consciences nightly and to overcome gluttony, sloth, sensuality, and anger. But the cults were also designed to fit alongside old pagan forms of worship, and in Europe, Christianity was sweeping them aside. "What has Athens to do with Jerusalem?" one Christian polemicist wrote. More sympathetic thinkers, such as St. Augustine of Hippo, adapted Plato's ideas to fit with the doctrines of Christianity. Aristotle, however, was neglected until the Middle

Ages, and Pythagoras is generally remembered in the West today only for his theorem regarding triangles.

In the Middle East, Greek philosophy was able to escape Justinian's edict, because that region was far from Byzantium, was partly ruled by the rival Persian Empire, and in less than a hundred years came under the rule of Islam. The Harranians still revered Pythagoras as a prophet as late as the eleventh century. Far from being hostile to Greek philosophy, many early Muslims were keen to see their own civilization as the true heir to ancient Greece. The great Arab philosopher al-Kindi argued that the Arabs and Greeks were kin: Qahtan, the father of the Arabs, was brother to the ancestor of the Greeks, Yunan. A later scholar, al-Farabi, saw the Muslims as having accepted Greek philosophical ideas that the Christians had preferred to ignore or suppress. An early Islamic caliph claimed to have encountered Aristotle in a dream and to have then debated philosophy with him. Their discussion convinced the caliph to authorize the translation of Greek works into Arabic.

Among heterodox Muslims, regard for the Greeks was even higher. A mysterious group of Muslims who called themselves the "Brethren of Purity" and lived in southern Iraq in the tenth century had a great reverence for Pythagoras, too (the conservative scholar Ibn Taymiyyah denounced their writings as "a few insipid crumbs of Pythagoras's philosophy"). Just like his followers the Pythagoreans, they felt that the universe was constructed around mathematics: "the nature of created things accords with the nature of number," as they put it. The Druze are very keen on the Great philosophers, too, especially some of them and not necessarily the ones that are best known in the West. "The Druze faith," according to Druze historian Najla Abu Izzeddin in a 1984 book, "reaches beyond the traditionally recognized monotheisms to earlier expressions of man's search for communion with the One. Hence its reverence for Hermes, the bearer of a divine message, for Pythagoras . . . for the divine Plato and for Plotinus." Three things in this sentence intrigued me when I read it in my room at Harvard as I prepared for my trip to Lebanon. Who was Hermes? Why was Plato "divine"? And why were Pythagoras and Plotinus so important? All eventually would become clear—or clearer, at any rate.

The Yazidi religious leaders, when I met them at Lalish, had told me that the Druze resembled them—"they even have the same kind of mustaches," one of them added. One Druze professor told me during my time in Lebanon that the Druze's relationship with Islam was like that of Mormons with Christianity. They have their own revelation and philosophy that mainstream Muslims would consider unorthodox. They are led politically, for the most part, by a single family: the Jumblatts, who have achieved the remarkable balancing act of remaining feudal landowners, based at a castle in Lebanon's southern mountains, while also running a modern radical socialist political party. The Jumblatts rely to a large extent on the tribal loyalty of the Druze, but their party is in theory open to all religions. During Lebanon's civil war, their political skills enabled them to outmuscle their longtime rivals for the Druze leadership, the Arslan family, which possesses an older lineage but less money and power. I was hoping to meet both Prince Talal Arslan and Walid Jumblatt, as well as the senior Druze clergyman.

In the center of Beirut, a small knot of people were protesting. I saw their slogans on lampposts and placards near the city's renovated center: "No to sectarianism," "No to bribery," "No to stupidity." They were asking for the right to civil marriage so that Lebanese from different sects could marry more easily. They had little chance of success. Lebanon is a liberal society in many ways; its bars and nightclubs are crowded every night with Muslims and Christians alike. But a deep strain of conservatism runs beneath the surface, and intermarriage is viewed with disfavor by the influential and conservative Christian and Muslim religious hierarchies.

Soldiers were stationed at key points around the city center. A dispute between political factions in the Lebanese Parliament had been ongoing for several months, preventing the formation of a government, and the troops were on the streets to prevent trouble. The Druze parties could play king-makers in these disputes, but never kings: Walid Jumblatt could call on the loyalty of at least six members in the 128-member Parliament, and the Arslans on two.

I was due to meet the British ambassador at a café, from where she and I would go together to see Jumblatt. I wandered toward our rendezvous through a beautifully restored section of the city. Located on the frontier of the civil war, it was once wrecked by shrapnel and gunfire, but Rafiq Hariri, Lebanon's billionaire prime minister in the late 1990s and early 2000s, invested huge sums in its restoration before he was assassinated near it by a car bomb in 2005—probably at the instigation of the Syrian government. The incident was all too reminiscent of the civil war and made some Lebanese expect that a new internal struggle would begin.

I passed a recently built mosque that towered over a neighboring church, and I saw that the church was in return now raising its tower to match the minaret. I was trying to decide whether this was a depressing sign of religious competition or a refreshing reminder of religious freedom when my attention was diverted by a discovery. Tucked away in a side street and relatively neglected beside these two newer and bigger buildings was a mosque built by a Druze governor of the city many centuries ago. When I looked in at the mosque from the outside, I noticed what looked like a pentagram woven into the patterning of its external ironwork.

The pentagram was a particularly significant symbol for the Pythagoreans, and one they could use to identify themselves to other members. It interested them because it is made of ten triangles—ten being a number that to them signified perfection, and the triangle being an emblem of Pythagoras's famous theorem. Pythagoreans believed that numbers, and the geometrical projections of numbers, were the building blocks of the universe. So when there was a pattern in geometry or mathematics, they read into it moral and practical messages. For them, Pythagoras's theory did not just prove that a triangle's hypotenuse must measure five if its other two sides measure three and four. In the Pythagorean language of numbers, two was the number for a woman, and three was the number assigned to a man, and so five was the number for marriage. Four represented justice because it could be equally divided twice over. So the three-, four-, and five-inch sides of the triangle spelled out a message written into the mathematical fabric of the universe: "Man must behave justly in marriage." Pythagorean husbands were renowned for their faithfulness to their wives.

What did it mean, I wondered, that this Pythagorean symbol was here? Was it a coincidence? I put this question aside for the time being, because I was late for my meeting. I hurried past expensive clothing shops and restaurants, elegant arches and shuttered windows, and reached the ambassador in time to catch my lift to Walid Jumblatt's house.

THE DRUZE NUMBER AROUND A MILLION PEOPLE, of whom half or more are in Syria and the remainder split between Israel (120,000) and Lebanon (250,000). In each country they have had to choose sides. In Israel the Druze serve in the army and distance themselves from the Palestinians. In Syria they have mostly supported Bashar al-Assad's government during the bloody aftermath of the 2011 uprisings. When Lebanon's civil war began in 1975, Jumblatt's Druze militia battled alongside a coalition made up largely of Muslims and leftists against the country's Western-backed and Christian-dominated government. The war became more complex as time went on. Both sides fragmented: Christian groups often fought each other and sometimes allied with majority-Muslim countries such as Iraq and Syria. The Druze fell out with other Muslim groups and especially the militias belonging to what became Lebanon's largest single religious group, the Shi'a Muslims. In the long to-and-fro of the conflict, the old heart of the city was devastated.

Now it is once more a fashionable district, and Jumblatt's street was quiet and prosperous-looking, his villa large and comfortable. A complement of guards stood around the entrance. We took an elevator to an upper floor, and as we emerged, a huge dog came bounding over to us. Jumblatt followed close behind. A mass of wild white hair protruded from the sides of his otherwise bald head. He wore a thick mustache and a shrewd expression. Before he succeeded his father, Kamal, as lord of a feudal estate, leader of a socialist party, and civil war guerrilla leader, he had been a history teacher. "He gives me a book every time we come," the ambassador had whispered to me in the elevator. "And I keep worrying, each time I see him, that he's going to test me on the book he gave me last time."

When we entered his study, I saw what she meant. Books and newspaper clippings were spilled across his multiple desks; on the wall hung eighteenth-century Ottoman portraits and an ornamental musket. He had discovered an antiques shop in Istanbul that he particularly liked, he told us.

Surely this man, I thought, would share my enthusiasm for tracing his own people's origins and uncovering their links to classical Greece. But when I asked him about the Druze faith, he gave me an unexpected reply. "I know nothing about the Druze," the preeminent leader of the Druze declared with a violent wave of the arm. From his piles of books he selected a couple by Tariq Ali and gave them to me as gifts. He invited me to visit him at his palace in the mountains. And then he said goodbye. Either the most powerful Druze man in Lebanon, an intellectual in his own right, had been excluded from the teachings of his own religion, or else he knew better than to pass them on to an outsider. I had every intention of taking up his invitation to spend time among Druze communities, but first I would have to find someone more willing to talk to me.

Luckily, a Druze man named Rabieh, who knew the ambassador and was keen to help us understand his community, had agreed to help. The only trouble was, he told us, that he did not know very much about it himself. He was not alone. Druze laypeople live essentially as they choose, provided they help defend and maintain the community and marry within it. But they are not allowed to know what their religion teaches. This is why they are known as *juhhal* (literally, "the ignorant ones"). Despite his power and wealth, Jumblatt was once one of the *juhhal.* Only the initiates—who are also known as sheikhs or *uqqal,* and who dedicate themselves to lives of contemplation and poverty—know the religion's teachings in full. That was why, Rabieh explained, he had arranged for us to visit the House of the Sect, the administrative headquarters of the Druze religion in Lebanon. It was a short ride away through Beirut's traffic-clogged streets.

When we arrived at this mysterious-sounding place I found that it was an unassuming two-story building in a Druze enclave of west Beirut called Verdun. Inside the building, men in black cloaks, baggy black trousers, and tall brimless *tarbush* hats wrapped in white fabric—the traditional garb of the Druze sheikhs—were walking the corridors. Occasionally I would see women, too, white fabric covering their hair and half their faces. These were female sheikhs (a female sheikh is called a *sheikha*).

We had an appointment with a figure called the Sheikh al-Aql. This man was the official head of the Druze clergy. I was forewarned not to take up too much of his time; he was known for being busy and rather bad-tempered. So I entered his office with some trepidation, along with Rabieh and the ambassador. I asked him about the relationship between the Druze and Islam, and he showed himself to be erudite about Islamic issues, quoting often from the Koran, keen to demonstrate that the Druze were orthodox Muslims. "We teach the need for good deeds. Everything forbidden in religion and international law is avoided. We respect others. Our religion is Islam. Our sect are the Muwahhidun, the Unifiers. Our title is Druze."

He made no apology for not telling me more. "It is about privacy, not secrecy," he said. "Doesn't a woman have privacy in her home? We're asking for the same privacy for our beliefs." He had intimidated me into silence. But Rabieh wasn't content to leave it there. He spoke up from the back. "Sheikh, tell us about *taqammus*. What is the basis for our belief in it?" The sheikh glared at him and shot back a question in the manner of a schoolteacher trying to suppress an impertinent schoolboy. Did Rabieh understand the meaning of *taqammus*? If not, then what was he doing asking the question? The message of his tone of voice was clear enough: Rabieh was violating the privacy of his own faith.

Taqammus was a new word to me. It sounded like the Arabic word for "shirt," *qamis*. Why did the sheikh not want to talk about it? Rabieh explained as we drove away that *taqammus* means "reincarnation." It is the idea that people can change bodies as they can change shirts: the body is just a cloak for the soul. I understood why the sheikh hadn't liked the question. Most Muslims do not consider reincarnation an orthodox belief. It did explain the Druze interest in Pythagoras, though. He was famous for his belief in reincarnation: one time he stopped a man from beating a dog, saying that he recognized in its yelps the voice of a friend who had died. For the same reason, Pythagoreans were often vegetarians. How deep did the Druze veneration for the Greek philosophers go?

I hoped I might find out more from my next meeting, which took place in a still grander location than the previous ones. The castle was set on a hill south of Beirut. At its doors we were met by a flurry of retainers. They escorted us to a reception room where Prince Talal Arslan, a large and jovial man in early middle age, was sitting under a portrait of his father, who looked even more jovial than the son, and who was depicted smoking a water-pipe. The prince—a title given him because of his descent from Arab kings in the period before Islam—confirmed what I had learned about *taqammus*. "We do not believe in death at all," he said. The Druze set no store by graves: the soul only occupied the body as a temporary casing, and was eternally re-born. It was not the custom to weep at funerals. The few "tombs" the Druze held sacred were in fact empty cenotaphs. "Three things are important in our beliefs," the prince explained. "Reincarnation, respect for all heavenly religions, and a belief in the Universal Mind."

But when I pressed him to say more, the answers I received were vague. A red-haired man who was sitting next to the prince told me that the Druze faith was more spiritual than ritualistic. It was more philosophical than re-ligious, said another of the prince's subordinates. "Not all the sheikhs un-derstand the philosophy," this man added scornfully. "Few of them would understand the Neoplatonism of Sheikh Abu Aref Halawi." Halawi was a Druze holy man, famous for his asceticism, who died in 2003 at the age of over a hundred; his religious poems, addressed to "the Creator of the Uni-verse," are displayed in Druze homes. But what did it mean to say that he was a Neoplatonist? And what was the Universal Mind?

———————

A PAINTING BY RAPHAEL shows all the philosophers of ancient Greece in one imaginary scene, with Aristotle and Plato standing side by side at the center of them all. Aristotle is pointing down toward the earth and Plato up toward the heavens. The picture neatly sums up the difference between two schools of thought. Aristotle's philosophy focused on the material world: the modern word "physics" derives from the title of one of his books. Plato saw the material world as a mere shadow of the world of ideas. His view was very influential with the writers who reshaped Greek philosophy in the early centuries AD, who are called Neoplatonists by modern scholars and among whom the most prominent was a third-century writer called Plotinus. Ploti-nus and his followers Iamblichus and Porphyry were all from the Middle East (having been born in the Egyptian delta, a Syrian town near Aleppo, and the

Lebanese city of Tyre, respectively)—a sign of how Greek philosophy had already become an integral part of Mediterranean or even Middle Eastern culture. These three, along with other less influential writers of the same period, attempted to create a synthesis of Greek philosophy that would iron out any disagreements between various different schools of Greek thought.

When I shut my eyes and think, it feels as if I can contemplate abstract concepts—numbers, say, or ideas such as love or truth—that are perfect and unchanging, in contrast with the things that I encounter in the physical world. Plato compared the physical world to shadows flitting on the wall of a cave; only if the mind turned in on itself and focused on the world of ideas would it glimpse the realities of which the physical world is merely a shadow. It was the thinking part of the person, rather than the body, that Plato believed might survive death. And yet this spiritual or intellectual world clearly had the ability to influence the physical world. By thinking, I can make a decision about what to do; then I move my arm to carry out my decision. So the Neoplatonists suggested that the soul or mind can operate on both the physical plane and on the intellectual one. They theorized about a hierarchy of planes of existence, and entities such as the mind that could cross from one to another. At the top of this hierarchy was the One.

Though called Neoplatonists, they were also enthusiasts of Pythagoras. Pythagoras appears to have been an exponent of monotheism, and one of the Pythagorean sacred symbols was a circle with a dot in the center. The circle represented the cosmos, and the dot was the One—rather like T. S. Eliot's "still point of the turning world," it was the unchanging and timeless "still point" on which the whole universe depended. That did not mean that the One had a will, or that it did things; its nature was so distant from our imperfect, transitory world that it was beyond the power of the human intellect to find even a single sentence to describe it, save that it existed and was changeless and perfect. It did not create the world: that would have marred its perfection by anchoring it in a particular moment in time. Instead, its existence entails the existence of everything else—just as the existence of the number 1 entailed the existence of all other numbers. The universe "emanates" from the One, to use the Neoplatonists' term, and the theory of why the universe exists is called emanationism.

What emanated from the One at the first level was the Universal Mind or Intellect, followed by the emanation of an entity called the Universal Soul; these three formed a sort of philosopher's trinity. From the Universal Mind and Soul emanated the physical and spiritual worlds. Some of the Neoplatonists suggested that there were a number of other spiritual beings that were intermediaries between the One and mankind. A moral code was built around this vision of the universe. To be good was to move toward the One— to unify oneself with it by turning away from the physical world. "He that has the strength," Plotinus wrote, "let him arise and withdraw into himself, turning away for ever from the material beauty that once made his joy." Selfishness and egotism were sources of division and the original cause of the separation from the One. Plotinus was keen that his philosophy should be kept secret from outsiders. "Nothing divulged to the uninitiated" was his rule, though this was broken after his death when his followers published his major works.

What I could not understand at first was how these ancient ideas had come to be at the heart of a modern-day Islamic sect in Lebanon. The prince was prepared to enlighten me. He looked out the window of the reception room where we were meeting at the narrow strip of land that separated his castle from the shore. The main road north to Beirut could be seen from this vantage. "It is a strategic place," said Prince Talal; "that is why the Abbasids gave it to us." He signaled to an aide, who a moment later held a heavy, elegantly bound Arabic book in his hands. It was the history of the prince's family over the past thousand years. The prince gave it to me. Reading it, and making my way through a collection of other books that I was given in subsequent days by Druze well-wishers, I pieced together at least a part of the Druze story.

———————

THE ARSLAN BOOK RECOUNTED HOW, in the eighth century, the family was sent from Baghdad by the Abbasid caliphs to defend the Lebanese coast from the Byzantines. The Arslans did this job effectively, but eventually a new and completely unexpected threat emerged. In 910 the Abbasids received disturbing news: in the neglected wilds of North Africa a man was claiming to be a descendant of the Prophet Mohammed and his rightful successor as the ruler of Islam. Thanks to a loyal lieutenant who had spread his message among the Berber tribes of the region, this man had many supporters, who had defeated and overthrown the Abbasids' local vassals. Al-Mahdi, as this man called himself, belonged to a small branch of Islam called the Ismailis. He and his descendants would over the subsequent centuries build and sustain the huge Fatimid Empire, encompassing not just North Africa but also Egypt and Lebanon. They founded Cairo. They proclaimed freedom of religion to their subjects, who included many Christians and Jews. And they amassed a huge library of Greek philosophy.

Fatimid Cairo was a particularly fertile environment for those who wanted to merge Greek philosophy with Islam. The Fatimids placed great emphasis on learning, building the al-Azhar mosque and a school that taught Islamic law, philosophy, and astronomy; Greek thought remained in fashion among Muslim scholars both in Cairo and in Baghdad. These scholars adapted the ideas of the Neoplatonists to fit with Islam. The One, naturally enough, was seen as Allah. The intermediaries between God and creation were identified as immaterial Minds or "archangels" by some scholars, and at least one philosopher, al-Farabi, said that these Minds took the form of the stars and planets.

A hundred years after al-Mahdi's dramatic revelation, his grandson's great-grandson was ruling in Cairo. Known as al-Hakim bi Amr Allah, he broke with the tradition of tolerance and imposed shari'a law on his subjects with unprecedented ruthlessness. He issued a number of controversial decrees: he demanded that curses against the first Sunni caliphs should be posted on mosques and bazaar entrances, banned his Christian subjects from celebrating Easter, ordered the city's raisins burned (because they might be used to make wine), called for the city's honey to be poured into the Nile (because it might be used to make mead), and declared that cobblers could no longer make women's shoes (as women were not to be allowed outdoors). He ordered non-Muslims to wear painfully heavy objects around their necks. He heard about the ritual of the Holy Fire, conducted at Jerusalem's Holy Sepulcher Church on Easter Sunday, decided that it was a trick, and was so outraged by it that he had the church razed to the ground. It was rebuilt only after his death. The destruction of the church helped to spark the Crusades, which would forever mar the relations between Christians and Muslims.

Although al-Hakim's behavior seemed cruel or even irrational to his victims (and many others), his admirers thought that his eccentricities were evidence of his closeness to God. A series of millennial events—the approach of the thousandth year after Christ, and the four hundredth year after Mohammed—stirred expectations that the end of the world might be close at hand. It was in this febrile atmosphere that a set of thinkers devised the philosophy of Tawheed—the Druze faith. Even the reason for the name "Druze" is mysterious. It probably was a version of the surname of Nashtaqin al-Darazi, an early adherent who was later excommunicated. And the religion's teachings gave rise to startling rumors. The Druze believed, or so the Cairo gossip had it, that al-Hakim was the human manifestation or epiphany of God himself. The Druze today deny these rumors. But Neoplatonism did allow for subtle ways to identify a person on earth with the divine. In its Arabic rendering, *lahut* was God in himself; *nasut* was God manifested on earth in human-like appearance.

Whatever formula the Druze may use to express this (and it might be as subtle and complex as the Nicene Creed), they appear to have considered al-Hakim to be a manifestation (*nasut*) of God on earth. What was more, they considered five of their own leaders to be earthly manifestations of other, inferior celestial beings: the Universal Mind, the Universal Soul, and three others called the Word, the Precedent, and the Successor. These five entities had appeared in human form before—as Jesus and his apostles, Moses and Aaron, Plato and Aristotle and Pythagoras, and Mohammed and his companions. Each time, they had ushered mankind into a new phase of understanding by instituting a new religion. Moses had brought Judaism, Jesus brought Christianity, and Mohammed brought Islam. Now the Druze religion was to usher in a new era of mankind's history, replacing orthodox Islam. Hamza bin Ali, the leader of the Druze movement, believed that he himself was the manifestation on earth of the Universal Mind. In previous incarnations, he had been Pythagoras and Jesus.

While al-Hakim was still alive, the Druze were tolerated. But when he disappeared mysteriously while walking on the Moqattam Hills above Cairo in 1021, his son succeeded him and was apparently less willing to tolerate a religion that held his father (but not him) in such high esteem. Thousands of Druze were killed. They gradually retreated into the hills of southern Lebanon, accepting converts for a time—their ethnic origins are very diverse—and recognizing each other through secret signs and code words. The five-pointed star, for example (each of whose points has a different color: white, blue, yellow, red, and green) represented the five Druze leaders and the five heavenly entities to which they corresponded. The community soon stopped accepting new converts, which only furthered the trend toward secrecy; as a Lebanese historian wrote, "The Druze religion thus became wholly hereditary, a sacred privilege, a priceless treasure to be jealously and zealously guarded against the profane." Pythagoras could not have put it better.

The new faith had a minimum of rules and rituals. The obligations of a faithful Muslim—prayer five times a day, fasting during Ramadan once a year, and pilgrimage to Mecca—were reinterpreted as more abstract requirements, such as to keep the faith, tell the truth, and help one's co-religionists. Druze laypeople were allowed to eat pork and drink wine. They could pray in whatever manner they wished—or not at all, if they preferred. Twice a year, one Druze layman told me, he was invited to a prayer session where he could in theory have asked questions about the faith. But there was no obligation, he explained: "If you ask me about theology, I couldn't answer you. Being Druze is a social allegiance to a community—one is born within it."

Unsurprisingly, the Druze's liberal take on Islam provoked the ire of fundamentalist clerics. In the fourteenth century, when the Arab lands were beset with enemies on all sides—Crusaders to the west, Mongols to the east—the scholar Ibn Taymiyyah wanted to use violence to crush all "deviant" ideas. He was so conservative that (it is said) he never ate watermelon because he had no evidence that the Prophet or his companions had done so. To do something that they had not was to risk "innovation," which conservative scholars regarded as dangerous. Unsurprisingly, Ibn Taymiyyah was a formidable enemy of the Druze. He issued a stern fatwa against both Druze and Alawites, calling them "deceptive unbelievers." Their food was not to be eaten, their women were to be enslaved, their money seized, their repentance denied, their scholars killed, their funerals boycotted: "They must be killed wherever found, and to be cursed as described." A period of persecution followed in which the Druze were forced to conform outwardly to orthodox Islam. But eventually their overlords, who by this time were the Ottomans, relented and granted them self-rule and (in effect) freedom of worship.

What about today? I wondered. What attitudes did the Druze encounter in Muslims who did not share their esoteric vision? In a trendy bar in downtown Beirut I met a woman whose father had died fighting in the civil war, as a member of the Druze militia. She arrived in a yellow Porsche. The bar gave the appearance of being a dive but was actually a haunt of Beirut's rich youth. "It's all down to politics," she told me as we sat on a couple of faded chairs. "When Walid Jumblatt is siding with the Sunnis, then the Sunnis are friendly, and when he is with the Shi'a, then they all say the Druze can't be trusted." The twists and turns of the civil war had given way to a less bloody, but equally changeable, set of political alliances.

She had encountered various unpleasant accusations at school—that the Druze have yearly orgies, for instance, or that they worship a golden calf hidden inside a box. These allegations are commonly directed against all minority groups in the Middle East. The first has been made against the Druze, the Samaritans, the Alawites, and the Yazidis. The second has been made against the Druze and the Samaritans. Both accusations were historically leveled against Christians, too, and some version of the same accusations has been thrown by Christians against Muslims. What lies behind this habit is unclear: not merely malice, but perhaps an element of prurient fantasy, and maybe, too, some vestigial memory of sects—a breakaway Zoroastrian movement, various ninth-century Sufi groups—that really did promote free love. Probably the biggest reason that the Druze were accused of sexual immorality is that they allowed men and women to pray together, and gave women something approaching equality. (The Pythagoreans likewise were known for allowing women as well as men to share in their mysteries.)

TO UNCOVER MORE OF DRUZE THEOLOGY, I was going to visit their heartland, in the Shouf Mountains of southern Lebanon. Every journey in

Lebanon is a religious education, because the country's different religions all tend to advertise themselves. One can go north on a huge coastal motorway, often choked with traffic, past casinos and supermarkets and the offered embrace of a huge statue of Christ; then up into the mountains, into villages populated with statues of the Virgin Mary, vineyards, and Aramaic names, on the edges of dizzying crevasses. Heading south from Beirut, one travels through crowded suburbs decorated with posters of Hizbullah's leader, Hassan Nasrallah. Past the sprawling cities of Tyre and Sidon, one descends to the pastoral open spaces of the Shi'a heartland; entering villages there, I might be greeted by the picture of a fist smashing down on the head of an Israeli soldier, and at the notorious al-Khiam jail, a list is posted of those who died while imprisoned during the Israeli occupation of southern Lebanon. These political symbols leave no doubt about the religious identity of the region's residents.

The route to the east, though, is rather more subtly adorned. An hour's winding, high-speed, brake-squealing drive in a car sent by Walid Jumblatt took me up into the Shouf Mountains, where the Druze community has traditionally been concentrated and where Jumblatt has his castle, and in the villages through which we passed I saw no sign of religion at all. Hassan, the driver, bought a piece of *konafa*, an oily and sweet cake made with cheese, at a shop where we paused on our route. As I ate it I looked out at the orange groves, tall mountains, and deep valleys of the Shouf. Tomatoes, olives, bananas, and lemons were grown here. Pink bell-shaped flowers gave extra color to the scene. Extensive construction had left the hillsides peppered with red-roofed concrete villas, covered with a thin layer of cream-colored limestone.

Far below, the sea sometimes showed through the encompassing hills. The scene was a figurative portrait of Lebanon, in addition to being a literal one. Sea and mountains together, I thought, have made Lebanon what it is—an intoxicating mixture of the international and the parochial, liberal modernity and stubborn tribalism, joie de vivre and fanatical religiosity. Holy men and women came into the Lebanese mountains early in the Christian era to live solitary lives sustained by donations of food from local villagers. After the arrival of Islam, medieval accounts show that Muslim hermits were similarly welcomed by Christian villages. When the first Druze preachers headed into the Shouf Mountains in the aftermath of their emigration from Egypt, preaching and practicing self-denial, they were treading in well-worn footsteps. "Go to the people who live in the shadow of Mount Hermon," says an early Druze text: "they are apt to follow."

The preachers would have found not only Christian villagers but the last remnants of a pagan cult. The Harranians had a temple at Baalbek in Lebanon—just sixty miles north from the Shouf Mountains, where I was now—at the time when the first Druze missionaries arrived. Perhaps some Harranians were among those who adopted the Druze philosophy, finding that it made Islam easier to accept, since it shared their belief in reincarnation and allowed them to continue revering Pythagoras and other figures from the ancient Greek tradition whom Christianity and Islam ignored.

I noticed curious shop names in one Druze town: Wisdom Pharmacy and Enlightenment Hospital, for example. At a dry cleaner's, I saw a Druze religious poem posted that began: "O Creator of the Universe . . . " It had been written by al-Halawi, the respected sheikh whose name I learned at Prince Talal Arslan's castle. One building, otherwise plain, had a single five-pointed star painted above its entrance.

One other quality marked Druze villages as unique: oddly ubiquitous men in brown coveralls, with white woolen caps on their shaved heads, working on houses and gardens and at gas stations. The only hair each of them had was a bristling mustache. I asked Hassan who they were. "Sheikhs," he said. These were *uqqal*—more junior versions of the ones that I had seen when I visited the House of the Sect. The laypeople among the Druze live as they choose, but the Druze clergy abide by a philosophy of self-denial. Male sheikhs are encouraged to live off the land, and it is particularly virtuous for them to eat only the food that they themselves have grown. They live austere lives, praying and meditating regularly, fasting during Ramadan, avoiding pork and alcohol, and never engaging in any kind of excess (a sheikh, for example, even when presented with a glass of water, is not supposed to drink it all down but only to sip at it without slaking his thirst). Druze clergy are proportionally a large group: perhaps 15 percent of all Druze, both men and women, are sheikhs. Joining the clergy was not a complicated business,

Hassan had told me: a person applied for admission, and over a period of time was evaluated for the level of his or her commitment and capacity for religious understanding.

Hassan's wife was a member of the Druze clergy. Just as the male sheikhs tilled the land, she and other women sheikhas worked on embroidery and other home crafts that allowed them to earn an income without going out into the world. If Hassan's wife did go outside her home, she would wear a white handkerchief on her head and half covering her face, like the women I had seen in the House of the Sect. Hassan was not a talkative man, but he was beginning to open up. Where had he been in Lebanon? I asked. "Down to Beirut, and back here." He had never left the Druze areas; his whole world, I guessed, could be no more than a square fifteen miles on each side. I guessed he had been a fighter in the civil war.

On our journey we passed through Druze towns and villages dotting the hillsides. The houses were large, some huge, and yet were used only as summer homes by wealthy Druze émigrés. Hassan told me that of the six thousand residents of his home village, between twenty and twenty-five had over $100 million each. Much of this wealth was the result of successful business ventures abroad, especially in West Africa. Many Druze villages had become ghost towns, with maybe only a third of the houses actually inhabited year-round. When we passed a village that was near Hassan's own, I asked whether there had been many killed there during the years of violence. Thirteen, he said: five when the village was bombed by Israel, the others killed at checkpoints when their ID cards showed them to be Druze. "It was a horrible war." When had it stopped? I asked. "It hasn't," he told me. "It's still going on."

When the civil war began, the Shouf Mountains saw some vicious fighting between the Druze and their Christian neighbors, who had been brought here by Druze rulers as tenant farmers in the seventeenth century. The Druze eventually gained the upper hand and cleared Christians from parts of the Shouf (though Jumblatt has recently encouraged them to return). Later in the war, the Druze were more often battling the Shi'a militias whose heartland was to their south. After the civil war was resolved in 1989, tension between Druze and Shi'a occasionally resurfaced. The worst single incident

The "tomb" of the Prophet Job, in Lebanon's Shouf Mountains, is a holy site for the country's 250,000 Druze. Since they believe in reincarnation, however, they consider it a cenotaph. Photo by the author

came in May 2008, when Hizbullah shelled Druze in the Shouf and took control of two strategically located Druze villages. In the ensuing fighting, the Druze resumed a trademark method of killing their enemies—cutting throats. Advisers to Jumblatt and Arslan later told the US ambassador (in conversations eventually published by Wikileaks) that the Druze were living in a "sea of Shi'a" and feared Shi'a vengeance. The events of 2008 served as an example of how communal violence could reemerge in Lebanon without notice, since there was no effective central authority that could resolve disputes: Lebanon's government is itself hostage to the same tensions. "We are a small people," was a refrain that I heard often in the Shouf hills.

ONCE IT HAD BEEN DIFFERENT. Fakhreddin, the preeminent Druze feudal lord in the early seventeenth century, carved out of the Ottoman domain a territory that was essentially independent, and whose borders were close to those of modern Lebanon. Fakhreddin is a figure of national importance: he gives Lebanon a native founder and a historical legitimacy

in the face of those who say that the country was a creation of the French
colonial powers in 1926. The Ottoman Turkish army eventually brought his
independent statelet to an end. Hassan took me to a ruined fortress at the top
of a tall cliff on the southern edge of the Shouf. Only fragments remained
of a great castle that had once stood there, commanding the plain below.
This, too, had been one of Fakhreddin's castles. "The Turks surrounded
this place," Hassan said, "but Fakhreddin would not give up. He carried on
resisting. And then the Turks poisoned the springs from where the castle got
all its water. But even then he refused to surrender. I'll tell you what he did.
He blindfolded himself and his horse, and together they jumped off this cliff
so that he would not be caught." I looked down. The fall must have been a
hundred feet or so. Hassan had walked back to the spot where the poisoned
spring had been. Now there was only dampness underfoot. But for him it
seemed almost sacred ground. Here was where a great Druze hero had been
brought low. "Forgotten kingdoms?" said Hassan when I told him my book's
title. "We have not forgotten."

Fakhreddin's story is a myth, symbolizing Druze courage. He was in fact
caught and put to death by the Turks. After him various other families competed to be preeminent among the Druze. Today's winners, the Jumblatts,
have been living in a castle at Moukhtara since the eighteenth century. In
1853 the castle was visited by the English peer Lord Carnarvon (whose son
would later fund the Tutankhamun expedition). The British had discovered
in the 1840s that the Druze were a minority community in need of a sponsor,
and had decided to fill that role. Carnarvon, who was on his way to becoming
a senior British statesman, wanted to make the acquaintance of his nation's
latest allies. Carnarvon's own stately home in England was itself fairly imposing—in recent years it has featured as Downton Abbey in the TV show of
that name. Even so, he seems to have been greatly impressed by Moukhtara,
which he described in a book published a few years later. Its finest scene is an
account of a medieval-style joust held in the castle courtyard: "The cavaliers
of the *maidan* in their gay colours, the 'varlets' standing by the horses and
handing fresh spears to the riders, the shouts of approval which hailed each
fortunate stroke, the ladies on the battlements . . . the armed and haughty

crowd . . . the square towers rising from the long sweep of wall on every side."

Carnarvon was certain that he had visited a relic of the Middle Ages that would not long survive. Even as he remembers the carnival of Moukhtara, he writes elegiacally of the Druze's "picturesque and feudal independence . . . which is possibly now doomed to extinction in the mountains in Syria." The Druze have outlasted that prediction, in part owing to the support of Carnarvon and others. In the 1860s Druze communities wrote in a collective petition to the British that "we Druses have, after God, no other protector than the British Government." The belief even spread among the Druze that they were British by origin, or at least that they and the British shared a common ancestry. Some Druze believed this as late as the early twentieth century, and Druze leaders apparently still sometimes ask the British for aid. When I later met one of the most senior of Druze sheikhs, Abu Mohammed Jawad, as he lay on his deathbed in a simple cottage—where homemade confectionery sat on a cart ready to be served to guests—the one thing he had the strength to utter was a reference to this old and curious alliance.

The pro-Druze policy may have seemed a surprising one for a Christian country to adopt, since one of the principal enemies of the Druze at the time were the Maronite Christians. In the eyes of the British, however, the Maronites' Christianity was far less important than the fact that they were backed by the French. There was another reason the British favored the Druze, though, a wonderful find for a conspiracy theorist. Among all the colorful theories about the origins of the Druze—as well as their putative British ancestry, they were said to be descended from a French count called Dreux, or, according to the Russian theosophist Madame Blavatsky, from Tibetan lamas—the most intriguing suggestion of all is in a volume deep in the London Library, dating from 1891. The book contains the proceedings of a Masonic lodge called Quatuor Coronati. Its first article, by Brother the Reverend Haskett Smith, argues "that, to this very day, the Druses retain many evident tokens of their close and intimate connection with the Ancient Craft of Freemasonry."

The Freemasons believed that they carried on the traditions of the masons who built Solomon's Temple. Brother Haskett thought that the Druze were the real thing—the masons' actual descendants—and he was determined to prove it. He spent several weeks in Lebanon, living among the Druze and trying out a simple test. The Freemasons believe that the code words they use were handed down from the builders of the Temple; Brother Haskett thus assumed that the Druze must know the same words. But since he had great difficulty penetrating their wall of secrecy—as he ruefully recounted, each time he asked them about their beliefs, "the whole subject is adroitly turned"—he realized he would have to overcome their secrecy with guile.

He summons up, perhaps sincerely, a fascinatingly bizarre image for us: "I have made many attempts to gain the ear of a Druse by words, mysteriously whispered, as a dramatic theatrical aside, solemnly pronounced, or casually uttered when the Druse would be least on his guard." This made me imagine a scholarly English cleric in his dog collar trying to surprise tough and wizened Druze farmers by coming up behind them and shouting words in ancient Hebrew. If the Druze knew the words, they nevertheless maintained their aplomb, for Brother Haskett never found proof of his theory. He presented it to his fellow Freemasons nonetheless, as the 1891 record shows—noting their skepticism as it does so. One of Brother Haskett's audience, indignant that his movement should be regarded as a mere offshoot and a Middle Eastern community presented as the original, claimed that the Druze must simply have borrowed their customs from the Freemasons. (In fact, the historian Philip Hitti claimed that the Knights Templar, whom Freemasons have attempted to imitate, might have been influenced by the Druze "organization and teaching." The concept of the self-denying, austere warrior-monk is one that the Templars and Druze shared, although there is not much evidence of philosophical ideas that they held in common.)

Whatever the reason for the cultural similarities between the two groups, a Freemason such as Carnarvon certainly would have spotted the resemblance. There is more than dispassionate observation in his description of the ascent of the Druze toward the higher secrets of the faith: "Gradually—very gradually—he is permitted to draw aside the successive veils which shroud the great secret . . . he is learning only to unlearn; he makes, and he treads on the ruins of his former belief: slowly, painfully, dizzily, he mounts each successive degree of initiation . . . and—as if to mock the hope of all return—at each stride

British war artist Anthony Gross painted this depiction of Druze religious leaders (seated in the circle, at center) accompanied by members of the British Druze Cavalry Regiment in 1942, during World War II. The Druze had a friendship with the British dating back to the mid-nineteenth century, though in fact this Druze regiment had been deployed by the Vichy French against the British before being won over to the British side. Image courtesy Anthony Gross/ Imperial War Museum

he hears the step on which he last trod crumble and crash into the measureless abyss that rolls below him. Few indeed scale these mysterious heights."

———————

HOW MANY SECRETS WOULD I LEARN, I wondered, at the Jumblatt castle? As Hassan drove me up toward it, he slowed to a more reverent speed. I noticed a simple stone up ahead, by the roadside. "It is a memorial to Kamal Bek," said Hassan, referring to Kamal Jumblatt, Walid's father ("Bek" is an honorific). The car stopped. "He was killed just here," Hassan said, and sat behind the steering wheel without moving, looking at the stone. Hassan could only have been a child at the time, but his tone and manner suggested that he had witnessed the scene that he was describing. "He only had one bodyguard, and his car was coming the same way we are heading now. Another car came in the other direction." I looked ahead, toward the next hairpin bend, where the road curved upward. "From there," Hassan said.

"There was a group of men in the car and they opened fire and killed him." He would not say who was responsible, but it is widely accepted that the attack was arranged by Syrian president Hafez al-Assad to punish Jumblatt for rejecting a Syrian-brokered peace deal intended to end the Lebanese civil war on terms Jumblatt found unacceptable. Hassan sighed. Another Druze hero had fallen.

He restarted the car and we climbed the last few hundred yards to Moukhtara village. Here I finally caught my first glimpse of Walid Jumblatt's castle. A huge building in honey-colored stone, it dominated the hairdresser's and grocery store and well-kept gardens of the hillside settlement. After dropping my bags at an outbuilding, I made my way to its gatehouse, where bodyguards sat chatting and drinking coffee in front of an old cupboard with a grimy glass door through which I spotted a selection of rifles and what looked like a rocket launcher.

Finally a familiar character with wild white hair came into view: Walid Jumblatt was here to collect me, his dog bounding along behind him. I avoided trying to ask him again about the Druze religion for the time being, and instead admiringly toured his ancestral home. The castle was built in what could be called the Lebanese classical style: a red tiled roof, patches of red and orange coloring on the walls, pointed arches between thin columns and a lantern hanging from the tip of each point. In the courtyard—perhaps the same place where Carnarvon had seen the jousting—there were fountains, pediments above the windows, and a Roman sarcophagus decorated with scenes of Bacchus dancing among grapes. The interior rooms were more lavish: huge marble floors, fountains, Damascene carved ceilings. A massive painting of the siege of Leningrad, a gift from the Soviet Union, was a sign of where the Druze had turned when British support ran dry.

Over dinner I tried him again on Druze religion, and he promised to introduce me to some of the clergy. But he preferred to talk about politics. Syria was descending into civil war, and the Druze there would have to take sides: to his embarrassment, he said over glasses of vodka and cups of steaming black coffee, there were many who wanted to back Assad. I asked how the Druze had ended up in Syria in the first place, and he told me that they had been forced to flee there in 1711 as a result of an internal battle among the Druze themselves, between two groups called Qaysis and Yemenis. The Yemenis had been driven out east, into what later became Syria. Their descendants are now the world's largest Druze community; most of them live on a basalt plateau called the Druze Mountain. The Druze in Israel (now numbering a little over 120,000) were separated from their brethren in Lebanon when national borders were imposed on the region after World War I.

The next day Walid Jumblatt fulfilled his promise and took me to meet the *uqqal* at a lunch in a garden higher up the hillside. He drove the car, rather to my surprise: wasn't he worried that what had happened to his father might happen to him, too? "It's down to fate," he said. A belief that certain events are destined to happen and cannot be avoided is common in the Middle East (and it is an old one; Babylonian astrology rests on this belief that human affairs are fore-ordained). It was an uneventful journey, except for people waving at Jumblatt in the one village through which we passed. When we reached the garden where the lunch was being held, it was like encountering an ocean of white fezzes and black cloaks: there were upward of a hundred sheikhs seated at the long tables, contemplating huge dishes of lamb and rice. The host, Sheikh Ali, came to greet us. He was an enormously jolly and rotund man, who in his nineteenth-century Druze dress of black baggy trousers and Ottoman fez looked like a pasha out of a 1930s film about the Orient. He was especially talented, I was told, at arranging picnics. I could believe it. Touring his house after the meal, though, I saw photographs on his living room wall that showed another side of the sheikh. They were from the early 1980s, when the civil war was just beginning, and showed a young Sheikh Ali training cadets for battle. In those times, the crisis was so great that the sheikhs had to fight despite their commitment to asceticism.

The sheikhs were keen to explain that this was not a normal practice—ordinarily they scrupulously avoid involving themselves in conflict of any kind. "We sheikhs are in the service of people," said Sheikh Ali, "maintaining customs that keep the sect going, preserve the Druze honor, and prevent social ills." But when Druze honor was at stake, he added, everything was permitted: "Yes, everyone in time of war must turn out, and fight with sticks if need be. Our community comes alive in war; it's in peacetime that we get fed up." The small group of young men gathered around the sheikh laughed in agreement. Sheikh Ali explained that his reference to sticks was meant seriously: that was how the Druze had fought the French in the 1920s, overcoming armed soldiers with swords, sticks, and stones before seizing their weapons and starting a full-scale insurrection. It all began because the French had arrested a guest of the local Druze chieftain, which the Druze considered to be an insult to their honor.

Another sheikh, blind in one eye, talked to me about the Greek philosophers. He told me how during the eleventh century, in a brilliant piece of polemic, the Muslim scholar al-Ghazali argued that philosophy was self-contradictory. It could not explain God and therefore could only lead those who studied it to skepticism. Al-Ghazali led the intellectual charge against the Greeks, and orthodox Sunni Islam gradually stopped taking inspiration from the philosophy of others. The Druze, though, isolated in their mountain villages and already determinedly unorthodox, were untouched by al-Ghazali. They continued to revere Plato, Pythagoras, and Aristotle.

After the lunch, back at Moukhtara, I wandered through alleyways and down stairs littered with oranges freshly fallen from trees. I passed a church, but its one tiny door was shut. Nearby there was a small restaurant where I sat writing for a while before a cheerful group of young men sitting at the next table invited me to join them for *arak*. They offered me *hummus* and *fattoush*. "We wish we could give you our local dish," they said. "There are little pigs in the hills that people shoot, and cook them in red wine. But it's not the season." There is no dish that could be more forbidden in Islam than pork cooked in wine. I knew they must be *juhhal*, the uninitiated Druze who are not bound by any religious laws governing food.

"Tell us what you think about reincarnation," they said. "Do you believe in it?" I tried to answer tactfully, but this wasn't enough for them. "No, it's real," one of them said. "We have proof." Another piped up: "My cousin could speak as a child in words that an ordinary person could not say, could do things that were remarkable for her age." Another told a story of a man who remembered that he had been killed on his wedding day and who was able to draw pictures of the dresses the women in attendance had worn. He even met the man who had killed his former self, and forgave him.

Later that day I met a woman who had changed her name because of a dream in which she was living in America. After considering the dream, her family decided that she was the reincarnation of a Druze girl who had gone to live there and had died young. That girl's name had been Carmen, so she was renamed Karima in honor of her dead self. The belief in reincarnation is so widespread, a Druze friend later told me, that a boy who appeared to have knowledge of the life of a man who had died around the same time the boy was born was accepted as the new incarnation of the dead man's soul and was trusted by the dead man's children to divide up their inheritance.

The Druze rejected the more outré versions of reincarnation that had been espoused by earlier Muslim groups (one of which saw the possibilities that rebirth in a new body can offer for poetic justice. A man who had had sex with a sheep, this group believed, might be reborn as a sheep in a future life.) Alawites believe that people can be reborn as plants, for example, but the Druze reject this. They believe that members of their own community are always reborn within it. The Druze existed as a people, on this view, long before the religion came into existence: their bodies are young but their souls are thousands of years old, and before they were the Druze community of today they were the companions of the prophet Mohammed and the disciples of Pythagoras. And the Druze have an answer to the age-old question of what happens to souls when there are not enough bodies to receive them: Druze souls go in that case, says Druze folk mythology, to China.

As I wandered through the streets of Moukhtara that night, I mused on the ways that belief in reincarnation has shaped the Druze community. In the beginning it may have helped them to win converts. To a Christian I imagined the early Druze saying, "By accepting Mohammed as a prophet you are not rejecting Jesus: for Mohammed is Jesus reborn." To a pagan who revered the Greek philosophers, they could argue that the Druze leader Hamza bin Ali was Pythagoras returned to life. In later centuries, the famous Druze characteristic of courage in battle was fortified by the belief that death would quickly lead to rebirth. Going into battle, Druze soldiers would shout, "Who wants to sleep in their mother's womb tonight?"

The belief also gives the Druze a profound sense of group loyalty. They consider themselves to have sworn the Covenant of the Lord of Time, a pledge of allegiance to the caliph al-Hakim. They made this pledge not in this lifetime, of course, but back in the eleventh century—in a previous incarnation, when they were the people who constituted the first Druze community.

Finally, the belief underpins their strict rules against accepting converts or intermarriage. One of the few requirements for the average Druze layman or woman is to marry within the faith. Since they have eternal life through their rebirth within the community, then having children by an outsider—who do not count as Druze—affects those children not only in this life but in their future ones, too. It can have some nasty consequences in this world, for that matter. In July 2013 a man married a Druze woman, telling her family that he was a Druze from another village. When they found out that he was a Sunni Muslim, they tracked him down and castrated him. The incident was condemned by Walid Jumblatt. The community was more tolerant when Amal Alamuddin, descendant of a famous Druze family, became engaged in 2014 to American actor George Clooney. One old Druze lady in Amal's home town, though, when interviewed by a female journalist, was unimpressed. "Aren't there any young Druze men left?" she asked. "God give you better luck, my girl."

THE SHOUF IS THE DRUZE HEARTLAND IN LEBANON, but they also inhabit a mountain further south, near the border with Israel. On this mountain there is a shrine called Hasbaya, and the day after the lunch with the *uqqal* I had the chance to visit it with the British ambassador and Rabieh, the same man who had asked the cheeky question about reincarnation when we met the Sheikh al-Aql back in Beirut. It was a long journey: we went up to the top of the mountain, then steeply down to a valley below the cliff where Fakhreddin had supposedly plunged with his horse, through a Christian village surrounded by vineyards, and then through a Shi'a village decorated with Hizbullah posters.

When we reached Hasbaya I saw that it was a town of old stone buildings. One of these was a ruined castle, one of its crumbling stone corners still inhabited by a family that had been there since the Crusades. They had relieved the starkness of its gray stone courtyard with flowers. Another corner, less habitable, was owned by a separate branch of the same family, which was using it to hold political rallies. On the inside of a tall stone arch a large portrait of Jumblatt's rival, Talal Arslan, was suspended, and plastic chairs had been set out for an impromptu reception in honor of the ambassador.

Once the reception had ended we went to visit the nearby hilltop shrine called al-Bayyada. It was a *khalwa,* or a place where a Druze person might seclude himself or herself from the world and pray—a hermitage, in Western terms. At its heart was a prayer room (simple and unadorned, as I could see from looking in through the window; the room itself was off-limits). Its outlying buildings served mostly as living quarters for a community of monklike Druze sheikhs. Five of these, one in sandals, had prepared a meal of pine nuts and honey for us. They sat and answered our questions patiently. The one in sandals had been there for forty years. As with other Druze sheikhs, it was their custom to eat only food that they had made for themselves. "This place was founded 350 years ago by a very spiritual man," another of them explained. "He became a very holy man and decided to build a *khalwa* here. It was below, and then it was moved to top of hill. He wasn't aiming for any worldly gain, so it became famous. People came and built private *khalwa*s."

The Druze had also at some stage built next to the shrine a curious thing—a circular slab of stone, surrounded by a low stone rim. It appeared to have some religious significance that our hosts did not explain, for I had to remove my shoes before stepping onto it. A darker stone, small and round, was set in its center: the whole, seen from above, was a point in the center of a circle. The symbol of a dot at the center of a circle was a sacred sign of Pythagoras, representing the One at the heart of the universe, the "still point in the turning world." Standing on the dot and speaking, I could hear my voice echoing clearly off the circular rim. This acoustic would have appealed to Pythagoras, too. He was the first to delineate the musical octave, spotting that pleasing harmonies operated according to mathematical formulae (halving the length of a metal rod means that the note it will sound when struck is an octave higher). He believed that the planets made music as they rotated across the sky, and that a person who concentrated long enough and knew what to listen for could hear the "music of the spheres." One of the sheikhs I had met had come across this idea. *Hanin al-aflak,* he called it in Arabic. And although I had studied Greek philosophy for years at Western universities, this was the first time I had heard it mentioned.

The shrine's guardian, whom we saw at his home in the town rather than at the shrine itself, was an elderly man with a long beard and a mischievous sense of humor. He showed us into his living room, where a table was laden with huge plates of food in our honor. The ambassador and he had a rather jocular conversation about the status of women in the Druze clergy: they could be sheikhs, but with a limited authority, he explained, before turning the tables on the ambassador by asking how the British Empire had ended. "Has the sun set on it?" he asked. (The phrase "The sun never sets on the British Empire" is a popular one in the Middle East, for some reason. I have lost count of the number of times it has been quoted to me.)

The guardian turned more serious when I asked him about Pythagoras. Could he explain why the philosopher had forbidden his followers to eat beans? The sheikh was amazed. Pythagoras, he said, had done no such thing. He pointed to the plates of food that his family had prepared for their visitors. "I wish we had prepared for you a plate of beans," he said, "so that you could see that the Druze are allowed to eat them!" His instant assumption was that if I was asking what Pythagoras had allowed and forbidden, then that was a question about Druze custom, too. (In a Lebanese Druze magazine that ran an article on "the wise Pythagoras," a list is given of his instructions that interprets them all as metaphors, which is the same approach that the Druze take toward the rules of Islam.)

AS A COMMUNITY, the Druze today are doing better than the Yazidis or Zoroastrians. They have managed, so far, to hold on to their land and their autonomy, in part because no single religious group dominates Lebanon. Jumblatt has so far escaped assassination and remains politically relevant in Lebanon; in Syria, their remoteness from the main cities and the size of their community have so far shielded them from the worst of that country's civil war; in Israel they have religious freedom, and many serve in the Israeli army. Threats abound. Lebanon is unstable, Syria is bloody, and Israel has confiscated a large proportion of Druze land to house the country's Jewish immigrants. The ignorance of lay Druze about their religion ill suits them ᵥ for maintaining it abroad. Yet in every region their clergy and secular leaders have succeeded in maintaining the unity and distinctiveness of their community. Having seen how wrong Carnarvon was to write off the Druze, I came back from Moukhtara and Hasbaya unwilling to do the same.

Back in Beirut I set up one final meeting, with a Druze professor at the American University of Beirut named Sami Makarem. He invited me to his flat, and when I arrived, he offered me a glass of sweet mulberry juice. "Our God is different from your Abrahamic God," he said. "In Semitic religion, God is known by his deeds. But for us, he is immanent and tran- ᵥ scendent at the same time." The Druze see God, like the Neoplatonic One, as unchanging—not the cause of the Universe, but the cause of the causes of the Universe (the One causes the Universal Mind and Soul; the Universal Mind and Soul cause the Universe). God cannot be described—and is therefore addressed by Druze only as "Creator of the Universe," because no other appellation can be used with any confidence.

True to the idea of emanationism, the Druze believe that the world is part of God in the same way as the dream is part of the dreamer. Makarem continued: "Separating oneself from God and thinking of one's separateness ᵥ is evil. The ego is in individuals who are otherwise emanations of God. The ego comes necessarily. And what can we fight it with? With love. Love, and by ᵥ accepting that we are dependent on the cosmic order." This notion reminded me of the words of St. Bernard of Clairvaux: "As a drop of water poured into wine loses itself, and takes the colour and savour of wine; or as a bar of iron, heated red-hot, becomes like fire itself, forgetting its own nature; or as the air, radiant with sun-beams, seems not so much to be illuminated as to be light itself; so in the saints all human affections melt away by some unspeakable transmutation into the will of God."

Were the Druze, I asked the professor, successors to the Pythagoreans? He smiled at me guardedly and did not reply. He had obviously decided that a non-initiate could not be given the answer to this question. As he told me, "Hermes Tresmegistus, the founder of astronomy, says that to reveal a truth to man unready to accept it is three sins at once. It makes him disbelieve in truth, makes him think wrongly about you, and makes him say the truth is nonsense." What, in Makarem's view, might make a person ready to accept the truth? Did my study of Greek philosophy qualify me? It seemed not. Makarem said that "it takes generations to adapt for truth. That is what re-incarnation means. True knowledge is recollection." Pythagoras had thought that by recalling his past incarnations he could accumulate more than a lifetime's worth of wisdom. Similarly, the Druze believe that since they are reincarnated in the community of the enlightened, only they can ever hope to attain real wisdom. It is a truly Pythagorean notion.

5

Samaritans

THE TEN LOST TRIBES OF ISRAEL must be the most found of all lost people. In the ninth century, they were reported to be in Arabia. A few centuries later, they were apparently near India—where, a medieval fabulist reported excitedly, they were guarded by Gog, Magog, and the queen of the Amazons and plotting the destruction of Christianity. Even when Europeans were exploring new continents they saw the Ten Tribes everywhere, like a ghostly army. Perhaps that was where the Native Americans came from, some suggested; Thomas Jefferson asked whether they might even want to return from America to their homeland in Zion.

I found the Lost Tribes myself when I was living in Jerusalem, between 1998 and 2001. I was there for a quite different purpose. As a political officer at the British consulate general in Jerusalem, my main task was to persuade Palestinians to support the Middle East peace process. At the time I was there, it seemed possible that some kind of deal would be reached. It would not have given either side exactly what they wanted, but it would have ended the cycles of rebellion and repression that had marked the Palestinian experience, and offered both Palestinians and Israelis the chance to live in greater peace and dignity.

Although this later proved a false hope, it meant that when I first arrived in Jerusalem in 1998 there was a sense of optimism—and it was safe enough to explore the fascinating region in which I was living. I saw the almost miraculous cities of Israel, in which a state and language and pioneering economy had all been developed in the few decades since Israel's founding in 1948, in the aftermath of the Holocaust. (The language, modern Hebrew, was actually devised from the 1880s onward as a simplified version of biblical Hebrew by a scholar called Eliezer Ben Yehuda. Ben Yehuda's son was brought up, at his father's insistence, to speak only Hebrew—a tough rule, because it meant that no other children could understand him. But eventually, in the face of skepticism and some hostility, Ben Yehuda's project succeeded and the language was widely adopted.) I saw, too, the Palestinian cities of the West Bank, which Israel had conquered in 1967. The Palestinians had one of the liveliest cultures of any Arab people: their desire for freedom had inspired them to develop a strong identity, expressed through film, art, and theater.

Several times I visited Nablus, a city of white limestone houses once famous for its beauty and its olive oil, which was about thirty miles north of Jerusalem. Its name came from the name given it by the Romans, Neapolis, which meant "new city." The old city that had existed nearby, and which the Romans had destroyed, was called Shechem, meaning "saddle," because just like a saddle dipping in the middle with a ridge on either side, two mountains here enclose a valley. These are Mount Gerizim, to its west, and Mount Ebal, to its east. They are close enough that jackals once could howl to one another across the valley between them. The site of ancient Shechem is now occupied by a United Nations refugee camp called Balata, which I had the chance to visit when the consulate funded a theater project there.

In 1950 Palestinians from villages near what is now Tel Aviv, fleeing or driven out by the victorious Israeli army, settled here in tents. Now the tents have been replaced with concrete houses, and the place has become a poor suburb of Nablus, though its people have never been reconciled to the confiscation of their original homes. A group of young men from the camp who were involved with the theater project gave me a tour of the local area. We walked through the city of Nablus and tried some of its famous sweet *konafa*, made with cheese and dripping with honey, which along with olive oil soap is one of the local specialties.

On the edge of Balata was Jacob's Well. Whether or not the Jewish patriarch Jacob did himself use this well, it certainly has been treated as a holy site for thousands of years. In the Christian Gospels, Jesus asks a woman to draw water from it for him to drink. The woman, a Samaritan, is amazed that he speaks to her, because "the Jews have no dealings with the Samaritans." The same conflict between Jews and Samaritans crops up in Jesus's parable of the Good Samaritan: a Jewish man lies wounded at the roadside, and a Jewish priest and a Levite pass him by (not because they are callous, but because it was taboo for a priest to touch a corpse, and they fear he may be dead). A Samaritan is the one who helps the wounded Jew, and so he is the one whom, Jesus says, his own Jewish followers should love. The fact that he is a Samaritan is the twist in the tale, because Samaritans and Jews were old enemies. They were almost identical in their religious practices, but different interpretations of history had set them at war.

The Samaritan interpretation goes like this. Back in the eighth century BC two kingdoms, Israel and Judah, occupied roughly the territory of modern Israel. The two kingdoms fought each other, but their inhabitants shared a religion and a common ancestry, because all of them belonged to one of twelve tribes descended from the twelve sons of Jacob. The kingdom of Israel was the older of the two and was originally the location of the religion's holy sites. When that kingdom was invaded by the Assyrians in the eighth century BC, though, tens of thousands of its inhabitants were carried off to northern Iraq. The kingdom of Judah was spared; its inhabitants came to be called Judeans, and then Jews. They, too, were taken into exile in Babylon, and came back with new ideas and changed traditions. As for the exiles from Israel, they were never heard of again, and came to be called the Ten Lost Tribes.

But not all the ten tribes were truly lost, say the Samaritans. Some were deported by the Assyrians, yes, but others remained. Revering Mount Gerizim was their tenth commandment. In Samaritan belief, Adam had been made from dust gathered from Mount Gerizim. It was here, not Mount Ararat, where Noah's ark came to rest; here, not Mount Sinai, where Moses was given the law; and here, not Mount Moriah in Jerusalem, where Abraham took Isaac for sacrifice. They had thirteen different names with which they honored it, such as Ar Gerizim, "Mount of the Commandments"; Gabat Olam, "World's Mountain"; and Ar Ashekina, "Mountain of the Dwelling Place of God." They built a temple on it, and each year they pitched tents on the mountaintop and reenacted the Passover sacrifice according to the ritual in the book of Exodus.

They did not call themselves Jews, but rather Hebrews or Israelites. They also called themselves Shamarin, an Aramaic word meaning "the guardians"—the origin of the word "Samaritans." The Samaritans saw themselves as keeping to the letter the ancient traditions that their southern neighbors the Jews had abandoned. They saw the Jewish Temple in Jerusalem as an unholy innovation by King David, who is a figure they particularly dislike: to this day, no Samaritan is ever given the name David. Jerusalem, as the Samaritans see it, is a pagan city unfit to be the site of the Temple.

The Jewish version is the same as far as the disappearance of the ten tribes, but then it diverges. The Jewish religious authorities ruled that the ten tribes were truly lost. The Samaritans were descendants of peoples from other parts of the Assyrian Empire, who were settled there in place of the ten tribes ("the king of Assyria brought men from Babylon, Cuthah, Avva, Hamath, and Sepharvaim," according to the Book of Kings, "and placed them in the cities of Samaria instead of the people of Israel") and who later adopted Jewish practices. These settlers eventually persuaded a renegade priest from the Temple in Jerusalem to set up a temple for them on Mount Gerizim. The Samaritans could conceivably be accepted as being on a par with Jews—but only "when they deny Mount Gerizim and confess Jerusalem and the resurrection of the dead," as the Babylonian Talmud says, because they "marry illegitimate women," probably meaning intermarriage with women of other races. For as long as they kept up these unacceptable customs, there could be no contact between Jews and Samaritans.

The Talmud's ruling was bound to cause tension, but political rivalries made relations worse: in a pattern that dated back to the ancient kingdoms of Israel and Judah, the two groups tended to back opposite sides in regional power struggles. When Alexander the Great fought the Jews, the Samaritans marched alongside him; when Alexander changed his mind and supported the Jews, he ended up at war with the Samaritans. When the Jews rebelled against Alexander's Greek successors in the Maccabee Wars of the second century BC, the Samaritans took the opposite side; in revenge, the Jewish rebels burned down the Samaritan temple. In the aftermath of those wars, however, the Jews were suppressed and the Samaritans prospered.

By Jesus's time the Samaritans may have numbered half a million people. Relations were worse than ever, though. In AD 9 a Samaritan gang infiltrated Jerusalem and polluted the Jewish Temple by scattering human bones in it. In AD 50 a Jew traveling from Galilee to visit the Temple in Jerusalem was murdered by Samaritans at a village on the site of modern-day Jenin. Jesus was preaching in between those two dates, and either for this reason or because of a fear for their safety, initially he told his apostles not to enter Samaritan towns when they went on their preaching missions. Later, though, he relented and himself planned to travel through Samaritan territory on his way to Jerusalem. Jesus's meeting with the Samaritan woman by Jacob's Well and the parable of the Good Samaritan show a friendlier attitude toward the Samaritans. In fact, at one point Jesus was accused of being a Samaritan himself. Perhaps because of this, Christianity attracted Samaritan converts early on.

What happened to the Samaritans afterward? As it turned out, my friends from Balata had a surprise to show me. We climbed a twisting road on the side of Mount Gerizim, entering a little village at its top. Spidery archaic Hebrew letters marked the buildings, and a man in white robes and the red and white *tarbush* of a cleric was walking along the street. A small museum explained who the man and the other residents of the village were. This mountaintop village, which they called al-Loz (meaning "the almond trees"), and a street in a suburb of the Israeli capital, Tel Aviv, were the two remaining places where the world's 750 Samaritans could still be found.

The Samaritans were spared the fate meted out to the Jews in AD 70 when Roman legions defeated a Jewish revolt and sacked the city of Jerusalem, destroying its Temple forever—and the even worse disaster inflicted on the Jews after another revolt in the 130s, when half a million Jews were killed and the remainder entirely expelled from their homeland. The Samaritans actually flourished in the absence of their old rivals. Their leader at this time,

Baba Rabba, was remembered afterward in legend as a reformer and miracle worker. Christian missionary work may have provoked a series of Samaritan rebellions in the sixth century, after which the emperor Justinian destroyed all of the Samaritans' synagogues, barred them from service in government and the imperial army, banned them from testifying against a Christian in court, and even stopped them from passing down their possessions to their offspring. Unsurprisingly, the Samaritans became hostile to outsiders: a Christian pilgrim named Antoninus of Piacenza reported that when he visited Samaritan towns, they "burned away our footprints with straw, whether we were Christians or Jews, they have such a horror of both." Likewise, it is no surprise that the Samaritans welcomed the coming of the Arab Muslims in 637.

It may seem odd, given that the Arab-Israel conflict has come to define the relationship between Muslims and Jews, that that relationship was once close and respectful. At one point Jews and Muslims both prayed in the same direction, toward Jerusalem, before Muslims turned toward Mecca instead. Although early Muslims fought the Jewish tribes of Arabia, several verses of the Koran teach respect and tolerance for Jews. Muslims and Jews generally regarded each other as more thoroughly monotheistic than Christians because both groups rejected the idea that Jesus was God incarnate, and they refused to depict God in any kind of image. The great Jewish scholar Maimonides (who knew Islam from the inside, having been forced to practice as a Muslim at one point in his life before being allowed to revert to Judaism) asserted that Muslims, "in attributing Oneness to God—they have no mistake at all." Muslim scholars drew on Jewish scholarship when devising the early jurisprudence of Islam, sometimes inserting Talmudic punishments in place of the less severe Koranic ones (adopting the practice of stoning for adultery, for instance). None of this guaranteed good treatment for Jews, whose refusal to convert to Islam could always be used against them. After the Islamic conquest, they faced legal discrimination and were always vulnerable to bouts of persecution. But they remained loyal to their Muslim rulers as late as the First Crusade, when they fought alongside Muslims to defend Jerusalem from the Christian Franks.

Early Muslim rulers doubted whether the Samaritans were truly a people of the book, and imposed extra taxes on them compared to their Christian and Jewish neighbors. Yet the Samaritans benefited, even more than the Jews, from the Islamic conquest. "The Arab conquest actually helped the inland Samaritan community," wrote Israeli historian Nathan Schur, "gave it a freedom of worship it had not known for centuries and made the medieval flowering of its religion and literature possible." Samaritans abandoned Aramaic and began speaking Arabic, and they devised distinctive names for themselves (Abed Yahweh, for example, meaning "servant of Yahweh," instead of the Muslim version, Abed Allah; unlike the Jews' version of the Ten Commandments, the Samaritans' version does not feature a taboo on using God's name).

Without persecution, Samaritans still converted to Islam—for economic benefits, social advancement, and theological reasons. So the community continued to diminish, and the good treatment did not last. Hard-line Muslim rulers, sometimes under pressure from the clergy, passed punitive and humiliating laws meant to encourage the Samaritans to convert, and those rulers who were liberal or friendly could do no more than grant temporary relief. One by one the communities of Samaritans in Cairo, Gaza, Aleppo, and Damascus shrank and disappeared, until Nablus was the only place where they could be found. By the sixteenth century, when contemporary Samaritans appear in Western records for the first time, they were desperate to find any of their number who might remain, scattered around the world. A French scholar named Joseph Scaliger tricked them at that time into thinking that he might be one himself, a member of a long-lost community in Europe, and so they wrote to him hopefully: "We ask thee for the Lord's sake, and we adjure thee by his Holy Name, that thou return not our Request unanswered . . . whether there be among you Priests descending from Levi, Aaron or Phinees, or whether you have any Priests at all?" (Aaron, from the tribe of Levi, was the ancestor of all Jewish priests in biblical times, and Phinees was Aaron's grandson.) It was their own version of the myth of the Ten Tribes.

The Samaritans saw themselves, though diminished in number, as heirs to a proud and ancient history. In their letter to Scaliger they boasted that they still had a high priest who was descended from Phinees ("The Jews have not Priests descended from Phinees," the letter writer added competitively). They remembered, as most Jews did not, the tribe to which they belonged—Samaritan priests like the Jewish priests, the *kohanim,* are descendants of Levi, while the Samaritan lay people trace their descent from Joseph. Joseph Wolff, a missionary, was told in the 1820s by a Samaritan called Israel el-Shalaby that the Samaritans had not forgotten that they were descendants of Joseph, who had been betrayed and sold into slavery by his brothers. The Samaritans had inherited his grievance and thus resented the Jews, he said: "We his children, can never forget that Joseph, our father, was so harshly treated by his brethren."

As late as 1772, Nablus's laws required Samaritans to wear bells in public and banned them from riding horses (in an emergency, they could ride mules). Local politics in Nablus were violent and fast-moving: various demagogues saw opportunities to attack the Samaritans as a way to burnish their own Islamic credentials. One such managed to start a riot in the 1850s, in the course of which some men started shouting that the Samaritans should be given the choice of conversion to Islam or death. The Jewish chief rabbi came from Jerusalem just in time to avert a disaster by certifying that they were genuine monotheists (a historic move, given the traditionally bad relationship between Jews and Samaritans).

An American missionary, the Reverend Pliny Fisk, whose posthumous memoir was published in 1828, recorded his encounter with the Samaritans: "They inquired whether there are any Samaritans in England, and seemed not at all gratified when we told them no. On learning that I was from America, they inquired if there are Samaritans there. I told them no, but they confidently asserted the contrary and that there are also many in India." A Welshman named John Mills, who had taught himself Hebrew, Latin, and Greek, headed to Nablus in the 1850s. Mills commented that he found the Samaritans an attractive people: "As a community, there is nothing in Palestine to compare with them . . . they are tall and of lofty bearing." Tellingly, he added that they had "an unmistakable family likeness." So they do today, including distinctively large earlobes. When the community asked him if there were Hebrews in his country, Mills thought they meant Jews and said yes. Once more, they became deeply excited at the thought that they might find a lost colony of Samaritans. The reality was that they were alone in the world.

They hoped for a Messiah, or Ta'eb, as they called him. John Mills wrote that they believed their Messiah would come "not to shed blood, but to heal the nations; not to make war, but to bring peace." They predicted, for reasons that Mills does not explain, that the Messiah would come in 1910, but he did not. On the other hand, the British Mandate, which came into force in Palestine in 1920, was a turning point. From that moment the community began to recover, with the encouragement of British Christians who viewed the Samaritans kindly because of their biblical connections. The relief came just in time: the community had reached an all-time low of 146 members.

They had continued through the centuries to copy out on parchment their ancient biblical texts, which they believed proved the claims that Mount Gerizim was God's sacred mountain. They remembered, too, the ancient quarrel between Israel and Judah. When the new Jewish state was proposed in the 1940s, a Samaritan priest explained to a British official with all the dignity of the last heirs of the house of Israel: "I am no enemy of the Jews having their kingdom once again. I am angry that they should be installed on land that is Israel's, that has never been theirs!" He was undeterred by the fact that the Samaritans at that time numbered two hundred people and the Jews about eleven million. As the British travel writer H. V. Morton remarked at around the same time, "I think that the Samaritans consider the Arabs who have been there since only AD 638 as interlopers!"

WHEN DOING THE RESEARCH FOR THIS BOOK, in 2012, I looked again at items that I had kept from my time as consul in Jerusalem. It was an assembly of memories. There was a ticket to Easter Mass at the Church of the Holy Sepulcher, where I had looked down from the church's dome to see the Orthodox Patriarch bring fire, apparently by a miracle, out of the small booth that is said to house the tomb of Christ. There was a photograph of the Western Wall, where Jews still go to lament the razing in AD 70 of the Temple by the Romans, who were determined to stamp out the Jewish religion because it had proven so resistant to their rule. (The Western Wall is actually the embankment on which the Temple stood, rather than being a part of the original building itself.) There was a picture, too, of the golden Dome of the Rock, built on the old Temple site after the Muslim conquest.

And I found a memento of the Samaritans: a newsletter printed in four languages—Arabic, English, Hebrew, and the same spidery script that I had seen on the buildings of their village in 1998. This was the ancient Samaritan script, an older version of Hebrew writing. At the bottom of each page of the little booklet was the legend *A.B.—The Samaritan News.* The booklet recorded that Passover, held in 2001 at the height of the Palestinian intifada, had taken place peacefully. The Palestinians had agreed to avoid any confrontation with Israeli forces. I was thanked for my involvement—after my first visit to the Samaritans, I had visited them several more times, including one occasion when they had asked me to encourage the Palestinians to suspend fighting during Passover.

Not that they had any difficulty themselves in dealing with the Palestinians, as the newsletter also reported: "Samaritans who went down the Mountain to Nablus to buy groceries for the Festival, received a warm welcome from the inhabitants. . . . The inhabitants of Nablus will treat a strange face with suspicion. . . . However, when the clients identified themselves as Samaritans, suspicions quickly turned into a wide smile accompanied by handshakes." As I read this, I wondered if the Samaritans might be something yet more remarkable than the lost Ten Tribes of Israel: they could be a bridge between Palestinians and Israelis.

So I hoped that they might make a good chapter for this book. Their ideas and customs, being similar to those of Jews, would be more familiar to most readers than those of the book's other chapters. But the existence of this community, described by the Israeli scholar Nathan Schur as "probably the smallest group of people to have retained over many centuries a national consciousness of their own," might help to shed light on what makes a people see themselves as a nation. What causes us to draw the invisible line between us and them?

When I visited the Samaritans for the first time, many still hoped that lasting peace was possible. More than a decade later, those hopes had receded. I was afraid of what I might find if I went back. But I was determined to go, because I had an invitation. I had written to the *A.B.* newsletter's editor, Benyamim Tsedaka (the Samaritan spelling of the name Benjamin), hoping that he might remember me from my brief time in the village. He did not reply at first. But some weeks later I received a curious email from his account: "The Paschal Sacrifice will take place this year on Friday noon, May 4, 2012." It was signed "Benny," and seemed to have been sent to a long list of potentially interested parties. There followed a list of readings from Leviticus and instructions on when they should be read. For the period of the Festival of the Unleavened Bread, it prescribed kosher matzos (unleavened bread) and forbade pasta. One should pray facing east—unless one was in India or Russia, in which case one should face southwest. The Paschal Sacrifice and the Festival of the Unleavened Bread were clearly Passover, though the Samaritan date differed from the Jewish one. (The two groups have slightly different calendars, and the Samaritan feast can be up to two days earlier or up to a month later than the Jewish version.)

I decided that May 4 would be a good time to visit Benny and the Samaritans. First of all, though, I would have to get past the Israeli border authorities. I had reason to believe that this would be tricky. My passport had stamps in it from just about every country that would make them suspicious: Iraq, Iran, Saudi Arabia, Afghanistan, and Pakistan. It had caused me to be detained on arrival at airports in Chicago and London; I could only imagine what would happen in security-conscious Tel Aviv. Long before, though, during my posting to Jerusalem, I had spent some weeks learning Hebrew. I thought this might help me break the ice a little with the authorities, but then realized that all I remembered was a love song. I doubted that that would win anyone over.

The border guard at Israel's Ben-Gurion Airport was puzzled. "You're coming for Passover?" she said. "But Passover is finished." I tried to explain that there was another Passover, celebrated in a little village in the West Bank by a group called the Samaritans—and as I said it, I realized she had never heard of them. I was ushered aside to a special waiting room in a corner of the arrivals hall, dedicated to suspect individuals who would need extensive interrogation. I sat on a bench. About a dozen Palestinian women were on a bench opposite me. Next to me was a dark-skinned boy who had the twisted *peyot* (long sideburns) and *kippa* (head covering, also called a yarmulke) of an Orthodox Jew and a huge sack of consumer goods with labels in Arabic. He was from Yemen, he told me, and had just come back from a visit to his family in a village near that nation's capital, Sana'a. Until a few months earlier, he had been one of Yemen's four hundred remaining Jews; he was now waiting for Israeli citizenship.

The interrogation was mercifully brief, because one of the staff in the airport had heard of the Samaritans and came to my rescue. So within a couple of hours I had boarded a bus to Jerusalem and was trying for the benefit of a fellow passenger, a tourist from Scandinavia, to describe the sights to her as the memory of them rushed back. Behind us was the seaside city of Tel Aviv, built in the twentieth century by Jewish migrants; here on the left was the Arab village of Abu Ghosh; and ahead was Jerusalem—"golden Jerusalem," as a hit Israeli song from the 1960s had it. The most golden thing about the city was the dome of its foremost Muslim shrine. But just as the white stone of its buildings reflected the changing light of the sun, Jerusalem was a city whose personality shifted according to the angle from which one saw it. It is the site of Israel's government, but also a major destination for tourists both religious and secular; an architectural jewel whose city walls are still a striking landmark that can be seen for miles around, but also a frontier city where religious and secular, Jew and Arab frequently find themselves in unhappy competition for space, and for freedom from fear.

After reaching my hotel that evening I called Benny Tsedaka and asked him how I could best reach the village of al-Loz, on Mount Gerizim. It was easy, he replied: all I had to do was get on a Palestinian minibus at Damascus Gate, in the Old City of Jerusalem. It would take me north, to the Palestinian-run city of Ramallah in the West Bank; there I could catch a different bus, with a Palestinian license plate, to take me to Nablus. From Nablus I could catch a taxi. This sounded feasible: I had ridden Palestinian minibuses before. But there was one more thing I wanted to check before starting the journey. Sometimes, I knew, there were travel restrictions placed on Palestinian vehicles in the West Bank. So I called the Palestinian governor of Nablus to make sure that I would be able to get through to the village. The governor sounded panicked. "They have closed all the roads for the

Samaritan Passover," he said. "You will never make it. Come next week." I tried to say that it was exactly Passover that I was coming for, but he hung up. I was baffled. But as I thought about alternatives, I realized that there was another way to reach the Samaritans.

When Israel took East Jerusalem and land beyond it, as far as the river Jordan, in the 1967 war, there were many Jews, including in Israel's government, who wanted to withdraw as soon as possible. Others had a more expansionist vision and wanted to keep the conquered territories. They argued that Israel's former borders were indefensible. Religious sentiment was on their side: Jerusalem's Old City, along with what remained of the old Temple, was in Jewish hands for the first time since AD 70. Israel held on to it, and ever since has taken a series of measures clearly designed to make East Jerusalem an inseparable part of Israel.

A wave of religious Israelis also believed that the rest of the land between Israel's former eastern border and the river Jordan—the area known as the West Bank—should also forever remain part of the state of Israel. They established settlements there, often using land that had been originally confiscated by Israel for military purposes. Because this represented a breach of the Geneva Conventions, which banned an occupying power from using confiscated land for civilian settlement, this move was instantly controversial. It also committed Israel to a constant confrontation with Palestinian villagers living near the settlements, while the settlers made easy targets for terrorist attacks. Nonetheless, the religious settlers were joined by others drawn by economic motives: the new land, many parcels of which were sited above valuable sources of water and in strategic locations, was made available at low cost to Jewish Israelis. The settlers had cars and buses with Israeli license plates, which were exempt from the road closures and movement restrictions that were imposed on Palestinians. Even if the roads were closed to Palestinians, these would get through—and so I clearly needed to be on one of them. I headed to the Jerusalem central bus station to see if I could find one that might take me anywhere near the Samaritan village.

The bus station was crowded, but the majority of people in it were going to conventional places—Tel Aviv, Netanya, Eilat. After consulting the bus guide I found that the West Bank was served from a special bay at the farthest end of the station. The bus, as I noticed when I boarded it, was armor-plated, and most of my fellow passengers were soldiers with machine guns. The ideologues of the settler movement saw their communities as a return to land that biblically belonged to the Jews, and as an aggressive defiance of terrorism. For Palestinians, they represented a racist exploitation of Israel's military conquest of the West Bank, and a creeping dispossession that would block their ambitions for an independent state. Over the years clashes between settlers and Palestinians have been frequent and bloody.

The bus headed north and passed through the "separation barrier": partly fence, partly high wall, it was built to reduce terrorist attacks on Israelis. It has cut off Palestinians from Jerusalem, controversially limiting their access to their holy places, whether Christian or Muslim. On the other side of the wall, I was both in and outside Israel. I was in an Israeli bus, heading to a town that felt like any Israeli town, along an Israeli-built road. Yet I was formally outside Israel: the region I had entered was run not by elected civilians but by a military governor, and non-Jewish children born there are not entitled to Israeli citizenship. A road for Palestinians, rather bumpy and pot-holed, ran parallel to the Israeli road at certain points and then disappeared. A message reached me on my cell phone, which was switching networks automatically: "Welcome to Palestine. Smell the jasmine, taste the olives!" The plate glass windows kept out the smell and taste, but radio signals, like memory and guilt, could not so easily be blocked. Even the Palestinian and Israeli cell phone networks, it seemed, overlapped and competed.

For years, the focus of the peace process between Israel and the Palestinians was on drawing a boundary between them. A boundary on a map is a mere two-dimensional thing, however, and during the Camp David negotiations in the year 2000, it was suggested that a three-dimensional one would be needed. The Haram ash-Sharif (known in English as the Temple Mount), which was sacred to Muslims, was on this proposal to have been Palestinian, and the remains of the ancient Jewish Temple beneath it would have been part of Israel. Perhaps even three dimensions are not enough. To understand the complexities of Israel and Palestine a fourth dimension is needed—invisible to the naked eye, but familiar to everyone who lives there: its history. Every place in Israel, the West Bank, and Gaza has a name in

Arabic and an alternative name in Hebrew; every place likewise has both Jewish and Palestinian associations and history. "Israel" and "Palestine" are still not really used by the inhabitants to describe two separate countries, but rather serve as alternative names for the land that lies between the river Jordan and the Mediterranean Sea. The one-fifth of Israeli citizens who are Arab increasingly call themselves Palestinians, while the Israeli settlements that are spreading across the West Bank are making the "two-state solution"—the idea of an independent Palestinian state—less viable with every year that passes.

The city of Nablus, toward which I was heading, is known to Israelis as Shechem—its old biblical name. It is a city with historic Muslim mosques but also houses Jewish holy sites such as Joseph's Tomb. Similarly, Tel Aviv's suburbs include the historic Palestinian town of Jaffa; many of the refugees who live on Nablus's outskirts have their origins there. Nor is it only the geography of the two peoples that is intertwined. The languages are, too: when Ben Yehuda invented the modern Hebrew language and could not find the words he needed in the Bible, he borrowed them from Arabic instead. The process has continued since, with Israelis adopting Arabic slang like *yalla,* which means "let's go," and Palestinians using the Hebrew word *mahsoom* for a checkpoint. The two people's DNA is also related. A study published in 2010 concluded that—setting aside south European influences on Jewish DNA, which might have come from conversions to Judaism—"the closest genetic neighbours to most Jewish populations are the Palestinians, Bedouins, and Druze."

Even if Jews and Palestinians are descended from common ancestors, their religious differences have trumped ties of kinship. The feeling of trust gained by praying together and sharing beliefs ended up mattering more than the trust gained by sharing a family or tribe. Something similar once happened between Jews and Samaritans. A genetics study in 2004 showed that Jewish *kohanim* and Samaritans are closely related—something that backs up the Samaritan claim that they are indeed descendants of Israelite tribes who were spared by the Assyrians.

Reaching the Samaritan village was not a simple business. The settlement that was closest to the Samaritans, I was told by my fellow passengers, was Har Brakha. It was small and fervently religious. Reaching it would mean taking three different buses. The first dropped me at Ariel, a large and bland university town created by ideologues in the 1970s in order to block the creation of a Palestinian state by sitting right in the middle of the West Bank; it had since managed to attract a sizable population, many of whom just wanted cheap housing. I wandered along its quiet tree-lined streets, hungry and looking for a town center that I never found. I gave up on the idea of buying food and waited for my next bus. It was emptier than the first, and now as we traveled I could see vineyards and gardens the local Jewish settlers had cultivated in an attempt to live more authentically biblical lives. If their relations with Palestinians were more peaceful, they might have perceived biblical scenes in a Palestinian village during the olive harvest, or in a Bedouin encampment with a sheikh sitting at the entrance to his tent at midday. Instead, theirs is in every sense a frontier existence.

The second bus dropped me just outside Nablus, at a roadside shelter protected by concrete blast walls with a gas station nearby; it was at the foot of Mount Gerizim, at the top of which was Har Brakha. Great imagination would have been necessary to find any history or holiness there, if not for the group of children standing and waiting for the next bus alongside me. They had the *peyot* of strictly religious Jews, like my Yemeni acquaintance at the airport, and gave me curious glances. Clearly, strangers did not often come this way. The next bus arrived, and took us—boisterous boys at the front, demure girls at the back—up the mountain to the collection of houses that made up Har Brakha. From the edge of the settlement, I could see the Samaritan village three or four hundred yards away; a road led toward it, with trees on one side and an open field on the other. I alighted from the bus and began to walk.

The Israelis call the Samaritan village Kiryat Luza, while its Palestinian name is al-Tor. The Samaritans had a name for it as well: al-Loz. In this as in much else, they studiously tried to be neutral between the two sides. The residents of al-Loz have identity papers from both the Palestinian and Israeli governments—and can also hold passports from neighboring Jordan. They are obviously not Muslims, but neither are they Jews. They manage, most of the time, to remain open to both groups. I had first come to the village in 1998 with a group of Palestinian refugees. This time around I entered the village in the company of a Jewish man, who drew level with me in his van as I was walking and offered me a lift. His front seat was littered with papers, which he swept aside. "There isn't often anyone in here but me and God," he joked, and explained that he was a traveling salesman who visited the settlements and Palestinian towns. It was not so dangerous, he said; things were calm just now.

The village itself looked as if it had been designed to be a showcase of diversity. It had only one street, where the village's teenagers socialized. A bunch of boys were talking in Arabic: some students from Nablus's university, meeting a Samaritan friend. Girls in miniskirts were sitting at a table in the main shop and speaking Hebrew. They were Samaritans from the suburbs of Tel Aviv and were more integrated into Israeli society (their clothes made that clear: the village's regular inhabitants were more conservatively dressed). I guessed that these visits might be a good chance for them to find husbands, since Samaritans—and especially Samaritan women—are not allowed to marry outside the religion.

I had some practical problems. I had come to the village without arranging for a place to stay the night and had planned to stay at a Nablus hotel, but it looked as though the security rules would stop me. I had no idea where I would sleep, but I assumed that at least I could get some food at the village's two shops. But during these days of preparation for the Passover, normal bread is not eaten or sold in the village. The best things I could find for a simple meal were a can of olives and a package of cheese. Lining up to buy them, I saw a selection of mugs and T-shirts hanging from the shop's ceiling, branded with the words "Good Samaritan." That also was the name of the village's welcome center, which was closed.

I made my way to the ruins of the Samaritans' temple, which were at the highest point in the village. A fence surrounded the ruins, which are still being excavated by archaeologists, who have made some remarkable finds there. A boy had offered to show me the place, for a fee. He let me through the gate, to which he had a key, and showed me the rocky foundations of what clearly was once a magnificent shrine. Archaeologists have worked out that this Samaritan temple was built twenty-five centuries ago, within a massive enclosure that measured 315 by 321 feet. Thousands of visitors could pray in the temple at a given time. So many animals were sacrificed there that four hundred thousand bone fragments have been found at the site. Inscriptions declared it to be "the House of the Lord." The chief archaeologist at the site has come to the controversial conclusion that the Samaritan temple was built before the first Jewish one.

From the edge of the enclosure we looked down at Nablus in the valley below. I could see the church of Jacob's Well. Jacob had had twelve sons, and each one of them founded a tribe: the twelve tribes of Israel. I asked the boy what tribe he was from. "Menashe," he said. Menashe was one of the two sections of the tribe of Joseph, so Joseph, whose tomb was visible below us, was this boy's ancestor. He may be the ancestor of many others, of course, who are not now Samaritans. Many of the Muslim inhabitants of Nablus and the villages around it must be of Samaritan descent. Some families were known to have converted to Islam only recently. A member of one of these families, Adli Yaish, was elected as mayor of Nablus by a 76 percent margin—as the Hamas candidate. Benny Tsedaka later claimed to me that more than 90 percent of Palestinians were descended from Samaritans and Jews. "If you ask a religious person from either side, they'll say nonsense. But it's true!" (Benny himself was conscious of the long history that tied him to the land where he lived. On a later occasion, I was with him in Britain when a Jewish man asked him how long Benny's family had lived in Israel. He misheard Benny's reply and said, "A hundred and twenty-seven years? That's a long time!" he said. "No," said Benny, "127 *generations*.")

———————

FROM THE TEMPLE RUINS it turned out to be just a short walk to Benny's house. He was something of a spokesman for the Samaritans; his comfortable summer villa doubled as the home of the community newspaper. The house had the cladding of rough cream-colored stone that is often used by Israelis and Palestinians alike to cover and ennoble the gray cement they use to build their houses. Benny lived on the upper story, with a view over the hillside. Here he received an endless stream of visitors in addition to me—a rabbi, a Christian evangelical couple, a film crew—and answered all of our questions. My questions had to do with the Samaritans' beliefs. The Samaritans reject Jewish religious texts such as the books of Daniel and Isaiah: for them, the Pentateuch (the first five books of the Old Testament, sometimes also called the Torah) stands alone. The Samaritan Torah is slightly different from the Jewish one. As previously noted, its version of the Ten Commandments does not include any ban on using the Lord's name in vain, but it does include a commandment to build an altar on Mount Gerizim. Benny argues that the Samaritan Torah is the more authentic version. His people preserved the text better over the centuries, as he sees it, because they stayed in one place, scrupulously copying the precious scriptures from old scrolls onto new ones.

But the biggest difference in practice between Samaritans and Jews comes from the Samaritans' rejection of all the Jewish traditions that developed after the Torah was written. For example, since the Torah does not explicitly tell men to cover their heads all the time, the Samaritans do not generally wear the *kippa*, as Orthodox Jews do; nor do Samaritan women wear wigs or veils to conceal their hair. Since it does tell them to sacrifice lambs at Passover and paste the blood of the lambs on the top and sides of their door frames, that is exactly what they do—as I would see. They do not celebrate the Jewish festivals of Purim and Hanukkah, which postdate the Torah.

They also reject any Jewish measures to abandon or relax the Torah's rules. They keep the ancient traditions of the priesthood. While the Jewish Temple stood, it was served by priests, who were led by a high priest. Judaism still has a role for its hereditary priests from the tribe of Levi, the *kohanim:* these deliver the priestly blessing in Orthodox Jewish prayer services, for instance, and are forbidden by Jewish law to marry divorced or converted women. They do not, however, offer sacrifice, and their leadership role in the Jewish community has largely been taken by rabbis. Among the Samaritans the priests' role is still as it was two thousand years ago. Benny told me that twenty-eight Samaritan men were priests, drawn from adult men in families that claim descent from Levi. They supervise circumcisions, readings of the Torah, engagements, marriages, divorces ("It's very rare," Benny assured me, "five times in a hundred years"), and lead prayers. They also sacrifice animals once a year, at Passover. The Samaritan high priest acts as a supreme court on religious matters.

Samaritan men, like Orthodox Jewish men, do not touch their wives when they are menstruating. The Samaritan rules go somewhat further: even the items that a menstruating woman touches are considered unclean, meaning that she must be segregated completely. Benny explained, "A woman during her period has a special room, where she stays for seven days. After the birth of a boy, it's forty days, and after a girl is born, it's eighty days. No touching is allowed, but she can speak—she sits at another table. But the great benefit," he claimed, "is that the husband does her duties in the home! The family helps her. It reduces natural stress." At the end of this period, the woman takes a ritual bath to purify herself.

The Samaritan Sabbath is from sunset on Friday till sunset on Saturday, just like the Jewish one—but stricter. They do not go quite as far as the Essenes, an austere Jewish sect who imposed on themselves the (surely painful) rule that they should not defecate on the Sabbath. But the Samaritans cannot kindle fire on the Sabbath, and in the days of candles and lanterns this meant sitting in darkness: unlike Jews, they may not ask people from outside their religion to light candles for them. They did not sleep with their wives on the Sabbath, they wrote to Scaliger in the sixteenth century. They left their houses only to pray. Even today, the Samaritans will not walk outside the village on the Sabbath, and they do not smoke on that day, either. They still dress for the Sabbath in clothes they believe are replicas of those worn by the Jews who took part in the biblical exodus from Egypt. Benny told me that he had even dressed in this way on Sabbath days when he was a student at Hebrew University.

Benny told me that Samaritans had to live in the land of Israel, which they interpret as including Egypt. (In fact, Samaritans did live on Greek islands in the second century BC, but the rules have since been tightened.) Benny can travel abroad, which he does to attend conferences, but may not eat meat outside the community: meat is not kosher for a Samaritan unless the animal has been killed by a Samaritan in strict accordance with the instruction of the book of Deuteronomy, which demands that its right foreleg should be offered to a priest. Benny could eat vegetarian food at a halal or kosher restaurant, though.

Benny also brought my knowledge of Samaritan history up to date. His family had a long history of poets and pioneers. His great-grandfather left Nablus in 1905 and founded a second community of Samaritans at Jaffa. Jaffa was a more cosmopolitan seaside city with a big Jewish community, compared to the remoteness and conservatism of Nablus, and it offered more diverse opportunities for work. There were more potential marriage partners, too, in this town where so many Jewish souls were living. Faced with a shrinking pool of available Samaritan brides—for reasons that have not been definitively identified, the community for many generations had a shortfall in female births—his son Yefet decided to break an ancient taboo: he would marry a Jewish woman. (Yefet was persuaded to do this by a future president of Israel, Yitzhak Ben-Zvi, who had become interested in the Samaritans when he encountered Yefet's father and was addressed by him in ancient Hebrew.)

Yefet succeeded against the odds. He married a Jewish woman from Russia named Miriam. Benny was their grandson. Sitting on the couch of his living room while his wife prepared dinner, he proudly pointed to his Einstein-like head of wildly curly white hair—an inheritance from his Russian side, he said. "If you ask me, it's also making me cooler," he told me, by which I think he meant more patient. But why did the Samaritans have a rule against marrying outside their community? One reason was that it protected them from becoming entangled with more powerful communities. In Islamic law (and Samaritan tradition, too) a couple's children take the religion of the father. A woman who marries out of her own community is taking her future children out with her as well, and depriving some man or other in that community of a possible bride. So communities in the Middle East tried (and try) to keep their women from marrying men of other religions—sometimes using violence. Until recently, for a Samaritan man, a member of the region's smallest minority, to provoke some other community by marrying one of its women would have put all Samaritans in danger. For a Samaritan woman to marry out would mean simply that the community would diminish. The ban on marrying others guaranteed that the Samaritans' culture and bloodline would survive and not be absorbed into the wider culture around them. In addition, the Samaritans treasure their genealogy as a close tie to their biblical forebears.

I asked Benny what had happened to his grandmother. The precedent hadn't been broken without some controversy, he said. "The elders didn't acknowledge her at first. But," he chuckled, "after she had six daughters they accepted her." Daughters were what the Samaritans most needed. Especially among the Jaffa Samaritans, intermarriage became more common. Benny himself had married a Jew of Romanian extraction who had accepted the particular customs of the Samaritans when she married him. "It's a bit racist to ask where you came from: 'Are you Jewish or are you Christian?'" said Benny. "She changed to join us. She became Israelite like us." These days, he said, about 25 percent of the community's marriages were between Samaritan men and non-Samaritan women, most of them Jewish. Some were from Eastern Europe. Two had come from Muslim families in Central Asia.

A documentary on the Samaritans, which interviewed two Ukrainian women who had married Samaritan men—and who apparently had adjusted well to life in their new community—also interviewed a member of the priestly family who disliked this new trend. "When we adopt foreign women into our nation," he said, "it makes me afraid for the future, afraid that we will not be able to control them. Our nation, which for 3,642 years has kept its unique traditions and customs, must continue keeping them in the future, otherwise it will plunge into chaos."

Marriages between Samaritan women and non-Samaritan men, meanwhile, are strictly taboo. A second documentary, made in 2008, looked at the anguish of a Samaritan woman, Sophie Tsadka, who was ostracized by the community for rejecting its rules and marrying a Jewish man. (She is a prominent actress on Israeli TV.) In an interview, Samaritan men showed her no sympathy. One commented that if his sister were to propose to marry out and leave the faith, "I would say OK . . . but when she slept at night, her life would be over. Like you slaughter a sheep." There is no evidence that any Samaritan woman has ever in fact been killed for this reason, but such harsh attitudes are what has protected the community from assimilation

over the centuries; they are the darker side of the warmth and communal spirit the Samaritans displayed and which, in the documentary, Sophie
clearly missed.

The Samaritans are strict traditionalists—were they not, they would not
exist—but Benny, like his grandfather, was finding new ways of interpreting
his faith's old traditions. One of his innovations was to spread the Samaritan
message and way of life so that non-Samaritans could imitate it. In 1864,
John Mills published a set of tables sent out some decades earlier by a Samaritan priest to the community in England. It was a Samaritan version of
the Lost Tribes myth, and just as forlorn. Mills said he had added the chart
for historical interest, "as it is, most probably, the last document of its kind
that ever will be drawn up by a Samaritan priest." How wrong he was. Benny
now produces similar charts and sends them around the world to people
who want to follow the Samaritan way of life. "It is a new phenomenon of
people wanting to join community—singles, families, tribes. I am in contact
with thousands of them through the Internet. I don't believe in including
thousands at once. We accept one family after one family. They want to live
according to the Torah. They send me a lot of questions and I send them
books. They find it exciting. They are from all over the world: India, the
former Soviet Union, Europe, America, Australia, Brazil. Some are Jews."

I realized that the mass email from Benny had been guidance for those
looking to adopt the Samaritan way of life. These emails show which readings from the Samaritan Torah correspond to which Sabbath dates on the
calendar and when the seven festivals of the Samaritan year should be celebrated. These festivals include Shavuot, when Samaritans make a pilgrimage
around their holy sites on Mount Gerizim (such as the places where they
believe Adam, Isaac, and Noah sacrificed to God); the fast day of Yom
Kippur, when the Samaritan prayer service lasts for twenty-four hours without interruption; and Sukkot, a harvest festival that Samaritans celebrate
by bedecking their houses with fruit (unlike the Jews, who build a shelter
outdoors, the Samaritans celebrate Sukkot entirely within their homes). A
particularly ambitious Samaritan family's living room might contain pomegranates, apples, and lemons, all of a huge size, with perhaps up to half a ton
of fruit hanging from the ceiling above the feasters, interwoven with palm

fronds and willow branches. Sitting under this cornucopia, Samaritans drink homemade beer and eat cakes and water-soaked almonds.

Very few of Benny's online followers had actually come to live in the village. "They don't have to join physically. You can live a Samaritan life in the home. If they send a representative, I host them. People are always looking for something to stop them being bored. But it gives us pride that people find in us the people of truth." As far as I could tell, Benny occupied a unique position in his community of just 750 people. But when I asked him who would publish the newspaper, attend conferences, and research Samaritan history when he was gone, he smiled and said: "We have a proverb: God makes a replacement in every generation. I think they will find a crazy like me in every generation."

So far, one family Benny had corresponded with had come to live in al-Loz. They were American and had previously been Christian. One member of the family, Matthew, visited Benny while I was there, and I had the chance to talk to him. Matthew told me: "My mother was more and more interested in the Old Testament." His mother, Sharon, wondered why Christians did not keep the Jewish law; wanting to observe it more closely, and searching on the Internet for information, she came across Benny's name. "Six to eight years ago Benny visited, and we slowly started doing everything that the Samaritans do. The separation of unclean women, staying in our neighborhood for Shabbat, and so on. The old high priest invited Sharon to come and join the community, so she looked for religious studies programs and was accepted by Hebrew University."

Eight years after the first encounter with the Samaritans, Matthew was in Benny's house preparing for the Passover sacrifice. Other members of his family had not stayed the course: Matthew's brothers had drifted away after growing tired of the need to attend regular prayers at the synagogue, and Sharon moved away to Jerusalem. Matthew, though, two years before my visit, had been invited to join the community's observance of Passover and to eat the meat of the sacrificed lambs, which was the ultimate sign of acceptance. "Families live together, that's what I love about the community," he said. In practice, making his home among the Samaritans would mean learning both Hebrew and Arabic, which he had yet to do, but he planned to take on the task, and then study business and settle permanently in the community's other neighborhood, in Tel Aviv, as the first American Samaritan. (The following year, I heard that he had abandoned this plan and gone back to America. No other outsider has since followed his lead by coming to live in the village.)

Benny gave me a tour of the village that afternoon, showing how the families were preparing for Passover. He simply wandered into people's houses, I saw, without even needing to ring the bell or ask permission. In the basement storeroom of one house, where cribs and strollers had been stacked against the wall to make space, a man with the Arabic name Ghaith (his Hebrew name was Moshe) was spreading dough, made only with flour and water, over a hot curved metal plate called a *taboon*. A large stock was needed: as in Jewish tradition, only unleavened bread could be eaten during the seven days of Passover, which were about to start. Benny passed out to us a couple of pieces of the cooked bread, hot and crisp and flavorless. In the lead-up to and during Passover, the men were expected to handle cooking and other tasks. Ghaith's wife sat nearby, in a slightly sour mood. "I do the cooking 364 days of the year," she said in Arabic, "and nobody comes to take pictures of me doing it. And he does it one day a year and everyone thinks it's amazing?"

There was one other Samaritan obligation that I had not yet seen, but I was given an intense introduction to it the next morning. Dozing fitfully in the guest hall where the Samaritans had put me up, I woke to an unearthly sound, a vigorous susurration echoing through the empty rooms around me. It was clearly no kind of conversation or argument, because there were around thirty voices speaking ceaselessly, but discordantly. For some minutes I could not work out where it was coming from. Then I realized: the guest hall was just next to the *kinsha,* the Samaritan synagogue. I went to see what was happening. At the entrance to the *kinsha* I had to take off my shoes and stow them in an outer room; just as Moses took off his shoes when receiving the Law on Mount Sinai (or Mount Gerizim, in Samaritan belief), so the Samaritans take off their shoes in the presence of that Law.

The prayer room faced east, and a niche at one end was sealed off with a yellow curtain, in front of which sat the white-robed high priest and his

The Samaritans have preserved carefully over the generations their ancient scrolls, which record a Torah that differs somewhat from the Jewish one. Here in 1905 a Samaritan priest displays one such scroll for curious visitors. Stereograph in *Views of Palestine* [1905], Getty Research Institute

brother. There was a small clock and a menorah, the seven-branched candelabra, on the white-painted wall alongside; chandeliers and ceiling fans hung above. The building was constructed in the 1980s, but the niche housed vellum scrolls that date back centuries, possibly even millennia. Mills called them "the desire and the despair of European scholars," and his determination to see them "grew almost into a fever." When he eventually did, he found writing on one of them that claimed the document was written in biblical times. This was unlikely—not even vellum lasts that long—but perhaps it had been copied from a document from that period. There are seven-hundred-year-old scrolls in the British Library that were bought from the Samaritans in the nineteenth century. In places where the scrolls contain blessings that the priest touched as he recited them, the vellum is dark and worn.

The great murmuring that I had heard was produced by all of the village's male Samaritans, dressed in thin cotton *jelaba*s that reached down to their feet, gathered in this room and reciting prayers, each in his own time and rhythm, using different words, not in unison. Every so often they would pause and prostrate themselves on hands and knees, touching their foreheads to the floor. Prayer time is when the Samaritans cover their heads, as some devout Jews do at all times with the *kippa.* The Samaritans had three different styles of headgear: a white prayer cap such as Muslims wear, a red *tarbush,* and a black beret. The last was favored by the Samaritans who lived in Tel Aviv, as they followed slightly more modern fashions. The effect was curiously transformative. A woolen jacket worn over the *jelaba* and a red *tarbush* made a man look as though he had stepped out of a book about the Ottoman empire; the man next to him, in a raincoat and beret, looked like a French artist.

For a week before Passover the Samaritans pray morning and night; on normal Saturdays, people pray either at home or at the synagogue. The prayers were extracts from the Samaritan Torah mixed in with religious poems written by Samaritans over the centuries. Most people seemed to know these by heart, but one teenager in spectacles was reading them from a book; at the back the younger children were less involved, and one fell asleep in the corner, *tarbush* falling to one side. His schoolmates, giggling, asked me to take his photo. This was as far as teenage rebellion went. Not turning up for prayer at all was apparently unthinkable. One of the teenagers, keen to chat in between prayers, told me a little about his family: he had a nephew who, as the firstborn son from a priestly family, would have the blood of the sacrifice smeared on his forehead that day, according to the tradition, and another nephew was studying computer science and wanted to serve in the Israeli army. The boy interrupted his life story occasionally to perform his prostrations with the others.

Later that morning, after the prayer service, I wandered along the main street. Toward the end of it was a shop selling beer and whisky, run by a Samaritan man called Jameel. We sat and drank coffee and talked for a while; some other men from the village joined us and looked at the photos I had taken. Why had I taken pictures of the sleeping boy? they asked suspiciously. Was I trying to make fun of them? Our conversation was interrupted several times by phone calls, from Palestinians in Nablus placing orders, after which Jameel would head off to fix some delivery or other.

"Yesterday was exhausting," he said. "I was preparing unleavened bread for the family. It's a big family!" His father had been a priest, and a huge picture of a Passover sacrifice ceremony had pride of place on one wall of the shop. I asked him how things were for the Samaritans. "I'm a bit worried," he said. There was peace in Nablus for the time being, which was good, but it might not last. "Things should stay as they are. The intifada was bad for both sides, the Palestinians and the Israelis. Now it's quiet, and safe. We need Nablus—we bring everything from there, all our food." It was also where several Samaritans maintained shops and owned other property. The Samaritans had lived in Nablus until the late 1980s, when the first intifada frightened them into moving to their own separate village.

Yasser Arafat often boasted of the fact that the Samaritans were treated well under Palestinian rule, suggesting that it could be a precedent for Palestinian sovereignty over the West Bank, which would at the same time be open to Jews. He created a seat in the Palestinian parliament reserved for Samaritans. Jameel's father had won the subsequent election, mostly on the back of Muslim votes: he was well known in Nablus, where his beer and whisky shop had apparently won him many friends.

Jameel's father stood in a long tradition of Samaritans who advised Muslim rulers. Although the community in past centuries was collectively vulnerable and disadvantaged, individuals in it were often favored for sensitive posts because they stood outside the deadly tribal rivalries that split local Muslims. Those rivalries could put a Samaritan advisor in peril, though. A man called Jacob Esh Shalaby was an unusual Samaritan: he showed an early love of money and adventure, accepting money from a missionary to climb down Jacob's Well and recover a Bible the visitor had dropped down it. Later he traveled to England (presumably breaking the Samaritan rules to do so) and wrote a memoir in 1855. In it he records the experiences of his great-uncle as treasurer for the governor of Nablus, as first one faction and then another seized power. This great-uncle was threatened with death, thrown into jail, and sentenced to execution—but fled, or was released, or was granted a reprieve. He managed to serve each of the rival warring families in turn. He survived, but his hair turned prematurely white.

Arafat's welcoming of Samaritans into Nablus politics ended more benignly. Their reserved seat was abolished, leaving the larger Christian community as the only minority with reserved seats in the Palestinian parliament.

As I sat with Jameel and a few other villagers joined us, I asked if the Samaritans felt slighted. No, they chorused; in fact, they were relieved. Involving the community in politics only caused trouble, and they would rather be neutral.

Neutrality can be hard to maintain, especially for a vulnerable minority community. So far, though, the Samaritans have hewed to their middle path with great skill. Later that day I wandered past the end of the village, through a gate that apparently had been put there to stop people from entering the village on the Sabbath. I walked by potato fields and thinly wooded slopes. On the same slopes in 1855, John Mills had heard jackals crying to each other at night and "vieing with each other in their antiphonal but hideous music." At the time nobody lived on the mountain, and when they arrived to perform the Passover sacrifice, the Samaritans would pitch tents that they could stay in overnight. It seemed unlikely that any jackals survived there now. Houses were springing up everywhere, including one particularly lavish one that belonged to a Palestinian billionaire, Munib al-Masri. Some local workers were busy on one of the construction projects. They eyed me a little suspiciously until I spoke to them in Arabic, which delighted them. Things were peaceful, they said, which was good news. Were these houses still part of the Samaritan village? I asked. "No," one of them answered, "the people living here are Palestinians." Weren't the Samaritans themselves Palestinians? "I suppose so," he replied hesitantly, "especially the older ones; I'm not so sure about the younger generation. All right, then: let's say these houses belong to Arabs."

The man's confusion was telling, because the Samaritans' status is ambiguous. By the mid-twentieth century Samaritans and Muslims were coexisting better than they had a hundred years before. In the 1950s an envoy sent by Baron Edmond de Rothschild wrote to the baron that the Samaritans "enjoy good relations with Moslems." Ahlam, a Muslim woman from Nablus, told me that she remembered going to Samaritan homes for the harvest festival of Sukkot in the early 1960s: "We went to their houses for festivals, and there was a particular one when they decorated their homes with fruit. They made a big effort to reach out, more than the Christians did, actually. They wouldn't take hospitality from us"—because of the rules of *kashrut,* which state that Samaritans, like Jews, must only eat food prepared in a specific way—"but they would invite us to have food with them." There were limits to this familiarity, as Ahlam discovered. She took private classes after school from one of the schoolteachers, who was secretly in love with a Muslim colleague. He dared to tell his pupil about it, but he could never tell the woman herself. Ahlam wondered why. She was too young at the time to understand the rigid codes that separated Samaritans from Muslims and other outsiders.

After the Israeli conquest of the West Bank in 1967, the Samaritans' position improved further because Israel found it useful to employ them in semiofficial administrative positions. The Samaritans simultaneously managed to stay on good terms with the Palestinians. After the intifada broke out, it was harder to escape the violence. One unlucky Samaritan priest was shot twice in a single night, once by Palestinian gunmen who mistook him for an Israeli settler, and then—as he lost control of the steering wheel—by Israeli soldiers who saw him driving toward them erratically and thought he was a suicide bomber. He survived and received apologies afterward from both sides. Peace now prevails, and the Samaritans are better off than they have been for many centuries, but they do not take this for granted.

Back at Benny's flat, as sundown and the start of the Passover observance approached, I waited while two women discussed with him a project of recording sacred music (various recordings of Samaritan music have been released on CD, sung by members of the community themselves). When they finished, I asked him about politics. "We are trying to be a kind of bridge between Palestinians and Israelis," he said. "Physically we have no power to contribute. We're struggling for our survival. If we take one side and the other side wins, where will we be? They'll say we are collaborators." But the Samaritans had no desire for their own territory. "We don't have territorial demands: we never say, 'Hey, our family used to have this, it's ours.' We see how much misery it has given to the whole area. I think myself I have more than I expected."

At a certain point the time came for me to leave Benny's house because he had to prepare himself to take part in the sacrifice. It was happening earlier than usual, because that year the Sabbath would begin at sunset—and so the sacrifice had to be complete before then, in the early afternoon rather than the usual evening ceremony. Following the tradition to dress as their biblical forebears did when fleeing Egypt, Samaritans wore robes, each with twenty-four buttons (one for each letter of the Samaritan alphabet). Priests wore special colors: red for the blood of the lamb, blue for the skies, white for purity of heart. The event was a huge tourist attraction, and this was a mixed blessing for the Samaritans. "I don't like to be exotic," said Benny, "but that's how it is. Anyone keeping a tradition is exotic." Keeping a tradition, he explained, was central to Samaritan identity.

Waiting in the street outside, I watched throngs of visitors arrive. Some Christians and many Jews were coming to see something that could not be seen anywhere else: the Passover marked by a sacrifice of lambs, as it was until the destruction of the Jewish Temple nearly two millennia ago. Parked cars were gradually filling up the streets, film crews were setting up their cameras, and the early arrivals were occupying the best places for viewing the event. I had an invitation to attend the reception that preceded the sacrifice, which would be held in the hall where I had slept overnight.

This reception was a series of speeches—which could easily have been dull, except that the audience for them was such an unusual combination. The head of the Israeli forces in the West Bank sat opposite the Palestinian governor of Nablus, and the two engaged in half-serious, half-mocking banter. An even stranger juxtaposition was evident at the other end of the hall, where representatives of the settler movement sat next to Palestinians who later gave impassioned speeches about the injustices of Israeli rule (in particular movement restrictions on Palestinians, which were crippling Nablus's economy).

All the speakers—the governor, the general, and Munib al-Masri, who was sponsoring the event—expressed their respect for the Samaritans. It reminded me of something Benny had said: the Samaritans were the one issue the Palestinians and Israelis could agree about. Finally a Samaritan, a short man with a distinctive face whose father had recently died, rose to speak. "Our people were on the verge of extinction," he said, "and we have pulled ourselves back and built up our community, and now we are going nowhere: we are staying here."

The event showed how carefully the Samaritans balanced their relations with Palestinians and Israelis. There were clearly some differing political

Samaritan priests, here assembled for the Passover sacrifice. © Hanan Issachar/Getty Images

views within the community—those who lived in Tel Aviv were comfortable in Hebrew and spoke more freely of their loyalty to Israel, while some of the Samaritans on Mount Gerizim were closer to the Palestinians. All of them understood the need to maintain good ties with both sides. Israel offered better opportunities for education and work, and its government had been generous to the Samaritans. Israel's prime minister, Binyamin Netanyahu, was said to have a picture of himself with the high priest: several of them had seen it when they visited him. The high priest had prophesied Netanyahu's rise to power, I was told. On the other hand, the Samaritans were less comfortable with Israel's conservative religious hierarchy. "We prefer to keep clear of the Jewish rabbis," one Samaritan told me. The Samaritans are regarded as a separate religious community in Palestinian law, meaning that (for example) marriages conducted by their priests are legally recognized; in Israeli law their status is much more ambiguous.

The gathering ended, and people began to file out. It was time for the sacrifice to begin. Decades ago the Samaritans used to come together in tents on the mountain for the ceremony, but now there was a enclosure specifically built for the event, enclosed by a wire fence. Hundreds of tourists were pressing against the fence, and some tried to clamber over it, eliciting shouts from the burly security guards. The Samaritans now gathered within the enclosure, squeezing through the crowds to enter it. The priests were in their colorful traditional robes; the other Samaritan men were wearing white aprons and baseball caps in preparation for the bloody work they were all about to perform. The women stood further back with the younger children. In accordance with the regulations for the Passover laid down in the Book of Exodus, each family that is large enough brings a lamb to sacrifice. So a small flock of lambs was gathered in the middle of the crowd of Samaritans, while—ominously for the lambs—large pits at one end of the enclosure were be-

A Samaritan priest relaxes after the Passover sacrifice, the blood of the lamb visibly marked on his forehead. Photo by the author

ing filled with wood for burning, and heaps of earth were prepared nearby.

The senior priests sang as the lambs were brought up to the place of slaughter, where metal frames stood ready. Then the Samaritans gave a great shout: the lambs' throats had been cut. The men in aprons got to work, hanging the carcasses from the metal frames so that they could be flayed. They began to chant with joy, singing in ancient Hebrew, "There is only one God!" as they gestured toward each other. They chanted verses from the Song of the Sea, the celebratory song sung by the people of Israel after their deliverance from Egypt: "Pharaoh's chariots and his host hath he cast into the sea." The blood from the lambs was collected, ready to be painted with a stick of hyssop onto the lintels of the village doors. Finally the sacrificed lambs were impaled on spits. Once the wood in the pits had burned down to charcoal, the lambs would be cooked with a layer of earth on top of them to keep in the heat. It was, as Benny had promised, a scene out of the remote past.

The Samaritans have defied centuries of gloomy predictions made by those who visited them during their long decline. An English writer in 1714 commented: "The Sect of the Samaritans hath now continu'd in the World about 2400 Years, and in the same Spot almost where it first appear'd. It is not therefore to be wondered at, that a Thing so remarkable should excite the Curious." But he concluded that "the Place where they have so long continued will in a little time know them no more; and that their Name is shortly like to be found no where but in History." The Welsh missionary Mills, in the 1850s, was just as pessimistic. "Before many generations more have passed away," he sighed, "this nation, in all probability, will have become extinct." They have all been proven wrong.

Here, on a sacred mountain in the Holy Land, the 132nd high priest (the first having been Moses's brother Aaron), wearing resplendent robes, was resting with his colleagues after the exertions of the Passover sacrifice. The women of the community came to kiss their hands. Firstborn sons were marked on their foreheads with the lambs' blood. Above this apparently Jewish scene, a sign declared that it was sponsored by the Palestinian Telecommunications Company. It was perhaps too easy to imagine that the Samaritan experience, limited and precarious as it was and dependent on the goodwill of both Israeli and Palestinian authorities, might provide a basis for coexistence between all the different communities in this troubled place. But surely it should give at least a glimmer of hope.

Copts

I T WAS GREAT FRIDAY IN THE YEAR 1727 of the Era of Martyrs. The month was Baramouda, when seasonal dust winds blow along the Nile Valley, a time for harvesting wheat and avoiding the increasing heat of the sun. At such a time, for thousands of years, Egyptians have prayed for the Nile to rise and irrigate their fields with silt-rich water in a land that was otherwise one of the driest places on earth. So they prayed now, gathered around me, for the "rising of the water of the rivers." If I shut my eyes at certain moments, I could have imagined myself in ancient Egypt. But in the Western calendar, the year was 2011, and the nearest river was the Thames; with open eyes, I could see the pretty façade of London terraces through stained-glass windows.

St. Mark's Church, Kensington, is dedicated to the first-century evangelist and missionary who, according to tradition, first brought Christianity to Egypt. Those Egyptians who remain Christian are known as Copts. Estimates of their numbers vary widely, from four million to twelve million, plus a diaspora in Sudan, Libya, and the West. Because of a split in the Christian Church in the fifth century over the nature of Christ, Copts have since then developed their own distinctive brand of Christianity, the Coptic Orthodox Church, under the leadership of the Patriarch of Alexandria. This Coptic form of Christianity spread south from Egypt to Eritrea and Ethiopia—and perhaps it once traveled north, too. When the Coptic leader (also called the "pope") Shenouda III, the 117th Patriarch of Alexandria, consecrated St. Mark's in 1979, it was then the only Coptic church in Europe. But it was not so much a new arrival as a return. An eighth-century Irish book of martyrs refers to "the seven holy Egyptian monks who lie in Disert Ulaidh." Coptic monks such as those, who settled in Ireland, may have had some role in shaping the early Irish Church—which shared the Copts' focus on monasticism, and their austerity.

Another difference between Egyptian and European Christians is that the Copts have kept or even toughened many of the rules that European Christians have relaxed. The congregation at St. Mark's had endured more than fifty days of the tough Coptic Lenten fast, during which they abstain completely from all fish, meat, and animal products such as milk and cheese. On Great Friday (called Good Friday in Britain and America) they eat nothing until sunset, and they pray all day: the service at St. Mark's had begun at dawn, when a cross had been laid out in the aisle of the church and decorated with candles and roses. One of the prayers involved four hundred reverences (and although, for some, a reverence just meant a bow of the head, one man got down on the floor to prostrate himself). Even though they were living thousands of miles from their home, the Copts' enthusiasm for their faith was undimmed.

Much of what I could see in front of me—an elaborate screen separating the altar from the congregation, icons of St. Mark and the Virgin Mary—dated to the early centuries AD, when Christianity supplanted Egypt's old polytheistic religion. But in the books helpfully placed in the aisles as guides to the service, I could see the church did not use either the Western calendar or the Islamic one sometimes found in the Arab world. Instead they used the calendar that the pharaohs would have known, with months called Baramouda, Kiahk (the "month when the spirits gather"), and Thout (named after the baboon-headed god Thoth). For that matter, the year was dated according to the Era of Martyrs, which starts in the Western year 284. This was when the emperor Diocletian massacred Christians—a persecution that is still remembered by the Copts.

The style of the chanting in St. Mark's that day would have been familiar to a Greek politician and scholar called Demetrius of Phalerum, who lived in Egypt's coastal city of Alexandria in the third century BC. "In Egypt," he wrote, "the priests, when they are singing hymns in praise of the gods, use the seven vowels, which they chant in a specific sequence; and the music made with these letters sounds so good that men prefer it to the flute and lyre." So they do now. *Oh-oh-oh,* the priest and deacons sang, wavering on a sequence of notes, and then *eh* and *ah,* the consonants of the words hardly audible. This chant was the "Pek Ethronos." It turns from sadness to joy at the prospect of the Resurrection, just as the ancient song on which it is based both mourned the pharaoh who had died and celebrated the accession of his successor. I was hearing the funeral music of the pharaohs in London's leafiest streets. How it came there, and what that means for Christianity in Egypt, is the subject of this chapter.

CAIRO WAS MY FIRST OVERSEAS POSTING, in 1997. I was then a language student straight out of London, a neophyte diplomat. "Welcome to the embassy," the ambassador had said, "and I hope you don't take it the wrong way if I tell you we don't want to see you here again. Get out there and spend time with Egyptians." Our small group of students needed little telling. The city was a revelation. It was a vast concentration of humanity, perhaps eighteen million people, with more arriving every day—leaving behind life in the villages along the Nile River and streaming into the capital by train, by bus, on foot, or in carts, settling in unplanned, chaotic shantytowns on the edge of the existing city, poverty side by side with wealth. I used to walk from my tree-lined street over to the slums and watch knife jugglers and street traders stand amid the raw sewage that trickled down the dirt lanes.

It was also a joyous, chaotic, confusing, overwhelming carnival of noise. I lived in Mohandiseen, a leafy modern suburb. But even there I would hear the mint seller call outside my window with his horse and cart at five in the morning, and the loudspeakers of the mosque at noontime, and then car horns blaring late into the night. I studied at the British Council on the banks of the Nile—made rather less romantic by the fumes of a crematorium that blew ash across the balcony on which I would sit to have lunch. But I could put up with that, and all the other irritations of that polluted, crowded city, because I was in love. Not with a person, not then. I was in love with Arabic. It was my key to a world hidden in plain sight. It admitted me into places where otherwise I could not have gone, let me read books and poetry that dated back over a thousand years—for it had changed little during that time, being the sacred language of the Koran—and opened up conversations I never could have had without it. The language also had an extraordinary system to its design. Take three letters, and it formed a root. That root, like a musical motif, could be treated in one of twelve different ways, each one changing its meaning in a subtly different way. The result was a language as sweetly mathematical as a Bach motet.

To most Westerners, Arabic is the language of Islam. But I found that Arabic-speaking Egypt had more Christians in its churches on Sundays than England. I joined them: each week I took a taxi or rode the Metro, smooth and clinically clean and Japanese-built, up to the slightly shabby, unremarkable suburb of Shubra. To escape expat life, there was no better place. It was almost Egypt's center of gravity, its definition of middle class with its small shops and one famous restaurant and paved streets. There was grit, there was noise, there was still the sour tang of polluted air—but these things did not seem to trouble my Egyptian friends as much as they did me. In Egypt villages are not places where the well-off choose to live, and the better kind of apartment (so my friends told me) was the kind on the noisy main street, not the quiet dirt roads behind. When one friend visited me in London she complained of the quiet, which had prevented her from sleeping.

No tourists went to Shubra, or do today. They are wrong, however, if they think it has nothing to offer them. It has at least one thing they will not find anywhere else in the Middle East: a station named after a European saint. Boarding the Metro in central Cairo, I would pass through stations named after Egyptian presidents—Nasser, Sadat, Mubarak; I would go through one named after the pharaoh Ramses; and then I would arrive at a station named Sainte Thérèse.

How did St. Thérèse of Lisieux, the Little Flower, come to be on the Cairo map? The answer can be found just off the main street of Shubra, in a very remarkable church. The church is named after St. Thérèse because it was founded by French Carmelites, and it is remarkable because the portico of the church is covered from top to bottom in votive plaques, in English and French, Hebrew and Arabic, left by Jews, Muslims, and Christians in testimony to miracles performed by the saint. The church still attracts some Muslim visitors who come to light candles at the back, and even when an Islamic militant came to vandalize the church many years ago, he attacked the cross but left the saint's pictures alone.

One day I walked into the small, asphalt-paved forecourt of the church and met what would be, for a year, my own community in Egypt. There was huge Atef, who looked like a bouncer but wanted to be a monk; there was Maggie, who was studiously training to be an architect; there was Samih, a self-confident engineer. I noticed among the congregation signs of its pharaonic past, names such as Rameses and Nefertiti. A man called Wael, who had ambitions to be a model, claimed that his features were exactly those of the pharaohs. Regally presiding over everyone was Father Paul, a priest from a Coptic Catholic family. (In the nineteenth century, the Catholic Church set up a Uniate church in Egypt, whose Coptic members could keep their own traditions while accepting the bishop of Rome's authority. This Uniate church has today more than 160,000 members.) He was a study for me in Egyptian courtesy. This was pretty much at the opposite end of the scale from the understated and distant courtesy of the English; I found myself navigating exaggerated compliments, half-meant invitations, and gargantuan hospitality. One particular exchange that the priest had with a flower merchant summed it up for me. After a lengthy negotiation over price, the flower seller declared: "Of course, I would like you to have them for free." Nimbler at this than I would ever have been, the priest had an equally insincere compliment ready in reply: "You know, I only came here for the pleasure of seeing you."

Endlessly generous in showing me around Cairo, the priest was more elusive when I tried to return his hospitality. On the one occasion that he came to my flat, he drank a single glass of water, and when I tried to persuade him to stay longer, he declared, "No: I have honored you enough." My Coptic friends' kindness to me, though, never dried up. The church was more than a church. The members of the congregation took holidays together, chatted to each other for hours in the forecourt, and met frequently during the week. They taught me Egyptian dancing and once invited me to join them on charitable visits to Cairo's poor: people living in makeshift shacks on the rooftops of tall apartment buildings. My new friends also regularly reproached me for the laxness of British Christianity. No wonder. A devout Copt should pray seven times a day, avoid drinking alcohol, and never smoke cigarettes. Copts fast not only during Lent but also during Advent and at other times of the year—210 days of the year in total. Though they are bound to give up meat and dairy products during these times (and fish during Lent), some go even further by eating only fruit, or the stewed beans that Egyptians call *fuul*. Some do not eat anything at all between midnight and sunset each day of Lent. This is more demanding than the Muslim fast of Ramadan. I was tempted to repeat a judgment made by Herodotus, who twenty-five centuries ago was an awestruck visitor to one of Egypt's great temples, which at one point became so wealthy from donations that they owned a third of the country's fertile land: "The Egyptians are religious to excess, more than any other country in the world." (In recent opinion polls, Egyptians have agreed with Herodotus: they believe themselves to be the most religious people in the world.)

I thought this not only about the Copts, but also when I heard the loud-speaker-enhanced sermons of local mosques on Fridays. Every taxi driver seemed to play the Koran on his cassette player, sometimes pointing out, like a connoisseur, the quality of the particular reciter. At a concert of Sufi music the lead singer, eyes hidden behind dark glasses, elicited rapturous applause, and some of his hearers went into a state of trance. This pervasiveness of religion meant that religious differences, too, were obvious. Several times when I was walking through Cairo's streets, people came up to me and asked which soccer team I supported. A few times they would ask instead—much in the same spirit, it seemed—if I was Muslim or Christian. My Arabic teacher told me that people asked her the same question, though not directly. They would ask her for her name, and then her father's name. (As a liberal Muslim, she evaded their questions on principle, feeling that people should have a right to keep their religion private.) Copts had their own way of asking the same question. One time at the local supermarket the cashier surreptitiously exposed his wrist to me, showing the tattoo of a cross.

Those differences expressed themselves violently from time to time while I lived in Egypt. The embassy forbade me to visit parts of the south of Egypt, and especially the city of Minya, because of Islamist terror groups that were attacking the security forces and local Christians there. In September 1997, when I was in Alexandria with friends from St. Thérèse, I saw on the television that German tourists had been gunned down in Tahrir Square. It was my first encounter with terrorism. "Don't be alarmed, Gerard. It is fate," said Samih. "We must all die on our appointed day." I was not comforted. Two months later, sixty-two people were killed in a massacre at Luxor, carried out by terrorists armed with guns and knives. A five-year-old child was among the victims. A note praising Islam was found afterward in the disemboweled body of one of the victims.

Yet interspersed with these terrible events were occasional reminders of a more humane form of coexistence. Take, for example, the attack in Tahrir Square, which so alarmed me when I saw it on the news at Alexandria. The men who carried it out escaped afterward, or so I read, to a neighboring district called Bulaq Abu'l Alaa. The people of the district shielded the killers. It happened that I knew this place. It was one of my favorite areas to walk in, where welders' magnesium flares garishly lit up once-elegant colonial-style buildings and the dust and dirt of neglected roads between them. Yet the priest in this area, a huge man in a huge Italianate church, told me the Muslims there were his brothers; he had no trouble from them, he said. Copts came and went to the church without ever being harassed. As I walked back out of the neighborhood, I passed through a street market selling clothes. Here were people of all kinds: men in turbans, men in suits, in jeans, in coveralls; women wearing veils, women without veils, and one woman, too poor perhaps to afford a veil, who had fitted a cardboard box around her head to protect her from the sun; and a girl with long plaited hair teaching her little brother how to make the sign of the cross.

I left Egypt in 1998 and went back only rarely and briefly. Then in 2011 I saw that Tahrir Square was in the news again. The Egyptian people had gathered there to topple a president. Christians and fundamentalist Muslims stood shoulder to shoulder. Paid thugs attacked the demonstrators. President Hosni Mubarak resigned. An army council took over. There were outbreaks of fighting between Christians and Muslims. Some churches were attacked. Several Christians were killed. I had planned to go to Egypt anyway, for this book, and the trip seemed more relevant than ever.

———————

AS THE PLANE LANDED AT Cairo in March 2011, I looked out at a well-remembered city. I could see the mansions of the rich, in the serene northern suburb of Heliopolis; I could see where the poorest of Cairo's poor, the Nile River dwellers who have no homes except their little uncovered skiffs, are rocked each evening by the backwash of luxury cruise boats. The road from the airport took me past a huge grand military barracks with murals showing the victories of Egypt's pharaonic armies; turning into a giant over-pass, it sped me over the grimy edifices of the state, its ministries, and the principal train station. It passed by the domes of the Coptic cathedral, and next to it a mosque—in solidarity? Or competition?

My hotel, on an island in the Nile called Zamalek, was a shabby but cozy relic of Cairo's elegant past. A retired architect had installed himself eccentrically on a faded chair in the lobby and appeared to be dictating various letters, usually of complaint, to an obliging member of the staff. Outside the hotel, a group of young women in *hejabs* were painting a mural representing people power. As I walked along the street I noted the signs on the shops and walls. One advertised in English the Libyan currency at its new low rate as Western and Arab allies threatened war: "Libian dinar buy 2 sell 3.65." Another said in Arabic: "In the name of God: there are many honorable policemen. Let us celebrate our police." A third, on the door of a shop, was starker, with just one word in bright letters: "Viagra."

The island of Zamalek appeared on the Nile just over a century ago, a composite of the silt that used to be washed down the river year by year, and which gave the Nile Valley its fertility. (After the Nile was dammed in 1970, the silt stopped flowing. For that matter, the "rising of the waters"—the annual ebb and flood of the river—ended, too.) Zamalek attracted the upper classes, who built on it palaces and parks that now have become frail and faded. I rode a taxi across the bridge to the older parts of Cairo, which are on the eastern bank of the Nile. As we crossed the Nile, the taxi driver proudly pointed out the burned-out shell of the former ruling party's headquarters, squatting on the river's edge. A presenter on the radio declared: "Corruption in society—we can talk freely about this now!"

My goal was a modest pink-stuccoed building stuck between a multi-layer concrete overpass and the expanse of Tahrir Square. Into this museum every day thousands of people would come to see 165,000 statues, figurines, sarcophagi, and mummies. Tourism in 2009 provided employment for up to 12 percent of the Egyptian workforce, but the Egyptian Museum has always been more than a moneymaker. It is a monument to Egyptian identity. On its front wall is another symbol—a long list of the dynasties that had ruled Egypt, as if to say to Egyptians: *You have always been ruled by kings.* In revolutionary Egypt in 2011 it was the one place where autocrats—though of the dead and mummified kind—were still in vogue.

Instead of elaborate traps and curses to ward off intruders, the mummies had a guardian in the form of Tariq el-Awadi, the museum's director. I found him in his office in the museum basement. His desk was surrounded by a collection of ornate gilded clocks, each showing a different time. I had come to ask him about history. "Egyptians are divorced from their past," Awadi said. "They are made to feel that they have nothing in common with it." The school curriculum, he explained, divided history into eras: pharaonic, Coptic, Islamic. It was the Islamic era that received most attention. But Awadi thought that learning more about previous eras could help Egyptians become more united as a people. A Muslim himself, he felt that the country's ancient past was a heritage that both Christians and Muslims shared: "Our country is a cohesive society, although it has more than one religion; customs, language, even certain religious traditions are the same for all Egyptians, and different from the Arabs." But for many decades, Egyptians had been told that they were Arabs. And so, as Awadi said, "Egyptians are asking, 'Who am I? Am I Arab or Egyptian?'"

After I saw Awadi I walked through the halls of the museum, looking at toys and models of ships and *ushabti* (funerary) figurines that might have been made yesterday, so perfectly were they preserved. It gave me a strange feeling—as though the veil of time had somehow grown thin, and the mummified pharaohs might really step through it and come alive in the modern day. Certainly the Egyptians had expected that their bodies might come alive again, something that most other ancient peoples did not foresee. For example, when Gilgamesh the king in the Iraqi epic descends beneath the earth to search for his dead friend Enkidu, he meets shades, not people of flesh. "Enkidu," as he says, "has turned to clay!"

The people of the Nile Valley, however, were surrounded by a sand that was a hundred times drier than the Iraqi desert—so dry that even pieces of paper buried in it for two thousand years have been discovered with writing on them still legible. Ancient Egyptians buried their dead in this sand, and even without the process that was later devised of removing the body's organs and stuffing the corpse with *natrun* salt to preserve it, the corpses were often naturally mummified by the sand's dryness and heat. Dug up years later, they would still have been recognizable. It was possible to imagine the soul (the *ka*) reentering them and bringing them back to life. An Egyptian inscription from the twenty-fourth century BC declares, "Let them who are in their graves, arise; let them undo their bandages. Shake off the sand from thy face" (here appearing to address the dead themselves), "raise thyself up on thy left side, support thyself on thy right side."

If the pharaohs really did come back to life today, rising from their gilt sarcophagi, they would find their country changed beyond recognition. Only in the countryside might they see familiar sights: families washing themselves and their pots and pans in the Nile, green palm trees and heaps of threshed wheat punctuating the fields, water buffalo wandering beside streams. Otherwise they would be amazed at the choking fumes and teeming apartment buildings of Cairo, now one of the world's biggest cities; at the population of Egypt, more than twenty times now than in antiquity; at the fact that the nation, once the breadbasket of the Roman empire, now imports 40 percent of its food. And they would discover that their religion of animal-headed deities, which once held so powerful a grip on Egyptian society, was gone.

Or not quite gone, as it turned out. I had an appointment in a hotel by

Tahrir Square with a couple who called themselves Osirites—modern-day Egyptian worshipers of the old Egyptian god Osiris. The husband, Hamdi (not his real name), looked just like the statue of an ancient Egyptian scribe, thickset and jovial. Bottles of Saqqara beer, named after the oldest pyramids, were brought to our table. Past the chintz sofas and glazed windows the river Nile flowed by, brown and ageless. According to Egyptian myth, Osiris, the god of the underworld, had floated down the river in a coffin after being tricked by his wicked brother, Seth. His sister, Isis, rescued him, but Seth found him again and chopped him into pieces. Isis found all the pieces except her brother's penis, which she rebuilt for him out of gold. Then she magically revived him. He became the god of resurrection—and was thought to control the ebb and flood of the Nile, themselves symbols of death and rebirth.

Osiris, Isis, and Seth—and other Egyptian gods such as Amun—were just one single deity, the Osirite couple told me. It was wrong, they added, to speak of the ancient Egyptians as polytheists or *kuffar,* as some Muslims did. They had given the world most of its contemporary religious ideas, including the word *amen.*

"When others say 'Amen,' I say 'Amun'!" declared Hamdi.

"We invented the Sabbath," his wife added. "And the psalms of David: they were written by the pharaoh Akhenaten. Look at the hymns he wrote to Aten, and you'll see they are the same as the psalms."

She told me about a modern Egyptian festival that could be traced to an ancient one. Two thousand years ago it was referred to as "Osiris coming to the moon"; now it is called Shamm al-Nessim, but it is still celebrated at the spring equinox. "There is a special holiness to the day. It is the only day when everything stops." There was no other festival in modern Egypt celebrated by both Christians and Muslims. "People eat green things, and fish and lettuce, and sit on the grass, and paint the eggs they eat." (There is an Egyptian specialty that they eat on Shamm al-Nessim: *fiseekh*, a kind of preserved fish that academics say dates back millennia. I tasted it once and found it shockingly pungent. But some Egyptians love it.) This old Egyptian feast was the origin of Easter, she insisted.

With deep nationalist pride, she listed the many and widespread religious customs and ideas that had originated in ancient Egypt: the customs of pilgrimage and prayer, fasting, the concept of the Messiah, Christmas trees and the name of Christmas, the lighting of candles in churches, and more. "The Egyptian flag is fourteen thousand years old," said Hamdi. "Red, white, and black have always represented national pride. And the eagle at its center is the sign of Horus." I could see that this couple, too, were looking for an identity that would be the property of all Egyptians. While I found it hard to imagine that there would be many people joining them in the cult of Osiris, their final declaration was boldly given: "The Egyptian religion is returning!" A year later, when the Muslim Brotherhood were running Egypt, I met this couple again, but they spoke differently and more cautiously. They were interested in the culture of ancient Egypt, they said, not the religion.

Still, they were right that the ancient Egyptians had an influence on later religions. Not only did the Egyptians pioneer belief in the resurrection of the body, but the pharaoh Akhenaten, father of Tutankhamun, was the first known monotheist in history. He abolished all gods except his beloved Aten, the sun god, and built epicene statues symbolizing the union of masculine and feminine. A hymn to Aten survives, written perhaps by the pharaoh himself: "The earth brightens when thou arisest in the eastern horizon and shine forth as Aten in the daytime. . . . How manifold are thy works! They are hidden from the sight of men, O sole God, like unto whom there is no other!" Jews, who lived in Egypt, share some of their customs with the pharaohs: the avoidance of pork and catfish was practiced by both Jews and Egyptians, as was male circumcision. Compared with the number of ancient traditions I found alive and well in Iraq, though, I noted few in Egypt. The country had no community like the Mandaeans or the Zoroastrians that kept pre-Christian traditions continuously into the modern era. And Egypt's folk customs, though many and colorful, are mostly medieval. I found only three that date back to pharaonic times.

One is the custom by which the Egyptians mark death. At the medieval cemetery of Cairo, a collection of miniature mansions is assembled in silent array along straight, empty dirt roads near the al-Azhar mosque. Although these mansions are actually lived in for much of the year by squatters, they are built above graves and exist for a particularly Egyptian custom: forty days after a relative's death, and on the death's every anniversary, many Egyptian families gather at these little mansions to eat a meal there. In the same way, their ancestors came to eat by the graves of their loved ones, offering food to their spirits. A doctor I met told me how in the south of Egypt, the ancient custom of hiring mourners for funerals continued, and, that for a week after a death, the bereaved family would shelter and feed visitors. The same doctor had once come across mourners who improvised chants while he was carrying out a surgical operation. They stood, dressed predominantly in black mourning costume, around the operating table and improvised a dirge for the occasion, since they refused to accept that the patient might survive. "Oh, you poor woman whose flesh was cut while you were still alive!"

Another, less attractive custom definitely dates back to pharaonic times. The Egyptians "practice circumcision for the purpose of cleanliness," wrote Herodotus, and a papyrus from the second century BC shows that it was performed on girls as well as boys. It still is. A UN-backed survey in 2008 shockingly found that over 90 percent of Egyptian women surveyed had undergone the procedure—though it is uncommon among better-educated Egyptians. Also known as female genital mutilation, it involves slicing off the clitoris and sometimes also the labia with a knife. It was banned by the Mubarak government in 2007 after a girl died during the surgery. Although its origin is not Islamic (it is practiced by some Christians as well as Muslims) this ugliest of all ancient Egyptian customs has survived better than any other, and—unlike those other customs—attracts support and not hostility from Muslim fundamentalists.

Yet another sign of ancient Egypt stares most visitors in the face at some point or other. Hanging from many car mirrors in Cairo is the blue-colored "Hand of Fatima," which today is believed to ward off the evil eye, the envy people attract through their good fortune. The "Hand of Horus" in ancient times, often made of blue lapis lazuli, served the same purpose. In the nineteenth century, Egyptians went to all kinds of lengths to avoid the evil eye—dressing up boys as girls, staining the faces of beautiful girls to conceal their looks, and giving themselves unpleasant-sounding names such as "Ugly" or "The Little Bird" or "The Donkey."

Very few Egyptians read any deeper significance into these customs, any more than most English people think of the god Tiu when they touch wood for luck. Both Christian and Muslim religious hierarchies, however, want their followers to abandon these traditions. In particular, Salafi Islam condemns them. In 2012 a Muslim fundamentalist politician, Murgan al-Gohary, called for the Sphinx and pyramids to be destroyed. Salafi groups in Egypt boycott the Shamm al-Nessim celebration and have called for it to be suppressed. *Pharaoh,* too, remains a dirty word for Islamists. When in 2011 the Muslim Brotherhood wanted to promote a new constitution on which there was to be a yes-or-no vote, it devised the slogan "Vote no, get pharaoh!"

EGYPT'S ORIGINAL RELIGION was weakened by centuries of foreign rule over Egypt—by Persians, Greeks, and Romans—starting in the fourth century BC. Even Cleopatra was of Greek and Persian descent, though her family tried to adopt Egyptian customs (one of the less savory of these being the tradition that pharaohs married their sisters; Cleopatra was descended from several generations of incestuous marriages). The native Egyptians came to be given their own special label, to distinguish them from the Greek settlers who owned most of the land and ran the administration. They were called Aiguptioi—from which the words "Egypt" and "Copt" are both de-rived. By the third century AD a Christian preacher could claim that the old religion was dominated by Greeks, and that Christianity was the religion of the Copts.

Roman rule, introduced after Cleopatra's death, did not displace the Greeks, but it did lead to the abolition of the role of the pharaoh—which in turn undermined the temples, which had depended on financial support from the pharaohs and had played a significant role in keeping the old culture alive. In the second century AD, we see an example of traditions dying out in the report of a guild of hieroglyph carvers at the city of Oxyrhynchus: they numbered only five, the guild reported, and had no apprentices to carry on the profession.

The temples survived several centuries of Roman rule, though their power was reduced. But in the fourth century the Roman Empire adopted Christianity and made strenuous efforts to suppress the old religion. Many

Egyptians enthusiastically joined in, attacking pagan philosophers and obliterating the gods' faces on murals in their temples so that their magical power would be annulled. In the narrow confines of Egypt's Nile Valley there is no record of any non-Christian community surviving at the time of the Muslim conquest. Even the ancient Egyptian language was flooded with new words brought by Christianity: a Greek word for "soul," *psyche,* replaced the *ka* of the pharaohs.

Some customs survived, as I learned in St. Mark's Church, because they were thought worthy of inclusion in new Christian rites. Early Christian clergy of Egypt were in many recorded cases either temple priests who had become Christian or children of temple priests. A hymn such as "Pek Ethronos," which I heard at St. Mark's in Kensington, would have been very familiar to them. It just needed some amendments so that it would be addressed to Jesus Christ. Cymbals, too, had been used in the worship of the old gods. For a time, they were banned by the Christian church, but it later relented; they are still used in Coptic rites today.

Coptic, Armenian, and Syrian churches, on one hand, and Byzantines and Europeans, on the other, disagreed with each other at the fifth-century Council of Chalcedon about the nature of Christ. Putting the difference crudely, the Copts felt that the council was not firm enough in taking a stand against those who wanted to distinguish between Jesus as man and Jesus as God. The Copts were emphatic that Jesus had only one nature, and they still refer to themselves as Miaphysites (*mia physis* meaning "one nature" in Greek). The upshot was that the Coptic patriarch rejected the council; although Egypt was then part of the Byzantine Empire, the patriarch and not the emperor was the true ruler of Egypt. Relations between the Copts and Byzantium suffered. The dispute reflected other tensions as well—perhaps among them the long-standing dislike that the Copts had for foreign rule. Certainly the religious divide deepened that dislike, and Copts did little to resist when the Muslim Arabs invaded Egypt in the seventh century. Relations soured somewhat when the new Muslim government imposed heavy taxes on the non-Muslim population; rebellions followed. Still, most Egyptians remained Christian until the tenth century, and Coptic was still a common language until the thirteenth century, when Arabic was gradually enforced. In the

fourteenth century, in the aftermath of the Crusades and the Mongol invasions, anti-Christian riots became more frequent, and the authorities imposed
laws to curb the Copts' influence and status. When the German monk Johann
Vansleb explored Egypt in 1672, he reported that the Copts were "so fearful
from continued tyrannies that at the least noise they trembled like leaves."

Admiration for the pharaohs is a recent phenomenon among both
Copts and Muslims. In the Koran, the pharaoh who famously refused to
allow Moses and the Jews to leave Egypt features prominently. He is described as "one of the corrupters," having set himself up as a god, exalted
himself, and despised the poor. Unlike the "Sabians" in Harran, therefore,
the pharaohs were always clearly defined as idolaters and their religious sites
were regarded with suspicion. One early Muslim ruler reputedly wanted to
demolish the pyramids. According to the medieval historian al-Maqrizi, a
fourteenth-century Sufi mystic did manage to smash the Sphinx's nose, apparently enraged by the fact that local peasants were making offerings to it
as a god (a rare reference to the possibility that, covertly, the old gods were
still worshiped). Nor would the average person living in Egypt necessarily
have seen "Egyptian" as an identity. William Browne, a British visitor to
Cairo in the eighteenth century, reported that the local merchants referred
to themselves simply as Arabs. The term *Copts,* originally used to describe
indigenous Egyptians, was by this stage applied exclusively to Christians.

During the nineteenth century, however, this attitude began to change.
The catalyst was a series of discoveries, initially by Western archaeologists,
that revealed the skill and artistic achievements of the ancient Egyptians.
Archaeologists uncovered the temple of Abu Simbel, guarded by sixty-five-
foot-high statues of Pharaoh Rameses II, in 1813. In 1817 they found the
tomb of Seti in the Valley of the Kings, complete with painters' brushes still
on its floor beneath bright blue and golden pictures showing the progress of
the pharaoh's soul in the afterlife. In Europe and America, these and other
discoveries contributed to "Egyptomania"—an enthusiasm for imitating ancient Egyptian architecture.

This coincided with cultural and political shifts within Egypt itself.
In the nineteenth century Egypt and Sudan, though officially provinces of
the empire of the Ottoman Sultan in Istanbul, were actually governed as a

separate entity by the Mohammad Ali dynasty—named after its founder, a successful Albanian adventurer who established his power base by inviting his rivals to a banquet and then slaughtering them all as they went home. Despite this bloody beginning, the dynasty was a force for reform and modernization in Egypt.

Ismail, the dynasty's third member, who ruled from 1863 to 1879, was particularly ambitious. He curbed the slave trade, built Africa's biggest railway, and began the digging of the Suez Canal. He also opened the first Egyptian Museum, a predecessor of the one that sits in Tahrir Square, in 1863. It was designed in a pharaonic style. To reassure devout Muslims who hesitated to emulate the polytheistic pharaohs, a religious scholar named Tahtawi offered reassurance that the pharaohs were really "Sabians" who worshiped one god in different forms. In 1864 a pupil of Tahtawi's named Abu'l Suud wrote a history of ancient Egypt calling on its modern-day people to imitate their ancestors "in working together as true Egyptians and true patriots, for the renaissance of Egypt." From 1867 onward, the pyramids appeared on Egyptian stamps.

This was not just a romantic movement of nostalgia for the past. It had relevance to Egypt's status in the world. The glories of Egypt's history enabled Ismail to look European rulers in the face. They also constituted a basis for seeing Egypt not as a province of the Ottoman Empire but as the independent country that Ismail wanted it to be. This emphasis on Egypt's separate identity influenced Ismail's attitude toward religion as well. Ismail reproved a Muslim minister who spoke of a government employee contemptuously as "this Coptic official"; he turned to the author and retorted, "All are Egyptians alike." This assertion of equality between Christians and Muslims (as well as of a unifying national identity) was significant: only in 1855 had Christians been released from the special *jizya* tax imposed on them as non-Muslims. But Ismail granted land for Coptic schools; included Copts in a sort of proto-parliament he created, called the Advisory Council of Representatives; and appointed one Copt as chief of the government's official press and another as head of the finance administration. At the end of his reign he appointed an Armenian Christian, Nubar Pasha, as his prime minister. The country's Jews also benefited from the new atmosphere of religious openness: Ismail encouraged the Jewish Egyptian playwright Yacoub Sanoo'a by praising him as "Egypt's Molière." Religious emancipation, the celebration of Egypt's ancient heritage, and the project of building an Egyptian state went hand in hand.

No wonder, then, that educated Copts embraced ancient Egypt, even though the Christian Bible is scarcely kinder about it than the Koran. They created a Rameses social club and a journal named *Pharaoh*. There were even efforts to revive Coptic as an everyday language. Vansleb had written in the 1670s that he had "had the satisfaction of seeing the man with whom the Coptic language wholly shall die out." Now, at the start of the twentieth century, a Coptic antiquarian named Claudius Labib insisted that his children speak the language at home. A Coptic Museum opened in 1908 to celebrate the Egyptian cultural achievements of the post-pharaonic age.

By 1919 Copts were at least as well off as their Muslim countrymen: they owned 20 percent of the country's agricultural land, according to a British estimate, which also assessed that this was well above their proportion of the population. The prime minister that year, Youssef Wahba, was a Copt (the third Christian to serve in that position). But by this time the political context had changed from Ismail's day. The government was dominated behind the scenes by Britain—which had become Egypt's biggest creditor, and then effectively its administrator, when Ismail's ambitious spending plans had sunk his country into debt. As well as featuring in the government, the Copts were also active alongside Muslims in the burgeoning movement for Egyptian independence from British control: demonstrators gathered in Tahrir Square in 1919 under the banner of a conjoined crescent and cross. When the Egyptian nationalist Wafd Party, led by a visionary leader called Saad Zaghloul, put together a delegation of seven Egyptian representatives to go to the British ambassador and demand independence, Zaghloul was careful to include a Copt. A Christian priest even preached from the pulpit of the country's premier mosque, al-Azhar, in 1919, for the first time in history. "If the British stay in Egypt under the pretense of protecting Copts," the priest, Father Sargious, declared, "let all Copts die and Muslims live free."

In Cairo during my visit in 2011 there were reminders of that time. Near Tahrir Square, opposite an antique bookstore whose outer wall was blotched with bloodstains, a man wearing a shirt that said "Guns don't kill. Governments do" was selling T-shirts marked with a crescent and cross. I saw that symbol painted on walls across the city. By evoking the spirit of 1919, the people who painted it were stressing national unity in the face of those who wanted to foment differences between Christians and Muslims.

This crescent and cross symbol, which I photographed in 2011, was in the strongly Muslim area of Cairo around the al-Azhar mosque. It symbolized the desire of Christians and Muslims to overcome their differences and work together for freedom. Photo by the author

Not all of the Egyptian politicians who called for independence in the 1920s and 1930s, though, were as open-minded as Zaghloul. In 1928, a group of laborers at the British military camp in the port city of Ismailiyya visited Hassan al-Banna, a well-educated opponent of secularism, and told him: "We see that the Arabs and the Muslims have no status and no dignity. They are not more than mere hirelings belonging to the foreigners." They took an oath to be soldiers for Islam, but al-Banna chose for the group a more innocuous title: the Muslim Brotherhood. Among the first demands that the Brotherhood made of the Egyptian government was that it ban alcohol and crack down on prostitution, which had become rife during World War I, when foreign soldiers were stationed in Egypt. The Brotherhood called for the British to withdraw from Egypt. But it also had larger ambitions: to unify all Muslim lands under a caliph who would impose strict Islamic law.

Coptic politician William Makram Ebeid tried to find common ground with the Brotherhood and was the only politician to protest when the Egyptian government dissolved the movement in 1948. He was also the only politician to attend Hassan al-Banna's funeral after the latter's killing by government agents the year after. In return, the Brotherhood claimed to have no quarrel with Copts. In practice, however, the new Islamist movements wanted to undermine their secular rivals. Attacking the Copts, who often played a part in the country's secular parties, helped them in this mission. In the 1940s, Islamist rhetoric led to church burnings, beatings of priests, and attacks on Coptic ceremonies. In the meantime, al-Banna's emphasis on the struggle against Christian foreigners inevitably colored the Brotherhood's discourse about Christianity in general. The Brotherhood did not share Ismail's enthusiasm for Egypt as a country in which all citizens would be equal. Instead, al-Banna was proud of Egypt principally because of its historical role in defending Islam against the Crusaders, which was not a vision of history that offered much real dignity to the Copts. The movement offered Copts a position of peaceful inferiority, not the equality offered by some secular nationalists.

When independence truly came, it brought to power neither Zaghloul-style liberals nor Islamists. In 1952 Farouq, Mohammad Ali's great-great-grandson, was deposed by a group of previously unknown army officers. One of these, Mohammad Neguib, became president. Four years later he was removed by Colonel Gamal Abdel Nasser, who then achieved the withdrawal of all British forces from the country and ruled Egypt from 1956 until 1970. Though he rid Egypt of all foreign control, the title of his biography is not *The First Egyptian* but *The Last Arab*. The author was referring to the fact that Nasser saw himself as an Arab, not an Egyptian: he wanted the Arabic-speaking peoples, living in disparate countries stretching from Marrakesh to Baghdad, to unite, rise up against their colonial overlords, and form one nation.

Nasser was not so much interested in Egypt as such. Indeed, for more than a decade the name "Egypt" vanished from the map, as Nasser changed the country's name to the United Arab Republic and sought to unify it with Syria. He also redistributed Egypt's land, crushing the old feudal order. This affected both Muslim and Coptic landowners, but since the Coptic lay elite had done well under the monarchy, it hit them particularly hard: one estimate suggests that the Copts lost 75 percent of their wealth and property. The upper-class Coptic laymen who were impoverished by this measure had often been the community's political leaders, and so the community was not only poorer but also less influential. The eighteen-member Revolutionary Command Council, which administered Egypt after the Revolution, did not include a single Christian. Nonetheless, while Nasser lived, violence against Copts was almost unheard of. That was in part thanks to his fearsome security services, which repressed Islamist movements ruthlessly, and to his own considerable popularity. Nasser never expressed any religious prejudice— Arab nationalism could have room for Christians as well as Muslims (and indeed, some of its early proponents were Syrian Christians). Nasser had a close relationship with the Coptic Pope, and made gestures toward the Copts such as attending the inauguration of their new cathedral in Cairo.

For one other community, Nasser's advent marked the beginning of the end. In 1956, after Israel joined with Britain and France in a secret conspiracy to destabilize Egypt and seize the Suez Canal, Nasser stripped many Jewish Egyptians of their citizenship. He went on to expel thousands from the country, and nationalize—that is, confiscate—their businesses. Judaism was the oldest religion in the country: there had been Jews in Egypt since at least the seventh century BC. "We had Jewish neighbors when I was a child," a Christian Egyptian doctor named Amin Makram Ebeid told me in his flat overlooking the Nile. "A Mr. Shoheit and his family. He told my father that he had found a husband for my sister. And then a few months later he disappeared. All of them disappeared. We suspected what had happened"— they were deported—"but none of us had the courage to ask, because then we would be implicated ourselves as Christians." The doctor sighed. "How can someone's belief within four walls affect his acceptance by the society?" He had hung a painting of a man in a Jewish prayer shawl in a spot where it would be the first thing a visitor would see, in the hope that it would shock people out of their prejudices. There is still one synagogue in Cairo, but only ten Jews remain in the whole country.

After Nasser's death the Copts faced a new challenge. Church burnings had been rare before Nasser and unheard of during his time in power. When Anwar Sadat became president in 1970, this changed. Sadat styled himself the "pious president" and, to outflank his left-wing critics, allied himself to the Islamists. Extremist gangs were allowed wide license to operate in Egypt's universities, where they attacked Sadat's leftist critics and also enforced their own version of shari'a law on campuses. In 1972, an arson attack on a Coptic church marked the start of a new era of sectarian violence.

Meanwhile, the government's approach to education was undergoing a wider change. Youssef Sidhom, editor of the Coptic newspaper *Watani* ("My Country"), recalled that period when he spoke to me in his office in downtown Cairo. "After the Islamization of Egypt in the late 1970s, Christian history was taken off the syllabus. There was pressure from those who had taken over education. Coptic history was stolen." In the new textbooks only 4 of 240 pages were given to Egypt's Christian past. The Koran replaced secular poetry in Arabic language classes, marginalizing the cultural heritage that Christians and Muslims had had in common. The state television networks allotted Islamic religious programs thirty hours a week but Christian programs only one time slot a year (at Christmas). In a thoughtful article for the Egyptian newspaper *al-Ahram* in May 2013, education expert Kamal Mougheeth recollected that in the 1980s, one of his schoolbooks declared that the Bible was fabricated. His Christian schoolmates were forced to memorize verses from the Koran.

George Ishak, a veteran opponent of the Egyptian military government, also pinpointed to me Sadat's time as the pivotal moment. A man in his sixties, he became famous ten years ago for his outspoken protests against the rule of President Hosni Mubarak. I met him in an artists' café called Groppi's. He was clearly popular with the clientele: while we talked, we were interrupted every two minutes by someone coming up and shaking his hand, or by his getting up and greeting someone at another table.

"Sectarianism in Egypt started with Sadat," Ishak said, in between these encounters. "When Sadat said, 'I am a Muslim and this is a Muslim state,' it frightened people beyond the literal meaning of the words. Whether it was good fortune or bad, it happened that the head of the Coptic Church at the time, a man called Shenouda"—he meant Patriarch Shenouda III, the man who consecrated St. Mark's Church—"was charismatic. He drew people into the church, and all their life came to be lived within the church." I nodded. I had seen the aftereffects of this at the church in Shubra, which had been so much more than just a place to pray. Shenouda had reformed the Coptic Church, giving power to a new generation of educated and dynamic clergy; he and his contemporaries had inspired a surge in monastic vocations.

"Then the tension began. Priests demonstrated when they were forbidden to build churches." An old Egyptian law required Copts to receive a permit before building a new church, or even restoring an existing one. Sadat's government was slow to grant these permits, causing great frustration among Copts. In 1981, a dispute over a plan to build a Coptic church led to bloody clashes in a poor and overcrowded suburb of Cairo: seventeen people were killed in the worst incident yet of Coptic-Muslim violence. Patriarch Shenouda III led a nonviolent protest over what he saw as government failure to protect the Copts; Islamists accused Shenouda of seeking a Coptic state, said that only an Islamic state would stop Coptic aggression, and called for a complete ban on new churches. Sadat responded by putting both Shenouda and a number of Muslim clerics under house arrest. Later that year, however, Sadat was assassinated by Islamic extremists angered by his peace deal with Israel. (The man who fired the fatal shots cried as he did so, "I have killed Pharaoh!") Hosni Mubarak replaced Sadat and ostensibly built a much better relationship with the Coptic Church, granting permits for church building and making Coptic Christmas into a public holiday. But Ishak saw things differently. "Mubarak found," Ishak went on, "that he could use this issue to distract attention. The security forces made tactical alliances with the Salafis." The Salafis were just as Islamist as the Brotherhood but stayed away from politics.

The security forces grew hugely in the face of the terrorist threat. Between 1974 and 2004, as attacks on Copts and on the police themselves increased, the Egyptian police force grew from 150,000 to 1.7 million men. Yet the Copts remained unequal. There are no Coptic university presidents or heads of public companies. One Egyptian banker, a Muslim, told me that the attitude toward the Copts was one "that you might have toward a younger brother—a half brother, really. Someone you know is there, but you'd really rather he wasn't." Nor did Mubarak's government completely protect the Copts. In January 2000, for example, sixteen Christians were killed in the village of al-Kosheh. The longest sentence handed down for the killings was two years, though one man was given an additional ten-year sentence for possessing an unlicensed firearm.

Yet the Coptic Church never confronted Mubarak in the way that it had briefly confronted Sadat. Nor did it call for democracy in Egypt, or sanction participation of Copts in the Tahrir Square demonstrations in 2011. It apparently felt that the alternative to Mubarak—the Muslim Brotherhood—would be worse. The Brotherhood did little to calm Coptic fears when it called in the 1990s for Copts to be shut out of senior positions in the army or in 2007 for the Egyptian constitution to specify that only a Muslim could be president. In 2006 the Brotherhood's supreme guide, Mehdi Akef, was quoted as saying, "At-tuz fi Masr," meaning roughly "To hell with Egypt"—apparently because, as an Islamist, he rejected the nation-state in favor of the restoration of an Islamic caliphate.

For some Copts the answer was emigration, made easier for them by their relatively high levels of education and a favorable attitude from Western governments. Between 1993 and 1997, 76 percent of requests from Egyptians for permanent emigration to the United States, Canada, Australia, and New Zealand were made by Copts. Others retreated further into the church, investing their energy in making it into a more effective and all-encompassing community. I met a Copt who had been wounded in a protest against church burning, during which Copts had thrown stones and the security forces opened fire. "As long as you feel threatened by the others," he said, still nursing his leg, "your identity will be strong." Nor is it only Christians who have come to prefer religious institutions over secular ones. Gallup reported in 2013 that 92 percent of all Egyptians, Muslim or Christian, had confidence in their religious institutions. No other institution came close. Put simply, Patriarch Shenouda and his Muslim equivalents have, owing to their acumen and dedication, acquired a great deal of influence. Some hard-line clerics have used this for ill. The overall result is that Muslims and Christians have had less and less to unite them.

All of this I learned in Cairo. But I knew that if I wanted to understand Egypt, and particularly to understand Christians in Egypt and how they related to their Muslim neighbors, then I would have to go to the place where most of Egypt's Copts originated: south of Cairo, where the Nile Valley winds through hundreds of miles of unremitting desert. The people of this area (which is called the Sa'eed, or Upper Egypt—the same name that it had in ancient times) were slower to convert to Islam, and as late as the 1920s, 80 percent of Egypt's Christians lived in the Sa'eed.

Although great numbers of Copts have since migrated northward—one scholar suggested to me that more than half of the Copts now live in Cairo and other northern cities—the Sa'eed is still their heartland. At least a quarter of the inhabitants of Minya city, for instance, 140 miles south of Cairo, are Copts—the largest proportion of Copts of any city in Egypt. The wider governorate is poor, with over 80 percent unemployment; more than a third of the governorate's population is illiterate (though the figures are better in the city). The governorate is also where the greatest number of clashes have taken place between Christians and Muslims—perhaps as much as 65 percent of Egypt's sectarian violence has happened there. I decided that to understand the Copts—their history, their beliefs, their future—I needed to get a better sense of the place. I did this in 2012, as Egypt's first democratic election moved into its second round. Soon after my visit, Egyptians would choose between the two remaining candidates: Ahmad Shafiq, a Jesuit-educated Muslim who had served under President Mubarak, and Mohammed Morsi, of the Muslim Brotherhood. (Minya was one of the most pro-Morsi areas in Egypt, giving him 64 percent of the vote, with 36 percent going to Shafiq.)

Cairo's main train station—called Ramses because a statue of the pharaoh once sat there—was first built in the 1850s, when Ismail commissioned the first railway in Africa to take cotton from Cairo up to Alexandria for export by sea. It was also the place where in 1923 Egyptian feminist Huda al-Shaarawi, returning from a conference in Europe, removed her veil in sight of the astonished crowd who had come to greet her—a step that inspired later generations of Arab feminists. I hurried through Moorish arches and past walls with faience tiles to buy my ticket. There was a special platform for the Sa'eed, I found, and a scattering of people waiting there to board the train. In a small bookstore on the platform was a display of books, several of which advertised with lurid pictures their subject matter: the tricks used by practitioners of black magic and how to combat them. I remembered the Salafi boys who thought they had found spell-casting equipment in the burned church's basement.

Soon the train began trundling slowly south, through Cairo's suburbs of cheap brick apartment buildings. At a tree-lined station in one of Cairo's poorest suburbs, boys came onto the train to sell scented tissues and cheap candy. About half an hour into the journey the train track was joined by a narrow, clogged-up canal running parallel to it. Eventually we left the city and headed into the Nile Valley's green fields, stopping frequently at one small town after another. Always the canal ran alongside the railway. I saw people wash dishes in it, and their clothes. In the evening, we reached Minya. As I emerged onto the platform an elderly porter grabbed hold of my bag and, despite my protests, held on to it grimly and carried it over the railway bridge.

There was one major hotel in the city, a huge concrete building called the Akhenaten, and I checked in there for the night. My room had fittings that had been elegant once—the 1970s, I reckoned. No tourists were staying there. The only people in the lobby were its staff, smoking cigarettes. I talked to them for a while, and they explained to me how superior the people of Minya were to those elsewhere. "You can't trust people in Cairo, and they're not as friendly as us," said one of them to me. "And if you go further south from here, to Assyut, the people there are too hot-headed. But here in Minya, the people are in between the two. They're just right."

I found as I walked about the town that Minya was indeed friendlier than Cairo and, in its own quiet way, beautiful, facing as it did the Nile and low sandy cliffs beyond. A small riverside park was full of families, with some people playing football, others smoking the *shisha* water-pipe. On a boat moored by the riverside a wedding party was in full swing, bride and groom dancing to the sound of a popular Egyptian song. The city's squares were full of people enjoying the evening breeze, men and women sitting together. Most of the women were unveiled, an almost certain sign—in this conservative city—that they were Christians. (In Cairo there are Muslim women who go unveiled; I never saw one in Minya.) This being a Sunday evening, I guessed that these couples had probably just come out of the churches and Christian community centers on the nearby streets. When I went to a roadside stall to get a glass of orange juice, a nun was on line ahead of me, ordering crushed sugar cane.

My friends at the hotel put me in touch with a local driver to take me to the villages and monasteries in the countryside. The next morning, as I waited for him, I walked through the park again. Across the river I could see

Christian monasteries flourish in today's Egypt, partly as a result of Christians' retreat into their own community. The Deir Abu Fana, dating back to the fourth century and shown here in 2012, is expanding rapidly. Photo by the author

an ox pulling a plow in the fields. The city's gentle nighttime revelry had left a trail of litter in the park, and a pickup truck came to collect it. A veiled girl—from a nearby village, I guessed—threw bags of garbage onto the truck and then pulled herself up after them. Her feet on the bags, she sang and laughed as the truck drove away.

When the driver arrived he was pleased to hear that we would be going to see some of the local Coptic monasteries. He was a Copt himself, and his name was George. (Although St. Mark is claimed as the founder of the Coptic Church, children are more commonly named after St. George—and the image of him plunging a lance into a dragon is a popular one in churches and homes, just as once ancient Egyptians used to depict the god Horus driving his spear into a hippopotamus.) "Tourists are never interested in Coptic sites," he complained. "They only ever want to see things from ancient Egypt. I tell them about our churches and they never want to visit them." And yet the monasteries are in certain ways modern-day versions of the ancient temples. In the early years of Christianity, monasticism was solitary: men went into a remote place, often in the desert, to pray. It was in Egypt in around AD 320 that St. Pachomius founded the first community of Christian monks. He intended it for those who could not manage the rigors of living alone. But the monasteries took a familiar pattern: a community of pious men, living in a walled enclosure and farming nearby fields, worshiping in chapels within the enclosure to which pilgrims came as visitors—it was the system by which Egyptian temples had always operated. Many early monasteries had points of resemblance to the temples in the way that their high walls sloped inward and in the carvings on their entrances.

George showed me pictures of local monasteries. One particular picture caught my eye. Glass cases, labeled to show that they contained the bodies of Christian martyrs who died under Diocletian, contained partly mummified corpses. These, with teeth flashing through black flesh twisted in pain, were reverently dressed in silver tinsel and wedding costumes as a symbol of the eternal happiness their sacrifice had won them. At first I found the pictures shocking, even grotesque. But they were, I realized, the expression of a profound and uncompromising faith. The Copts' belief in martyrdom has helped them endure difficult times. George and I drove past fields with piles of reaped wheat and others where the sugar cane stood tall. George pointed to the sugar cane. "That's where the gunmen used to hide," he said, "back when the troubles happened here. I had a friend who was a policeman, and that was how he was shot." Between 1992 and 1998 a militant Islamist group called al-Gama'a al-Islamiya operated in Minya and other towns in southern Egypt, attacking both the security forces and local Christian civilians. Now, in 2011, the Gama'a had formed a political party and made an effort to show that it had changed: it persuaded five Copts to join, called for a free market economy, and won one of Minya's sixteen parliamentary seats.

The journey took us along country roads where there was little other traffic. A man on a donkey, pulling a cart full of alfalfa, passed us; next came a wedding party in a bus, lively music pumping out from a stereo. "They are coming from the monastery," said George, referring to the Abu Fana monastery, our first destination. "They went to get a *baraka* from the monks before the wedding." *Baraka* means "blessing" in Arabic, and was a word I found myself using often during this visit to Minya. When we drew up to the monastery I found that it was also a *baraka* simply to meet a priest or monk: "I came to see you, to take a *baraka* from you," the young men would say when they came to greet the monks in their trailing black robes and tight-fitting black caps ornamented with gold crosses. There were plenty of young men visiting the monastery. Some were more respectful than others. One of them, when he thought he was unobserved, went to sit in the abbot's throne in the monastery's chapel—he was drawn to it by the carving of a lion on its arms, which was the symbol of St. Mark the Evangelist.

The monastery, fronted by a high wall and gate, sits on the very edge of the Nile Valley, where the valley meets the desert. Some think there may have been an old temple on the site; the nearby town of Hor was likely named after the god Horus. An Egyptian named Abu Fana came to this place in the fourth century AD, giving away all his money on the way there. Known for his asceticism (one of his miracles, according to tradition, is to have gone without food for thirty-seven days), he raised the dead and read minds, and spent eighteen years on a pillar. By the Middle Ages the monastery had fallen into neglect. Only two monks were there, according to al-Maqrizi, an Arab scholar of the fifteenth century.

Now there are more than two dozen monks, many of them young, a product of the Coptic Church's renaissance. One of them, who was looking after the monastery shop—which sold crucifixes and religious posters—told me he had been a medical student before entering the monastery. He gave me a *baraka* in the form of a loaf of bread elaborately carved with holes in the pattern of sacred symbols and Coptic writing (Egyptians in pharaonic times, as we can see from tomb paintings, sometimes decorated loaves by perforating them with holes). The life of a Coptic monk consists of praying for hours communally—including every day at 3:00 A.M.—praying alone, and sometimes engaging in tough manual labor.

George introduced me to the abbot, and we sat together in a hot, rather dusty room packed with sofas. They served me tea and an endless supply of saccharine soft drinks. Later we walked out into the sunlight. "There, in that tower, is where the monks used to hide if bandits came into the monastery," the abbot told me. Similar problems persist. A monk came up to us and, on an order from the abbot, he reluctantly lifted his sleeve: his upper arm was shriveled where the bone had been broken. A few years before, he had

This bread, inscribed with Coptic letters, is given by monks as a blessing to visitors. Ancient Egyptian wall paintings show that the custom of decorating bread in this way goes back many thousands of years. Photo by the author

been captured by a Bedouin group who lived nearby. Though the kidnapping was related to a land dispute—the monastery wanted to build on land the Bedouin used for grazing—it turned sectarian. His captors had told him, the monk said, to spit on the cross. When he refused, they broke his arm. "When we found him, he had been starved of food and water and could not move," the abbot said. This particular monk was a talented artist who had painted many of the monastery's murals. It had taken him months to relearn how to paint.

BACK IN MINYA THAT EVENING, I moved out of my hotel and into a boat on the Nile, which turned out to be run by a Coptic Protestant group in the city. (As well as those Copts who joined the Catholic Uniate Church, there were others who joined various Protestant denominations during the past 150 years, and many villages around Minya had Protestant and Catholic churches as well as Coptic Orthodox ones.) The water lapped all night against its side, inches from my head. A year after my visit, the houseboat would be burned by a mob of Islamists protesting the overthrow of President Mohammed Morsi, and in the boat next to it, two men, a Christian and a Muslim, would be burned alive—while other Muslims formed human chains to protect Christian churches in the city. The rampage would infamously be punished with 529 death sentences, given not for the burning of churches so much as for the killing of a policeman in the course of the riots.

I had persuaded a Coptic priest to show me around his parish the next day. Father Yoannis lived in a top-floor apartment in a simple building just down the road from his church, in a village called Qufada, several miles from Minya. George drove me to see him. We all sat in his kitchen, and I nibbled at a piece of slightly stale and very sweet cream cake that the priest had bought to mark the occasion. I discovered that his father and grandfather had been priests before him. He had a natural gift for reaching out to others, and a distinctively Egyptian way with flattery. He asked George where he was from, and when George replied Minya, the priest said what turned out to be his standard compliment: "Minya? The people from that place are the *best* people."

Of forty thousand inhabitants in Qufada, more than 90 percent were Muslim. The mayor (*umda* is the Egyptian word), however, was Christian. His family had once owned the village's land, until Nasser's government confiscated and redistributed most of it. Although now much poorer, the family was still respected. "Back in 1940," the priest said, "soldiers came from the government to tell the *umda* that he had to punish the local people because they had failed to pay their taxes. But instead of punishing them, he paid their taxes himself." The villagers never forgot the incident and had been happy for the family to keep the title of *umda*—even though the family was Christian and mostly lived elsewhere.

"Hardly any of them live here now," the priest told us as he drove us around the town in his car. "The old house is almost empty. The present *umda* is a dentist in the city, and it is his sister who lives in the house. The younger generation are selling off their land. Our problem as a community," he added, honking his horn at someone he recognized, "is that we leave the villages and don't come back. Muslims go away for work but they keep their houses in the village. Christians go to the cities for higher education and stay there. I end up seeing my old parishioners around once a year, at weddings in Cairo."

The *umda*'s white-walled old house stood in a small unpaved courtyard set back from the main street. Father Yoannis's church was next to it, and I found a seat in the back of the nave while Father Yoannis gave a talk to the local Christian children. They sat attentively, girls separate from boys, while he told them about the monks at one of Egypt's oldest monasteries, who were so holy that they could fly. And he instructed the children on how to behave themselves in church. "You should know that this is a holy place," he said. "When you come in here, the angels are watching you. So behave with respect!"

The village had never seen sectarian violence, and one of the reasons became clear to me when Father Yoannis took me to see his friend Sheikh Hassan, who occupied the position of Muslim registrar of marriages—a position of religious and social authority. The priest pulled into the driveway of a large and well-appointed house and parked his battered car next to an expensive sedan. The owner's wife came out and greeted the priest warmly, then ushered us into a small conservatory-like room. The registrar was a powerful figure in the village: out of respect, he was called a sheikh. Unlike the *umda*, he was very much present in the village's daily life. He liked Father Yoannis and had helped him in various ways, most recently protecting the church from a gang of criminals who—taking advantage of the collapse of law and order that ensued when the Mubarak government fell—had come to plunder it.

The good relationship between the Christian priest and the Muslim official was crucial to keeping peace in the village. With the impoverishment of the Christian upper classes by Nasser's land reforms, and then their departure for the cities, the Coptic Church was the only institution that could mediate on behalf of their community in a country where strength and power matter more than legal rights and justice. And, seeing Father Yoannis's good humor, simplicity of life, and connection with his people, I found it easy to understand why people would trust him. But the more that people invested in religious institutions to represent them, the less they would invest their time and money in other institutions—political parties, trade unions, or secular social groups—that were shared between people of different faiths. The police, meanwhile, preferred not to intervene in disputes, even violent ones, if it meant making themselves unpopular. So if the religious leaders could broker peace between Muslims and Christians, religious strife could be avoided. Otherwise, the communities had almost nothing that would stop an incident from escalating into bloodshed.

"We in the Sa'eed are a fiery people," said George afterward as we set off again in Father Yoannis's little car. "People are friendly one minute and then they may be violent the next. It just takes a small thing to make the difference." Father Yoannis gave an example from a nearby village a year or so before. A local Christian couple had married their daughter to an acceptable Coptic husband, but without their knowing it she fell in love with a Muslim man and had an affair with him. Both took drugs. When the parents were away, the daughter used their house for trysts. One evening, the parents came back unexpectedly and found their daughter in bed with her lover, both in a stupor. The mother did not hesitate: she strangled them.

She spent that night in the kitchen, chopping up the body of the dead man and stuffing it into a plastic bag. She told her husband to dump it somewhere in the desert. He chose a bad spot, dropping it in an area that turned out to be an archaeological site. The lights of his car were noticed and guards came to investigate. He escaped, but the bag was found and its ghastly contents uncovered.

The guilty parents knew it wouldn't be long before they would be identified. The dead man's family was looking for him, and their own daughter had disappeared; people would soon understand what had transpired. So they fled. The dead man's family took revenge in the old way. Seven people from the guilty family were murdered before the blood feud was considered settled. And then, said the priest, the guilty couple returned. "And at the wake for one of the people who had died, the mother of the murdered Muslim man turned up. She said to the couple, 'If you had only told us what you had done, we would have thanked you for killing him. We would have killed him ourselves, if we had known.'" But the insult of leaving his corpse unburied had to be avenged.

Love and death have a long association in Egypt. Near Minya I saw the tomb of Isidora, daughter of a pagan priest under the Ptolemies, who died when she swam across the Nile for a clandestine nighttime meeting with her lover, whom her father had forbidden her to see. The tomb became a pilgrimage site for young lovers. They face even greater obstacles today: love affairs between Christians and Muslims are frequent causes of violence between the two communities. Egyptians are not often left free to choose whom they marry, and under both Islam and Egyptian law marriage is not an equal relationship. Islam does not allow a Christian man to marry a Muslim woman, and in Egyptian law the children of a couple take their father's faith, not their mother's. So Christian women who marry Muslim men will be unable to bring up their children as Christian. Most of those who marry Muslims are ostracized by their families; many convert to Islam. A Coptic bishop estimated in 2007 that between five thousand and ten thousand Copts convert to Islam every year, and Coptic priests have separately commented that the large majority of these converts are girls under the age of twenty-five. The fear of losing their daughters to Muslim suitors is yet another reason for Copts to build social networks that do not cross the religious divide.

Other conversions have happened because of the Coptic Church's almost total rejection of divorce: Pope Shenouda tightened the rules until only adultery could be a basis for ending a marriage. Copts who want to leave their husbands or wives for any other reason must first leave the church. Some join another Christian denomination; others become Muslims. Some of this last group try afterward to return to the Coptic Church, but by doing so they risk sparking conflict, for an apostate from Islam must, according to the shari'a, be put to death. In such disputes, religion becomes a way for husbands or wives to rally a wider community to their side. Abeer Fakhry, for example, a Coptic woman living in Minya, fell in love with a Muslim man and left her husband for him in 2011. She was traced by her family and detained by the Coptic Church, which tried to persuade her to return to her husband. It was rumored that she had already converted to Islam, however (a rumor she subsequently confirmed), and so her detention provoked riots and church burnings by Muslim fundamentalists and a gunfight that caused twelve deaths. In Atfih, a suburb of

Coptic priests remain significant figures in their communities. By the law of their church, they all must marry. Some of the children here are from priests' families. Photo by the author

Cairo, a love affair between a Coptic man and a Muslim girl sparked riots in which, again, a church was burned.

External factors could spark conflict, too. A few months earlier, Father Yoannis said, a television station run from Cyprus by a Coptic priest called Zakaria Butros had become famous for its attacks on Islam. At the peak of its infamy in Egypt, Coptic priests had experienced exceptional hostility from local Muslims. A group of Muslim women, for instance, had spat at Yoannis. "People who broadcast hate against Islam, insults to the Koran and who burn Korans," he said, "this all has very serious, bitter consequences for us."

———————

I ASKED FATHER YOANNIS whether Copts ever lived in entirely Coptic villages. It was unusual, he replied, because so few Christians in Egypt practice agriculture. Two villages that he knew of were entirely Coptic, though, and he agreed to take us to one of them, Deir al-Jarnoos. George was a little doubtful. The people in Deir al-Jarnoos, he said, were "toughs." "Nobody gives them any trouble," he said. "In fact, all the villages round about are scared of them. When they gather as a group and come out of their village, everybody else runs away." Father Yoannis knew how to handle them, though. As he drove us in, he rolled down the window and called out endearments to every man, woman, and child he could see: "How are you, honey? How beautiful you look!" He had an effusive style—and perhaps wanted to make sure that people would look at him and see his clerical dress and the cross hanging from the rearview mirror. Cars carrying strangers were not a common sight in this place.

The state had no presence inside the town. In this, Deir al-Jarnoos was a Christian equivalent of militantly Muslim towns of southern Egypt that the police never dare to enter. And just as those towns (and sometimes suburbs of Cairo) can enforce their own rules without much regard for Cairo, so Deir al-Jarnoos was building a huge church that dwarfed the humble houses that crowded around it. On the roof of the church, men in gray *jelaba*s were constructing domes and towers to make it stand even higher on the horizon. We climbed up to meet them, and Father Yoannis asked them where they were from. Asyut, they said, referring to a city another hour or so south. "Ah, Asyut," he said. "The *best* people are from Asyut." We climbed back down and inspected the old stone church next door. A villager pulled the wooden lid off a well just inside the church door and lowered a metal cup by a rope into the water below. He invited me to drink. It was a holy well, he said; when Jesus was brought to Egypt as a baby, his family had drunk from it. He hoisted the cup up and I sipped the cool water.

THE FOLLOWING DAY George came with me when I went to see a whole group of Coptic priests, courtesy of Father Yoannis—who also came. We met in a village not far from Minya, in a house attached to the village church. A black-bearded man named Father Mousa was our host, and a friend of his called Younus sat with us, too. Younus remarked, "The older generation treat Christians like brothers. Most of my friends are Muslims. They come to our festivals, they pray in the church. There is a priest here who exorcises demons; he is very popular with Muslims as well as Christians. But then the Salafis come from the universities. It's the Salafis and the Muslim Brotherhood who mistreat Christians. They tell Muslims not to greet Christians in the street. And the new generation, those between eighteen and twenty-seven years old, they are a bad generation. They have had very bad teachers. It started with Sadat." There was a new tradition, he added, according to which Muslim boys would hit Christians on the last day of a school term. "The teachers don't seem to encourage it," Younus said, "so far as we can see. Soldiers used to go to the school to stop it, but they couldn't be everywhere. And after the government fell, there were no rules at all. No fear of soldiers, no fear of guards, no fear of God."

Education was the problem, Mousa agreed. He had served in the army, three decades earlier or so, alongside a man from northern Egypt. Muslims and Christians mostly go to school together, in state-run schools (there are Christian-run schools that were set up by Western missionaries in the nineteenth century, but they are too expensive for poorer Copts to afford; they cater to upper-middle-class Copts and Muslims). Because Christians had historically lived mostly in the south, this northern man had never met one before. When he saw the cross that Mousa was wearing, he shrank away. "What is this cross?" he asked Mousa, and added, "I was taught that it was a demonic symbol." In a Pew poll in 2011–12, only 22 percent of Egyptian Muslims said they knew anything about Christian beliefs or practices—the schools' syllabus does not provide an adequate understanding of religions other than Islam—and 96 percent thought that Christians would go to hell.

Despite their stories, this group of Copts still had great affection for their country. Mousa's nine-year-old daughter was sitting in a corner of the room, writing on a piece of paper; when I looked at what she had written it was in English, in pens of different colors: "Egypt is my mother. Egypt is my blood. I love you EGYPT." But Copts were leaving Egypt, I said to George as he drove me back to Minya one last time. "Everyone would go if they had the chance," George said. "Muslims are a bit better off than Christians because they can work in Saudi Arabia. And security is a special problem for Christians, but it's bad for everyone. I have a good place and a nice job, but I'd give it up tomorrow to go to America and work in a restaurant, if it would provide my son with a good safe future." Emigration to the West is the Copts' preferred way out. In the United States there are more than two hundred Coptic churches and an estimated three-quarters of a million Copts.

The next day I took the slow train back to Cairo. There was one more thing for me to do before leaving Egypt. I got on the city's Metro and returned to the church of St. Thérèse, fourteen years after my last visit. I arrived about halfway through a service. There was Father Paul saying Mass, and two men I knew, Ashraf and Magdi, were acting as deacons—clashing cymbals at the holiest moments, just as their forebears had done for thousands of years. I caught up with the three of them after the service as they walked across to the presbytery. Father Paul had a slight stoop, and Ashraf's hair was white, but they remembered me. Where was Samih? I asked. He had gone to America, they said; he went to study and ended up staying. What had happened to Maggie? She had married a French man and gone to Paris. Where was Wael? He had followed his dream of becoming a fashion model in Beirut. It was not the Copts who would lose from all this outflow of talent, I thought: it was Egypt.

I went back to the church. A woman in a black Islamic *niqab*, with only her eyes showing, had waited for the Mass to end before coming forward from her seat at the back. She lit one of the thin wax candles that stood in a tray of sand by a pillar, then slowly descended the steps that led down to the crypt chapel. I followed, to say goodbye to the saint whose effigy lay down there. As we stood in front of it, the Muslim woman leaned down and touched St. Thérèse's side.

7

Kalasha

IN SUMMER 2007 I WAS ON A FLIGHT to Kabul from Islamabad, which had meant several hours of sitting on my bags in Islamabad's departure terminal. It was easy to tell when foreigners were heading for Kabul: they were mostly burly, muscular characters with North Face backpacks. I was an exception—a very unmuscular diplomat headed for a year's assignment running the political team at the British embassy. The landscape I saw out of the plane's window looked as if it had been unchanged for centuries. "Mountains brown like snuff," one British traveler had called them, "ten-thousand-foot mounds with the track snaking its way through for mile on heavy mile." Looking closely, I could spot thin green threads between the hills, which were the valleys. Human habitation was not visible at all.

Gazing eastward, I saw high peaks rising sheer above the green valleys and the brown mountains, up to a height of twenty-four thousand feet. These were the Hindu Kush, a great mountain range that runs along the eastern borders of Tajikistan, Afghanistan, and Pakistan and separates those countries from China. They are really part of the Himalayas. Though they are called the "Roof of the World," it is more apt to think of them as a wall or a rampart: many times over, they have been the furthest point eastward that any people has reached. These mountains are to human cultures what coral reefs are to marine life: rich and diverse. In the Afghan section of the Hindu Kush, for example, in an area the size of New Jersey twenty indigenous and mutually unintelligible languages are spoken.

Alexander the Great reached these mountains but made no effort to cross them—thinking, perhaps, that they formed the very easternmost edge of the world. Their inhabitants taunted him, undaunted by the fact that he was the conqueror of Persia and ruler of the greatest empire the world had yet seen: to capture their inaccessible hideaways, they said, he would need "soldiers with wings." In one of these battles, Alexander was wounded in the shoulder by an arrow. The great commander had never lost a battle in the eight years since he had left his homeland in northern Greece. But these opponents, one of Alexander's chroniclers recorded, were the toughest fighters that he encountered in his entire Indian campaign. Alexander was so impressed that he married a local girl, Roxane ("the loveliest woman they had seen in Asia," his soldiers thought, with the exception only of the Persian empress).

Alexander was not the only conqueror to be withstood by the inhabitants of the Hindu Kush. The Arab armies that brought Islam to Afghanistan and northern India from the seventh century onward seem to have satisfied themselves with governing the rich lowland cities, and left the mountain people well alone. In the fourteenth century the brutal central Asian conqueror Tamerlane came close to conquering them: he fought his way up to the mountains' highest citadel. He could not maintain his control, however, and the local people never converted to Islam. Long after Tamerlane, the people of this place still offered sacrifices to their gods Imra and Gish, drank wine, and danced—women and men together—on wooden platforms they precariously rigged up in villages clinging limpet-like to the steep mountainsides. Their frightened Muslim neighbors called them *kafir*s (unbelievers), a label they appear to have accepted with relish at the time. The region where they lived was called Kafiristan.

Marco Polo did not care for them when he passed by in the thirteenth century. "They are idolaters and utter savages, living entirely by the chase and dressed in the skins of beasts," he wrote. "They are out and out bad." That was not wholly inaccurate—the Kafirs did indeed wear animal skins, and did not practice agriculture—but it is doubtful that Polo ever went near them. A long time passed after Alexander's visit before any Westerner looked on the Hindu Kush again.

———————

TWO CATHOLIC MISSIONARIES are believed to have entered Kafiristan at the end of the eighteenth century (based on stories told by its inhabitants to later visitors). One was killed by the Kafirs after being mistaken for an evil spirit; neither left any record of what they saw. In the 1820s, an Illinois-born, part-Hispanic, Irish-accented, Jesuit-educated Unitarian named Alexander Gardner traveled to central Asia in search of adventurous employment (he would become, for a time, a highwayman). In the words of his admiring biographer, his time in the region was marked by "ambuscades, fierce reprisals, hairbreadth escapes, episodes sometimes of brutality and cruelty wellnigh inconceivable, at other times of hearty charity and fidelity unto death." He took the local name Gordana Khan.

Gardner claimed to have entered Kafiristan twice, but his original record of the visit was lost when Sir Alexander Burnes, the British envoy to Kabul, who had the only copy, was killed by a mob at the start of the Afghan war (some at the time said that the mob were urged on by Afghan men whom the flamboyant Burnes had cuckolded). Burnes, cousin to the Scottish poet Robbie Burns, was a fluent Persian-speaker and did leave a record of testimony that he had received from Kafirs in Kabul, testimony that reveals their practices of burying their dead in coffins in the open air, selling off their girl children at a price determined by their size, and men reconciling blood feuds by sucking each other's nipples.

After Burnes's death many years passed in which Kafiristan went unvisited. It came to be called the "dark spot on the map of Asia"—a place that even the British imperial government of India, which sent spies to map out the most inaccessible and forbidden places on its borders, could not penetrate. At the end of the nineteenth century, the British planned to produce a gazetteer about Kafiristan, as they had for every other area that bordered India, but in this case—uniquely—they gave up.

Yet the British authorities had a strong interest in learning more about places such as Kafiristan, which abutted the northern edge of their British possessions: the biggest outside threat to their empire in India in the late nineteenth century was Russia, which was swallowing up central Asia and progressing south at a rapid pace. Scouting out the areas like Kafiristan that lay between the British and the Russians, with the goal of either winning them as allies or taking them as possessions, became a decades-long endeavor known as the Great Game. This was how a certain Lieutenant McNair, veteran of the second Anglo-Afghan War, found himself at the border of Kafiristan in 1883 during his official leave, darkening his skin with walnut juice and packing measuring instruments into a disguised medicine bag. He was transforming himself into "Sahib Gul McNair Hussain Shah" and hoping to enter Kafiristan in the company of two friends from a local Pashtun tribe. It must have given McNair pause to climb down a path lined with cairns of rocks that imperfectly covered the corpses of previous travelers murdered by the Kafirs, who were brutal in protecting their separateness. "Of all notable deeds," McNair recorded, "among Kafirs that of slaying a [Muslim] is reckoned first." The head of the victim would be put in a tall tree. Luckily, the two men who were with McNair belonged to a tribe that was regarded by the Kafirs with superstitious dread and whose members were therefore generally allowed to pass without harm.

McNair's visit to the Kafirs was very brief, and he discovered little. He estimated their number at two hundred thousand. He added that "their idols are legion, each valley, glen and dale has some that are unknown except in that particular locality: these are supposed to represent heroes who lived among them in days of old and who now as spirits intercede with Amra in their behalf." Their wine was weak, he thought, and they were amazed by the whisky he had thoughtfully brought with him. Most significant, he noted that they were "exceedingly well disposed towards the British . . . they would not hesitate to place their services, should occasion require, at our disposal." He recorded all of this in a pamphlet stamped "Secret" that he lodged with the intelligence division of the British War Office. As an appendix to it, he wrote a vocabulary list showing what he thought a future visitor might need to say, such as "It is steep and I may fall" and "I will offer a goat to Amra."

McNair's insights were shallow, and Kafiristan remained an enigma until the arrival of George Scott Robertson. Robertson, originally an army doctor, was from the wild and remote Orkney Islands. He perhaps found some echo of home in the "veritable faery country" that he spotted from a mountaintop during a posting as an administrator in the very northwestern tip of British India. "Stretching far into the nothingness beyond" was how he described this view of Kafiristan. From that moment, as he tells us in a book that he later wrote about his expedition, he was hooked. While resident as the British political officer in nearby Gilgit he kept an eye out for any Kafirs that he might find there, and eventually some visited the region and were introduced to him. At first he found their appearance off-putting, but then he saw that "the vile brown robe, trailing at the heels, conceals active and athletic forms: that the bland insinuating faces are keen and well-formed, and can give at times the bold fixed stare, or the wild, quick glance of the hawk; and that the men playing the part of cringing beggars . . . are capable at any moment of throwing off the mask of humility and assuming their proper characteristics." He discovered just how true that was when he managed to get permission not just to visit the Kafirs but to live among them for what turned out to be an entire year.

He discovered that the people called the Kafirs were divided into many tribes, whose languages and practices differed. The Kafirs' religion, moreover, had once been shared by other neighboring peoples who now lived under Muslim rule. One of these peoples was called the Kalasha. Unlike those Kafirs in the high mountains who had remained free, the Kalasha's lower-lying territory had been conquered by the *mehtar*s (princes) of Chitral, and they had been compelled to pay tribute in the form of forced labor. The Kalasha were of no use to Robertson, who wanted to find fighting men: they were "a thoroughly servile and degraded race," he sniffed. The tribe with which he chose to live, the Kam, were by contrast the most warlike of all the Kafirs. When trying one day to describe to the Kam what a fat man looked like, he had trouble getting them to understand. Few of them had ever seen such a thing. He met with success only when he talked to the local priest, who "for a long time was puzzled. My meaning dawned on him as he exclaimed, 'I remember killing a man near Asmar who was just as you describe—the word is *skior*.'"

The priest was not alone in being a killer. Blood feuds were not just an occasional mishap among the Kam; they were a way of life. The nearest Muslim villages were targets for murderous raids, often conducted for spoils (in such a poor community, it might be worth killing a man just to have his clothes) or as revenge for the steady encroachment of Muslim tribes on Kam land. Robertson made a list of the qualities that the Kam admired, at the top of which was an ability to kill—the other being "a good hill-man, ever ready to quarrel, and of an amorous disposition." The Kam often had vendettas against each other, but a neat custom enabled them to dodge these if they wished: a man needed only to pretend to hide from his would-be killer, who then pretended not to see him.

Members of a tribe who failed to kill the tribe's sworn enemies might be pelted with ashes by their own people. They might become the target of practical jokes, and at public banquets their wives would turn their faces away when serving them with food. *Gal,* shame, was a powerful motivation among the Kam. So was caste. Those who slipped down the social ladder might end up among the low-caste *brojan,* who were liable to be bought and sold like medieval serfs. On the other hand, a young man who had killed five victims was allowed to wear a blue scarf made from their clothing; Robertson saw quite a few of these during his visit. He also met Torag Merak, a man who appears to have walked straight out of a Victorian adventure novel. Merak, "the richest man in Kafiristan," came to see Robertson dressed in a bright red robe and carrying a bronze shield. "He had strong Semitic features, and his long locks, matted into rat's-tails, fell upon his gaudy shoulders, while occasionally he turned a proud glance to see if the stranger appreciated his grandeur."

Merak claimed to have killed more than a hundred people, many of them women and children, and to celebrate the fact, he had tied a small bell to the end of his staff. "In his gloomy eyes," Robertson wrote, "there is a world of pathos. They belie him utterly. He is at heart a howling savage, while in repose his features are those of a man saddened from gazing on the sufferings of a troubled world." Luckily for Robertson, being a Christian meant that he was regarded as a fellow non-Muslim and a kind of honorary Kafir. The British already had a reputation among the Kam, though of a rather peculiar kind: they told Robertson that Gish, their god of war, had gone to live in London.

Death, in any case, was hard to ignore among the Kam. All Kafirs buried their dead in the open air, probably just because it was usually too hard to dig in the frozen ground. The stink of the rotting bodies, Robertson commented, would waft through the village when the wind blew in the wrong direction. And when there was a funeral, it was marked with a dance—with the corpse propped up on a chair in the midst of the dancers.

Robertson's portrait was as unflattering in its way as Marco Polo's had been centuries before. He wrote that the Kam never washed, that they stole from him incessantly, and that "lying comes as easily to them as breathing." But to Robertson, steeped as he was in the British Empire's martial tradition, these qualities were outweighed by "their splendid courage, their domestic affections, and their overpowering love of freedom." In other ways, he says, they were made what they were by circumstance. "For them, the world has not grown softer as it has grown older . . . if they had been different, they would have been enslaved long ago."

For all that he admired the Kam for their love of freedom, he was the inadvertent harbinger of their subjugation. His journey had a covert purpose: the British authorities were trying to decide whether the Kafir tribes were worth including in their Empire. Robertson's mission, disclosed in the India Office's secret papers, was "to examine their tribal organisation and discover their value as friendly disposed but neutral allies, or active partisans in war." His verdict was that they should be left alone. The Kafirs had, he wrote to his superiors, "no strategic or political importance whatever . . . and ought not to be interfered with in any way." It was perhaps wise policy, proposed for good motives, but it spelled the end of Kafiristan.

Afghanistan, whose territory the Kafirs abutted, was then ruled by Abdur Rahman Khan, called the "Iron Amir" by the British. In his memoirs, the old amir claimed that he wanted the Kafirs in his army because "they were such a brave race of people that I considered that they would in time make very useful soldiers under my rule." (He was right: in due course they became the elite of the Afghan army.) He also wanted to outdo Tamerlane by conquering Kafiristan. And although he was not a religious zealot—he employed, for instance, a Hindu secretary—he wanted to claim the glory of a jihad against nonbelievers. In 1895 three military units loyal to Abdur Rahman advanced on Kafiristan in a pincer movement. They struck in the depths of winter, when the Kafirs would find it hard to escape. Given that his enemies, however brave and brutal, had not yet mastered the use of the rifle and were mostly fighting with bows and arrows, Abdur Rahman's victory was guaranteed. The Kafirs were given the choice of Islam or death; in the 1950s, the British travel writer Eric Newby was shown a stone red with the blood of those who chose execution. Abdur Rahman won the title Zia ul-Millat wa ul-Din, "light of the nation and the faith." The territory that Abdur Rahman conquered was eventually renamed Nuristan, the "land of light," to celebrate its forced conversion.

MUSLIM IT NOW MAY BE, but Nuristan is as fierce and untamable as it was before Abdur Rahman. At dawn on July 13, 2008, forty-nine US soldiers in a makeshift camp in Wanat, Nuristan province, woke up to a sinister sight: figures in the half-light emerging over distant ridges. Closer observation revealed that the figures were Taliban with rocket launchers. More and more of the silhouettes appeared, until there were nearly two hundred of them. Suddenly they opened fire, taking out the US camp's heavy weaponry in the first few minutes. The next few hours were a confusion of blood and noise. At one point the attackers broke through the camp's defenses, and when they finally withdrew after a few hours of sustained assault, they left nine Americans dead and twenty-seven wounded. The battle of Wanat, as it came to be known, was the costliest American engagement in Afghanistan since 2001. Reports of the battle in the American press highlighted Nuristan's reputation as the "deadliest place on earth" and "Al-Qaeda and Taliban central." Three things made it especially attractive to Islamic militants: its stark topography (the mountains that make up the province are up to 19,500 feet high), the fact that it sits alongside the border with Pakistan, and the religious fervor and battle-hardiness of its people (it was the first province to declare jihad against the Soviets in 1979). Just as in Alexander's time, they and their neighbors in Kunar province, a little to the south, proved to be the fiercest fighters in the region.

Yet during the battle, and just a few miles away from it as the crow flies, a Greek teacher peacefully slept through it all. Athanasios Lerounis lived in a village called Bomboret and dressed like a local, with flowers tucked into a flat brown woolen cap. Though he was an outsider, he was allowed to join in the local solstice celebrations: the sacrifice of goats to their many gods and goddesses, the drinking of homemade wine and powerful brandy, and all-night dancing that saw women in bright red-and-yellow costumes and cowrie-shell headdresses form circles around the men and sway decorously to the sound of chanting. Almost right at the geographical heart of militant Islam, he was living among the last pagans of Pakistan.

These people were the Kalasha. They survived the forced conversion of their Kafir cousins in the high mountains: the *mehtar*s of Chitral were under British protection and Abdur Rahman could not enter their territory. It is for this reason, too, that their valley is in Pakistan, which annexed Chitral in 1969. There was a time, the Kalasha say, when all of Chitral followed their religion—but now all save four thousand are Muslim. The four thousand remaining Kalasha all live in three valleys in Chitral next to the border with Nuristan. Living in the mountains has left them no choice but to practice subsistence agriculture—growing wheat for bread and grapes for wine, herding wiry goats and sheep and rather bony cattle—and in winter their land freezes and they become snowbound. The mountains, however, have also protected them from almost all invaders, and their valleys can still be peaceful even when there is chaos and violence just a few miles away.

In 1839, the first British political agent in Afghanistan, Sir William Macnaghten, was told by the Afghans: "Here are your relations coming!" They meant a delegation from Kafiristan. The notion that the people of this delegation were "poor cousins of the European," as they were sometimes described, was a result of their pale skins and various habits that were seen as distinctively European—sitting on chairs and shaking hands instead of, like most Afghans, sitting on the floor and grasping the shoulders. At some point, the theory of European origins for the people of the Hindu Kush took on more detail. It was said that they were descendants of Alexander the Great and his soldiers. The story spread, in Athens and Thessaloniki and beyond, that the Kalasha specifically were a lost Hellenic tribe. Donations poured in. At one point Greek tourists arrived in Pakistani villages bringing pictures of Alexander to compare his features with those of the Kalasha, some of whom have blond hair and blue eyes. The idea has caught on among the Kalasha, too: one local boy changed his name to Alexandros when he turned eighteen. Lerounis, meanwhile, used the donations to establish a clean water supply, latrines, schools, and a museum that celebrated and preserved the Kalasha's heritage and religion.

There might be more than one explanation for the European-seeming traits of these isolated tribes in the Hindu Kush. Living in Afghanistan from 2007 to 2009 and learning its languages, I often encountered English-sounding words. In one of Afghanistan's two main languages, Dari, the words *lip, bad,* and *am* are used, and carry the same meanings as they do in English. *Madar, baradar,* and *dokhtar* sound almost exactly like their English meanings: "mother," "brother," and "daughter." *Tu,* the word for "you," is close to the old English *thou.* Entire sentences might almost match their English equivalent. *Baradar e-tu am* means "I am your brother." Whenever I heard these phrases in the often alien-seeming environment of Kabul, amid its snowy mountains, from men in multicolored *chapan* coats and flat woolen *pakol* caps who had lived through more mayhem and murder than I would ever see, it felt as if—borrowing a phrase from Alan Bennett about the feeling of finding sympathetic characters in history—"a hand has reached out, and taken yours."

The reason for this goes back three to four thousand years, long before the British Empire or even the earlier Afghan empires came into existence, when both Europe and Afghanistan were colonized by the same people: nomadic herdsmen from the Caucasus who spread their Indo-European language across a vast swath of land. In the Taklamakan Desert, east of the Hindu Kush, a mummified corpse of one of these settlers was discovered in 1980. Dating back approximately 3,800 years, the mummy is called the "Loulan Beauty." She had auburn hair, high cheekbones, and a high-bridged nose. Her presence in what is now western China shows how far the Indo-European settlers reached. No wonder Alexander, when he reached the

Hindu Kush, was reminded of home and sought places that featured in his people's mythology. He hoped to find in the Hindu Kush the mountain where Prometheus had been bound in chains, punished by the gods for teaching man the secret of fire; as he marched south toward India, he was persuaded that he was treading in the footsteps of the god Dionysus, whose ceremonies he thought he recognized among the local customs. Perhaps he believed he had reached the end of the world—a place where myths came true—and was overinterpreting coincidences. Or perhaps he was seeing cultural similarities that dated back to that earlier settlement.

So blond hair and blue eyes among the Kalasha do not prove them to be descended from Alexander's soldiers, but there was never anything impossible about the idea. After Alexander's death, Greek kings ruled southern Afghanistan and a large part of Pakistan for more than two centuries. Their "empire of a thousand cities" was famously wealthy and conducted commerce with China and diplomatic relations with Indian kings. The name Sekandar (Alexander) remains popular in Kashmir, and the Afghan city of Kandahar still recognizably bears the Greek king's name. The Muslim rulers of Badakhshan, a province just north of Kafiristan, continued to claim descent from Alexander himself as late as the fifteenth century. Greece's neighbor Macedonia, which also lays claim to Alexander's heritage, was not willing to be outdone by the Greeks and their Kalasha connection. It invited the prince of Hunza for a special visit in 2008, for this prince, living in a region just north of Chitral, also claims descent from Alexander. The Kalasha have an oral tradition tracing their origin to "Shalak Shah," a possible reference to Alexander's general Seleucus. Indeed, a study of the DNA of the Kalasha population conducted in 2014 seemed to bear out the Kalasha legend. It showed that at some point between 990 and 206 BC foreign genes, possibly European, entered the Kalasha gene pool.

———————

I LEARNED ABOUT NURISTAN soon after I arrived in Kabul. The white-capped mountains that tower over the Afghan capital on its eastern side—part of the Hindu Kush—were not even visible then, because of the summer haze of fumes and smoke that hung over the city, but when mortar shells landed in the city, I was told they had been fired from those mountains. From then on I saw them as places of terror as well as beauty. The name Kush, after all, sounded very much like the Afghan word for "killing," *kushtan*. Even so, it intrigued me that there were still places in those mountains that were beyond my reach; I read avidly the books of people who had visited Nuristan, including Robertson and also Eric Newby, a British travel writer who reached the province in 1956. I sometimes came near the place, and I saw pictures of its extraordinary and precarious mountainside villages, but I never actually set foot on Nuristani soil.

Instead in 2008 I decided to venture into the Hindu Kush from the other side. From Beijing, I traveled by train and road west through China's troubled province of Xinjiang and into a northern province of Pakistan called Hunza. Robertson had visited this place and wrote afterward how he found himself obliged to shin up a tree in his full ceremonial uniform, sword and brass helmet, since the local ruler lived in its branches to avoid assassination. The area was in many respects very similar to Afghanistan, but free of danger. I could ride the local minibuses, go shopping in the markets, and talk freely to people (in a little Dari, and mostly English widely spoken because the region has no single universal language). It was an exhilarating feeling. Since it was winter, the polo fields, which I imagined in summer must be full of local notables on horseback jostling and shouting and chasing after a white ball, were empty. Bony cattle grazed on the unused lawns of local hotels, which in previous summers had hosted tourists. A boy in the mountains practiced cricket with me and said he wanted to play for England—though his name was Saddam Hussein. Girls sat in a schoolyard overlooking the main road and teased boys as they walked past. I went unteased: all their insults would have been lost on me. Instead they summoned me into a singing contest, each in our own language.

I was staying at the home of a man named Hussein, and he invited me to visit the local shaman, as he called her. We walked to her house along the little footpaths of the village. "She lives right by the mountainside," he said. "All shamans do." In her house—traditional, built of stone, the hearth fire smoldering under a pan of almost-cooked bread—she stooped over a tray on which she had scattered a collection of pins. Hussein, a powerful local figure from a wealthy family, got a rather pointed set of predictions: "Some people in the village will dislike you—they feel that you are away too much, that you pay your community too little attention." For me, she prayed in Arabic and declared good fortune: "You will finish your book." I had not told anyone that I was writing one.

Leaving, I asked Hussein how a person living in a house huddled under the great mountains became a shaman. He said it was a matter of spending some months up in the high peaks, where the ibex lives, eating only bread and drinking only tea. When the ibex delivered her young, the would-be shaman had to drink its milk, and then descend to the valley to test his or her newfound powers of prophecy. A belief that fairies (*peri* in the local language) inhabit the high mountains is partly what lies behind this tradition. Spending time among the fairies is thought to give a person supernatural powers (and the word *perichahra,* "fairy-face," is a local compliment). Traditions and beliefs like these were once so widespread in that region, even among Muslims, that one book proposed that the whole Hindu Kush region, Hunza and Wakhan and Nuristan and Chitral, could be called "Peristan"—the land of the fairies. Hussein told me that there was a tribe called the Kalasha that had not yet converted, and offered me the chance to go and see them. It was a journey of a few days by jeep over unpaved mountain roads from Hunza to Chitral. I could not spare the time for it then, but promised myself that I would come back.

IT WAS FOUR YEARS BEFORE I TRIED TO RETURN, and this time acquiring a Pakistani visa had become much trickier. I was summoned by the country's High Commission in London, many months after I applied. I introduced myself at the counter. "Ah yes," said a small, energetic man with a long beard, "Mr. Russell. We all know about you. Yours is a famous case!" They had been working on it for weeks, he told me. Perhaps that was why the file on me had become so thick. I saw it when I was asked to call on a polite but weary official in a huge, once-elegant office. The file was open on the desk in front of him. "Someone in Pakistan has been putting a finger on your reputation," he said. "What is the reason for that?"

When I said I had worked in Kabul, a look of comprehension flickered briefly in his eyes, and he stopped asking me any further questions. I knew that Afghanistan and Pakistan regarded each other with a large measure of mutual suspicion: clearly, even just having lived in one was a hindrance to visiting the other. Eventually the visa came through, and a few weeks later I was in the somewhat chaotic airport of Islamabad, Pakistan's all-modern capital city. But I still faced one more challenge before I could reach my destination. Chitral sits 150 miles to the north of Islamabad, on the Afghan border. The region is surrounded by mountains, and there is only one low-altitude road leading in or out, which (thanks to the British-drawn border, as the locals pointed out to me) ran through Afghanistan and was now blocked off. So I would have to take a plane to get there, and although Chitral was a popular and sunny tourist resort in summer, the delay in getting my visa meant that it was now midwinter, when snow and high winds are common. The compensation was that if I made it to the Kalasha valley I might be in time for the winter solstice, when they hold a week-long festival called Chaumos.

My first flight attempted to reach the Chitral airport but, owing to the weather, ended up flying in wide circles around the next valley, giving me a spectacular view of the Hindu Kush. I could understand how Alexander the Great had imagined that the mountains were the edge of the world: even from a plane, nothing was visible but peak after peak, cliff after cliff, as far as the eye could see through the bright clouds and mist that covered them. Below me, and above Chitral, the clouds were darker and very thick: the plane tentatively nosed its way down through the top layers of cloud but soon gave up and turned back. It would be a few more days and trips to the airport before I managed to make it to the valley beneath those clouds.

Each time I came to the airport, I saw a sign saying farewell. *Allah hafez,* it said—a reminder of how the linguistic legacy of the region's ancient Indo-European settlers is now being contested. *Khoda hafez* was the old phrase for "goodbye" in Pakistan, as it still is in Afghanistan and Iran. Some Muslims, however, believe that the old word for God, *Khoda* (a cousin of the English word, with *kh* instead of *g*), is less truly Islamic than the Arabic *Allah*. I had seen in Iran how Persian poetry had emphasized the difference between Persian and Arab by reviving the ancient pre-Islamic language. Pakistan was going in the opposite direction—partly influenced by its commercial and political ties to the Arab world, where tens of thousands of Pakistanis work, and which traditionally views Iran and everything Persian with some suspicion.

The campaign to replace Persian words with Arabic ones dates back to the time of Zia ul-Haq, the military dictator who deposed Pakistan's democratic socialist president, Zulfikar Ali Bhutto, in 1978. Despite his politics, Bhutto had already put Pakistan on a road toward Islamic conservatism by passing a law against blasphemy, many of whose victims have been from religious minorities. Zia took things much further, imposing public whipping as a penalty for drinking alcohol and stoning to death as a penalty for adultery. Pakistan backed the most brutally militant of rebel groups in neighboring Afghanistan against the Soviets. Promoting Islamic causes gave a clearer, unifying purpose to Pakistan, a country stitched together in 1948 from a collection of provinces—including Chitral—that had little but religion in common. Constant tension with India, Pakistan's majority-Hindu eastern neighbor, also helped create a feeling that being more Islamic was the same as being more patriotic. Widespread corruption created a sense that only the pious could be trusted to run things honestly. Zia's successors never quite rolled back the changes he had made.

When eventually a plane reached Chitral, with me on board, I saw that the valley's floor was flat and green with buildings scattered across it haphazardly; a wide river flowed down its southern edge, and steep and bare mountainsides rose on either side. At one point we passed the steep slope down which McNair had come, past corpses of dead travelers. A slight mist hung over the valley, the only trace that remained of the thick storm clouds. This valley had been an independent princely state, ruled by *mehtar*s, when McNair and Robertson came through. I headed for a hotel that belonged to a cousin of the present *mehtar*. His great-grandfather had ruled the valley in Robertson's time, and done everything possible to stop Robertson from reaching the Kam Kafirs—even going as far as bribing the Kam to kill him—out of fear that the British might be hoping to annex Kafiristan and Chitral along with it. (In reality, Chitral remained a princely state, with control over its internal affairs, until its 1969 annexation by Pakistan.)

His descendant, Shahzada Siraj ul-Mulk, was by contrast immensely helpful. He had once worked as an airline pilot, and his wife, Ghazala, had a degree in catering. When they were not entertaining diplomats at their elegant salon in Islamabad, they were looking after hunters, hikers, and writers at the hotel they ran together. As I sat by an open fire in its dining hall Siraj handed me an eighty-year-old book, falling apart at the spine, written by Colonel Reginald Schomberg. A speaker of six languages and holder of several military medals and one from the Royal Geographical Society, Schomberg visited Chitral in the course of twenty years spent exploring central Asia. (At the end of his life he would join the Catholic priesthood.) He wrote this book, *Kafirs and Glaciers,* during his travels. Marginalia written in irritation showed where Siraj's father had once disputed the book's unkinder observations on the Chitralis. Schomberg had made a gloomy prediction about the Kalasha, the only non-Muslims in Chitral, in particular. "Before very long," he had written, "they will be persuaded—so gently, so blandly, but so firmly—to become Mohammedans and will be bad Muslims instead of good pagans."

I was soon to have a chance to come to my own conclusion on the subject, because I set off the next day to see the nearest Kalasha valley in the company of Siraj himself, a driver, and a Pakistani photographer called Zulfikar who was also staying at the hotel and was keen to see the Kalasha. Given that there are three hundred thousand Chitralis in all, and only four thousand are Kalasha, I was not surprised that the road we drove along was lined with signs showing the Muslim names for God: the Merciful, the Glorious, He Who Grants Power, He Who Takes Power Away. After half an hour we crossed the Chitral River, which I had seen running along the southern side of the main valley, and turned into a narrow gorge whose shale sides, lined with complex striations, looked like a frozen waterfall. Thirty feet or so below us a tributary of the Chitral, the Kalasha River, thundered at the gorge's bottom. The road headed upward, higher into the mountains.

The springs of our car groaned as it bumped over the road's rocky surface, and there were stretches where the gorge was barely wide enough for

The village of Grom, in the Kalasha valley of Rumbur, has the benefit of electricity but still must contend with cold and snow for much of the year. The Kalasha's poverty and remoteness have protected them from pressure to adopt Islam. Photo by the author

the car and the driver had to concentrate to make sure that he had chosen the precise angle that would neither scratch its doors on the cliff to our left nor send its wheels over the edge of the precipice on our right. I was amazed to learn that a minibus made this journey regularly. Electric wires stretched all along the length of the road, for miles and miles—showing that even if the Pakistani state was fragile and inefficient, it was still capable of delivering some services to its people.

After a time the gorge opened out to become a valley. We passed occasional houses by the roadside: at first these belonged to Muslim families, as I could see from the fact that the girls standing outside were veiled. After we had driven for another hour or so I saw much brighter clothes hanging out to dry on branches of roadside trees, and then a woman dressed in a black gown with complex red, white, and yellow embroidery and a headdress made from many-colored wool, white cowrie shells, and a red pompon, plus jangly earrings. We were among the Kalasha of Rumbur valley, one of the three in which they still can be found. They were in the midst of celebrating their winter solstice festival. Our car came to a stop in a small village called Grom. The valley, which here was around two hundred yards wide, had steep sides covered in snow and dotted with fir trees, while its fields were mud-brown. It was around 2:00 P.M., but the sun would soon dip beneath the hilltop. We headed for a house built in the style of a Swiss chalet with slate rock and wooden beams. A Kalasha man called Azem Beg—Beg being an honorific title rather than a surname, for the Kalasha do not generally use surnames— came out and greeted Siraj by hanging several brightly colored garlands around his neck. (Many of the Kalasha were wearing these for the festival.) He invited us into a wooden barn still under construction, where we stood shivering for a few moments as a cold wind came through its windowless window frames. Azem Beg seemed not to notice the cold. His two small children, a boy and a girl, joined us, bringing more garlands in different colors, and necklaces of threaded almonds. "Ishpata," they said, which means "hello" in the Kalasha language.

An older man brought a bowl of burning embers to warm us and offered us tea and wine. "I add wine to my tea," he said; "it improves the flavor." In the seventeenth century before their mountain kingdom was reached by Westerners, the Kafirs' wine somehow reached the Portuguese Jesuit Bento de Goes and won his approval. I found it surprisingly good, too, and invited Azem Beg to try some. He reached out his hand for it and then drew it back. "I forgot," he said, "that we are in the middle of the festival, and this house is unclean. I may not eat or drink in an unclean house."

This rule turned out to be central to Kalasha life. The Kafirs, as Robertson described them, were a collection of tribes whose customs varied (the Kam were much more warlike than the Kalasha, for instance) but who shared essentially the same religion. All Kafirs, for instance, had a whole series of opposing principles that governed their lives. The right hand, the male sex, the high mountains, purity, odd numbers, and life all were affiliated with each other; to these were opposed the left hand, the female sex, the low valleys, impurity, even numbers, and death. So the men sat on the right-hand side of their houses and the women on the left. Likewise, it was men who herded the goats and women who planted crops, men who went into the mountains and women whose place was the valleys, and women who were prone to all kinds of impurity.

Many of these rules are still kept by the Kalasha. In particular, the higher places of the mountains are reserved to men only during the months that follow Chaumos. A house that is clean for the festival is one that has been purified with juniper branches and which has no impure house higher than it on the mountainside. A short while after our sojourn in the barn, I was scolded for touching a village house as I passed it, since even this made it impure, and meant more juniper branches would need to be burned to restore its pristine state.

Yet the Kalasha are tolerant, when issues of purity are not involved. As we stood in the barn, Siraj Ulmulk's long-bearded Muslim driver meekly bowed his head to receive a festival garland from a small Kalasha boy. The Kalasha did not bat an eyelid when the driver, a few minutes later, got up onto a trestle table—a cleaner surface than the floor—and prostrated himself in Islamic prayer. They are accustomed to living side by side with Muslims, because some Kalasha in the village have converted to Islam. The female converts are obvious because of their demure pastel-colored dresses and headscarves. Male costume is the same for Kalasha men as for local Muslims. It was a rather eerie thing, as I walked through the Kalasha village, to see a man looking just like the fiercely Muslim Pashtuns, wearing the shift and trousers known as the *shalwar kameez,* topped with a blanket to fend off the chill, and a flat Chitrali cap on his head, regarding me with a fixed stare— and only the brightly colored garland around his neck and a feather in his cap would tell me that he was not a Muslim but a festival-going Kalasha on his way to honor one of his gods.

Siraj returned to the hotel, while Zulfikar and I—who were going to stay the night—walked toward the center of the village, where the villagers were going to dance later to mark the solstice. On the way we passed the *bashali*, a house in the middle of the village where women must stay during their menstrual periods. Schomberg, back in the 1930s, had made it sound like a terrible place, where even a midwife could only enter after stripping naked, and which no man could even approach. Seventy years seemed to have changed this custom somewhat for the better. The *bashali* is now a wooden building constructed recently with funds raised by Dr. Lerounis, and the three women staying there were standing by the entrance and cheerfully talking to passers-by.

Kalasha women must go to the *bashali* while menstruating, to live apart. The rule is not harshly enforced however, and these three women have come out to socialize with passers-by. Photo by the author

We crossed a wooden bridge over the Kalasha River, gripping the handrail tightly to avoid skidding on the bridge's icy surface. On the other side huge wooden casks stood by the river's edge. There was no need to lock these, I noticed: they were left open, and each family stored their own supply of wine and nuts inside. I saw an example of the way two religions coexisted here, spotting a herdsman leading goats for the Chaumos sacrifice past the Voice of the Koran madrasa. The preparations for the festival were accompanied by an Islamic call to prayer, broadcast by loudspeakers from the mosque and echoing off the snowy hillsides.

When my fellow guest Zulfikar and I went to the dance, we were shown to a place a little apart from the dancers. In front of us a row of curious Muslim girls stood quietly, demurely rearranging their head scarves from time to time, watching their more boisterous cousins. In terms of the Kalasha religion, Muslims are considered impure at festival time because they do not undergo the purification ritual with which the festival begins (for which men must sacrifice a goat and women be censed with burning juniper). If they stay in a house or touch a dish of food, they make it impure, and they may not join in the religious celebrations, but must watch from a distance. Schomberg recorded a similar example of segregation while attending the Kalasha spring festival in 1935. "A very melancholy-looking party of [Muslim converts] were huddled apart on a roof," he recorded, "watching with longing eyes the merriment of their former co-religionists."

Azem came up to Zulfikar and me. "I am sorry that you cannot join us," he said. "Only those who are here in the valley at the start of the festival can take part. But if you had been here," he said to me, "it would not have been a problem: Muslims cannot join in, but foreigners can." And in fact I could see a German man, with camera around his neck, and his wife twirling themselves around and waving

Akiko, a Japanese woman, joined the Kalasha community when she married a Kalasha man twenty years ago. Photo by the author

their arms almost as gracefully as the Kalasha. Presumably he had been there for the goat sacrifice. There was also a lady in full Kalasha costume, complete with cowrie shells—but, unlike any others among the Kalasha women, she was also wearing spectacles. And her features were certainly not Kalasha. She was Japanese. Later I had a chance to speak to her briefly. Her name was Akiko and she had been living in the valley, she said, for twenty-five years. She had come to photograph the region and had fallen in love with a local man. She felt part of a family there, she said: when she visited Japan now, it felt like an alien, individualistic place.

Zulfikar, a Muslim, took his exclusion with good grace, and even apologized to Azem for having shaken his hand (which must have made him impure). "It's useful for them to have this rule," he commented to me. "It stops them from being overrun by visitors." This was not a potential problem in the winter, but I was told that the summer festival attracted many Pakistani tourists who were as intrigued as those from Greece or countries even further afield. Many of the visitors were friendly, but some came with the wrong idea: they expected that because Kalasha women did not wear veils and were not Muslims, they would be available for sex. Lurid tales of a custom called the *budhaluk*—when a Kalasha man once a year was chosen from the community, consecrated himself by spending time in the high mountains, and then impregnated as many women as possible—had helped spread this idea. In fact, the Kalasha are very reserved about sex, and during Chaumos it is completely forbidden even between married couples. This does not stop prostitutes from coming from other parts of Pakistan to exploit the legend by dressing as Kalasha women, though, trading on this desire for the exotic.

In any case, though Zulfikar and I did not actually take part in the afternoon's dance, we had a good view. It began with a great milling about of Kalasha women—for whom synthetic fabrics have opened up an entire rainbow of colors to wear, oranges and pinks and yellows alongside the traditional red and black—and men, who dressed much more tamely in *shalwar kameez* and Chitrali cap. Kalasha boys had adopted Western clothes and baseball caps. In the midst of the crowd I could catch sight of some brave individuals dancing while surrounded by a circle of chanting and cheering onlookers. Gradually, men and women formed human chains and began to dance in earnest.

Men and women danced not as partners but in separate groups, and they chanted as they danced. I asked Azem Beg what the words meant. "It is about the return of the god, coming to rejoin us," he replied. "And they say our uncles' sons and our aunts' daughters have come to celebrate with us." Every twenty minutes, he said, the chant changed. Over the course of the festivities, the various chants made up a lengthy paean to Balimain, the god of the festival, who comes from afar on a winged horse to collect the petitions of the Kalasha. Children dashed about among the dancing adults, playing games of chase. They were almost never told off. Sometimes the boys would form little groups, linking arms and chanting at the girls. This proved to be a strategic error. One girl realized that the boys, having linked arms, would find it hard to disentangle themselves in time to chase after her. So she kicked the middle boy between the legs and sped away, laughing merrily.

After a while the daytime dancing started to subside, and the Kalasha headed home to prepare for another dance that would take place at night. I went to the guesthouse where we were spending the night, which was run by

Zarmas Gul prepares a traditional meat chapati for the festival of Chaumos, the winter solstice, when days begin to grow longer and nights to shorten. Photo by the author

Azem's relative Zarmas Gul and her husband. (Again, Gul is not a surname but a term of endearment—it means "flower"—stuck onto the end of her given name.) I watched as Zarmas Gul sat by a wood stove making mutton bread, which resembled a Cornish pasty, but was far better because it was made with fresh meat. An old computer was playing Hindi music alternating with American pop, and while waiting for the stove to heat up, our Kalasha hostess, in her elaborate embroidered dress, moved gently in time with the rhythm of Rihanna. Her daughter sat nearby, wearing a track suit instead of the traditional embroidered dress ("She's a tomboy, but she does agree to wear Kalasha dress for school," Azem Beg told me later), and occasionally taking over the computer to play a game on it.

Despite these intrusions of a more modern way of life—made possible, of course, by the power lines that I had seen running along the gorge—the Kalasha daily routine otherwise remains unassisted by modern conveniences. Even the smallest meal in the village took preparation—wood had to be cut, collected, stored, and kept dry, and even to fry an egg, the fire had to be lit. How hard it must be to wash clothes in this freezing winter, I thought. The consolation was that the stove quickly made the room very warm and felt all the more so because we knew how cold it was outside.

Conditions must have been unimaginably tougher for the Kam in Robertson's time—in an even higher place in the mountains, and without electricity or income from tourism. Yet Robertson said that they were "never melancholy"—perhaps because they were so unremittingly social. They never understood, for instance, that he sometimes wanted to be alone. When he retreated to his room in the hope of writing in peace, he noted in frustration, they assumed that there was something wrong with him and would make a special point of coming into his room and trying to cheer him up. (He could get rid of them only by asking them to teach him their language: teaching him bored them so much that they would invariably walk out almost at once.) The Kalasha, too, seemed content in their valley. Few of them, even among those who had converted to Islam, chose to leave for a career in the cities. From my own Western standpoint, every day seemed to be a struggle for them, but I reflected that they also never had to deal with the problems modern urbanites face: being in a crowd of strangers, being the odd one out, being lonely.

That evening, the second round of dancing began after dark. From our guesthouse Zulfikar and I could see blazing torches appear farther down the valley, and hear the distant sound of singing. Then a group of young men and women materialized slowly out of the darkness and headed toward a nearby field. We followed them, keeping a respectful distance. At the field we saw dots of light appearing all over the hillside, which turned out to be brushwood torches carried by Kalasha descending from their mountain villages. A hubbub arose as people greeted each other, sometimes after months of separation. The dancing lasted through the night, lit by the flames of a huge fire. Even though snow fell steadily, the Kalasha seemed not to notice. Warmth and light and human vigor were driving away the dark and cold, presaging the summer to come. When I got up the next morning, Azem Beg was still awake—he had gone in the early morning, after the dancing, to congratulate a number of couples that had gotten married the day before.

Azem's father had been an elder among the Kalasha, but they were traditionally an egalitarian and democratic people without permanent leaders. Robertson found that when Kam leaders had to make important decisions, they always waited for other members of the tribe to express an opinion and then agreed with whatever the majority said. In cases where there was a serious division and no clear majority, Kam politicians had recourse to a tactic only rarely employed by politicians in Western democracies: they would literally hide so that they could avoid making a divisive decision. Among the Kalasha, there are elders called *gaderakan* who check to make sure that the community performs its rituals correctly; they are unpaid volunteers, not really priests in the normal sense.

THAT NIGHT I SLEPT IN A KALASHA HOME, glowing embers in the stove keeping the room warm. In the morning, after the rising sun had taken the edge off the valley's nighttime chill, I had the chance to see a different style of dancing. Another of the Kalasha valleys—the farthest from Rumbur, called Birir, being several hours' journey by car—had solstice celebrations of a slightly different kind. Zarmas Gul was from the valley and had told us about the festival, though my own Kalasha companions did not even seem to know about it—it seemed that news did not travel much between Birir and Rumbur, perhaps because few Kalasha either have cars or see strong reasons to leave their own valleys to make the tough journey by foot to see the other Kalasha communities. Azem and Wazir, a Kalasha who had converted to Islam, came with me.

Birir gets few tourists and is poorer than Rumbur, and many of the Kalasha in Birir were living in a large wooden building on the hillside. It was in the old style—built on several levels with staircases linking communal balconies, off which each family had a room. The steep slope of the hillside meant that each balcony was set just a little way back from the one below it. It was far more picturesque than the newer buildings in Rumbur (let alone those in the middle valley, Bomboret, which has been extensively modernized) but also much more cramped.

There was also a collection of houses on the valley floor, and we walked through this and beyond, up the valley a distance and then a short way up the hillside, to a vantage point where there stood a temple called a *jestakhan*—sacred to Jestak, goddess of the family. This was where the festival was taking place. A police guard outside the door had to see my passport before he allowed me into the temple—which was a single room, lined with pillars, all made of wood. Although it had been built recently, it had an air of great antiquity. Perhaps this was because of its interior pillars, which looked like an exoticized version of Ionic columns; perhaps it was the cobwebs on those pillars, which obscured the symbols carved into the wood. Most of the room was in shadow, except that through a square opening in the roof two thin rays of sun lit up the temple wall, and a window looked out onto the icy mountainside. A crowd of boys and girls were staring down at us through the opening, sitting on the roof—I guessed that they might be Muslims barred from entering.

There were maybe eighty or even a hundred Kalasha in the room. Some sat on a bench at the back, but most were standing; the women in their multicolored dresses were lined up in the shadows. Friends greeted each other as they met, and stood chatting for a time. Others stood quietly listening to three men in *shalwar kameez* and Chitrali caps: one wore a sparkling cloak of synthetic fiber colored red and gold. These three were singing a simple chant in a minor key, consisting only of two notes suggesting sadness. In the corner of the *jestakhan*, two men beat different-sized drums to accompany the chant. Around its edges forty or fifty women formed a long line with linked arms and repeated the chant after the singers; they did not keep strictly to time, and the room was filled with discordant, melancholy notes. Standing among the men in the center of the circle, I had an experience quite different from that at Rumbur. The latter had been rough-and-tumble, while this felt solemn and mystical. The drums beat slowly, the women moved counterclockwise around the edges of the room, and the men sang on. Kalasha men came up to the singers from time to time and put crumpled rupee bills in their caps, a traditional way of rewarding good singing.

Interpreting the song, Azem told me that it had come to one of the singers in a dream, and that it related to a place in the valley where the Kalasha in the past had danced for the festival. "The god is asking, why do we not use the whole valley for Chaumos?" he translated. The scope of the festival had shrunk over the decades as the community had dwindled. Places where celebrations had once taken place were now owned by Muslims and counted

A Kalasha singer has been rewarded for his singing at the Chaumos festival with a shiny cape. Here, outside the temple where the festival is being celebrated with dancing, he wears it proudly. Photo by the author

as impure. How many people, I wondered, must have made this lament over the years as Islam, Christianity, or other missionary religions arrived in their homelands?

The rhythm changed. The drums sped up. The women broke into groups of four and some of the men joined them, dancing around more informally and sometimes spinning about. The drumbeat became loud and fast, and I along with Wazir and his friends joined in the new dance. Groups of four, men and women separately, sped around the dance floor—counterclockwise as before—and whenever they caught up with the group ahead of them, they would bump into them. Both groups had then to face each other and laugh loudly. Alternatively, a group could spin around to face the group behind them and do the same. When I sat out one round, I saw that the insistent

In January 2013 Kalasha women celebrated Chaumos, the winter solstice, with dancing in a temple called a *jestakhan*. The Kalash have many gods: Jestak is their goddess of the family. Photo by the author

thump of the drums, the staccato and slightly manic-sounding laughter, and the sight of people rushing around the room made for an extraordinary madcap atmosphere. And then the drums subsided and the more stately dance resumed.

When the dancing eventually ended and we left the *jestakhan,* we heard more laughter and singing down the valley, near the old wooden house I had seen when we arrived. "Those are the pure boys," Azem Beg told me: he meant virgin boys, a group who were considered especially pure in a ritual sense. In the festival they were thought to represent the community's dead ancestors, and they went from house to house, bringing good luck and receiving presents of new clothes in return. The boys were still singing as we walked back down the valley from the *jestakhan*, passing as we did so a covered arcade where some of the valley's Muslim converts were cooking themselves kebabs.

"Our hearts are open," Azem explained to me on the journey back to his home valley of Rumbur, "so we pray in the open air." In fact, Rumbur had a couple of stone temples, but these were small and not the focus of communal worship. The outdoor place of worship was called the *sajjigor* (which was also the name of the god that was worshiped there) and was located in a grove of trees beyond the northern edge of the village, which had been off-limits to me while the festival lasted. When we returned to Rumbur, however, the festival had ended and Wazir agreed to escort me there. It meant walking out of the village on its northern, higher end (the valley had hills on either side, but the valley floor, too, had a noticeable slope at this point) and heading along a path, slippery with ice, to a bridge across the river, on the other side of which the grove stood in an open field. Young men that we met along the path told us that we could look at the *sajjigor* provided we touched nothing. So we stood on the edge of the grove and looked through the trees at five wooden effigies, which we were careful not to approach. These, Wazir said, taking pains to defend his relatives against charges of idolatry, were not meant to represent gods. They are in fact effigies of important men in the community who have died, and are remembered a year later by their families. A stained patch on the ground near them showed where a hundred goats had been sacrificed in the previous days. A stone mound piled with twigs was where a ceremony had been held for boys who had reached the age of wearing trousers—each of them had thrown a twig on the pile as part of the ritual.

I looked again at the wooden effigies, which made me think of an episode in Rudyard Kipling's *The Man Who Would Be King*. In it, two disreputable ex-soldiers decide to set themselves up as pagan kings. "They call it Kafiristan," one of them says to the other. "By my reckoning it's the top right-hand corner of Afghanistan, not more than three hundred miles from Peshawar. They have two and thirty heathen idols there, and we'll be the thirty-third." Thanks to their knowledge of Freemasonry symbols, which turn out in Kipling's story to have come down to the Kafirs from their long-dead ancestor Alexander the Great, the two get away with their ruse for a while before being turned on by the Kafirs—one is killed, the other goes mad. These wooden figures reminded me of Kipling's story and of the Kafiristan fever that had gripped Victorian British society when it was written.

IT WAS SOME TRACE OF THAT FEVER that made me want to walk further north up the valley and nearer the border with Nuristan. Between the Kalasha village and the Afghan border, Wazir told me, there was a village of Nuristanis. These were descendants not of the Kalasha tribe but of the Kam whom Robertson knew; during Abdur Rahman's invasion their ancestors had escaped forcible conversion by fleeing across the border and taking refuge in Rumbur. In a later generation their community had adopted Islam anyway, finding the rules of impurity impossible to maintain when all their cousins back in Nuristan had become Muslim. In Schomberg's time they were called Red Kafirs and were blamed by the Kalasha for all kinds of mischief. I asked Wazir if he could take me to their village, and he said that he knew them and could introduce me. So we carried on walking northward from the *sajjigor*, recrossing the river by sliding across a precariously icy log, and clambering up to regain the main track. Above the track on the hillside at this point were some Kalasha summer houses, which were taboo for women after Chaumos. A small boy descended from one of them carrying a goat, placing his feet carefully in the packed snow that clung to the steep hill-side. We clapped when he made it down safely, and he ran shyly away with the goat toward the village. We walked on, and I spoke to Wazir about religion.

Wazir was a Kalasha who had converted to Islam, which meant he could give me some insight into the challenges that faced the community as it tried to hold on to its few remaining members. Wazir told me that he had been the only Kalasha boy in his class at secondary school. "The teacher asked if there were any Kalasha pupils, and I put up my hand," he told me. "I was the only one. I was made fun of a lot." When they asked him questions about his beliefs, he had no answers to give them. As he told me: "If I ask Kalasha people, 'Why do we do this thing?' or 'Why do we follow that tradition?' they will only say, 'That was how our grandparents did it.' They don't know what it means." As a thoughtful boy, not having any answer to give to the other boys and teachers when they challenged him, he eventually agreed to become Muslim—a step that takes only the recitation of a single sentence ("I witness that there is only one God and that Mohammed is his prophet") and which is effectively irreversible. If Wazir after conversion were not to continue practic-ing as a Muslim, he would expose his whole community to danger. Although abandoning Islam is technically not against the law in Pakistan, 76 percent of Pakistanis polled in 2010 said that it merited the death penalty. Even just a rumor that a person has left Islam can spark mob violence.

Because of this kind of experience, many Kalasha families had chosen not to send their children to school at all. The community's Greek support-ers, however, had built primary schools in all three valleys, and a second-ary school in Bomboret which was open to both Kalasha and Muslims. At these schools at least some of the teachers were Kalasha, and the girls could wear their traditional outfits. The community has also begun to celebrate its own heritage: at the *jestakhan* in Birir, I had seen Kalasha men carrying a big old-fashioned recording device while others took videos of the dancing on their mobile phones. A museum in Bomboret has begun to compile the community's oral heritage. Perhaps because of this renewed pride in their identity, educated Kalasha (Wazir told me) no longer converted to Islam. It remained true, however, that very few Kalasha had much to say about their beliefs, in contrast with most Muslim communities, where Islam will often have at least one outspoken advocate. Robertson, incidentally, encountered much the same problem as Wazir: "if the perplexed stranger asks the explanation of practices and usages," he wrote, "the reply will almost invariably be . . . it is our custom."

Historically, other factors had also encouraged Kalasha to convert—ones that appear again and again in the history of religions. The Kalasha, like other Kafirs, had serfs called *baira*s who were bought and sold by Kalasha and barred from marrying Kalasha of higher rank. Unsurprisingly, these unfortunates were the first to convert to Islam, as Schomberg noticed when he visited Rumbur in the 1930s (just forty years after Kafiristan had been forcibly converted). Schomberg saw a huge difference between the graves of *baira*s before conversion, which he compares to a pile of packing cases, and their graves after conversion, which revealed a jump in status and self-respect. (Similarly, some of Pakistan's nearly three million Christians were once low-caste Hindus. It seemed in Iran, too, that the priestly caste of Zoroastrians had been the ones who held on to their religion the longest.)

Conversion could save a family money, too. During each festival, a Kalasha family has to give three or four goats for the sacrifice. Funerals can be cripplingly expensive: they last three days, and can involve the sacrifice of more than 80 goats and four cows. Islam involves much less personal expense. The clothing of Kalasha women is another cost that converts no longer have to take into account, since Muslim women tend to wear simple, cheaper fabrics. Conversion could also open new opportunities, especially for women, who Wazir told me formed the majority of recent converts. That surprised me, given that it meant surrendering their freedoms. But some women, I learned, had fallen in love with officials or policemen visiting from Chitral, and marrying one of these men would mean for them a more comfortable life.

In Wazir's case, by contrast, conversion had done little good. In fact, it had complicated his life immensely, since he was the only Muslim in his village and was having difficulty finding a wife. I wondered if he ever regretted his choice. He spoke of the Kalasha virtues almost wistfully. People trusted each other, he said. Goats could be left unwatched because nobody would steal them. Theft was punished with the most draconian penalty the Kalasha imposed: expulsion of the culprit from the community. Sex before marriage was not punished, and if a woman wanted to leave her husband and marry someone else, then her husband had no right to prevent it (though he did have the right to be paid double the original bride price). In Islam wives have more difficulty initiating divorce. "And when I visit a Kalasha home," Wazir added, "I can sit with the whole family in their room. But when I visit a Muslim friend, I must sit in a separate room," because in strict Islamic households, a woman should only be seen by her close male relatives.

In the 1890s, Robertson had picked up on the relaxed attitude that prevailed among the Kafirs and was shocked by what he called their "gallantry." He found that they regarded adultery, for the most part, as a matter of general hilarity. When a man and a married woman were caught making love, the tribe would come to watch and laugh; the man did not find it nearly as amusing, as he would have to pay the cuckolded husband a heavy fine (the woman did not pay a penalty). Wooden "Nuristani" chairs, recognizable by the circular patterns carved on their backs and the tall horned finials that stick up from them, decorate the salons of sophisticates and expatriates in Kabul; few of their owners know that the circles were originally intended to represent vulvas, the protruding finials were once copulating couples, and the chairs (only ever used by men) were fertility symbols. The Kalasha have a more reserved attitude than Kafirs did, but—as Wazir noted—are more liberal than Muslims in certain ways.

As Wazir and I were walking up a mountainside on our way to the border with Nuristan, we encountered a group of his Muslim friends. "Here's a mix of everyone around," Wazir said as he introduced me: "a Chitrali, another Kalasha convert like myself, a Gujar, and a Nuristani." The second-to-last man he named was from an especially dark-skinned nomad group, and the last man had brown hair and was notably fair-skinned. The Kalasha convert was stolidly carrying a big box that he had tied around his shoulders, which he planned to deliver to a shop in the Nuristani village. As we walked, the box burst and six bags of sweet bread fell out. We each gave him a hand by taking one. I had often imagined visiting a village of Nuristanis, but I had never imagined that in a snow-swept wilderness hard by the borders of Afghanistan I would be delivering them their daily supply of brioche. Nor did I expect them to be playing golf—"Nuristani golf," that is, as Wazir called

This village of Nuristanis stands at the top of the Kalasha valley of Rumbur. It was founded by refugees from the forcible conversion to Islam of the peoples of the region now called Nuristan. Photo by the author

it. A group of Nuristani youths were standing on the edge of the ravine the Kalasha River—here, more like a stream—had carved in the narrow valley, hitting wooden balls across it with long pieces of wood shaped like hockey sticks while smaller children scampered to recover them. The winner was simply the person who hit the balls the farthest. Wazir was a champion player.

The village itself consisted of a single building made of wood, like the one that I had seen in Birir. Each family had a room, and the rooms were linked to one another by balconies and exterior wooden stairways. Once inside, I found that the passages smelled of urine. An old man lay, weak and coughing, on a bed; the hearth was in the center of the room, other beds lined the walls, and a collection of shiny metal crockery was displayed on a set of shelves. (Displays of silver are mentioned by Robertson as a status symbol among the Kafirs.) The old man's wife made tea for me and Wazir while two small boys, obviously her grandchildren, sat and stared at everything I did. One of them asked to have one of my Kalasha garlands. I gave it to him, and then the other could barely leave me alone, tugging at one of my remaining garlands in the hope that I would let him take it. I asked to take a photograph of a small girl who had been watching us from outside, but the question apparently offended the grandmother: taking pictures of the boys was allowed, but not girls. Still, the family was not quite as strict as some, because they had allowed us into their room. This was perforce shared between women and men, so some Muslims would not have allowed us to enter it. As I got up to go, a pile of bedclothes at the side of the room moved, and a woman underneath them spoke.

After our tea, Wazir and I went down to the floor below, and he knocked on the door of another house, to say hello. At the mention that there was a foreigner outside, two small girls popped their faces around the door for just a second and then were gone and could not be persuaded to emerge again. The village men, however, were very happy to be photographed, pointing out to me their own distinctive features and light-colored hair, and gesturing proudly to their village mosque, the only freestanding structure they had besides their village house.

―――――――

WHEN THE TIME CAME TO LEAVE THE VALLEY, Azem Beg rode with me in the car to Chitral, and asked if we might stop at a house at the foot of the Kalasha valley, where the people are all Muslim (it was in the same town, in fact, as Wazir's school). He was paying a condolence call on the family who lived there and invited me to join him. I noticed what a good ambassador he was for his people, and that a part of this was how he played down his Kalasha identity. His name could be taken for a Muslim one (it was twenty years, one person told me, since any child had been given an old-style Kalasha name). He prayed with the family Muslim style, extending his hands and symbolically wiping his face with them. Earning Muslims' respect in such ways could come in very handy when needed. Some Kalasha had once been taken as hostages in the course of a dispute over land, and Azem had worked with this family to set them free.

The Kalasha needed diplomacy because they were vulnerable. A book written in 1982, by a passionate Pakistani Muslim defender of the Kala-sha, presented a gloomy picture of Kalasha-Muslim relations: vandalism of

The Kalasha are famous for their homemade wine and brandy, which their religion does not prohibit. Here Wazir Ali (left), Azem Bek (third from left), and the author (between them) sample it during the Chaumos festival in January 2013.

Kalasha holy sites, money offered to Kalasha who converted, "missionary activity of the school teachers and a continuous denigration of the Kalasha culture by them." The writer believed that, as he put it, "outsiders suffering from a feeling of superior culture" were destroying the old traditions. He was in part reflecting the efforts made in the 1950s, shortly after independence, to convert the Kalasha forcibly to Islam.

Azem Beg and Wazir said that things had improved over the past few decades. The Pakistani police were controlling access to the valley and keeping out some of the most aggressive missionaries. Their own numbers, they told me, were increasing. Tourism—though it has decreased—has clearly benefited their villages, which now have a number of new, well-built houses. Even so, I was told by one Kalasha man that Muslim visitors would always nag him by asking, "Why have you not yet converted?"

I feared that much worse might await them. Pakistan was a country of contradictions. It was founded by a liberal Shi'a Muslim, but in the past twenty years, four thousand Shi'a have been killed there, a blasphemy law has been deployed oppressively against the country's minorities, and religious extremists have carved out areas of virtual self-rule in the Pashtun areas near Chitral, where they are challenged only by controversial, lethal US drones. Pakistani politicians who see a whole range of difficult constituencies that they must buy can see one that is cheap: religious fundamentalists will give their support for free if they are given influence over education and the morality of the people. All that is needed is to mortgage the future.

However, a vein of tolerance can still be found in Pakistan wherever the fundamentalists have been kept out, and Chitral had long been largely cut off from the rest of Pakistan by its topography and by the British-drawn border, which put part of the valley in Afghanistan. In winter, the only land route for a long time had been a very tough climb over the Lowari Pass (at ten thousand feet) or else a trip through Afghan territory. But at the time of my visit a tunnel had been dug under the pass, which when it was fully opened would create an easy route between Chitral and the rest of Pakistan. It would boost the local economy but might also bring other, less desirable changes. "When that tunnel is open," the Pakistani photographer Zulfikar gloomily said to me, "I wonder how long the Kalasha will last."

Epilogue

DETROIT

IN A SUPERMARKET IN METROPOLITAN DETROIT, a conurbation that houses half a million people whose roots lie in the Middle East, I overheard a woman in a white smock take a break from stacking shelves to address a customer in a language that was half familiar to me; it was like Hebrew and Arabic, but different, its words unknown to me, smooth-flowing but laden with harsh consonants. It was Aramaic. Amid the Muzak and synthetic fruit drinks in a suburban American store, I was hearing the language of Christ.

Aramaic was once the pre-Islamic lingua franca of the Middle East. Its different dialects all closely resemble both Hebrew and Arabic, to which Aramaic is essentially a linguistic cousin. (For example, "peace be with you" in Arabic is *salaam aleikum,* in Hebrew *shalom aleichem,* and in Iraqi Aramaic *shlama lokhum.*) It is still the language traditional rabbis in Jerusalem use when they curse. One of the most famous of Jewish rituals, the Kaddish prayer, has an Aramaic name, not a Hebrew one. (*Kaddish* is Aramaic for "holy.") In the Middle East, Aramaic has now been all but displaced by Arabic, but in the distant northern villages where Iraq's Christians endured over the centuries, it remains in use. When people from those villages watched Mel Gibson's 2004 film *The Passion of the Christ,* which was in the language that would have been used in Jesus's time, they could understand it without subtitles.

Originally these villagers' ancestors belonged to the Baghdad-based Christian Church of the East. Hardly known in Europe, this was once one of the world's great churches; it had the allegiance during the Middle Ages of 10 percent of all Christians in the world, and its Patriarch, based in Baghdad, had bishops and monasteries across a wider swath of the world than the Pope in Rome. Its missionaries brought Christianity to China in AD 635, a fact recorded on the so-called Nestorian Stele in Xi'an. In the thirteenth century it was the only Christian church to have at its head a man of East Asian origin (his name was Yahballaha, and he was Chinese or Mongolian; he came to Baghdad on an extraordinary four-thousand-mile pilgrimage from Beijing). Both Mongolia and Tibet have alphabets based on the Syriac script introduced by Iraqi Christian missionaries more than a millennium ago.

The Church of the East evolved among Christians living under the Persian Empire, who found that their ideological differences with Western Christians usefully protected them from suspicion that they might be secretly in league with the rival Byzantines. Its members have sometimes been called Nestorians, a name that identifies them with Nestorius, who rejected the idea that a Christian could say on Good Friday that "God is dead." He wanted to distinguish between Jesus as God and Jesus as man. The Church of the East never quite adopted the teachings of Nestorius, but it did reject the use of icons and play down the role of the Virgin Mary. British missionaries called them the "Protestants of the Middle East," choosing to ignore their un-Protestant cult of saints and practice of monasticism.

This church is today hardly even a shadow of what it once was. Much of this is due to Tamerlane, who sacked Baghdad in 1401 and left ninety thousand skulls on its ruins. He was particularly hostile to Christians, and from his time onward, it seems, the Church of the East clung on only in the mountains of northern Iraq, northeastern Syria, and southern Turkey. In the 1830s its members faced a similar threat when a militia sent from a nearby Kurdish chieftain, probably at the behest of the Ottoman government in Istanbul, killed twenty thousand Christian men, women, and children. The Church of the East—sometimes called also the Assyrian Church—had a number of splits over the centuries, some of them provoked by disputes over the church's leadership which often historically went from father to son, leaving other potential claimants disappointed. Often the dissident group would pledge loyalty to the pope in Rome, who eventually created a Uniate "Chaldean" Church for them that was recognized by Rome but preserved its distinctive rite and customs. Today, as a result, there are both "Assyrian" and "Chaldean" Christians, as well as a small number of Christians from other traditions.

After the supermarket, I went to a nearby church—a prefabricated building set back from the road, surrounded by parked cars. Outside, it was suburban America (an area with no trace of the urban decay that has blighted the city of Detroit—Detroit's metropolitan area is far larger than the city and more prosperous). Once inside, however, I was back in Iraq. There were stickers in Arabic on the collection boxes. A deep male voice was chanting the Chaldean liturgy, which dates back to the fifth century AD and is the oldest Christian service still in use, in Aramaic. "Kaddisha, kaddisha, kaddisha," recited the priest: holy, holy, holy. Chaldean cookbooks were on sale at a little bookstore at the back, and the Catholic-style altar was decorated in gold leaf and bunches of artificial fruit. A black-and-white poster by the church door showed a picture of Mar Addai Scher, after whom the church was named. *Mar* is the Aramaic word for a holy man, and Addai Scher was a Chaldean bishop executed by Turkish soldiers in 1915. Alongside the more than one million Armenians who died in that terrible year, hundreds of thousands of Chaldeans and Assyrians were also killed, and still more fled to Iraq. In Mardin, which is now a beautiful holiday resort near the southern border of Turkey, there are houses bearing the names, carved above the door, of their onetime owners who were killed or driven out.

After 2003 it was the turn of Iraq's Christians to flee, this time to the West. As late as the 1990s there were still 1.4 million Christians in Iraq. Now the country is not stable enough for a survey to be carried out, but probably only a third of that number remain, or even fewer. This enormous wave of emigration is not just because of the dangers that Christians have been facing there, but also because of the possibilities of building a better life elsewhere—and perhaps most of all the feeling, as one Iraqi Christian put it to me, of no longer being wanted in Iraq.

My own Arabic teacher in Baghdad, whose name was Nadia, was a Christian whose first language was Aramaic. She told me in 2006 that she dreaded every journey that took her out of her home. She never knew if kidnappers might see her as a viable target, or whether the family who lived across the street and who seemed to stand at their window all day long watching people come and go might perhaps be passing information to terrorists. (The family's Muslim neighbors were otherwise friendly and supportive, she said.) And there was always the risk of being caught in a bomb blast meant for others. Going to church was especially dangerous. When she got home in the evening, she said, neither she nor her parents had the energy to say anything to one another. They ate in silence and went to bed dreading the next day. Nadia left in 2007. Her parents stuck it out for another year and then moved north to Kurdistan. They didn't know Kurdish and had to accept lower salaries and living standards, but at least there they were safe. Nadia, reaching Detroit, had a better experience. She found Rafi at the church she had begun attending. They had known each other when they were children in Iraq, but they had not seen each other for years, because he had emigrated before the war. At their wedding, the priest was the same one who had officiated at their local church in Baghdad. He had moved to Detroit, too. It was as if an entire community had been transplanted halfway across the world.

The head of the Assyrian Christians, Patriarch Mar Dinkha IV, lives in Chicago. There are more speakers of Aramaic in metropolitan Detroit than there are in Baghdad: over a hundred thousand Iraqi Chaldeans live in the city and surrounding areas, and they have established nine churches, restaurants, a newspaper called the *Chaldean News,* a radio station, an annual festival, and (for the richest among them, which generally means the longest-established) a multimillion-dollar club. Sadly, they have not brought the Iraqi aesthetic with them, the beautiful houses and shrines of the hill villages where the Chaldeans have traditionally lived. When I traveled by bus around northern Iraq in 2012, each village seemed to have a monastery or saint's tomb, or else a ruined citadel that related in some way to the community's long history. This is something that emigrants cannot re-create in their adopted country. In greater Detroit there is little that distinguishes one home from the next in the rows of neat, all-American suburban houses. The

Egyptian Copts, Iraqi Chaldeans, Lebanese Shi'a, and Syrian Sunnis who live here and in the nearby towns keep their national cultures strictly within the home.

Other Middle Easterners agree that the Chaldeans are among the most conservative of immigrant groups. Church attendance is high and two new priests were lately ordained. Certainly the community newspaper, the *Chaldean News,* gives little sign of the stirrings of rebellious youth. I thought it might when I started to read a review of a play at a community cultural center—a play whose hero is a man who tries to resist his parents' pressure to marry. An edgy examination of changing values and a community coming to grips with secularism and modernity, perhaps? But no, the play had a happy ending, the paper reported: the hero finds a nice Chaldean woman and marries her.

The play was true to life. In America as a whole, according to a 2013 book by Naomi Schaefer Riley, the interfaith marriage rate is 42 percent, and parents care more about the political views of their possible sons- and daughters-in-law more than they do about their religious identity. That is not true of its Middle Eastern communities, among whom exogamous marriages remain very rare. The Assyrians of Chicago claim that only 10 percent of their community marry out. Some families will go far to control their children's marriage choices: I met an Iraqi Christian woman at a dinner party in Ann Arbor, near Detroit, who told me that she had run away from home, where she had no freedom to meet men. "As a teenager?" I asked. "No, I was twenty-six," she told me.

Although Chaldeans and Assyrians do not see themselves as Arab, their history parallels closely that of other communities from the Middle East, both Muslim and Christian. Large-scale emigration from the Middle East began in the late nineteenth century, driven by growing poverty and land shortages in Lebanon and Palestine, as well as Ottoman oppression and conflict. Most of the migrants were Christian, and Latin America was a favored destination because it both encouraged immigration and offered plenty of economic opportunities. As a consequence, it attracted the lion's share of Arab Christian migrants, with some startling results: today, for example, 5 percent of Latin America's population is ethnically Arab; there are more Christians of Palestinian descent in Chile than in Palestine; eight presidents of South and Central American countries have been of Middle Eastern descent; and the world's richest man (Carlos Slim Helú, a businessman), one of its best-known singers (Shakira), and the actress Salma Hayek all have Lebanese ancestry. The 2004 presidential election in El Salvador was contested by two politicians, one from the radical left and the other from the right—and both of their families were Christian Palestinians from the same small town near Bethlehem.

In the United States it is Michigan that has a higher proportion of Arab Americans than any other state. Their history is explained by the Arab American Museum in Dearborn, a city where 20 percent of the population are Arab. When I reached the museum, I found a small knot of people outside. They were staring at a man on the other side of the road, who was standing on the steps of Dearborn's city hall. He had set up a lectern with the words "Kafir! Infidel!" written on it against a backdrop of black cloth. The man at the lectern was managing to make himself heard over a hubbub of voices from supporters and opponents. "An end to Muslim immigration!" he demanded. "No Muslims in senior government posts!" Pastor Terry Jones, author of the book *Islam Is of the Devil*, whose well-publicized plans to burn a copy of the Koran had caused riots in Afghanistan, was aiming to provoke the people of Dearborn.

Many of the Arabs he was haranguing, I saw, were wearing crucifixes. A majority of Arab Americans are Christian, although the demographic is changing fast thanks to new waves of immigration from the Middle East. A sign in the museum's blue-mosaic-tiled lobby reflected this change, declaring that it was "an institution that makes a 4th-generation Arab American Christian whose great-grandparents came from Syria and a newly arrived Muslim immigrant from Iraq feel that the museum tells both of their stories." Until recently, Arabs who came to America tended to arrive with very little and achieved success only through hard work and luck. They were peddlers in the 1850s, $5-a-day manual laborers at Ford in the 1920s, and shopkeepers in the 1960s. Henry Ford's auto factory at Dearborn, Michigan, which was completed in 1928, was a particular magnet for Middle Eastern migrants (mostly at that stage Iraqi and Lebanese Christians) because it offered work to people who spoke poor English. They formed the nucleus that subsequently attracted others, both Muslim and Christian, who could see better opportunities for themselves in a place where their culture and communities were already established. There are now nearly 3.5 million Americans with roots in the Arab world, according to the Arab American Institute. The big success stories were all featured in the museum: politicians such as Donna Shalala; businessmen such as the founder of Kinko's, Paul Orfalea; and poets such as Kahlil Gibran.

I was browsing in the museum's shop when Yusif turned up. A friend of a friend, he was to be my guide to local Arab landmarks. He arrived dressed in a wooly hat, cowboy boots, and a jacket decorated with antiwar badges, one of which declared, "I'm already against the next war." We went to a boot

shop so he could look for a new pair. He was every inch a Palestinian and yet somehow had managed also to fit into a particularly American category: the rebellious hippie. Though he was in his seventies, he was in better shape than me, due to a routine of swimming in an ice-cold lake every day.

That evening was the first night of an Arab-American festival in Dearborn, and the festival was our next stop. When we arrived, an Egyptian band was playing at full volume, and a closed-off section of the street was crowded with people, many of them standing in a semicircle and watching. A small group in the center of the circle were dancing the *dabkeh,* an

Yusif Barakat shows a younger member of the Arab American community how to perform a traditional Arab dance, the *dabkeh,* in Dearborn, Michigan, in summer 2012. Photo by the author

Arabic dance that involves people holding hands and stepping swiftly and rhythmically from side to side. To my horror, Yusif bounded straight onto the dance floor; lacking rhythm, balance, and the confidence not to mind about either, I skulked to one side. A couple of young men, who looked as if they were Yemeni, started to take instruction from Yusif in the finer points of the *dabkeh*. An old woman in a veil moved her feet to the tune as we passed her.

When he had danced enough, Yusif offered to drive me around the area. He showed me the Orthodox church where he had been altar server and nearly became a priest, and the Ford factory, where, like so many other immigrants, he had worked to support his family. Near the factory stood an Arab cultural center that he had helped to set up. He also showed me the young offenders' school from which he had only lately retired as a volunteer. In the verdant countryside around the school lived many of his friends, several of whom were Jewish peace activists.

Yusif had come to America as a refugee, denied the right of return to his family home in what had been Palestine. He remained bitterly angry at Israel. Yet his own life in America seemed, like those of several other American Middle Easterners that I met, to be bound up with the Jewish community. Soon after arriving in America he had two children by a Jewish woman and, feeling that he was too young to marry, had decided with their mother to give them both up for adoption: one to a Jewish charity and one to a Catholic one. Decades later, in middle age, he wanted to find his children and succeeded in tracing his daughter, who had been brought up as an Orthodox Jew. He was still searching for his son.

———————

YUSIF'S RELATIONSHIP was an unusual one not because his girlfriend was Jewish—several of the émigrés that I met in Britain and America, from religious minorities, said they found an instant affinity with American Jews—but because these minority communities tend to keep to themselves, and certainly to discourage cross-religious sexual relationships. "Sterling Heights is where we live," one Chaldean told me. "Dearborn is Muslims." The suburb of Troy was the best place to find Egyptian Copts. To find Maronites, I was advised to head to Grosse Pointe.

Immigrant churches both benefited from and helped cement communal identity. The priest at Livonia's magnificent Orthodox basilica, Father Shalhoub, proudly showed me around. His community—Arabic-speaking Syrian and Palestinian Christians who follow the same traditions and teachings as the Greek and Russian Orthodox—are called Antiochan Orthodox and have five hundred churches in the United States. Father Shalhoub's church looked like it might be one of the very best of the five hundred. "Here is marble from Syria," he said as he pointed out the beautiful icons, which had been painstakingly painted in Syria and shipped over. The whole church was modeled on the church of St. Simeon Stylites near Antioch.

Their communities back home were, by contrast with the Chaldeans, not especially religious. But that changed when they came to America. "People make more effort to go to church here than in the old country," he said. "What keeps the Orthodox Christian is the church. It preserves their culture, keeps their identity as Arabs. The first thing that families do when they come to America is look me up—the church becomes like a haven, a memory of home. The neighborhood at home"—meaning the Middle East—"protected people from outside attack, and here the church takes the place of the neighborhood. People come here and they see others who look like them, and they hear Arabic spoken. It's a fellowship not just of religion, but of ethnicity and culture." The priest's room was full of books and photos and cards from the Middle East. "In this envelope is five dollars from *my money*," a child had written on one of them. "Please give it to a needy person." The Orthodox, he felt, would not assimilate in any meaningful way. Unlike Chaldeans and Maronites, they could not be tempted by their local Catholic parish, because they were not in communion with Rome. And so, it seemed, this Orthodox church would not just keep its people Christian: it would also keep them Arab.

A member of this Orthodox community later said something similar. After she arrived in the United States from Lebanon in the 1970s, the church was her link to home. It helped her make the transition to American life. "It's a family away from family," she said, although she added that her son had taken a different view, wanting to be Arab first and Christian second, and staying away from church as a result. The good thing about being religious in America, she said, was that it was not politicized: one's livelihood does not obviously depend on one's religion. She was drawing a contrast with her home country, Lebanon, where Orthodox Christians rarely get government jobs. What she did miss was the easy way that people in Lebanon mixed with those of other communities, such as Muslims and Druze. She believed Muslims in America were more religious than those in Lebanon, and all the *hejab*-wearing women she saw in Dearborn made her feel like an outsider among them. "People here group around religion rather than nation. People feel if they stick to their own, then their children will marry someone from their own religion."

Just a hundred yards from the huge Greek Orthodox church was a Shi'a mosque, almost as large. A serious-looking receptionist with a strict *hejab* ushered me in for an impromptu meeting with its Iraqi imam, Hassan al-Qazwini. He was very optimistic about his community's prospects in America. "It's a pluralist society, where Muslims can integrate very well. It offers unparalleled freedoms. We can flourish here not just in the economic sense but in a religious sense." To make sure that even the unreligious could stay involved, he preferred to call the mosque an "Islamic community center," which could host wedding parties, for instance, as well as religious ceremonies. The majority, though, were devout. "In the second and third generations, the connection with the region is much less. People aren't keen to go to the Middle East; they'd rather spend their summers here. But they keep their food traditions, their social traditions, and many are devoutly religious." And the Iraqi Shi'a, who had just arrived, had more time to attend religious services. "Religion is a magnet, it often proves stronger than any other kind of affiliation, even racial."

GEORGE KHOURY WAS AN EXCEPTION to the rule that Middle Eastern communities in Detroit tended to huddle around their place of worship. He was a Christian Palestinian living in a largely Jewish neighborhood. He had married a non-Arab woman. None of this meant that he had changed his identity, as I could tell as soon as I was dropped off outside his house. The clue was the license plate: PAL 4 EVR. It was cleverly ambiguous. It might just mean he was a good friend. But I knew that the PAL stood for Palestine, which his family had left as refugees in 1948. George told me that he had chosen to live in a Jewish neighborhood in part as a challenge to the voluntary segregation most immigrants practiced. He was also thinking about his children. "The crime report here is close to zero," he said as I sat in his home drinking a cup of Turkish coffee, its cardamom scent reminding me of countless cups drunk in Jerusalem, Bethlehem, and Jaffa. "High school grads at 100 percent, those who go to college above 90 percent, that's what I want for my children. Peer pressure controls kids. And they had Jewish friends, which made me happy—that we can coexist." There had been some trouble with the older children at the school, and one time the teacher had told the class, "There's no such thing as Palestine." George's children had come back confused and wondering whom to believe. So he had given them special classes of his own on Sundays, teaching them their history.

Quite unlike the Chaldeans, he saw his identity through a political lens. The history that he taught was the history of Western injustice. Indeed, George did not think that Arab Christianity would last long in America. "The death of the mosque is far away," he said, "but I think it's the beginning of the death of the church." Encounters with Americans weren't helping. "When we Arab Christians have a dialogue with American Christians, they say they're Baptists or Unitarians. And they have no Mass, no Communion, no fasting. So the Arabs start wondering, are we the only ones left still doing these things?"

There was an elegiac side to George. He was telling me the story of the great poet and epic hero Abu Zayd when he stopped and sighed. "I am from the last generation that will understand these stories," he said. This mattered a great deal to him. "The stories shape you—they teach you to think about the group more than yourself, to be generous. I try to transfer that to my children. But Abu Zayd fought only with a sword. In America they have tanks! These days he wouldn't stand a chance." He was thinking not just of the man Abu Zayd but of the culture that he had hoped to hand down to his children. "Coming here was the worst decision I ever made," he said gloomily. "I thought it would be like a salad, every ingredient taking on flavor from the other. It's more like a blender—everything ends up gray." For the moment, though, George's generation still held on to their identity. "It is an era of Arab Christians' life," George said, "when they are on the verge of being totally American and yet they have allegiance to their Arabism." Still, he knew that other Americans would never understand who Arab Christians really were. "I was asked many times, 'When did you convert?' Our local priest was asked the same."

———————

I TRIED TO UNDERSTAND why Yusif and George were both so much unhappier with American life than the other refugees that I had met, especially those from Iraq. My sense was that it had to do with being Palestinian; the experience of exile had been poisoned by the knowledge that it was forced. And they had been in America so much longer and were more integrated, to the point that they were looking complete assimilation full in the face. I wondered whether coming to the West must always be a back-loaded contract for immigrant communities—get the benefit of prosperity now, pay the price of loss of identity later. Or was it up to them to fashion an identity and communal structures that could endure? I discussed this with Yusif at a shop run by a Druze émigré from Lebanon. "We are melting," Yusif agreed, quoting a line of Palestinian poetry. "We are to blame. We didn't find the glue."

The shop was an Aladdin's cave of scents and tastes from the Middle East: bags of oregano and aniseed, tins of vine leaves and olives, and flour-dusted Lebanese treats. Halim, the Druze shopkeeper, came over from behind a stack of boxed Alwazah tea bags and added his gentle voice to the conversation. "You have to hold on to your culture, faith, and heritage if you don't want to be lost here, in a huge ocean. But we Druze have no church. We have no mosque. We have no teacher. We practice our religion individually. In Lebanon there are sheikhs who keep us united. There are none in America; maybe we're too materialistic here. And so many people lack faith in the Universal Mind," he said. Their community schools taught children Arabic, not religion. And their small numbers made it hard for children to find Druze husbands and wives.

I knew the Druze had much trouble explaining themselves in the overtly religious culture of America. Milia, a Druze woman who was brought up in Dallas, Texas, had told me of the embarrassing day at school when she and the rest of the class had to stand up and describe their religion: What was its holy day in the week? What were its beliefs? What kind of prayers did it have? She said: "I'm a Druze. We don't have a holy day, I don't know our beliefs and I never have to pray." The teacher said, "You're making it up! I'm going to tell your mother." Of course, when she did, Milia's mother could confirm it was all true. "It's really strange for others who conform to rituals to understand what it's about," Linda, a Druze academic based in the quiet and cerebral town of Ann Arbor, told me. "It's like the Chinese system—we have traditions but no rules." Despite these markers of difference, Linda had noticed a growing interest in religious identity among the younger generation of American Druze. "My daughter's now thirty, and she is asking questions about Druze culture. She's more interested in that than Lebanese culture. The younger generation are identifying more as Druze," she said. "They are more fanatical." I could hardly imagine how one could be fanatical in pursuing a faith that has no rules or rituals. Apparently, though, where American communities of Druze are larger, there is greater enthusiasm for tradition. California, she said, even had a Druze sheikh.

On the other hand, the liberty that children enjoyed in America made raising them more challenging than if the families still lived in the Druze homeland. "Raising children was hard," Linda admitted. "We couldn't impose our moral principles on them. At twelve, thirteen years old they saw cousins doing drink and drugs; they asked, 'Why can't we?'" Cross-religious marriages were another challenge. American Druze have established regular social events to bring Druze families together, with the not-very-hidden motive of encouraging young Druze to marry each other. They have also had to adopt a more pragmatic approach to outmarriage and no longer completely ostracize those who do marry out. A Druze sheikh once offered some consolation to a worried expatriate mother whose daughter had left the religion. "When your child dies," he said, "she will be reincarnated back in Lebanon as Druze again."

Druze communities in America are remarkably tight-knit. They look for work in the same towns, so that at least six or seven Druze families can live together in a neighborhood rather than staying apart. Like Yusif and George, Milia's family had also found unexpected common ground with American Jews. "Wherever we went we ended up meeting and connecting with Jewish people without knowing. There's a similarity of culture," she said. Many Middle Eastern émigrés from these smaller religions find common ground with Jews—especially because the latter practice their traditions and customs in private, keeping their identity and community alive but outwardly assimilating into secular society.

There is another obvious similarity between Jews and Druze. Judaism doesn't seek converts. The Druze go even further by *refusing* converts. Some American Druze want to change this, along with the culture of secrecy that prevents them from learning about their religion and explaining it articulately to others. In Boston, I attended a seminar of young American Druze during which they discussed their faith. What were they to make, they asked of the older people who were present, of the traditional belief that the souls of the dead who are not reincarnated in Lebanon are reborn in China?

BOSTON, WHERE I LIVED IN 2010 AND 2011, has witnessed not just Druze religious seminars but also a Mandaean baptism. The ceremony was described by the scholar Edmondo Lupieri at the start of his fascinating book *The Mandaeans: The Last Gnostics*: "Sunday, June 13, 1999. A man dressed in a long, white robe, his long beard concealed by a kind of white scarf that covers his mouth, his long hair wrapped in a white turban, stands in the river, holding in his left hand a long, wooden stick." The river is the Charles, and the book describes kayakers paddling past the ceremony without giving it a second glance. Wisam Breegi, a silversmith and Mandaean activist who organized the ceremony, remembers the kayakers. That was the good thing about Massachusetts, he told me when we met at his silver shop near the center of Boston: nobody was bothered.

The ceremony should have drawn a second glance, because it was the first Mandaean baptism ceremony in the New World. It was as significant, to those who took part, as the first Thanksgiving was to the Puritans and native Americans who celebrated it. And the Mandaean Pilgrim fathers have followed in its wake. Wisam was the only Mandaean in Massachusetts at the time. Now, just twelve years later, he told me that there were 650. In his shop he held classes to teach traditional Mandaean skills to the new arrivals. In Worcester, to the west, he was trying to found a community center for members of his faith. He saw the Jews of America as the model for his own community. But the specific model that he had in mind was the Syrian Jewish community of Brooklyn, who passed a decree in the 1920s against accepting intermarriage even with converts to Judaism. Wisam approved: such marriages, he thought, would dilute the Mandaeans to the point that they would become wholly secularized and the community would vanish. They should never be allowed.

As we talked calls came persistently on Wisam's cell phone from Iraqis who wanted his help in getting to the United States. Born in North Africa, he had been brought up as a Mandaean—"but," he said, "I never knew what it meant." As with many émigré Druze, the secrecy of religion sat uneasily alongside exile; separated from the temples and priests, Wisam found it hard to keep his faith. But he persevered, and worked to draw Mandaeans in the United States together and cement their group identity. Asylum was necessary but double-edged, rescuing Mandaeans from harm but also speeding up their departure from Iraq: "saving Mandaeans, and killing Mandaeanism," he said.

WHAT, THEN, WOULD HAPPEN to a religion that was even less understood in the West, that had strict and complex marriage rules, and whose teachings remain largely secret? Chapter 2 described the life of Mirza Ismail, a Canada-based activist campaigning for Yazidi rights. When I wrote to him in 2011, he invited me to join him that summer on a trip to Buffalo, New York, just over the border from Canada. He was there to see his old friend Abu Shihab, with whom he had escaped from Iraq, and whose house was in a quiet suburb. When Mirza knocked, one of Abu Shihab's children opened the door—and instantly knelt to kiss Mirza's hand. It was a custom the family had kept from the days when they lived in Iraq, because Mirza was Abu Shihab's "brother in the afterlife." Mirza saw himself, he said, as more like a Christian family's godfather, someone who gives spiritual guidance and explains some of the teachings of the religion to his "other family."

We sat in Abu Shihab's living room, and as we talked it seemed that every few minutes another of his children appeared. A boy grinned cheerily, his hair dyed a startling orange color and an ornate crucifix hanging around his neck (a statement of style, not faith, apparently), and then went into a bedroom, where he played a loud computer game. A girl passed silently to and fro in the kitchen without ever looking into the living room. Later Farhan, an older son who had been stranded in Iraq for twenty-one years, appeared. Abu Shihab had eleven children in all. It was as if he was aiming to repopulate the world with Yazidis to make up for the many killed in successive wars.

The oldest son, Shihab, who joined us with his wife, had just gotten a new job paying $9 an hour; he had lost his previous job after failing an English test. Shihab's English seemed good enough to me, especially given that he spoke two other languages—Arabic and Kurmanji—but apparently questions about synonyms had tripped him up. He had had no chance to go to school in Syria because the refugee camp where he lived had not issued him the necessary certificate. In any case, he needed to work so that his wife would not have to—so that she could focus on her studies and qualify as a nurse. "Then I can work and he can have a rest," she said with a smile.

Abu Shihab was no fan of America and Britain's foreign policy. They had failed, as he saw it, to solve his country's problems—especially those of his own region, Sinjar, in northwestern Iraq. But he wanted me to know how much he appreciated the help he had gotten from the United States since his arrival. "If it wasn't for America, my son would be dead," he said, pointing to one of his teenage sons, who promptly ducked out of sight. This son, and one of Abu Shihab's daughters, had a kidney condition that required frequent injections of a kind that the family could never afford. In Syria, where he had first taken refuge after leaving Iraq, the state does not pay for this kind of medical care, and Abu Shihab's family were poor even by Middle Eastern standards. In Sinjar, his chances of securing adequate medical care for his sick children would have been even lower. He told me that there was only a single ten-bed hospital in the area, which is home to half a million people. Abu Shihab put his hand up to his black-dyed hair. "It is on my head!" he said, meaning that he acknowledged the debt he owed his adopted nation. "We never fought against any other country for America, and we aren't from here, but we get health care for free because of people's humanity. In Iraq we are people of the country, and we get nothing."

Their relations with their neighbors, in this largely white working-class suburb, seemed good (a neighbor came in while I was there, and explained to me that he wished he could do something to help the Yazidis in Iraq, because from what he had learned from Abu Shihab, their lives sounded terrible). The one thing that upset the family about American culture was the way their religion was represented. Abu Shihab said he had heard a CNN reporter describe the Yazidis as "the most hideous religion in the world." I found this hard to believe, but he was very sure he had heard it, and he said he hoped that if I wrote my book, then at least nobody would say it again. Indeed, I came away impressed by the family's hospitality, the cleanliness of their home (a well-known characteristic of both Yazidi and Mandaean households in Iraq), and the closeness between generations. This being my first time in a Yazidi home, I was also struck by how little evidence there was of their religion. There were two signs of it: a picture of Lalish—an artist's impression rather than a photograph—standing on a sideboard, and, of course, the obligatory peacock image.

The other pictures in the living room were all of the family—especially of its youngest member, Abu Shihab's three-year-old daughter, Naalin. She provided relief during some of our more depressing conversations, usually by lying upside down on the sofa with her legs in the air, or curling her hands like binoculars and peering at us through them. She was particularly fond of her grandparents, Mirza explained, and they treated her with a great deal of affection. I wondered what life would be like for her when she grew up—specifically, when she was old enough to get married. Yazidi rules on marriage are complicated and very strict. Not only must a Yazidi woman marry a Yazidi man, but he must be from the right caste and the right clan. Some Iraqi families from the smallest caste (the middle-ranking *pir* caste) have to find husbands or wives in other countries. An Iraqi man might find a wife in the Yazidi community in Russia, for example. To ensure that marriage follows these rules, some families force their children to marry when they are only fifteen or sixteen. Abu Shihab's family were *murid*s, the lowest caste. In America there might be a handful of suitable men for Naalin. In a religion that otherwise made few demands of its followers, this was one they could not disobey.

The family wanted to show me the local sights, so we visited Niagara Falls, and they put a CD of Yazidi music into the car stereo. The singer, Abu Shihab told me, was called Khidr Faqir. He had been gifted with musical talent suddenly. When he was a young man in the fields of Sinjar, the Yazidi saint Khidr Elias had appeared to him in a dream. When he awoke, he could sing and play the lute (the *baghlama*, which resembles a guitar) better than any Yazidi alive. Khidr Elias had risen in Abu Shihab's eyes when he refused to perform wearing in Kurdish clothes. "He would only wear Yazidi clothes," said Abu Shihab. Both he and Mirza were keen to stress the Yazidi identity as something separate from the Kurdish one, and derided me for having spent time in Iraq with pro-Kurdish Yazidis.

This family of Yazidis was quite alone in Buffalo, a thousand miles from their nearest coreligionists, who lived in Lincoln, Nebraska. It seemed though that their desire to be themselves, to hold on to their traditions, remained strong. The family had attended a Christian church when they first arrived in America, Abu Shihab told me. The people at the church had helped them when they were new there, and they still felt a bond of friendship with them. "But we did not give up our own beliefs," he added with emphasis. Internet telephone services such as Skype allowed dispersed Yazidis to remain linked to each other. Virtual groups had sprung up across the world, opening new avenues to find potential marriage partners for their children. And yet a major challenge for Yazidis in America remains: as with the Druze, very few of them know the theology of their religion. There was a plan, his son Shihab said, to set up a community center in Nebraska where people could meet to play cards and learn the basics of the religion. "The problem is that the older generation, like my dad, are closed-minded. He knows things about the religion but he won't tell us. It's only Sheikh Mirza who will tell us things." His wife chipped in, "You probably know more about our religion than we do." The Yazidis are at a loss when they have to explain their beliefs to others or take part in theological debate.

Nor do they have a counterpart in American society. Middle Eastern Christians have an instant bond with American Christians, and Muslim immigrants now can easily find communities of American Muslims who will give them some kind of practical assistance and a place to worship. The Yazidis are alone—except, that is, for Amaru Mark Pinkham, the grand prior of the International Order of Gnostic Templars. The grand prior told me that he had been meditating in South America, experimenting with new ways to experience reality, when he suddenly found himself surrounded by a flock of peacocks. Puzzled by the vision, he later asked his friends about it, and one of them pointed him toward the Yazidis. To his series Secrets of the Knights Templar (both books and online videos) he added a new and final episode: *Mysteries of the Peacock Angel*. On its website, his order describes itself as "dedicated to the revival of Gnostic Wisdom and the Goddess Tradition of the Original Templars." The organization, which Grand Prior Pinkham (pictured on the website along with his wife, both wearing very tall red-and-white miters) traces back to John the Baptist via Mary Magdalene and the Knights Templar, had thirty to forty members when I spoke to him in 2013. But he hoped that "Jedi Templar" training, offered from 2014 onward, would raise its numbers.

I was skeptical of his genuine historical continuity with John the Baptist, but his help was welcomed by the Yazidis—though they could not allow Pinkham himself to join their religion. That, anyway, was what the Yazidis of Lincoln told me when I visited them in 2013. Having heard from Abu Shihab and Sheikh Mirza that there was a much larger community in Nebraska, I was keen to find out how one of Iraq's esoteric faiths was surviving in middle America. When I arrived at Lincoln's little airport, a group of twenty Yazidis was waiting to greet me—Iraqi hospitality in the Cornhusker State. Many were recent arrivals and had reached Lincoln courtesy of the federal refugee resettlement program.

Basim, who had been there several years, was my host for the visit and proved to be something of a community organizer. He arranged for six Yazidis to meet me at a café in downtown Lincoln. One of them was a *pir,* and one of the others in the group used him as an example of how they have had to change their customs. "He is a *pir,* and back home we would normally kiss his hand when we meet him. But we don't do that here." He looked at the bare wooden floor and chic-austere interior of the café, whose other customers were all wearing headphones and staring at their iPads. "People would think it was odd." Most of these men had arrived in the past three years. One who had been in the country longer than that and had attended high school in Lincoln experienced his culture shock early. "Seeing boys and girls kissing by the lockers," he said, "that was hard for me to accept. And I had never seen a big city before." Another, a recent arrival, had been shocked by something else. "The assault rifles that they sell openly in the shops here," he gasped. "In Baghdad you would never find guns like that for sale!"

They worried that their community would not keep up the Yazidi religion for long. "We have no money for our own festivals," said Basim. "So the Fourth of July will end up more important than the Yazidi New Year, because everyone else celebrates that. Yazidis are doing Christmas and not Charsema Sor." One sheikh, he added, still lit 366 candles at home for religious festivals, and Basim himself organized an occasional quiz about the religion, testing Yazidis on their knowledge of Yazidi lore. But they were all hampered by not knowing enough. "If my children ask what is a Yazidi," lamented one of them, "I can't tell them." And the *pir* told me that he faced a particularly difficult challenge. He was meant to marry within his specific subcaste, which has now almost died out. "In my home city there were fifteen thousand Yazidis," he said, "but I could not marry a single one of them."

I asked if they had trouble explaining their religion to people in America, but the response was that there was not much interest in hearing about it. "People don't want to ask open-ended questions. They just ask, 'Are you Muslim?' There was some trouble after 9/11 because people thought we were Muslims." As with Abu Shihab, their sentiment toward America was gratitude, with their complaints mostly directed at governments back in the Middle East. They talked about a Jordanian customs official who had laughed at

Basim, a Yazidi in Lincoln, Nebraska, shows his reverence for Melek Taoos by decorating his living room with the image and feathers of a peacock. Photo by the author

and thrown away the sacred earth from Lalish that one family tried to take with them on the plane. They talked about Turkey, where Yazidis still (they said) had to declare themselves Muslims, and where rocks could still be seen on which Yazidis who had refused to convert during the massacres of 1917 had been beheaded. They were concerned at news from Kurdistan, where rioters had burned a Yazidi-owned alcohol shop a few months before (they showed me the video). They had no nostalgia for the Middle East. "There are more rights for prisoners here than for free men there," the young man who had gone to high school in America said. "I don't suppose any country treats immigrants better. I just have to explain to new arrivals that it's normal for people not to greet you here." People in American small towns, especially in the midwestern areas, are often considered unusually friendly, but to these Yazidi villagers they seemed cold and distant.

FLEEING THE DECLINE and diminution that their communities are suffering in their homelands, these immigrants were for the most part thriving in the United States, putting up new places of worship and increasing in confidence. Christians in Syria live fearfully in the shadow of what happened to their co-religionists in Iraq. But in Detroit Father Shalhoub is putting the finishing touches on another set of spectacular icons. The churches of Baghdad are emptying, but in Boston, an Iraqi nun who acted as chaplain to Boston University has now founded a new religious order for women in that American city. In London Nadia Gattan, married to a British man, is teaching her children about their Iraqi heritage, and Shahin is preparing the water that Zoroastrian children can spray over each other to celebrate the summer solstice, just as their Persian ancestors did for Tirghan every year.

———————

I BEGAN THIS BOOK with some observations on why minorities are leaving the Middle East. After spending four years meeting them and reading their history, I care about them more than ever. So what can be done? It is the people of the Middle East who most of all must stitch together their frayed communities. A better understanding of history may give them something in which all, regardless of religion, can share a common pride. I was struck by something that a devout Muslim friend of mine from Iraq said after she had visited the British Museum: "It was amazing to discover that Babylon had an even greater history than Egypt, that it was the cradle of civilizations; I had never understood what that meant. Hearing the Epic of Gilgamesh and realizing that a massive part of my heritage was in the British Museum gave me more than Saddam to relate to." Best of all, a knowledge of history can help us all—wherever we are—to see that any civilization, whether Roman or Arab or British or America, is at its most successful where it is most open to others and the ideas of others.

What can people outside the Middle East do to help? Anything that outsiders want to do to help minorities must be founded on a policy of goodwill toward the entire population. Christian schools, for example, have done more good for Christians in Iraq, Palestine, and Lebanon than just about anything else because they have been open to Muslim children, and so have fulfilled a triple purpose of making Christians better able to earn a living, earning goodwill from Muslims, and providing a humane education to everyone. (Crucially, they have not tried to convert their Muslim pupils.) By contrast, Western military interventions have generally set back the cause of minorities, not advanced them. Members of a minority need protection from their own fellow countrymen and -women, not from foreigners who stay briefly and then leave. Instability usually unsettles minority groups, who feel (and are) particularly vulnerable. Most recently, the invasion of Iraq precipitated a huge emigration of Christians and Mandaeans from the country as it spiraled down into civil war.

At the same time, the governments of the United States, United Kingdom, and other countries are involved in the Middle East in many other ways. They give funding for development. They offer military support. They also, by engaging with people and organizations, confer on them implicit support and recognition. In doing so, they can and should take a firm stand against those who incite religious hatred, whatever their religion (recall from Chapter 6 how a Coptic priest criticized anti-Muslim propaganda broadcast from Cyprus by one of his fellow priests). Focusing on extremism only when it turns violent ignores the fact that violence comes at the end of a long process of radicalization, which begins with the encouragement of anger and hatred. Western governments should take religious belief seriously, understanding it well enough to tell the difference between a fervent believer and a preacher of hate.

Lastly, asylum is on offer in countries such as the United States, Canada, and Australia to religious minorities, and this in itself tempts them to leave their countries of origin. Asylum saves Iraqi Christians, Yazidis, and Mandaeans from immediate danger, and I found them to be deeply grateful and to have strong feelings of loyalty to their new homes—but it also diminishes their communities back home. There is a partial solution to this problem, which is to help these groups hold on to their traditions and build communities in their new homes. I would like to think that this book, by celebrating their traditions and history, might encourage them to do that.

Sources and Further Readings

I want to thank first of all the people who are the subjects of this book. Without the help of Nadia Gattan, Mirza Ismail and Abu Shihab, Shahin Bekhradnia, Sami Makarem, Benny Tsedaka, Fr. Yoannis, and my friends at Sainte Thérèse, Azem Bek and Wazir Ali, my Yazidi friends in Nebraska, and those, including George and Yusif, who saw me in Detroit, it could not have been written.

As well as kindly writing the foreword to this book, Rory Stewart was director of the Carr Center of the Harvard Kennedy School for part of my eighteen-month research fellowship there, which gave me the opportunity (among other things) to begin the research for this book. I would also like to thank the Jerwood Fund for granting me a prize in 2011 that helped meet the costs of some of the traveling this book required: between 2010 and 2014 I visited Egypt, Lebanon and Iraqi Kurdistan twice each, Pakistan, Israel, and the West Bank.

Lara Heimert and Dan Gerstle at Basic Books, Mike Jones at Simon & Schuster, and George Lucas of Inkwell Productions steered me through the editing of this book through their patient and diligent comments. Jack Fairweather, Dr. Lana Asfour, Sir John Jenkins, Dr. Brigid Russell, Professor Philip Kreyenbroek, Dr. Jorunn Buckley, Wynne Maggi, Felicity Devonshire, Dr. Nadim Shehadi, Alice Bragg, Dr. Barbara Jefferis, Gur Hirshberg, Dr. Cornelis Hulsman, and Dr. Amin Makram Ebeid helped me by reading drafts of this book or individual chapters; they bear no responsibility for the opinions expressed in the book, nor for any mistakes that remain.

I also benefited from the lectures and advice of Professor Ali Asani, Professor Oktor Skjaervo, and Dr. Charles Stang of Harvard University.

Choosing any book to highlight as an introduction to Islam, Christianity, and Judaism, other than their sacred texts, is an invidious business. Hans Kung's series on these religions, including *Christianity* (Continuum, 1996), *Judaism* (Bloomsbury, 1995), and *Islam* (Oneworld Publications, 2008), told me much that I had not known. So did Albert Hourani's *A History of the Arab Peoples* (Faber & Faber, 1991) and Eugene Rogan's *The Arabs: A History* (Basic Books, 2011) on a more secular front. The *Encyclopaedia Iranica*, the *Oxford History of Islam,* edited by John L. Esposito (Oxford University Press, 1999), and the *Shorter Encyclopaedia of Islam,* edited by H. A. R. Gibb and J. H. Kramers (Brill, 1953), were all useful reference documents throughout.

On the specific issue of conversion to Islam, I read *Conversion to Islam,* by Richard Bulliet (Harvard University Press, 1979); *Rise of Islam on the Bengal Frontier,* by Richard Eaton (University of California Press, 1996); *The Formation of Islam,* by Jonathan Berkey (Cambridge University Press, 2002); and "The Age of Conversions: A Reassessment" by Michael Morony in *Conversion and Continuity,* edited by M. Gervers and J. Bikhazi (Pontifical Institute of Medieval Studies, 1990).

Three other books that are referred to in multiple chapters are Michael Morony's *Iraq After the Muslim Conquest* (Princeton University Press, 1984), Patricia Crone's *The Nativist Prophets of Early Islamic Iran* (Cambridge University Press, 2012), and Christoph Baumer's *The Church of the East: An Illustrated History of Assyrian Christianity* (I. B. Tauris, 2006).

Quotations from the Bible are from the Authorized King James version unless noted otherwise below. Quotations from the Koran are from the Saheeh International version. Quotes from Herodotus are taken from Aubrey de Sélincourt's translation of *The Histories* (Penguin, 1954).

INTRODUCTION

On Identity by Amin Maalouf is available in English in a translation by Barbara Bray (Harvard Press, 2004).

Al-Ghazali's polemic against Greek philosophy was called *Tahafut al-Falasifa.*

The kaiser's remark is taken from Kamal Salibi's *Bhamdoun: Historical Portrait of a Lebanese Mountain Village* (Centre for Lebanese Studies, 1997).

Ambassador Morgenthau's assessment of the Armenian genocide can be read on the website of the Armenian National Institute, at www.armenian -genocide.org/statement_morgenthau.html.

Suha Rassam's observation comes in her *Christianity in Iraq* (Gracewing, 2010), page 196.

Arthur Balfour's memorandum of August 11, 1919, can be seen in Woodward and Butter, *Documents on British Foreign Policy, 1919–1939* (HMSO, 1952).

CHAPTER 1: MANDAEANS

I met the High Priest when I was head of the political section of the British embassy in Baghdad between 2005 and 2006. I subsequently met Mandaeans in Erbil, northern Iraq, in 2010 and 2013, in the United States, and in Britain. To read more about them, as well as the books listed here, I recommend the Mandaean Associations Union, whose website is www.mandaeanunion.org.

Those who helped me with this chapter included Nadia Hamdan Gattan and her aunt, Sheikh Sattar, and Wasim Breegi, who all generously gave me their time and confidence. Professor Jorunn Buckley of the University of Maine, author of a learned and humane study called *The Mandaeans: Ancient Texts and Modern People* (Oxford University Press, 2000), patiently answered my numerous questions. The staff of the Bodleian Library allowed me to see the Drower collection; likewise the Bibliothèque Nationale in respect to its collection of Syriac and Mandaic manuscripts and books.

For a general introduction to the Mandaeans, there can be nothing better than E. S. Drower's books, especially *The Mandaeans of Iraq and Iran* (Gorgias Press, 2002)—labeled hereafter as *MII*—but also *The Secret Adam* (Oxford University Press, 1960). *Mandaeans: The Last Gnostics,* by Edmondo Lupieri (Eerdmans, 2001) was the source for my stories of Western missionaries' encounters with the Mandaeans, including the Isa-Iahia quote, and also for the Mandaean magical potions that appear later in the chapter. Another major scholar on the Mandaeans is Edwin Yamauchi, who wrote *Gnostic Ethics and Mandaean Origins* (Harvard University Press, 1970).

Excavations at Ur, by Leonard Woolley (E. Benn, 1954), is the source of Woolley's remark on the Flood. I used Andrew George's excellent *The Epic of Gilgamesh: A New Translation* (Penguin, 2003) for the excerpts from the epic in this chapter, including the prostitute's curse. "Therefore is the name of it Babel . . . " comes from Genesis 11:9.

For background on Babylon I read *The Sumerians,* by Samuel Noah Kramer (University of Chicago Press, 1964), and *Everyday Life in Babylon and Assyria,* by Georges Contenau (W. W. Norton, 1966). *Babylon: Mesopotamia and the Birth of Civilization,* by Paul Kriwaczek (Atlantic, 2012), is a description of the legacy of Babylon in the present day. My account of Saddam's reconstruction of Babylon was informed by the September 1997 documentary *The New Babylon* by Journeyman Pictures.

The Patriarchs' salutation "From my cell . . . " is quoted in Baumer's *Church of the East.* Insights into the sectarian bloodshed that ravaged Iraq after 2003 can be found in *Sectarianism in Iraq,* by Fanar Haddad (Hurst, 2011), and *Eclipse of the Sunnis: Power, Exile and Upheaval in the Middle East,* by Deborah Amos (PublicAffairs, 2010). The guidebook to Baghdad alluded to in this chapter was the Bradt travel guide by Karen Dabrowska, published in 2002.

Jaakko Hameen-Anttila's *The Last Pagans of Iraq* (Brill, 2006) was my source on the *Nabatean Agriculture,* of which it is a translation with an added commentary (I am grateful to Philip Wood for the tip).

Al-Mas'udi can be read in *Islamic Historiography: The Histories of Al Masudi,* by Tarif Khalidi (State University of New York Press, 1975).

Caliph Omar weeping at the conversion of Arameans is reported in Crone, *Nativist Prophets,* page 10.

Biruni's comments on the Mandaeans are in his *Chronology of Ancient Nations*, which he wrote in AD 1000 at the age of twenty-seven. It was his eighth book. For more on Biruni, see the *Encyclopaedia Iranica* (e.g., at www .iranicaonline.org). Sarton's remark comes in his book *Introduction to the*

History of Science (Williams & Wilkins, 1927). Ibn Qutaybah's quote is taken from Dimitri Gutas's *Greek Thought, Arabic Culture* (Routledge, 1998).

I used my Arabic edition of the *Ginza Rabba;* an English translation is now available. I read Wilfrid Thesiger's *The Marsh Arabs* in the Longmans 1964 edition. The *Drasa di Yehia* is translated in part in G. R. S. Mead's *Gnostic John the Baptizer,* republished by Jürgen Beck (Altenmunster, 2012).

The religious environment in the late Roman Empire is described in *A World Full of Gods: Pagans, Jews and Christians in the Roman Empire,* by Keith Hopkins (Weidenfeld and Nicolson, 1999). Statistics for the Jewish population of Iraq before the coming of Islam come from Morony's *Iraq After the Muslim Conquest,* page 308; this book was also a source on the survival of paganism in Iraq. My interest in the Marcionites and like movements was originally kindled by Henry Chadwick's *The Early Church* (Penguin, 1993).

Information on Manichaeism came from Ibn Nadim's *Fihrist,* trans. Bayard Dodge (Columbia University Press, 1970); Samuel N. C. Lieu's *Manichaeism in the Later Roman Empire and Medieval China* (Manchester University Press, 1985); and Peter Brown's paper "Diffusion of Manicheism in the Roman Empire," *Journal of Roman Studies,* 1967. The quotations from Augustine's *Confessions* are from Pine-Coffin's translation (Penguin, 1961). The Mandaean funeral prayer can be read in full at http://gnosis.org/library /tsod.htm.

The Sumerian poem "Schooldays" was originally translated by Kramer in 1949; I here used the translation of A. R. George, 2005. The "umannu" prayer is taken from *Astrology: A History,* by Peter Whitfield (British Library, 2001). The Aristokrates horoscope is quoted in *A History of Astrology* by Derek and Julia Parker (London, Deutsch, 1983). Herodotus's remark on Babylonian washing habits is in his *Histories,* I:198. Drower's quote from Hermez on the *melki* comes on page 282 of *MII.*

Drower told of the priests' anger on page x of *The Secret Adam,* and described Krun on page 270 of *MII.* The description of Dinanukht is a translation from the *Ginza Rabba,* reworded by Eliot Weinberger for *An Elemental Thing* (New Directions, 2007). Drower relates the cure to the Baghdad boil in *By Tigris and Euphrates* (Hurst & Blackett, 1923), page 228. The Libat spell is in *MII,* page 26. The Bel and Nebu amulet is mentioned in Drower's article

"A Mandaean Book of Black Magic," *Journal of the Royal Asiatic Society*, vol. 75 (October 1943). The scorpion amulet and the reconstructed Ishtar Gate of Babylon can be seen at Berlin's Pergamon Museum.

The Mandaean Human Rights Group's 2011 report can be seen at www .mandaeanunion.com/images/MAU/MHRG/MHRG_Docs/MHRG%20%20 Report%202011.pdf.

CHAPTER 2: YAZIDIS

I visited Lalish in July 2011, visited Yazidi refugees in Kurdistan in August 2014, and met Yazidis in the United States in 2012 and then again in 2013. I am grateful to those who talked to me, who are named in the book; most of all I want to single out Mirza Ismail, who was very generous with his time, and Abu Shihab, whose family kindly looked after me in Buffalo, New York. In Nebraska Basim gave me a wonderful introduction to his community. The Spiritual Council of the Yazidis were generous in giving me their time, as were Khairi Buzani, Ayad, and Dakheel. Professor Philip Kreyenbroek very kindly corrected some of my early mistakes, while of course not being responsible for any that may remain.

For more information on the Yazidis, there is some useful material at www.lalish.de. For general books on the Yazidis, I suggest *Yazidis: A Study in Survival,* by John S. Guest (Routledge, 1987), E. S. Drower's *Peacock Angel* (John Murray, 1941), and Philip Kreyenbroek's *Yazidism: Its Background, Observances and Textual Tradition* (Edwin Mullen Press, 1995).

For details on Sinjar I am indebted to Nelida Fuccaro's 1994 Durham University e-thesis, "Aspects of the Social and Political History of the Yazidi Enclave of Jabal Sinjar (Iraq) Under the British Mandate, 1919–1932." Details on the history of Edessa and Harran are mostly taken from *Edessa: "The Blessed City,"* by J. B. Segal (Clarendon Press,1970). *Egeria's Travels* can be read in a translation by John Wilkinson (Aris and Phillips, 1999).

"God help the Romans" comes from Walter Emil Kaegi's book *Heraclius, Emperor of Byzantium* (Cambridge University Press, 2003). Surat al-Rum is the thirtieth sura of the Koran. I used Paul-Alain Beaulieu's translation of

Nabonidus's inscription, found online at www.livius.org. Shahristani's remark on the Sabians comes from his *Al-Milal wa al-Nihal.* The Harranians' story is told by Ibn Nadim in his *Fihrist,* ii:14–17. The quotation from Thabit ibn Qurra is taken from Berkey's *Formation of Islam.*

Yaron Friedman's *The Nusayri-Alawis* (Brill, 2009) is a thorough study of what is known of the Alawites from medieval sources. The Reverend Samuel Lyde's experiences are described in his book *The Asian Mystery Illustrated in the History, Religion and Present State of the Ansaireeh or Nusairis of Syria* (Longmans, Green,1860). *After the Moon* is cited online as a publication of Dar al-Shimal publishers in Beirut, but I could find no copy of it. I have drawn on a review of it published at the online magazine *Al-Maaber* in November 2003 by Nadra al-Yaziji (in Arabic at http://maaber.50megs.com/issue _november03/books4.htm). Jacob de Vitriaco is quoted in Lyde, *Asian Mystery.*

Marco Polo's reference to the Kurds comes in Ronald Latham's translation of *The Travels* (Penguin, 1958). *Nestorians and Their Rituals,* by G. P. Badger (Joseph Masters, 1852), describes Badger's experiences in northern Iraq, including Yazidi rituals, the *sanjak,* and Sheikh Adi's prayer quoted in this chapter. Matti Moosa's *Extremist Shiites: The Ghulat Sects* (Syracuse University Press, 1987) was my source on the Shabak. *Nineveh and Its Remains,* by the archaeologist A. H. Layard (John Murray, 1849), was the source of remarks attributed here to Layard.

Al-Hallaj's life was examined with depth and sympathy by Louis Massignon, *The Passion of al-Hallaj,* available in an English translation by Herbert Mason (Princeton University Press, 1982). Herbert Mason wrote his own shorter and useful biography, *Al Hallaj* (Carson, 1995).

Montanus's quotation is taken from Crone, *Nativist Prophets.* The quotations from Yusuf Busnaya and Isaac of Nineveh are taken from Christoph Baumer's *The Church of the East,* pages 134-5. I also drew on *Rabi'a the Mystic and Her Fellow-Saints in Islam,* by Margaret Smith (Cambridge University Press, 1928).

Plutarch's description of haoma-offerings in caves is in his *Isis and Osiris,* chapter 46. Yohannan bar Penkaye's words are quoted from Berkey's *Formation of Islam.*

CHAPTER 3: ZOROASTRIANS

My visit to Iran was in the summer of 2006. I saw Balkh in the spring of 2008. I am very grateful to the World Zoroastrian Organisation and its former president, Shahin Bekhradnia, as well as to the Zoroastrian Trust Funds of Europe, for their very kind cooperation. I several times was given hospitality and an open-hearted welcome at the Zoroastrian fire temple in Rayners Lane, London.

Mary Boyce is so well regarded as an outside expert on the Zoroastrians that I saw her picture hanging in the London fire temple. In particular, her *Zoroastrians: Their Religious Beliefs and Practices* (Routledge and Kegan Paul, 1979) and her *A Persian Stronghold of Zoroastrianism* (Clarendon Press, 1977) were very useful to me in writing this chapter. An older but important and thought-provoking book on the religion is R. C. Zaehner, *Dawn and Twilight of Zoroastrianism* (Weidenfeld and Nicolson, 1961). Paul Kriwaczek's *In Search of Zarathustra* (Knopf, 2003) traces the broader influence of the religion as far as the modern day.

Zoroastrians' conception of their own religion differs somewhat from one individual believer to another, so there is no single book to read that will explain it. Zoroastrian explanations of their own faith include *The Religion of Zarathushtra,* by I. J. S. Taporewala (Sazman-e-Fravahar, 1980) as well as "The Parsee Religion," a talk given by Dadabhai Naoroji in 1861 to the Liverpool Literary and Philosophical Society.

For a broader understanding of Iran there is a wealth of choice. I particularly enjoyed Roy Mottahedeh's *Mantle of the Prophet: Religion and Politics in Iran* (Oneworld, 2008). I also recommend *The Turban for the Crown: The Islamic Revolution in Iran,* by Said Amir Arjomand (Oxford University Press, 2009).

Shapur's criticism of Christianity is quoted by Richard Foltz in *Religions of the Silk Road* (Palgrave Macmillan, 2010). Herodotus's observation on Persian education is in his *Histories,* I:136. Excerpts from the *Avesta* were taken from the translation provided by D. J. Irani at www.zarathushtra.com. The quote from the Book of Daniel (12:2) is taken from the NET Bible, available online at netbible.com. Nietzsche's remarks on morality are taken from the introduction to his book *Thus Spake Zarathustra,* translated by Thomas

Common, released as a Project Gutenberg e-book in 2008. Edward Browne's encounters with the Zoroastrians and Baha'i of late nineteenth-century Iran are described in his *A Year Amongst the Persians* (Adam and Charles Black, 1893), which was the source also for the poem inscribed at Persepolis. Diodorus Siculus's words are from the translation of his *Histories* by Peter Green (University of Texas Press, 2006).

Details of the Shah's feast come from an article by Spencer Burke for the *Harvard Advocate*, Winter 2012 issue. My copy of *My Uncle Napoleon,* by Iraj Peshehkzad, was published by Random House in 2006. The shah's remark is quoted by his then minister of education, Manouchehr Ganji, in *Defying the Iranian Revolution* (Praeger, 2002). The ayatollah's declaration that the commandments of the ruling jurist are like those of God was made in 1988 and is recorded by Arjomand in *Turban for the Crown,* page 34.

Herodotus writes on Persian sacrifices in his *Histories,* page 96. The quotes from the *Shahnamah* were taken from Dick Davis's translation (Viking, 2006). Crone, *Nativist Prophets,* gave me the lines that I have quoted from the Arab poet Al Ja'di. "This is their religion—to kill Arabs" comes from a poem by the Umayyad general Nasr Ibn as-Sayyar, referring to the Iranian followers of Abu Muslim. Boyce's *Zoroastrians* provided me with the reference to the writer Narshakhi, who is the source of the account of Arab conquerors' actions in Bukhara.

Kasravi's experience is described by Mottahedeh in *Mantle of the Prophet.* Khomeini's judgment that Plato was "grave and solid" comes in his *Kashf ul Asrar,* where he also described Aristotle as a "great man"; see www.irdc.ir/en /content/19569/print.aspx.

Browne's *Year Amongst the Persians* described his encounters with the Zoroastrians and Babis. Poems from the *Divan* of Hafiz are taken from Gertrude Bell's translation (W. Heinemann, 1897).

Hataria's words are quoted from his 1854 report to the Society for the Amelioration of the Conditions of the Zoroastrians of Persia (which can be read, for instance, in Dr. Daryoush Jahanian's lecture "The History of Zoro-astrians After Arab Invasion" on the website of the Circle of Iranian Studies at www.cais-soas.com/CAIS/History/Post-Sasanian/zoroastrians_after_arab _invasion.htm). The quote "the last mass forcible conversion of Zoroastians," the statistic on priests' decline in Yazd, and the address of the bier carriers are all taken from Boyce, *Persian Stronghold*. Herodotus writes on funerary customs in his *Histories,* page 99. Khamenei's words on Charshanbeh-e-Suri were reported by CNN on March 16, 2010: http://edition.cnn.com/2010/WORLD /meast/03/15/iran.new.year.crackdown.

The History of Parliament (www.historyofparliamentonline.org) helped me with some details on the life of Dadabhai Naoroji, which I also partly pieced together from newspaper reports and from *Dadabhai Naoroji: The Grand Old Man of India,* by Sir Rustom Pestonji Masani (Allen & Unwin, 1939).

I took some statistics, and the quoted remark of the Zoroastrian Cricket Club, from John Hinnells, *The Zoroastrian Diaspora: Religion and Migration* (Oxford University Press, 2005).

CHAPTER 4: DRUZE

I have been to Lebanon many times between 2000 and the present day, but most of the encounters in this chapter were during a trip dedicated to meeting the Druze in 2011. Without the support and help of the British ambassador, Frances Guy, and our mutual friend Rabieh Kays, this would have been a much less fruitful visit. Nadim Shehadi at London's Royal Institute for International Affairs corrected me on modern Lebanese history and joined me in the search for *After the Moon*.

I am very grateful to those who met me in Lebanon, especially Walid Jumblatt, Prince Talal Arslan, Dr. Sami Makarem of the American University of Beirut, and Sheikh Ali Zeinadin. The late Abu Muhammed Jawad, a very saintly man, was greatly mourned by the Druze when he died in 2012. Eyad Abu Shaqra gave me some useful insights into the community's view of reincarnation. Abbas al-Halabi gave me his book, which is cited below. Rifaat Eid, Badr Wannous, and Sheikh Ahmed al-Assi were kind enough to see me when I was in Lebanon in 2012, on a return visit, to discuss the Alawite religion.

There are enough books on the Druze to justify a bibliography: *The Druzes: An Annotated Bibliography,* by Sami Swayd (ISES, 1998). General books on the Druze religion include *The Druze,* by Robert Brenton Betts (Yale University Press, 1988); *The Druze Faith,* by Sami Makarem (Carnarvon Books,

1974); *A History of the Druzes,* by Kais Firro (Brill, 1992); *The Druze: Realities and Perceptions,* edited by Kamal Salibi (Druze Heritage Foundation, 2006); and *Origins of the Druze People and Religion,* by Philip K. Hitti (Columbia University Press, 1928). This last book was much criticized by those Druze whom I met, because they disliked certain of its conclusions. It does, however, honor them by declaring the Druze riddle to be "one of the most baffling in the history of religious thought."

The *sheikh al-aql* gave me a brief official guide to the Druze religion: *The Path to Monotheism,* issued in ah 1431/AD 2010 by the Office of Druze Sheikhdom. *Les Druzes: Vivre avec l'Avenir,* by Abbas al-Halabi (Dar an-Nahar, 2006), forms part of a trend among Druze intellectuals to question how to keep their esoteric religion alive in a globalized world.

Matthew Arnold's words are taken from his poem "Dover Beach."

Between 2009 and 2011 Gallup discovered that 76 percent of Lebanese adults would not object to someone of a different religion moving in next door to them—more than the percentage in the United Kingdom, which was 57 percent, and Israel, which was 23 percent.

Gibran's *Garden of the Prophet* is widely available in English, e.g., from UBS Publishers (1996), but I amended the translation to reflect the Arabic better.

"Like ants or frogs around a pond" is a remark made by Socrates in Plato's *Phaedo.* On Pythagoras and his legacy, I recommend *Lore and Science in Ancient Pythagoreanism,* by Walter Burkert (Harvard University Press, 1972); Leonid Zhmud, *Pythagoras and the Early Pythagoreans* (Oxford University Pres, 2012); *The Fifth Hammer,* by Daniel Heller-Roazen (Zone, 2011), which looks particularly at Pythagorean interest in music; and *Measuring Heaven,* by Christiane Joost-Gaugier (Cornell University Press, 2006), which discusses medieval European (i.e., Christian) interest in Pythagoras.

The Arabic book *Pythagoras* I read in Beirut was written by Hubert Husun (1947) and translated by Shawqi Dawud Tamraz. The autumn 2013 edition of the Beirut-based magazine *Al-Duha* was the issue that contained an article about Pythagoras. Justinian's edict is quoted from John Malalas's *Chronicles,* 18:46, translated by Elizabeth Jeffreys, Michael Jeffreys, and Roger

Scott (Australian Association for Byzantine Studies, 1986)—which is also what tells us of the sequel. "What has Athens to do with Jerusalem?" was a rhetorical question asked by the Christian polemicist Tertullian in *De Prescription Hereticorum,* chapter 7.

Ikhwan al-Safa', by Godefroid de Callataij (Oneworld, 2005), gives more detail on the mysterious Brethren of Purity. A complete edition of the *Epistles of the Brethren of Purity* was published in 2008 by Oxford University Press, edited by Nader el-Bizri. Ibn Taymiyyah's fatwa comes as number 35 in the collection of Ibn Taymiyyah's fatwas edited by Ibn Qasim and Ibn Muhammad (Matabi' al-Riyad, 1961–67) and can be seen at http://archive.org/stream /mfsiaitmmmfsiaitm/mfsiaitm35#page/n159/mode/2up. Najla Abu Izzeddin's book, referred to in this chapter, is *The Druzes* (Brill, 1984)

For an understanding of neo-Platonism, the best insight of all can be gained from Plotinus's *Enneads,* available in an English translation by Stephen MacKenna (John Dillon, 1991). Books that examine the ways in which early Muslims adopted and adapted neo-Platonism include *The Cambridge Companion to Arabic Philosophy* (Cambridge University Press, 2005); *Muslim Neoplatonists,* by Ian Richard Netton (George Allen & Unwin, 1982); and the particularly useful *Greek Thought, Arabic Culture* by Gutas. *A Short History of the Ismailis,* by Farhad Daftary (Edinburgh University Press, 1998), explains more about the Ismaili Muslim context from which the Druze emerged. *Caliph of Cairo,* by Paul E. Walker (American University of Cairo Press, 2010), is a biography of al-Hakim bi Amr Allah.

The US telegram published by Wikileaks can be seen at https://www .wikileaks.org/plusd/cables/09BEIRUT972_a.html.

Recollections of the Druses of the Lebanon, by the Earl of Carnarvon (John Murray, 1860), contains his account of visiting Moukhtara and speculations on the Druze religion. "Druses of Syria and Their Relation to Freemasonry," by Haskett Smith, can be read in the 1891 edition of *Ars Quatuor Coronatorum.* I gathered a broader knowledge of Freemasonry's history from *Freemasonry: A Celebration of the Craft*, edited by John Hamill and R. A. Gilbert (Angus Books, 1993). Hitti's observation comes in his *Origins of the Druze People.*

The July 2013 assault was reported in the Lebanese newspaper the *Daily Star,* July 23, 2013. The old lady commenting on George Clooney's marriage was quoted by Zeina Hariz in an article in Arabic for the *Al-Nahar* newspaper, April 29, 2014.

Details of Israeli land confiscation came from "The Druze in Israel: Questions of Identity, Citizenship, and Patriotism," by Mordechai Nisan, *Middle East Journal* 64, no. 4 (Autumn 2010). Chapter 10 of "On Loving God" by St. Bernard of Clairvaux can be read at the Christian Classics Ethereal Library website, www.ccel.org.

CHAPTER 5: SAMARITANS

I lived in Jerusalem for three years as a British diplomat between 1998 and 2001 and visited the Samaritans twice during that time, but the Passover sacrifice described in this chapter happened in 2012. I would like to thank the Samaritan community and Benny Tsedaka in particular for their cooperation and help, and also their representative in London, Felicity Devonshire.

General books on the Samaritans include *History of the Samaritans,* by Nathan Schur (Peter Lang, 1989) and *The Keepers: An Introduction to the History and Culture of the Samaritans,* by Robert T. Anderson and Terry Giles (Hendrickson, 2002). *A Companion to Samaritan Studies,* by Alan David Crown, Reinhard Pummer, and Abraham Tal (Mohr Siebeck, 1993), is a good reference work.

Jesus's encounter at Jacob's well is told in John 4:9. Tudor Parfitt's *The Lost Tribes of Israel* provided much of the material on the legend of the Ten Tribes and its influence on medieval Europeans, with which the chapter begins. The Book of Kings quote is from verse 17:24. The quote from the Babylonian Talmud is taken from a translation by Professor Mahlon H. Smith at http://virtualreligion.net/iho/samaria.html.

The estimate of the Samaritan population in Jesus's time is taken from Alan David Crown, *The Samaritans* (Mohr, 1989), who estimates their numbers in the Helleno-Roman period on page 201. Jesus's instructions to avoid Samaritan towns are in Matthew 10:5, and his first visit there himself in Luke 9:51; the accusation that he was a Samaritan comes in John 8:48; and Samaritan converts are mentioned in Acts 8:14.

Antoninus of Piacenza's observations are taken from John Wilkinson's *Jerusalem Pilgrims Before the Crusades* (Aris and Phillips, 2002). *Maimonides,* by Joel Kramer (Doubleday, 2010) is the source of the sage's remark on Islam. Schur's assessment of the initial effects of the Arab conquest is given on page 93 of his *History of the Samaritans.*

Joseph Scaliger's letters are quoted from *An Account of the Samaritans in a Letter to J—— M—— Esq.* (R. Wilkin, ca. 1714). Another quote at the end of the chapter is taken from this book.

Travels and Adventures of the Rev. Joseph Wolff was republished by Cambridge University Press in 2012. *Memoir of the Rev. Pliny Fisk,* by Alvan Bond, was published by Crocker and Brewster in 1828. *Three Months' Residence at Nablus,* by John Mills, was published by John Murray in 1864.

The Samaritan high priest commenting on the foundation of Israel is quoted by Douglas V. Duff, a British policeman in Palestine during the 1930s and a prolific writer who recorded his experiences in *Palestine Picture* (Hodder and Stoughton, 1936). H. V. Morton's observation comes in his book *In the Steps of the Master* (Rich & Cowan, 1934). Schur's remark about "probably the smallest group" is on page 11 of his *History of the Samaritans.*

The 2010 genetics study is by Gil Atzmon, Li Hao, and others and is published in the *American Journal of Human Genetics* 86 (June 11, 2010). The 2004 paper by Peidong Shen, Tal Lavi, and others was published in *Human Mutation* 24 (2004) and can be read at http://evolutsioon.ut.ee/publications/Shen2004.pdf.

Yitzhak Magen's excavations of the Samaritan temple are described in "Israel's Other Temple," *Der Spiegel International,* April 2012.

The two Israeli documentaries made about the Samaritans are *New Samaritans* (Journeyman Pictures, 2007) and *Lone Samaritan* (Heymann Brothers Films, 2010).

Jacob Esh Shalaby's life is described in *Notices of the Modern Samaritans,* by E. T. Rogers (Sampson Low & Son, 1855).

Lord Rothschild's envoy's positive appraisal of Samaritan-Muslim relations is quoted in Schur's *History of the Samaritans*, page 194.

The Song of the Sea is Exodus 15:1–18.

CHAPTER 6: COPTS

I lived in Egypt for a year from 1997 to 1998, and returned twice for this chapter: once in April 2011, and once in May 2012. It was during this last visit that I spent a week down in Minya.

I am very grateful to Dr. Cornelis Hulsman and his Arab-West Report for their introductions and information. This charity tries to produce objective analysis of violence between Muslims and Christians in Egypt; its website can be visited at www.arabwestreport.info. I am also grateful to those quoted in the text: Tariq Al Awadi, George Ishaq, and Yousif Sidhum. Fr. Yoannis of Qufada kindly showed me around his parish on several successive days. Others in the text are unnamed, but not for lack of appreciation of how generous they were with their time and thoughts.

Christianity in the Land of the Pharaohs, by Jill Kamil (Routledge, 2002), and *Two Thousand Years of Coptic Christianity,* by Otto Meinardus (American University of Cairo Press, 1999), were both useful on the Copts in general. On Copt-Muslim relations, I read *Christians Versus Muslims in Modern Egypt,* by S. S. Hasan (Oxford University Press, 2003)—a book whose authorship somewhat belies its gloomy title, since it was written by a Muslim Egyptian with great though not uncritical sympathy for the Copts; *The Copts of Egypt,* a document issued by Minority Rights International and written by Saad Eddin Ibrahim and others, published in 1996; *Copts and Moslems,* by Kyriakos Mikhail (Smith, Elder, 1911); and *Motherland Lost,* by Samuel Tadros (Hoover Institution Press, 2013).

The travel writer Anthony Sattin also looked at the survival of ancient customs in Egypt, though without much focus on the Copts, for *In the Pharaoh's Shadow* (Eland, 2012). Max Rodenbeck's book *Cairo: The City Victorious* (Vintage, 2000) is an excellent history of the city since its medieval Islamic foundation. The Osirites recommended to me *Dawn of Conscience,* by James Breasted (Macmillan, 1976), for evidence of the spiritual sophistication of the early Egyptians. More than one Egyptian directed me to *Fellahin of Upper Egypt,* by Winifred Blackman (Harrap, 1927), for evidence of ancient customs that are still practiced.

The number of Copts in Egypt is a matter of controversy. The official

Egyptian census found that Copts were 8.34 percent of the population in 1923, 5.87 percent in 1986, and an estimated 5.50 percent in 2000. Cornelis Hulsman, in *Mélanges de l'Institut Dominicain d'Etudes Orientales à Caire* 29 (2012), defends the census findings against skepticism expressed by many Copts, who estimate their own numbers at anything up to 20 percent of the population.

The Egyptians of Disert Ulaidh are mentioned in the Litany of Aengus the Culdee, dated to 799. This is discussed by the *Middle East Journal*'s editor in a 2009 blog: http://mideasti.blogspot.co.uk/2009/03/saint-patricks-day -special-patrick-and.html.The chanting of the seven vowels is described by Demetrius of Phalerum in his book *On Style*, chapter 71. The number of Coptic Catholics is given by the Roman Catholic agency CNEWA as 162,000 in a February 2013 estimate. Herodotus's comment on Egyptian religiosity is on page 143 of de Sélincourt's translation of *The Histories*. Shibley Telhami in "Egypt's Identity Crisis," a Brookings Institution paper of August 16, 2013, concluded from ten years of opinion polls in Egypt that "Egyptians see themselves as the most religious people in the world."

The Gilgamesh quote is from the George translation (see notes to Chapter 1). The twenty-fourth-century BC inscription is from Samuel Mercer's 1952 translation of the Pyramid Texts.

It was the Greek historian Plutarch, in chapter 43 of his *Isis and Osiris,* who tells us that in his time the Egyptians called the spring equinox "Osiris's coming to the Moon" (translation by Babbitt; Loeb Classical Library, 1936). Akhenaten's hymn is taken from Cyril Aldred's book *Akhenaten, King of Egypt* (Thames and Hudson, 1991). Dr. Amin Makram Ebeid has written several books on religion and culture in Egypt including *Egypt at a Crossroads* (El Hadara, 2010). It was he who told me the story of the Copts who sang dirges for a patient while he tried to operate on her.

"Prevalence of Female Genital Cutting Among Egyptian girls," by Tag-Eldin and others, in the *Bulletin of the World Health Organization* for April 2008 (www.who.int/bulletin/volumes/86/4/07-042093/en) lists some of the surveys by the UN and others showing the remarkably high prevalence of FGM in Egypt. Murgan al Gohary called for the Sphinx and Pyramids to be destroyed on November 10, 2012, during an interview on Egypt's Dream TV.

For Egypt's pre-Christian religion I read *Religion in Roman Egypt,* by Max Frankfurter, which provided me with the Oxyrhynchus hieroglyph guild's lament that their profession was dying out.

The voyages of J. M. Vansleb (aka Wansleben) are recounted in his book *Nouvelle Relations d'un Voyage Fait en Egypte* (an Elibron Classics facsimile of Estienne Michallet's 1677 Paris edition). Al-Maqrizi tells the story of how the Sphinx lost its nose in his *Kitab al-Mawa'iz wa-al-I'tibar bi-Dhikr al-Khitat wa-al-Athar;* this is also the source for his observations on the Abu Fana monastery. William Browne can be read in *The Modern Traveller* (Cawthorn, 1800).

On Egyptomania and its effects on Egyptian nationalism, I owe much— including quotes from Tahtawi and Khedive Ismail—to *Whose Pharaohs? Archeology, Museums and Egyptian National Identity from Napoleon to World War I,* by Donald Malcolm Reid (University of California Press, 2002). Ismail's appointments are given in Iris Habib al Masri's *Story of the Copts* (Saint Anthony's Coptic Monastery, 1982). For the events of 1919, including Father Sergious's sermon, I am indebted to Tadros's *Motherland Lost.*

The Muslim Brotherhood and other Islamist parties' activities are described by S. S. Hasan in chapter 3 of her *Christians Versus Muslims,* and also in *The Muslim Brotherhood,* by Carrie Rosefsky Wickham (Princeton University Press, 2013).

The Last Arab is a book by Sa'id Abu Rish (Duckworth, 2005). The figure of 75 percent losses for the Copts from Nasser's nationalizations comes from Ibrahim et al., *The Copts of Egypt. Out of Egypt,* by Andre Aciman (Farrar Strauss Giroux, 1994), evocatively tells how the diverse Egyptian community in which the Jewish Aciman was brought up was dispersed.

Kamal Mougheeth's recollections came in the article "M Is for Mosque," by Yasmine Fathi, for Ahram Online, May 4, 2013. Mehdi Akef's "at-tuz" interview was published by Rose al-Youssef on April 9, 2006 (as reported by International Crisis Group, "Egypt's Muslim Brothers," June 18, 2008). The 92 percent reference comes from a Gallup poll in March-April 2011: www.gallup .com/poll/157046/egypt-tahrir-transition.aspx#1.

The damage from the Minya riots is listed by the Egyptian Initiative for Personal Rights (which gave me the names of the two men who died) at its website, www.eipr.org/en/content/2013/08/25/1796. The estimate of 65 percent of violence taking place in Minya is from an article by Soliman Shafiq in the February 15, 2014, issue of *Watani*, online at http://wataninet.com /watani_Article_Details.aspx?A=51783. Statistics on poverty and unemployment in Minya can be found in Al Monitor, "Egypt's Minya Province Flashpoint for Muslim-Christian Violence," www.al-monitor.com/pulse/originals /2014/04/egypt-sectarian-violence-minya-province.html#. The statistics from the Pew poll 2011–12 are from "The World's Muslims: Religion, Politics and Society" at www.pewforum.org/2013/04/30/the-worlds-muslims-religion -politics-society-interfaith-relations.

For more detail on the Egyptian curriculum, including recent reforms, see "New Approaches in the Portrayal of Christianity in Egyptian Textbooks," by Dr. Wolfram Reiss, Cairo, November 2006.

CHAPTER 7: KALASHA

I made my visit to the Kalasha valleys in December 2012. That came after two years spent in Afghanistan between 2007 and 2009 and a visit to the northern areas of Pakistan in 2008. Siraj Ul-Mulk's excellent hotel in Chitral, where I stayed, is called the Hindukush Heights. I am very grateful to him and his wife, Ghazala, and more especially to the Kalasha people, who received me so kindly. Azem Bek and Wazir Ali Shah deserve special mention. Humira Noorestani very kindly gave me insights into what it is like to be a contemporary Afghan American of Nuristani origin, and helped provide a corrective to the perception of her people as poor and fanatical.

The quotation in the first paragraph is from Peter Mayne's *The Narrow Smile* (Murray, 1955). The references to Alexander the Great's travels in the third paragraph come from Arrian's *Anabasis* in Martin Hammond's translation (Oxford University Press, 2013). Marco Polo's remarks are in Latham's translation of Polo's *The Travels* (Penguin, 1958).

For context on the Great Game, details on the death of Alexander Burnes, and a great read, I recommend Peter Hopkirk's *The Great Game: On Secret Service in High Asia* (John Murray, 2006). News of Burnes's death reached Britain only in February 1842, which is when his various obituaries were published.

The Memoirs of Alexander Gardner were edited by Major Hugh Pearse and published by William Blackwood & Sons in 1898.

In 1873 a British missionary called E. Downes wrote *Kafiristan: An Account of the Country, Language, Religion and Customs of the Siah Posh Kafirs: Considering Especially Kafiristan as a Suitable Field for Missionary Labour* (W. E. Ball, 1873), in which—perhaps feeling the need to attract less spiritual interest in the place—he hinted at fabulous reserves of gold and an aphrodisiac plant that might be found there.

McNair's visit to Kafiristan resulted in two publications: one for the general public, "A Visit to Kafiristan," by W. W. McNair (Wm. Clowes & Sons, 1884), and one for the Indian government, "Report on the Explorations in Part of Eastern Afghanistan and in Kafiristan in 1883" (Dehra Dun, 1885). He died not long afterward, and his biography, *Memoir of W. W. McNair, the First European Explorer of Kafiristan,* was written by J. E. Howard (Keymer, 1889). A British attempt at cataloguing, *Dardistan and Kafiristan: In Three Parts* (Superintendent of Government Printing, India, 1885), only ran to two parts, with that on Kafiristan absent.

G. S. Robertson's book *Kafirs of the Hindu Kush*, published first in 1896, was reprinted in 2001 by the Lahore-based publisher Sang-e-Meel. His secret report for the British government can be seen at the British Library under the title "Report on Journey to Kafiristan" (HMSO, 1894). His biography, *The Unlikely Hero,* by Dorothy Anderson (Spellmount, 2008), defends him against accusations that he should have done more to protect the Kafirs. Abdur Rahman Khan's memoirs, *The Life of Abdur Rahman, Amir of Afghanistan,* were published by John Murray in 1900.

The Macnaghten quote "Here are your relations coming!" is from a talk that McNair gave to the Royal Geographical Society in January 1884, quoted in Howard's *Memoir of W. W. McNair.* The Alan Bennett quote is from his play *The History Boys* (1995). The 2014 DNA survey, "A Genetic Atlas of Human Admixture History," by Garrett Hellenthal, George B. J. Busby, and others, was published by *Science* magazine on February 14, 2014, and an interactive map of its data be seen at http://admixturemap.paintmychromosomes.com.

Books on the post-conversion people of Nuristan include Max Klimburg's *The Kafirs of the Hindu Kush: Art and Society of the Waigal and Ashkun*

Kafirs (Franz Steiner Verlag, 1999). Eric Newby gives Nuristan some attention in his travel memoir *A Short Walk in the Hindu Kush* (Harper, 2010), and a trio of Kabul-based diplomats, Nicholas Barrington, Joseph T. Kendrick, and Reinhard Schlagintweit, visited the region and wrote down their impressions in *A Passage to Nuristan: Exploring the Mysterious Afghan Hinterland* (I. B. Tauris, 2005).

The brothers Alberto and Augusto Cacopardo wrote a book called *Gates of Peristan* (IsIAO, 2001), which looks at the customs of Kafiristan, the Kalasha, and the people of nearby Gilgit and Hunza. R. C. F. Schomberg's observations on the Kalasha are in *Kafirs and Glaciers: Travels in Chitral* (London, 1938), which is now out of print. *The Man Who Would Be King,* by Rudyard Kipling, is available through Wordsworth Editions in a 1994 reprint.

M.S. Durrani's book on the Kalash, *Kalash Kafirs—The Urgent Need to Save a Vanishing People* was written in 1982 but did not get published; I found a copy at the University of London's SOAS Library.

EPILOGUE: DETROIT

Thanks to Dr. Elaine Rumman, Yusif Barakat, George Khoury, Imam al-Qazwini, Wisam Breegi, Mirza Ismail, Abu Shihab, and the Yazidi community of Nebraska.

Information on Iraq's Christians comes from Dr. Suha Rassam's *Christianity in Iraq* (Gracewing, 2005) and also Dr. Christoph Baumer's *The Church of the East*. The story of Markos is touched upon in *Voyager from Xanadu,* by Morris Rossabi (Kodansha International, 1992). *Telling Our Story: The Arab American National Museum* was published in 2007. Lupieri's book is cited in the notes to chapter 1. Naomi Schaefer Riley's book *Til Faith Do Us Part* was published in 2013 by Oxford University Press.

Index

Aaron, 127, 153, 180

A.B.—The Samaritan News, 156, 157

Abbas, Hajji, 57

Abbasid Empire, 61, 92

Abbasids, 63, 125, 126

Abdullah, Abdul-Jabbar, 32

Abraham, 10, 13, 18, 28, 43, 45
Isaac and, 149–150

Abu Shihab, 54, 72, 73, 272–273,
274–275, 277
daughter Naalin, 273, 275
foreign policy and, 272
photo of, 40
son Farhan, 272

Abu Simbel, temple at, 196

Abu Zayd, 267

Abu'l Suud, 197

Academy of Plato, 95, 116

Adam, 2, 6, 10, 13, 23, 25, 62, 69

Adi, Sheikh, 57, 58, 59, 63, 65, 67–68

Adultery, 233, 251

Advent, Copts and, 186

After the Moon (Haidar), 53

Ahura Mazda, 77–78, 79, 81, 87, 101,
108

Akef, Mehdi, 204

Akhenaten, 191, 192, 206

Akiko (Japanese Kalasha), 239
photo of, 239

al-Ahram, 202

al-Aql, Sheikh, 121–122, 142

al-Azhar mosque, 126, 188, 192, 198

al-Banna, Hassan, 199, 200

al-Bayyada, 143

al-Darazi, Nashtaqin, 127

al-Farabi, 117, 126

al-Gama'a al-Islamiya, 208

al-Ghazali, xxii, 140

al-Gohary, Murgan, Sphinx/pyramids
and, 194

al-Hakim bi Amr Allah, 126, 128, 142

al-Ja'di, 90

al-Khattab, Omar ibn: assassination
of, 90

al-Kindi, 117

al-Loz, 151, 158, 162, 170

al-Mahdi, Caliph, 17, 126

al-Maqrizi, 209

al-Masri, Munib, 175, 178

al-Mas'udi, 7, 8–9

al-Qaeda, 226

al-Qazwini, Hassan, 266

al-Shaarawi, Huda, 205

Alamuddin, Amal, 142

Alawites, 117, 141
  Assad regime and, 53
  criticism of, 128–129
  described, 51, 52
  moon/planets and, 52–53
  prayer by, 54
  violence against, xxiii
Alexander the Great, 5, 11, 45, 52,
      141, 226, 227–228, 248
  Arab world and, 81
  Aristotle and, 94
  death of, 5, 229
  Hindu Kush and, 220, 221,
      228–229, 232
  Kalasha and, 228
  Persian Empire and, 81, 220
  Samaritans and, 150–151
Ali (son-in-law of Mohammed), 53,
      92, 99
  Alawites and, 52
Ali, Mohammad (ruler of Egypt), 197,
      200
Ali, Sheikh, 139–140
Ali, Tariq, 121
Ali, Wazir, 243, 245, 247, 249, 250,
      253, 254
  on Islamic households, 251
  on Nuristani golf, 251–252
  photo of, 254
American University of Beirut, 145
Amulets, 30, 31, 67
Anderson, James, xxix
Angels, 44, 60
Anglo-Afghan War, 222
Angra Mainyu, 64, 77–78, 79–80, 83,
      105
  battle against, 92
  Satan and, 80
Anti-Semites, 34
Antoninus of Piacenza, 152

Arab American Institute, 263
Arab American Museum, 262
Arabian Nights, The, 6, 88
Arabic, xxviii, 25, 56, 185, 232–233,
      257, 272
  Islam and, 184
  slang/adopting, 161
  speaking, 153
Arabs, 40, 45, 71, 81, 196
  Islam and, 89
  Kurds and, xxiv
  Persian culture and, 90
  Samaritans and, 155
Arafat, Yasser: Samaritans and, 174,
      175
Aramaic, 45, 130, 257, 259, 260
  abandoning, 153
  Mandaean dialect of, 25
Aristokrates, 26
Aristotle, xx, 14, 95, 116, 117, 127, 140
  Alexander and, 94
  Plato and, 123
Armenians, 18, 86, 195, 198
  massacre of, xxiv, 259
Armstrong, Neil, 53
Arnold, Matthew, 113
Arslan, Prince Talal, 118, 122, 125,
      131, 133
  Jumblatt and, 143
Arslan family, 118, 125–126
Artemisia, 23
Asceticism, 11–12, 13–14, 18, 123, 209
Assad, Bashar al-, 51, 120
Assad, Hafez al-: Jumblatt and, 138
Assyrian Church, 258
Assyrian Empire, 5, 40, 44, 64
  Samaritans and, 150
Assyrians, xxiv, 57, 86, 149, 161, 260,
      261
  Church of the East and, 57

religious practices of, 49
sun and, 44
Aswad, Du'a Khalil: murder of, 70
Ateshkadeh
   photo of, 103
   visiting, 102–103
Avesta, 77, 78, 79, 100, 106
   interpreting, 110
   messiah and, 91–92
Awadi, Tariq el-, 189
Ayad, 67, 68, 69
   Kurdish identity and, 66
   theory of, 64–65
Azeris, 86

Baalshamin, 64
Baalzebub, 64
Baba Sheikh, 68
Babak, 90
Babis, 96
Babylon, 2, 12, 40, 81, 150
   Aramaic in, 25
   astronomy of, 26, 139
   civil war in, 5
Babylonian Empire, 5
Babylonian exile, 12, 149
Babylonians, 19, 22, 40
   influence of, 88
   Iraqi Marshes and, 7, 9
   Mandaeans and, 11, 25, 27,
     28–29
   predictions by, 26
   religious practices of, 4–5, 49
Bacchae (Euripides), 94
Bacchus, 138
Badger, Percy, 53, 59
Baghdad, 200
   demonstrators in, 35
   Jewish community in, 33
Baha'i, 96, 107

Balfour, Alfred, xxvi, 107
Balimain, 240
Baptism, 10
   Christian, 42
   Mandaean, 2 (photo), 23–24, 24
     (photo), 27–28, 270, 271
Bar Anhar, Hermez: on worship, 27
Bar Penkaye, Yohannan, 29
Barakat, Yusif, 267, 270
   photo of, 263
   relationship of, 264–265
Bedouins, 161, 162, 210
Beg, Azem, 236, 239, 241, 242, 243,
     247, 253, 254
   on dancing, 240
   Kalasha song and, 244–245
   photo of, 254
Beirut, 121, 125, 130
   described, 113
Bel (sun god), 11
Belem, 21
   photo of, 20
Belshazzar, 5
Ben Yehuda, Eliezer: Hebrew and,
     148, 161
Ben-Zvi, Yitzhak, 167
Bennett, Alan, 228
Berbers, 126
Bhutto, Zulfikar Ali: Islamic conserva-
     tism and, 233
Bible, 10, 65, 174, 202
   Egypt and, 198
Bin Ali, Hamza: Druze and, 127
Bin Musafir, Sheikh Adi: controversy
     over, 58–59
Biruni, xxii, xxix, 50, 54
   described, 8–9
Blavatsky, Madame, 135
Blood feuds, 213, 224
Bodleian Library, 28

Book of Daniel, 165
Book of Exodus, 150, 179
Book of Genesis, 2
Book of Isaiah, 165
Book of John, 27
Book of Kings, 150
Boyce, Mary, 78–79
Bread, Coptic letters on, 210 (photo)
Breegi, Wisam, 270, 271
British Druze Cavalry Regiment, illustration of, 137 (fig.)
British Library, 172
British Mandate, 155
Browne, Edward, 96, 99–100
Browne, William: Egyptian identity and, 196
Buckley, Jorunn, 11
Buddhism, 12
Budhaluk, described, 240
Burnes, Sir Alexander, 221
Burns, Robbie, 221
Bush, George W., 9
Busnaya, Yusuf, 61–62
Butros, Zakaria, 215
Buzani, Khairi, 63
Byzantine Empire, xxii, 46, 90
    Egypt and, 195
    religious minorities in, 95
Byzantines, 45, 49, 126, 195, 258
    defeat of, 46
    holy fire and, 89
Byzantium, 46, 95, 117
    Copts and, 195
    Persian Empire and, 7

Cairo, 192–194, 201, 204, 206
    Copts in, 205
    described, 191
    Samaritans in, 153
    visiting, 183, 184, 185–186, 188

Calendars
    Mandaean, 21
    Muslim, xxviii
    Samaritan, xxviii, 157
    Western, 181
    Zoroastrian, xxviii
Carmelites, 185
Carmen (Karima), reincarnation of, 141
Carnarvon, Lord, 136, 138, 145
    Druze and, 134–135
Castes, 224
    Yazidi, 57, 274, 276
    Zoroastrian, 89
Catalhuyuk, 103
Catholic Uniate Church, Copts and, 210
Chaldean News, 260, 261
Chaldeans, 115, 264, 265, 267
    conservatism of, 261
Charsema Sor, 59, 276
Charshanbeh-e-Suri, described, 105
Chaumos
    celebrating, 232, 237, 238, 240, 241, 244, 248
    photo of, 245, 246, 254
Cheops, Pharaoh: Great Pyramid and, 4
Chitral, 223, 227, 231, 250, 253, 255
    annexation of, 233
    described, 232
    visiting, 233–234
Christianity, x, 1, 47, 116, 194, 245
    Constantine and, xxix
    conversion to, 141, 151, 161, 214
    in Egypt, 181, 183
    Greek philosophy and, 131
    Islam alienation with, xx
    Mandaeans and, 18
    monotheism of, 152

Roman Empire and, 194–195
spread of, 182, 258
understanding of, 217
Christianity in Iraq (Rassam), xxvi
Christians, xxiv, 50, 61, 185, 186
Arab, 261, 267, 268
asylum for, 279
Egyptian, xxvi–xxvii, 195–196
emigration of, 279
Iraqi, 259, 262
Jews and, 177
Lebanese, 262
massacre of, 182
mistreatment of, 217
Muslims and, 8, 118, 127, 129, 188,
197, 198, 199, 204, 205, 213,
214, 217, 263, 279
Orthodox, 265, 266
Palestinians and, 262, 266–267
Samaritans and, 155
sects of, 1
Syrian, 201, 265
tolerance for, 90
Yazidis and, 41
Chronicles of Narnia, The (Lewis), 78
Church of the East, 57, 258
Church of the Holy Sepulcher, Easter
Mass at, 155
Church of the Nativity, 77
Circumcision, 166, 192, 193
Citizenship, 69, 201
Israeli, 158, 160
Cleopatra, Egyptian customs and, 194
Clooney, George, 142
Communism, xxv, xxvi, 33
Constantine, Christianity and, xxix
Coptic Museum, 198
Coptic Orthodox Church, xxiv, 181,
195, 202, 210, 212
conversions and, 14

divorce and, 214
Mubarak and, 203–204
renaissance of, 209
in US, 217–218
Coptic priests, 214, 216
photo of, 215
Copts, xx, xxii, xxiv–xxv, 186, 187,
188, 194, 261, 264, 279
Byzantium and, 195
Catholic Uniate Church and,
210
Egyptians and, 196, 197, 198–199,
203
emigration of, 204, 205, 217, 218
history of, 202, 207
influence/status of, 196, 200
Islamic movements and, 200
Jesus and, 195
leadership of, 181–182, 201
monasticism and, 182
Muslim Brotherhood and, 204
Muslims and, 200, 203, 215, 217
number of, 181, 182
persecution of, 182, 208
social networks of, 214
Council of Chalcedon, 195
Crassus, 46, 94
Creator of the Universe, 123, 131,
145
Crescent and cross symbol, photo of,
199
Crusades, xxiii, 45, 127, 142–143, 152,
196, 200
Culture, xiii
Babylonian, 7
Druze, 269
Kalasha, 254
Middle Eastern, 124
Palestinian, 148
Persian, 90

Culture, *continued*
  religions and, 7
  Zoroastrian, 79
Cyrus, King, 80, 84

Dabkeh, 263, 264
  photo of, 263
Dakheel, Qahtaniyah attack and,
  70–71
Dakhma, 102, 103, 105
  photo of, 104
Dari language, 228, 230
Darius, 82, 110
David, King, xxv, 150, 191
de Goes, Bento, 236
De Vitriaco, Jacob, 53
Death
  Assyrians and, 259
  Chaldeans and, 259
  Copts and, 201
  Druze and, 128
  Kam and, 225
  Mandaeans and, 17–18, 37–38
  Shi'a and, 254
  Zoroastrians and, 79
Deir Abu Fana, 208, 209
  photo of, 207
Deir al-Jarnoos, 215–216
Demetrius of Phalerum, 183
Deuteronomy, 167
Devil, 60, 62. *See also* Satan, Sheitan.
Dinkha IV, Patriarch Mar, 260
Diocletian, Emperor, 182, 208
Diodorus, 81
Dionysus, 229
Divorce, 214, 251
Diwan (Hafez), 97
Dome of the Rock, 156
Drasa da Yehia (Book of John), 10,
  23

Drower, E. S., xxviii–xxix, 67
  magic and, 29–30
  Mandaean community and, 28
  planets and, 27
Druze, 71, 115, 121, 127, 161, 266,
  268, 270
  blue and, 69
  criticism of, 128–129
  folk mythology of, 141
  Freemasons and, 135–136
  Hizbullah and, 133
  illustration of, 137 (fig.)
  immigrant, 132, 271
  Islam and, 118, 122, 128, 129, 144
  Knights Templar and, 136
  leadership of, 118
  Lebanese civil war and, 138
  Maronites and, 135
  number of, 120, 139
  Palestinians and, 120
  Pythagoras and, 114, 115, 117, 122,
  143, 145–146
  reincarnation and, 123, 140,
  141–142, 142–143
  Shi'a and, 129, 132–133
  Sunnis and, 140, 142, 192
  theology of, 130
Druze clergy, 131–132
Druze militia, 120, 129
Druze Mountain, 139
Druze religion, xx, 117, 121, 123, 127,
  131–132, 136–137, 138
  conversion to, 141, 142, 270

Easter, 59, 155, 191
Ebeid, Amin Makram, 201
Ebeid, William Makram, 199
Egeria, fish and, 44, 45
Egypt
  Byzantine Empire and, 195–196

Islamization in, 202
reform/modernization of, 197
Egyptian Museum, 189
Eid al-Sawm, 43
Einstein, Albert, 32
el-Shalaby, Israel, 154
Elagabalus, 12
Elias, Khidr, 274
Eliot, T. S., 124
Elphinstone, Mountstuart, xii
Emanationism, 124–125, 145
Era of Martyrs, 181, 182
Erbil, 56, 70, 71
growth of, 57–58
Esfahan, described, 95
Esh Shalaby, Jacob, 174
Euclid, 114
Euripides, 94
Eve, 6, 23
Evil eye, avoiding, 193
Ezid, Sultan, 58

Fakhreddin, 133–134, 142
independent territory and,
133–134
Fakhry, Abeer, 214
Faqir, Khidr, 274
Farouq, deposing of, 200
Farsi, xviii, 56, 74, 110, 111
Fatimah al-Maasoumah, 92
Fatimid Empire, 126
Female genital mutilation, 193
Ferdowsi, 92
Festivals
Arab-American, 263
Egyptian, 191–192
Kalasha, 232, 236–237, 238,
239–240, 241, 244, 248
Mandaean, 19, 22
Samaritan, 157, 169

Zoroastrian, 105, 108
Fire temples, 109, 110, 261
photo of, 103
visiting, 102–103
Fisk, Pliny: on Samaritans, 154
Ford, Henry, 262
Fravahar, 81, 102, 111
photo of, 82
Freemasons, 248
Druze and, 135–136
Funerals
Egyptian, 192–193
music for, 183
Zoroastrian, 102–104, 108, 110–111

Galen, 14, 94
Gandhi, Mahatma, 106
Ganzibra, 22–23, 26, 27
Garden of Eden, 2, 13, 60
Garden of the Prophet (Gibran), 114
Gardner, Alexander, 221
Gattan, Nadia, 18–19, 20, 21, 23–24,
36, 37, 38
baptism of, 24 (photo), 27–28
discrimination and, 35
education and, 35
festivals and, 19, 22
Hadeel death and, 37
inequality of the sexes and, 22
Mandaeans and, 21
religious name of, 25–26
rules violation by, 19–20
sabbath and, 34
spells and, 30–31, 32
Gibran, Kahlil, 114, 263
Gibson, Mel, 257
Gilgamesh, 4, 43, 190, 278
Ginza Rabba, described, 10
Gladstone, William Ewart, 107
Gnostics, 14

God, xxix, 62
  Messiah and, 52
Goliath, David and, xxv
Good Samaritan, parable of, 149–150,
    151, 163
Gospel of Luke, 13
Gospel of Matthew, 77
Governments, weak, xxiii–xxiv, xxvi
Great Flood, 22
Great Game, 222
Great Life, 10, 11
Greek Orthodox, 265, 266
Greek philosophy, xxix, 11–12, 116,
    117, 122, 123, 140, 146
  Christianity and, 131
  Islam and, 126, 131
  Middle Eastern culture and, 124
Greeks, 79, 194
  Egypt and, 194
  Persians and, 80
Grom
  photo of, 235
  visiting, 235–236
Gross, Anthony, illustration by, 137
    (fig.)
Gul, Zarmas, 241, 243
  photo of, 241
Gushnasp fire, 87, 88, 89

Hadeel, death of, 36–37
Hafez
  magi and, 99, 111
  poetry of, 96–97
  tomb of, 98 (photo)
Haidar, Ahmad Mohammad, 53
Halawi, Sheikh Abu Aref: Neopla-
    tonism of, 123
Hallaj, Hussein ibn Manosur al-, 61, 63
  on monotheism, 62
  Satan and, 62

Hand of Fatima, 193
Hand of Horus, 193
Handshake, 48, 73
Hanukkah, 166
Har Brakha, 161–162
Hariri, Rafiq: assassination of, 119
Harran, xxii, 45, 47, 48, 49, 50, 52,
    196
Harranians, 52, 53, 131
  beans and, 69
  Muslims and, 50
  planets and, 49
  prayer by, 54
  Pythagoras and, 117
  reincarnation and, 49
  shrine of, 54
  theology of, 49
Hassan (driver), 109, 131, 132, 134
  on Kamal Jumblatt, 137–138
  Jumblatt castle and, 137
  on Zoroastrians, 105
Hassan, Sheikh, 42, 212
Hataria, Maneckji Limji: on Zoroas-
    trians, 100
Hayek, Salma, 262
Hebrew, 148, 161, 185, 257
Hebrew University, 167, 171
Hebrews, 150
Helú, Carlos Slim, 262
Hermes (Tresmegistus), 117, 146
Herodotus, 27, 97, 103, 114, 186, 193
  on Magians, 78
  Persians and, 88
Hibil Ziwa, 10, 18
Hindu Kush, 219, 227, 230, 231
  Alexander the Great and, 220, 221,
    228–229, 232
Hinduism, 12, 250
Hinnels, John, 107, 108
Hitti, Philip, 136

Hizbullah, 130, 133, 142
Holy fire, 89, 111, 126–127
Holy Sepulcher, 126–127
Homer, 4, 114
Horus, 192, 207, 209
House of the Sect, 121, 131, 132
Hussein, Imam, 19, 91, 92, 99, 102
    death of, 22, 76
    tomb of, 75
Hussein, Saddam, 3, 5–6, 70
    Babylon and, 5
    Iraqi Marshes and, xxiv, 7, 8
    Kurds and, 55
    Mandaeans and, 32
    statues to, 83
    support for, 35
    Yazidis and, 40–41

Ibn al-Nadim, xxii, 17
Ibn Taymiyyah, xxiii
    Druze and, 128–129
    Pythagoras and, 117
Ibn Wahshiyyah, 7, 27
Ibrahim, 45
Immigration, 132, 262, 271, 277, 278
Immortality, 77, 79, 104
Indian National Congress, 106
International Order of Gnostic
    Templars, 275
Iranian clerics, astronomy and, 95
Iranian revolution (1906), Zoroas-
    trians and, xxiii, 100
Iranians
    Parsees and, 110
    Zoroastrianism and, 89
Iraq War (2003), 60, 83
Iraqi Marshes, xxiv, 7, 8, 14, 19–20,
    40, 84
    Babylonians and, 9
    photo of, 8, 20

Isaac, son of Abraham, 149–150, 170
Isaac of Nineveh, 62
Ishak, George, 207, 208, 209, 211, 215,
    216, 217
    on Mubarak, 203
    Sadat and, 202
    on Sa'eed, 213
Ishtar, 4–5, 26, 30
Isidora, tomb of, 214
Isis, 12, 191
Islam, 46, 47, 50, 58
    Arabs and, 89
    conversion to, 100, 109, 153, 161,
        214, 226, 227, 249–250, 251, 254
    Druze and, 118, 122, 128, 129, 144
    Greek philosophy and, 126, 131
    intolerance towards, 262, 277
    Kalasha and, 250
    language of, 184
    mob violence and, 249
    non-Arabs and, xxii
    spread of, 90
    tolerance in, 8
    understanding of, 217
    Zoroastrian challenge to, 62
    See also Muslims
Islam Is of the Devil, 262
Islamabad, 219–220, 232, 234
Islamic Brotherhood, 200, 203
Islamic law, 168, 199
Islamic Revolution (1979), 82, 83, 96,
    108
Islamists, xxv–xxvi, xxvii, 194, 200,
    201, 204
Ismail
    Copts and, 198
    religion and, 197–198
Ismail, Mirza, 41, 53, 54, 58, 69, 70,
    272, 274, 275
    birth of, 40

Ismail, Mirza, *continued*
    four elements and, 43–44
    described, 39
    migration of, 73
    photo of, 40
    on Shams/sun, 53
    sheikhs and, 42, 43
    Yazidi rights and, 271
Israel
    Judah and, 149, 150, 155
    Palestine and, 161
Israelis, 159
    houses of, 164
    Palestinians and, 147, 160, 162,
        176–177
    Samaritans and, 177–178
Israelites, 115, 150
Izzeddin, Najla Abu: on Druze
        religion, 117

Jacob's Well, 149, 151, 164, 175
Jaffa, 161, 267
    Samaritans in, 167, 168
Jawad, Abu Mohammed, 135
Jefferson, Thomas, 147
Jerusalem, 155, 158, 159, 267
    optimism in, 148
    Palestinians and, 160
    sacking of, 151
Jestak, 243
    photo of, 246
Jestakhan, 243, 247
Jesus, 80, 127, 130
    Copts and, 195
    John and, 1
    language of, 257
    Mohammed and, 52
    Moses and, 140
    rejection of, 14, 18
    Samaritans and, 149, 151

Zoroastrians and, 77
Jewish Temple, 135, 156, 160
    destruction of, 151, 155, 177
    ruins of, 164
    Samaritans and, 150, 151
Jews, 50, 162, 185, 264
    Babylonian exile of, 12
    Christians and, 177
    converts and, 270
    Egyptian, 201
    Iraqi, 33–34, 37
    kingdom and, 155
    Koran and, 152
    liberation of, 80
    Mandaeans and, 13, 29, 34
    monotheism and, xxi, 152
    Muslims and, 8, 34, 152
    Orthodox, 264
    Palestinians and, 161
    Samaritans and, 149–150, 151, 153,
        154, 165, 176
    Syrian, 271
    tolerance for, 90, 152
Jinnah, Mohammed Ali, 106
Jizya tax, 100, 197
Job, Prophet: tomb of, 133 (photo)
John the Baptist, 1, 10, 275
John the Evangelist, 1
Jones, Sir William, xxix
Jones, Terry, 262
Joseph, Samaritans and, 154, 164
Joseph's Tomb, 161
Judah, Israel and, 149, 150, 155
Judaism, xxix, 47, 127, 141, 152, 201,
        271
    conversion to, 12, 161
    See also Jews
Julius Caesar, 115
Jumblatt, Kamal, 10, 137
    death of, 137–138

Jumblatt, Walid, 118, 121, 130, 132, 133, 137, 142, 144
  Arslan and, 143
  Assad and, 138
  Druze militia and, 120
  Lebanese civil war and, 138
  meeting with, 138–139
  Sunnis/Shi'a and, 129
Jumblatt castle, 134, 137, 138
Justinian, Emperor, 116, 117, 152
  expulsion by, 95

Kabul, 291, 221, 228, 232, 251
  arrival in, 229–230
Kafiristan, 220–227, 229, 248, 250
  annexation of, 233–234
Kafirs, 220–221, 233, 248, 252
  adultery and, 251
  *baira*s and, 250
  conversion of, 227
  freedom and, 225
  idols of, 222
  principles of, 236
  religion of, 223
Kafirs and Glaciers (Schomberg), 234
Kakais, 57
Kalasha, ix, 223, 228, 229, 231, 242, 244
  clothing of, 235, 250
  conversion of, 227, 249–250, 251, 254
  dancing and, 240–241
  described, 239–240
  diplomacy and, 253–254
  divorce and, 251
  Islam and, 250
  Muslims and, 238, 249, 253–254
  photo of, 238, 245, 246, 254
  religion of, 238
  traditions/customs of, 236–237, 240, 243

  virtues of, 250–251
Kalasha River, 234, 238, 252
  photo of, 252
Kalasha valley, 232, 234, 243
  photo of, 235
Kam, 223, 233, 242, 243, 248
  blood feuds and, 224
  social ladder of, 224
Kasravi, Ahmad: anticlerical writers and, 95
Kemal, Mustafa "Ataturk," 54
Khadhouri, Moshe, 34
Khadhouri, Yvonne, 34
Khamenei, Ayatollah, 85, 105
Khan, Abdur Rahman, 225, 226, 248
Khan, Gordana, 221
Khan, Reza, 100
Khatami, President, 84
Khomeini, Ayatollah Ruhollah, 82, 83, 93–94
  penal laws and, xxvii
  Plato and, 95
  poem by, 97
  power for, 86
  secularism and, 85
  Zoroastrians and, 94
Khorramiyah, 90
Khosro, 89, 97, 99
Khoury, George, 266–267, 268, 270
Kipling, Rudyard, 248
Knights Templar, 136, 275
Koran, 8, 10, 19, 32, 49, 50, 65, 81, 95, 97, 122
  burning, 215
  Egypt and, 198
  Jews and, 152
  language of, 184
  pharaohs and, 196
  Satan and, 62
  Zoroastrians and, 102

Kurdish language, 54, 56
Kurdistan, 55, 56, 57, 58, 65, 71
Kurds, 39, 45, 57, 86, 258, 260
   Arabs and, xxiv
   described, 56
   independence for, 55
   Turks and, 54
   Yazidis and, 40–41, 61, 65–66, 70,
     71, 274
Kurmanji language, 39, 45, 47, 54, 66,
   272

Labib, Claudius, 198
Lalish, 42, 43, 58, 69, 73, 118, 277
   described, 67, 273
   temple at, 65 (photo)
   visiting, 44, 64, 66
   Yazidis around, 71
Lalish Cultural Center, 64
Lawrence, T. E., xii
Layard, Austen Henry, 61
Lebanese civil war, 118, 119, 120, 129,
   138
   Druze and, 132–133, 138
   end of, 113
Lerounis, Athanasios, 227, 228
Levi, 153, 154, 165
Lewis, C. S., 78
Light-World, 1, 2, 11
Lord Sin, 4, 42, 48
Lost Tribes, 147, 149, 153, 156, 169
Louis XVI, King, 25
Loulan Beauty (mummy), 228
Lucifer, 60, 64
Lupieri, Edmondo, 270
Lyde, Samuel: Alawites and, 52–53

Maccabee Wars, 151
Macnaghten, Sir William, 227
Magi, 77, 78, 79, 97, 99, 111

Magic, black, 29–30, 79, 205
Maimonides, 152
Makarem, Sami, 145, 146
Man Who Would Be King, The
   (Kipling), 248
Mandaean Human Rights Group, 37
Mandaean priests, 1, 26
Mandaeanism, 12–13, 19, 271
   converts to, 23
   Iran/Iraq and, xxvi
Mandaeans, x, xix, xxviii, 8, 14–15, 32,
   40, 43, 50, 71, 192
   asylum for, 279
   Babylonians and, 11, 27, 28–29
   baptism of, 2 (photo), 10, 11, 23,
     23–24, 24 (photo), 27–28, 271
   blue and, 69
   celibacy and, 14
   Christianity and, 18
   cleanliness of, 27, 273
   curses by, 32
   descent of, 2
   described, 20–21
   emigration of, 37–38, 279
   festivals of, 21–22
   harassment of, 9, 35
   holidays of, 29, 30
   holy books of, 7, 19
   Jews and, 12–13, 29, 34
   language of, 10–11, 25
   number of, 18
   photo of, 21
   polytheism and, 27
   tribes and, 37
Mandaeans: The Last Gnostics, The
   (Lupieri), 270
Mani, xix, 14–15
   on antagonistic masses, 15–16
   Christian asceticism and, 18
   followers of, 16–17

Jesus and, 15
  representation of, 15 (fig.)
  statue of, 17
  theory of, 16
Manichees, xix, xxii, xxix, 16, 18
Manicheism, 16–17, 18
Mansur, Caliph al-, 6
Marcionites, 13
Marduk, 5, 26
Maronites, 135, 264, 265
Marriage
  Chaldeans and, 261
  Christians and, 214
  Copts and, 214
  Druze and, 269
  Mandaeans and, 26–27
  mixed, 110
  Muslims and, 214
  Samaritans and, 167–169
  Yazidis and, 274
Mary Magdalene, 275
McNair, Lieutenant (Sahib Gul
    McNair Shah), 222, 223, 233
Mecca, 19, 46, 102, 128, 152
Mehr, Farhang, 100
Melek Taoos, 59–60, 64, 67, 277
  Yazidis and, 60–61, 63
Merak, Torag, 224
Messiah, 52, 192
  Christian, 91
  Jewish, 91
  Samaritan, 155
  Zoroastrian, 92
Mills, John, 154, 175
  on Messiah, 155
  Samaritans and, 169, 172, 180
Minorities, 279
  crushing, xxiv–xxv
  Islam and, xxiii
  racial/religious, xxv

Minya, 187, 214
  visiting, 204, 205, 206, 208,
    210–211
Missionaries, 131, 254, 258
Mithraists, 2, 47, 64
Mithras, xix, 12, 53
  depiction of, 48 (fig.)
  handshake and, 73
  worship of, 47
Mohammed, Prophet, xxi–xxii, 43, 46,
    76, 91, 92, 126, 128
  Ali and, 52
  Islam and, 127
  Jesus and, 52
Mohammed Reza Shah, 82, 86
Monastery, Egyptian, 207 (photo)
Monasticism, 17, 18, 207–208
Mongols, xix, xxiii, 50, 128, 196
Monotheism, xxi, 7, 8, 62, 65, 124, 154
Montanus, 61
Morsi, Mohammed, 205, 211
Morton, H. V.: on Samaritans/Arabs,
    155
Moses, 127, 149, 172
  Aaron and, 180
  Jesus and, 140
Mougheeth, Kamal, 202
Moukhtara, 138, 140, 145
  carnival of, 135
  castle at, 134
Mount Ararat, 149
Mount Ebal, 148
Mount Gerizim, 169, 171
  altar on, 165
  Samaritans and, 148, 149, 150, 151,
    155, 158, 162, 178
Mount Hermon, Druze and, 131
Mount Moriah, 149
Mount Sinai, 149, 171
Mousa, Father, 216, 217

Mubarak, Hosni, 184, 202, 205, 212
   Copts and, 203–204
   Muslim Brotherhood and, 204
   resignation of, 188
Mughtasila, 14, 15, 18
Music, 274
   funeral, 183
Muslim Brotherhood, 192, 194,
     199–200, 205
   Christians and, 217
   Copts and, 204
   fall of, xxvii
Muslims, xxvii–xxviii, 20, 185, 186,
     266, 277
   Arab, 152
   Christians and, 8, 118, 127, 129,
     188, 198, 198, 204, 205, 213,
     214, 217, 263, 279
   Copts and, 200, 203, 215, 217
   Harranians and, 49–50
   Iranian, 86
   Iraqi, 35
   Jews and, 8, 34, 152
   Kalasha and, 238, 249, 253–254
   Samaritans and, 174, 175
   tolerance by, 9
   Yazidis and, 39, 60
   See also Islam
My Uncle Napoleon, 83
Mysteries of the Peacock Angel, 275

Nabatean Agriculture, 7, 27, 28–29, 63
Nabateans, 27, 28
Nablus, 158, 161, 162, 164, 177
   economy of, 178
   Palestinians in, 174
   Samaritans in, 153, 154, 156, 163,
     167, 173, 174, 175
   visiting, 148–149, 163
Nabonidus, 48–49

Naoroji, Dadabhai, 106, 107, 110
Nasrallah, Hassan, 130
Nasser, Gamal Abdel, 184, 200
   Copts and, 201
   land reforms and, 212
Nationalism, xxv, xxvi
   Arab, 33, 201
   Iranian, 82
   Kurdish, 68
   radical, xxvii
Nebu, 26, 30
Nebuchadnezzar, 5, 30
Nefertiti, 185
Neguib, Mohammad, 200
Neoplatonism, 123, 124, 125, 127
Nergal, 64
Nestorians, 52, 258
Nestorius, 258
Netanyahu, Binyamin, 178
New Year
   Mandaean, 21–22
   Zoroastrian, 90, 96, 105
Newby, Eric, 226
Nicene Creed, 127
Nietzsche, Friedrich, 77, 80
Nile River, 183, 184, 188, 189
Nimrod, 44, 45
Nineveh, 45, 56, 62
Noah, 3–4, 10, 149, 169
Nowruz, 90, 96, 105
Nuristan, 30, 229, 230, 231, 248, 251
   described, 226–227
Nuristanis, 248, 251–252
   village of, 252 (photo)

Odyssey (Homer), 4
Old Testament, 13, 165, 170
Omar, Caliph, 7, 84
Orfalea, Paul, 263
Osiris, 191, 192

Ottoman Empire, 32, 54
    Armenians and, xxiv
    non-Muslim subjects and, xxiii
Ottomans, 41, 134, 196–197
    oppression by, 261

Pagans, ix, xi, xii, 22, 44, 50, 78, 95,
    99, 195, 227
    monotheists and, 7
    polytheist, 32
    tolerance for, xxii
Pahlavi shahs, 82, 100, 101
Palestinian intifada, 156, 174, 176
Palestinian Telecommunications
    Company, 180
Palestinians, 163, 174, 262, 264
    Druze and, 120
    houses of, 164
    Israelis and, 147, 160, 162, 176–177
    Jews and, 161
    racist exploitation and, 160
    relations with, 162
    restrictions on, 159, 177–178
    Samaritans and, 174, 175, 176, 178
    state for, 161, 162
Parsees, 77, 100, 103, 106, 107
    identity of, 110
    Iranians and, 110
Parthian Empire, 16, 46
Parthians, 16, 46
Pasha, Nubar, 197
Pashtuns, 237, 255
Passion of the Christ, The (movie), 257
Passover
    celebrating, 156, 157, 176–177
    sacrifice of, 150, 165–166, 179, 180
    Samaritan, 157, 158–159, 163–166,
        170–174, 175, 176–177, 178
        (photo), 179 (photo), 180
Paul, Father, 185, 218

Peacock Angel, 44, 60, 67
    representation of, 60 (photo)
Peacocks, 275
    image/feathers of, 277 (photo)
"Pek Ethronos" (chant), 183, 195
Pentateuch, 80, 165
People of the book, xxii, 8, 49–50
    Mandaeans and, 32
    Samaritans and, 152–153
Persepolis
    Persian Empire and, 81
    Zoroastrians and, 80–81, 82, 101
Persian Empire, 81, 89, 117
    Byzantium and, 7
    Hinduism/Buddhism in, 12
    Roman hostilities with, 46
Persian language, 92, 232–233
Persians, 45, 84, 85, 88, 194
    Greeks and, 80
Pharaoh (journal), 198
Pharaohs, 190–191, 194, 196
Pinkham, Amaru Mark, 275
Plato, 52, 80, 117, 124, 127, 140, 141
    Academy of, 95, 116
    Aristotle and, 123
    Khomeini and, 95
    philosophy of, 94, 95
    St. Augustine and, 116
    vision of, 95
Plotinus, 117, 123, 125
Plutarch, 64, 104
Polo, Marco, 56, 220, 221, 225
Polytheism, 27, 32, 50, 182, 191, 197
Prayer, 43, 54, 171–173, 237
    communal, 66
    kaddish, 257
Priesthood
    Jewish, 165
    Mandaean, 22, 23, 24
    Samaritan, 165

Prometheus, 229
Ptolemy, 14, 95, 214
Purim, 166
Pythagoras, 50, 124, 127, 128, 131,
        140, 143–144
    Druze and, 114, 115, 117, 122, 143,
        145–146
    Harranians and, 117
    Ibn Taymiyyah and, 117
    pentagram and, 119
    Socrates and, 116
    theory of, 117, 119
Pythagorean Brotherhood, 114, 115
Pythagoreans, 115, 119–120, 122, 129

Qahtaniyah, 40, 41, 70
Qassem, Abdul-Karim, 32
Qom, 92–93, 95–96

Rabba, Baba, 152
Rabi'a of Basra, 62
Ramadan, xxvii, 3, 96, 128, 131, 186
Ramses, 184, 185, 196
Raphael, painting by, 123
Rashid, Haroun al-, 6
Rassam, Suha, xxvi
Red Cross, bombing of, 36
Red Kafirs, 248
Reincarnation, 44, 49
    Druze and, 123, 140, 141–142,
        142–143
Religions, xxix
    Celtic, xx
    cultures and, 7
    Egyptian, 194
    as magnet, 266
    in Middle East, xvi–xvii (map)
    minority, xxi, xxiii
    Norse, xxi
    origins/evolution of, ix

    pervasiveness of, 186
    pre-Christian, xxi
    state-backed, xxvii
    understanding of, 217
Republic (Plato), 95
Revolutionary Command Council, 201
Reza Shah, 101
Rihanna, 241
Riley, Naomi Schaefer, 261
Rituals, 2, 52, 94, 99, 101
    Babylonian, 27, 49
    doctrines and, xii
    Druze, 269
    Jewish, 257
    Kalasha, 243
    Mandaean, 27
    Zoroastrian, 109
River Tigris, photo of, 2
Robertson, George Scott, 223, 230,
        233–234, 250, 252
    Gish and, 225
    Kafirs and, 225, 236, 251
    Kam and, 224, 225, 242, 248
    on Merak, 224
Roman Empire, xix, 194, 195
Romans, 40, 45, 148, 194
    defeat of, 46
    Jewish revolt and, 151
Rothschild, Baron Edmond de:
        Samaritans and, 175
Royal Geographical Society,
        Schomberg and, 234
Ruha, 1, 21, 69
Rumbur valley, 235, 243, 244, 247, 250
    photo of, 252
Russian Orthodox, 265
Rustam, 89

Sabbath, 191
    Jewish, 26

Mandaean, 34
Passover and, 176–177
Samaritan, 166, 167, 169, 175
Sabians, 8, 32, 50, 196, 197
Sacrifice
animal, 40, 165
bull, 40, 42–43
Sadat, Anwar, 184, 201, 217
Copts and, 202, 203
sectarianism and, 202
Sa'eed, 205, 213
Sahak, Sultan, 57
St. Augustine, 2, 15, 17, 116
St. Bernard of Clairvaux, 145
St. George, 102, 207
St. Mark the Evangelist, 207, 209
St. Mark's Church, 181, 182, 183, 195,
202
St. Pachomius, 208
St. Paul's Cathedral, 5
St. Simeon Stylites, 265
Sainte Thérèse of Liseux, 184, 185,
187, 218
Salafis, 194, 203, 216–217
Salisbury, Lord, 106–107
Samanids, 92
Samaritan priests, 169, 179
photo of, 165, 173, 179
Samaritans, xxiv, xxix, 158, 161, 163,
164
accusations against, 129
Arabs and, 155
conversion of, 153
documentary on, 168
endurance of, 179–180
flourishing of, 151–152
genealogy and, 167–168
Greek islands and, 166
history of, 170
Israelis and, 177–178

Jews and, 149–150, 151, 153, 154,
165, 175, 178 (photo), 176
memento of, 156
Muslims and, 174, 175
Palestinians and, 174, 175, 176, 177
predictions about, 179–180
rebellions by, 152
traditions/customs of, 165,
168–169, 170–171, 172–173,
176–177, 177, 180
visiting, 154, 156–157
*Sanjak*s, 59, 64, 67
Sanliurfa, 44–45, 47, 54
Sanoo'a, Yacoub, 198
Sargious, Father: on Copts, 199
Sarton, George: on Biruni, 8–9
Satan, 60, 62. *See also* Devil, Sheitan.
Angra Mainyu and, 79–80
cursing, 60
Sheitan, Arabic word for, 60
Sattar, Sheikh, 9–10, 22, 37
Mandaeans and, 10–11
Scaliger, Joseph, 153, 166
Scher, Mar Addai, 259
Schomberg, Reginald, 234, 237, 248
Kalasha and, 238–239
Schoolbook, Hebrew, 33 (photo)
Schur, Nathan, 153, 156
Sebastianus, 17
Secularism, 85, 109, 261
Seth, 2, 10, 191, 207
Shabak, 57
Shafiq, Ahmad, 205
Shahnamah, 78, 89, 92
Shahristani, on Harranians, 49
Shahrvini, Laal, 99, 100, 106, 108
memorial service for, 110–111
as midwife, 101
purity and, 75–76
Zoroastrianism and, 77, 80, 107

Shahrvini, Shahin, 108, 278
Shahrvini, Shahriar, 101, 108
    memorial service for, 110–111
    wounding of, 106
    Zoroastrians and, 107
Shakira, 262
Shalala, Donna, 263
Shalhoub, Father, 265, 278
Shamash, xxii, 4, 42, 43
Shamm al-Nessim, 191, 194
Shams, Sheikh, 42, 43, 53
Shapur, 78
Shatt al-Arab, 83, 84
Shavuot, 169
Shechem, 148, 161
Sheikhs
    Alawite, 51, 52, 53
    Druze, 121, 131, 132, 135, 139–140,
        143, 144, 269
    Edizi, 42, 43
Sheitan, 60. *See also* Devil, Satan.
Shenouda III, Patriarch, 182, 202, 203,
        204, 214
Shi'a, xxiv, xxv, 3, 19, 51, 58, 91, 92,
        93, 99
    Ashura and, 21–22
    disillusionment with, 95
    Druze and, 129, 132–133
    government and, 95
    massacres of, xxiii
    processions of, 22
Shihab, Farhan, 272
Shihab, Naalin, 273, 275
Shiraz, described, 95–96, 96–97
Shirazi, Ali, 95–96
Shouf Mountains
    Druze and, 129–130, 131, 132, 133,
        134, 142–144
    photo of, 133
Sidhom, Youssef, 202

Sizdah Bedar, 90
Smith, Haskett, 135, 136
Socrates, 114
    Pythagoras and, 116
Solomon, King, 88
Spells, casting, 29, 30–31, 32, 205
Sphinx, 124, 196
Strauss, Richard: Zarathustra, 80
Sufis, 7, 62, 97, 99, 186
    conversion by, 58
    Sphinx and, 196
Sukkot, 170, 176
Sun, 26
    as god, 65
Sunnis, xxiii, xxv, 3, 51, 91, 99, 126,
        261
    Druze and, 129, 140, 142
Syriac, 45, 258
Syrian Orthodox Church, 195

Tahrir Square, 187–188, 189, 191, 197,
        198, 204
Tahtawi, 197
Taliban, 226
Talmud, 12, 150
Tamerlane, xix, 220, 225
Taqammus, 122, 123
Tawheed, 127
Tel Aviv, 148, 151, 157, 158, 159, 161,
        163
Temple Mount, 160
Ten Commandments, 153, 165
Ten Lost Tribes of Israel. *See* Lost
        Tribes
Thabit ibn Qurra, 50
Thermopylae, 82, 84
Thesiger, Wilfrid, 20–21
    photo by, 20 (fig.), 21 (fig.)
Thor, xix, 26
Thoth, 182

Three Wise Men, 77, 106
Tirghan, 108, 278
Tolerance, ix, xxii, 90, 152, 255
    spirit of, xxiii, 8, 9
Torah, 80
    photo of, 172
    rules of, 166
    Samaritan, 165, 169, 170, 173
Trajan, Emperor, 85
Tsadka, Sophie, 168
Tsedaka, Benyamim, 157, 158,
    164–165, 179
    marriage of, 167
    Passover and, 170, 176–177
    sabbath and, 167
    Samaritan history and, 166–167
    Samaritan tradition and,
        169–170
    Samaritans and, 167, 178
Tsedaka, Miriam, 167
Tsedaka, Yefet, 167
Turkmen, 57
Turks, 40, 45, 56
    blue and, 69
    Kurds and, 54
Tutankhamun, 4, 134, 192
Twelfth imam, 91
Typewriters, photo of, 33 (fig.)

ul-Haq, Zia, 233
ul-Mulk, Ghazala, 234
ul-Mulk, Shahzada Siraj, 234, 237
Unani-tibb (Galen), 94
Uniate "Chaldean" Church, 259
Uniate church, 185, 210, 259
United Nations, sanctions by, 31
Universal Mind or Intellect, 123,
    125, 127, 145, 268
Universal Soul, 127, 145
Utnapishtim, 3

Vansleb, Johann, 196, 198
Virgin Mary, 102, 130, 182, 258
Vishtaspa, 97

Wafd Party, 198
Wahba, Youssef, 198
Wanat, battle of, 226
Warner Brothers, 82
Watani, 202
West Bank, 157, 158, 159, 161, 162,
    177
    conquest of, 160, 176
    Palestinians and, 148
White Days, 21, 21–22
Wolff, Joseph, 154
Woolley, Leonard, 4
Wordsworth, William: paganism and,
    xii
World of Darkness, 18
World Zoroastrian Organisation, 108
Wotan, xix

Xerxes, 81, 84

Yahweh, 45
Yaish, Adli, 164
Yazd, 75, 76, 81, 107, 108
    dakhma in, 104 (photo)
    fire temple at, 109
    photo of, 76
    Zoroastrians in, 99, 100, 101, 102,
        105, 109
Yazidis, ix, x, 52, 53, 58, 59, 64, 67,
    118, 144
    attacks on, xxiv, 70–71, 129
    beliefs of, 39–40, 42, 43, 54, 276
    challenge for, 72–73
    Christians and, 41
    cleanliness of, 273
    creation and, 42

Yazidis, *continued*
    education of, 71
    fish and, 54
    folklore of, 276
    handshake and, 48, 73
    identity of, 66, 274
    Kurds and, 40–41, 61, 65–66, 70,
        71–72, 274
    Melek Taoos and, 60–61, 63
    missionary work and, 69
    Mithraists and, 47
    Muslims and, 39, 60
    Ottomans and, 71
    photo of, 60
    prayer/fasting by, 43
    reading/writing and, 42
    refuge for, 41, 279
    reincarnation and, 44
    rights of, 271
    scripture of, 43
    shrines of, 41, 66
    sun and, 44, 65
Yemeni, 138, 139, 264
Yoannis, Father, 211, 212, 213, 215,
    216
Yohannan bar Penkaye, 64
Yom Kippur, Samaritans and, 169

Zaghloul, Saad, 198, 200
Zagros Mountains, 84
Zamalek Island, 188–189
Zarathustra, 92, 97, 102, 110
    immortality and, 77, 79

    moral law and, 80
Zendan-e-Soleyman, 87, 92, 106
    temple at, 88 (photo)
Zenobia, 23
Zoroastrian priests, 79, 90
Zoroastrianism, 46, 52, 88
    conversion to, 109, 110
    free choice and, 78
    human history and, 84–85
    Iranians and, 89
    liberal interpretation of, 108
    modern, 109–111
    Muslim practices of, 89–90
    signs/emblems of, 81, 82
Zoroastrians, 8, 60, 61, 62, 64, 77, 81,
        83, 86, 87, 91, 96
    animals and, 78–79
    Baha'i and, 107
    in Britain, 106, 107, 108
    cleanliness of, 101, 104, 105
    customs of, 99–100
    disrespect/hostility for, 80
    encountering, 109
    Gabri language and, 76
    Hafez and, 97, 99
    Jesus and, 77
    monotheism and, xxi
    Parsee, 106
    talking with, 111
    wine and, 97
Zulfikar (photographer), 234, 237,
        239, 240, 242
    on Kalasha, 255